America

Since 1945
Third Edition

America

Since 1945
Third Edition

Edited by

Robert D. Marcus

and

David Burner

St. Martin's Press

New York

Library of Congress Catalog Card Number: 80–52375
Copyright © 1981 by St. Martin's Press, Inc.
All Rights Reserved.
Manufactured in the United States of America.
54321
fedcba
For information, write St. Martin's Press, Inc.,
175 Fifth Avenue, New York, N.Y. 10010

cover design: Mies Hora
ISBN: 0–312–03116–5

Preface

In 1971, when we wrote the preface to the first edition of *America Since 1945*, it was easier for us to comprehend the quarter century between 1945 and 1970 as a unit than it is for us today, as we prepare the third edition, to perceive the more than three decades from 1945 as a clear continuity. For all the variety of American experience between 1945 and 1970, certain recurrent themes gave the period a narrative coherence. The presidency always waxed greater; the Cold War was ever a looming presence; prosperity attenuated only by short recessions was the steady experience of most Americans and a visible goal toward which the others could aspire. Now even these few enduring themes have been transformed. Our uncertain present demands a fresh view of our recent past, a new mapping of the road leading to today.

The United States since the end of World War II has contained all the makings of a great historical subject. More powerful yet more vulnerable than ever before, this nation became in the 1950's and 1960's the world's major military and economic power and the center of the world's culture. Then in the 1970's, facing major challenges from the Soviet Union, China, and the Third World and wracked with increasing economic uncertainty, Americans sought anxiously for a new perspective on their place in the world.

Keeping in mind this search for a perspective, we have selected articles that deal with—and link together—the most significant political and social events of the past thirty-five years. For example, in foreign affairs the articles include the views of Averell Harriman and Barton Bernstein on the Cold War, Walter La Feber on the Korean War, and Michael Herr's discussion of American involvement in Vietnam. In the domestic realm we have included not only political articles, such as Garry Wills's reevaluation of Richard Nixon's famous Checkers speech, but also articles that deal with some of the social transformations of the period—including selections from Betty Friedan's *The Feminine Mystique*, Michael Harrington's *The Other America*, and Lester Thurow's *The Zero-Sum Society*. Throughout we have attempted to offer an interesting combination of primary and secondary materials; thus we have included excerpts from such primary sources as the Army-McCarthy hearings, the speeches of John F. Kennedy, Lyndon B. Johnson, and Malcolm X, and the memoirs of Richard Nixon and Henry Kissinger.

There are ten new selections in the third edition. Besides the readings by Herr, Thurow, Nixon, and Kissinger mentioned above, the new material consists of accounts of the Kennedy presidency and the Greensboro sit-ins, excerpts from Sara Evans's *Personal Politics* and Barry Commoner's *The Closing Circle*, and analyses of both Jimmy Carter's and Ronald Reagan's approach to the presidency. We have also updated the Suggested Further Readings section.

Robert D. Marcus
David Burner

Contents

America

Since 1945
Third Edition

PART ONE

1945-1952

In 1945 World War II ended and the atomic age began. It was a year of high drama: of the final defeat of the Axis powers, the establishment of the United Nations, and the beginning of what people hoped would be a great "American century" in which, under our guidance, the world would know a long era of peace and progress. Americans eagerly awaited demobilization, the sweet harvest of victory. Yet they were uneasy. The great leader, Franklin D. Roosevelt, was dead and in his place a modest ex-haberdasher from Missouri. Victory in Europe had left that continent devastated. Victory over Japan had introduced the world to the horror of nuclear weapons. And in America victory raised the question of whether an economy which had been depressed for a decade would not lapse into the same dismal state from which war production had roused it. Moreover, the unusual homefront harmony had suppressed intense conflicts that would break out again in an era of peace.

Many of the hopes and even more of the fears were realized in the next few years. The United Nations survived, the United States remained the greatest world power, and the domestic economy showed little inclination to slip back into depression. But the image of an "American century" rapidly gave way before the reality of a cold war. New Deal reforms were continued but not expanded, as bipartisan forces vigorously pursued the ideological conflict with the Soviet Union. Amid confusion and ill-feeling the nation rearmed, fought an inconclusive war in Asia, created an economy dependent on military spending, and moved irregularly toward a social order which in the 1950's seemed more stable than in fact it was. In reaction to a threatening world, Americans in 1952 closed ranks behind a popular and decidedly unmilitaristic general whom they hoped—correctly as it turned out—would put the sour era of postwar adjustment behind them.

Russia and the Cold War

AVERELL HARRIMAN

From 1926 when he bargained with Leon Trotsky in Moscow over a manganese concession until 1968 when he conferred in Paris with the North Vietnamese, Averell Harriman has probably been our most experienced and influential representative to the Communist world. His reminiscences are important not only for the insights he has acquired about Communist governments over the years, but for what they reveal about developing American foreign policy.

Harriman never conceived of American-Soviet relations as a struggle to the death between hostile forces, one destined to conquer, the other to die. He had contempt for the crusading cold-warrior mentality in international affairs and strongly criticized Eisenhower's Secretary of State, John Foster Dulles, for taking "the position that Communism was evil and that countries were either for us or against us in our struggle with it."

Harriman's opinions are quite typical of American policy makers in the immediate postwar era. He himself called it "a fairly glorious period, perhaps the most creative period in American foreign policy." The idealism he expresses—as in his account of the Marshall Plan—is undoubtedly genuine. Although some critics such as Barton J. Bernstein (in the next selection) have suggested that those liberal ideals actually defined the world in a way that made the Cold War inevitable, Harriman contends that Stalin's intransigence led to an unavoidable collapse of the wartime alliance.

There has grown a myth about Yalta that somehow or other Roosevelt and Churchill sold out Eastern Europe to Stalin. That wasn't true at all. I can't imagine why Stalin went to such extreme lengths in breaking the Yalta agreements if it had been true that they were so much to his advantage. It was agreed that the people in these countries were to decide on their own governments through free elections. But Stalin didn't permit it.

One wonders why he broke his agreement on Poland so soon. It's rather hard to guess. Personally, I think one of the reasons was that Bierut, the leading member of the Lublin Polish government—the Communist government—was in Moscow on Stalin's return from Yalta. He may have told Stalin that if he carried out his plan for free elections, Bierut and his comrades couldn't deliver Poland. Stalin had the idea that the Red Army would be accepted as a liberating army. In fact, he told me so. In this regard, perhaps the Communist partisans had reported too optimistically to Moscow. At any rate I think the Kremlin leaders were awfully hurt when they found that the Red Army was looked upon by the Poles, the Romanians, and others as a new invading force.

In addition, there appeared to be two schools of thought in the Kremlin hierarchy—the Politburo itself. One is apt to think of the Communist government as one single brain; it isn't. It is made up of men with sometimes differing views; this was true even under Stalin. I was conscious of the fact that members of Politburo even during the war had different views on different subjects. Let me quickly say that there was free discussion in the Politburo on *new* subjects only. On anything Stalin had decided, that was it. That couldn't be questioned. I think it is fair to say that in these discussions about new matters, Stalin listened, smoked his pipe, and walked up and down the room. Then, when he had heard enough, he said, "This is what we are going to do." If anyone left the room with a shrug of his shoulders, he might find himself on the way to Siberia the next afternoon. That may be somewhat of an exaggeration, but I think it's pretty nearly right.

In any event, I feel sure that there was a difference of opinion as to whether it would be wise for the Soviet Union in the immediate postwar period to soft-pedal Communist expansion for a time and continue to collaborate with the Western Allies to get the value of loans and trade, technical assistance, and other cooperation for the terrific job of reconstruction they faced; or whether they should push ahead and use the extraordinary opportunities in the dislocations in Europe and elsewhere to extend Communist control. Stalin once told me, "Communism breeds in the cesspools of capitalists." In this sense, Europe looked as if it were going to be in a mire.

I was so concerned about this that in early 1945, I sent messages about the need to help Western Europe, urging that the recovery of Europe would require much more than most people thought. I said that UNRRA would not be enough, food would not be enough. We would have to supply working capital and raw materials to get trade going again. Imports would be needed for raw materials for industrial production as well as for reconstruction. Without that, there would be vast unemployment and misery, in which the Communists might well take over.

I believe that Stalin hoped to get to the Atlantic, and that was perhaps the reason why he didn't carry out the Yalta agreements. The prospects for Communist takeover simply looked too good.

He said a number of things on different occasions, some of them contradictory, and it is hard to know what he had in mind. After Teheran he sent President Roosevelt a telegram in which, among other things, he said, "Now it is assured that our people will act together, jointly and in friendship, both at the present time and after the completion of the war." This is only one of the many expressions of that kind which gave some indication that he had in mind postwar cooperation. But that didn't happen. Roosevelt died, and I know that before he died he realized that his hopes had not been fully achieved; he knew Stalin had already broken some of the Yalta agreements. I know that from the telegrams I received from him to deliver to Stalin and also from some of the people who talked to him just before his death.[1] . . .

While I was home, I did spend several weeks in San Francisco during the United Nations Conference. At the request of Ed Stettinius, the Secretary of State, I had three off-the-record talks with editors, columnists, and reporters to give them some background on our growing problems with the Soviet government. I told them we would have real difficulties with the Soviet Union in the postwar period. This came as a great shock to many of them. At one meeting, I explained that our objectives and the Kremlin objectives were irreconcilable; they wanted to communize the world, and we wanted a free world. But I added that we would have to find ways to compose our differences if we were to live in peace on this small planet. Two men were so shocked that they got up and left. Some of the press at that time criticized me for being so unkind to what were then known as "our gallant allies," and some even suggested that I should be recalled as Ambassador. It was one of the few times in my experience that members of the press have broken the confidence of an off-the-record talk.

People ask when and why I became convinced we would have difficulties with the Soviets. This judgment developed over a period of time. . . .

A talk I had with Stalin at Potsdam in July 1945 is illuminating. The first time I saw him at the conference I went up to him and said that it must be very gratifying for him to be in Berlin, after all the struggle and the tragedy. He hesitated a moment and then replied, "Czar Alexander got to Paris." It didn't need much of a clairvoyant to guess what was in his mind.

I don't think there is any doubt that, with the strong Communist Parties both in Italy and in France, he would have extended his domination to the Atlantic, if we had not acted to frustrate it. In all probability, the Communist leaders in those countries had reported to Moscow that they could take over, and I think they would have succeeded if we had not helped Western Europe to recover. Some of Western Europe would have had Communist governments under the control of Moscow. One doesn't know what the rest of Europe would have been like, but perhaps some countries would have been something less independent than Finland and allowed to be cautiously neutral at the grace of Moscow.

But that isn't what happened. I know that some young people

1. Mrs. Hoffman wrote me a letter some years later describing her conversation with Roosevelt on March 24, 1945, his last day in Washington:

The President was in his wheel chair as we left the room, and both Mrs. Roosevelt and I walked at his side. He was given a message which I learned later was a cable from you which had been decoded. He read it and became quite angry. He banged his fists on the arms of his wheel chair and said, "Averell is right; we can't do business with Stalin. He has broken every one of the promises he made at Yalta." He was very upset and continued in the same vein on the subject.

These were his exact words. I remembered them and verified them with Mrs. Roosevelt not too long before her death.

think that everything that has been done before them wasn't just right, but we did have a fairly glorious period, perhaps the most creative period in American foreign policy, immediately after the war. It was due to the leadership of President Truman and the effective cooperation of Senator Vandenberg, the Republican Senator from Michigan, who was then Chairman of the Foreign Relations Committee. The undertakings included aid to Greece, which was under Communist attack, and Turkey, which was threatened at that time; the Marshall Plan, which was an extraordinarily ambitious and successful venture in co-operation; and that led to NATO. These things developed one from the other. Public opinion in the West was deeply disturbed by the Czech coup of March 1948 and then the Berlin blockade three months later. . . .

I was involved in the Marshall Plan, in charge of operations in Europe for more than two years. This was a European effort, with United States help. By the way, I should recall that General Marshall's offer of aid was made to all of Europe, including Russia and Eastern Europe. In fact, Molotov came to the meeting of Foreign Ministers of the European countries called in Paris in July 1947 to consider Marshall's offer with a staff of sixty, including senior economists. However, he demanded that each country act independently. He wanted the European nations to reply to the United States along these lines, "Tell us how much money you will give us, and we will divide it on the basis of those who suffered most will get the most. Then each country will look after its own recovery." But Marshall's proposal was that the European countries should cooperate together in a mutual recovery program. Bevin and Bidault, the British and French Foreign Ministers, stood firm for the cooperative concept, and Molotov left in a huff. The Czechs and the Poles had wanted to join the Marshall Plan, but the Kremlin ordered them not to do so.

At that time the Soviets organized the Cominform and declared war on the Marshall Plan, calling it an "American imperialist plot to subjugate Western Europe." Needless to say, that was just exactly the reverse of what we wanted. We wanted a strong, united and independent Europe. Everything that we did was to minimize our role and maximize the cooperative effort of the Europeans. "Self-help and mutual aid" was the slogan. It was amazingly successful—a spirit of cooperation and unity developed within Europe which had never before existed. They abandoned some of the restrictive business and labor practices of the intra-war years and accepted the necessity of an expanding economy as the basis for a rising standard of living. . . .

Now, Western Europe is more vital and dynamic than ever. When De Gaulle was in control, France was, perhaps, a little too nationalistic. But today the Europeans are again moving toward greater integration and closer cooperation. This was part of the objective of the Congress, and certainly of President Truman in initiating the Marshall Plan. . . .

The Berlin blockade in June of 1948 was a startling event and led to the pressure for NATO. You have to remember that never in history has a nation destroyed its armed strength as rapidly as we did after the

Second World War. The demand for bringing the boys home was irresistible. No one was to blame; it was the deep desire of the American people. We thought we had won the war and everyone in the world would want peace. We had the strongest military force in being at the end of the war, but after the Japanese surrendered, it was dissipated. The Russians didn't do that. They strengthened their forces. They developed new weapons. We in Moscow reported to Washington in late 1945 evidence which indicated that Soviet research expenditure was being doubled, that production of certain new weapons and military equipment was continuing at wartime levels, and that combat training for the Red Army was being emphasized.

Although for a time we had a monopoly in nuclear weapons, Stalin ordered the highest priority be given to developing nuclear capability. Much to the surprise of most people at the time, the Soviets exploded their first nuclear device in September 1949.

The Berlin blockade was countered not by direct force. There has been a lot of argument about that at the time and since. People can argue whether Truman's decision was right or wrong—whether to try to drive our forces through and threaten a nuclear attack, or whether to supply Berlin by airlift. In any event, the least provocative of these responses—the airlift—was chosen, and with full British cooperation it was successful. The Soviets lifted the blockade a year later.

We have had difficulty over Berlin ever since, some times more dangerous than others. Of course, one can criticize the arrangements which made Berlin the capital of occupied Germany. Frankly, Ben Cohen and I favored at the time a capital in a new location, where the three zones came together, just north of Magdeburg. I was influenced in part by the appalling way in which the Soviets had stripped Berlin of most everything they could take out, between V-E Day and the Potsdam meeting. The factories, particularly, were emptied of all machinery and machine tools. But these arrangements had been made by the European Advisory Commission in London. They had been accepted by the three Allies and would have been pretty hard to change at Potsdam.

Sometimes I have thought our presence in Berlin was of great value. Other times I have wondered if it was worthwhile. These are things that historians can argue about. But we are there in West Berlin, and the division of Germany continues along the line of the Soviet occupational zone.

Some think that General Eisenhower should have taken Berlin, but if he had done that, our Third Army wouldn't have been in Austria, and Austria, which is a free and independent country, probably would have been occupied largely by the Red Army and might have been turned into a satellite.

These are all questions which one can weigh. It is hard to say what might have been done. If one objective had been gained, something else would have been lost. I think by and large with the Soviet recalcitrance it would have made very little difference.

Some people have even argued that if General Eisenhower had

liberated Prague somehow or other Czechoslovakia would be free today. That's nonsense! The Czech government under President Benes was set up under an agreement in Moscow, negotiated by Benes with Czech party leaders, including the Communists. This government returned to Czechoslovakia from the East, as the Red Army, joined with four or five Czech divisions, advanced. Under the agreement Benes had to take Communists into the government.

I had several talks with Benes when he came to Moscow from London in March 1945 before returning to Czechoslovakia. He told me that he was not too well satisfied with the composition of the new government, but he added, "It might have been worse." Benes was confident he could control the situation in Czechoslovakia as he believed the people would support him. He told me that Stalin had assured him that the Soviets would not interfere in Czech internal affairs.

Unfortunately, Benes was ill in March 1948 when the coup took place. Of course, the Red Army had long since retired. It had withdrawn from Czechoslovakia more than two years earlier. Our troops had also withdrawn long before, so nothing we did in 1945 would have affected the outcome. Whether or not it would have been different if Benes had been well and vigorous, and whether he could have held his own, I don't know. But the Communist coup was successful without the participation of the Red Army, but undoubtedly with Moscow's collusion.

I had long talks with Jan Masaryk in San Francisco in May 1945. He was Benes' Foreign Minister. He told me I must understand that in the United Nations he would have to vote with Molotov. The Soviets were insisting that the Czech government support them in foreign policy. In return, he thought they would have a free hand at home. Unfortunately, it did not work out that way, and Masaryk himself came to a violent end in March 1948.

The Truman period was an exciting period. President Truman was a man of great determination. He was very humble at the start. He said he had not been elected; Roosevelt had been elected, and it was his responsibility to carry out Roosevelt's policies. He did the best he could. Very early he showed that he recognized the unique problems facing the United States in the world, and he had the extraordinary courage to undertake new policies and programs. And I think they were extraordinarily successful.

President Truman proposed in January 1949 the Point Four Program, announcing that since science and technology had developed to such a point that the old enemies of mankind—hunger, misery, poverty, and disease—could be overcome, it was the obligation of the United States and other more technologically advanced nations to help. That concept has moved ahead. There have been some outstanding successes in some ways and in some countries—some disappointments in others. Unfortunately, our development assistance is in rather a low state today —one of the casualties of Vietnam.

There have been lasting constructive results from the Truman period. Germany has revived and has become a strong ally; Japan has revived and is becoming a strong partner. Western Europe is more productive and united than ever. Other countries have made progress as well and are on their way to sustained economic development, for example in Asia, Korea, and Taiwan, and in Latin America, Mexico, Venezuela, and Colombia. There have been disappointments, of course. The developing countries as a whole have not been able to advance as rapidly as had been hoped, and the gap between them and the industrial nations has widened.

China was an enigma. Roosevelt first of all wanted to get the Soviet Union into the war against Japan. There was never any doubt in my mind that Stalin would attack Japan when it suited him. We could not have kept him out. The question was whether that would be soon enough to do us good. Our Chiefs of Staff estimated that it would take eighteen months after the fall of Germany to defeat the Japanese and would require an amphibious landing on the plains of Tokyo. American casualties were estimated to run up near a million with perhaps a couple of hundred thousand killed. This was a grim prospect to President Roosevelt. Yet, if the Russians attacked the Japanese Kwangtung Army in Manchuria, the Japanese strength to defend the home islands would be reduced. President Roosevelt had a deep sense of responsibility to protect American lives, and it was hoped that possibly, with Russia in the war and with American use of Soviet airfields in Siberia, we could bring Japan to surrender without invasion. Therefore, Soviet intervention seemed of vital importance.

It didn't turn out to be important because, unexpectedly, the nuclear bomb became operative and events moved so rapidly. At Yalta, when plans about Soviet entry into the war against Japan were agreed to, the nuclear bomb had not yet been completed, and nobody knew whether it would work. Even five months later at Potsdam, after the first test explosion took place, one of the most distinguished Navy officers bet an apple that it would not go off as a bomb. Of course, after things happen they seem so easy and so obvious that people say, "Why didn't you think of this at the time?"

Apart from Soviet entry into the war, Roosevelt also wanted to get Stalin to accept Chiang Kai-shek's Nationalist government as the government of China. And that, too, was part of the agreements reached at Yalta about the Far East. This was formalized in a treaty negotiated by T. V. Soong, Premier of the Nationalist government, with Stalin six months later. During these negotiations in Moscow I saw T. V. Soong almost every day. He was finally well satisfied, and in fact the world applauded the agreement. . . .

There were certain concessions to the Russians related to the railroads and ports in Manchuria for a thirty-year period, but the important point for Chiang was that the Soviets accepted Chinese sovereignty over the area. Some of us had been concerned when the Russians got into Manchuria they would establish a "Manchurian People's Republic" just as they had the Mongolian People's Republic. The fact that the Soviets accepted Chinese sovereignty was the thing that impressed Chiang.

Curiously, Stalin did not have much respect for Mao Tse-tung. During the war he spoke about him several times, and at one time he called him a "margarine Communist." That created a great deal of puzzlement in Washington. Some didn't know what it means. It would be entirely clear to any dairy farmer what he meant—a fake, not a real product. I gained the impression from several of my talks with Stalin that he was not keen to support Mao Tse-tung in China and that, perhaps, he wanted to see a new group more amenable to Moscow, take over the Chinese Communist Party before he gave his full support.

After the war, in January 1946, he told me that he had "poor contacts with the Communists." He said that the Soviet government's "three representatives in Yenan had been recalled" and that the Soviet influence with the Chinese Communists was not great. I think there is other evidence to that effect. For example, the Red Army not only stripped Manchuria of its industrial machinery for use in the Soviet Union but also blew up facilities such as blast furnaces. However, the Mao Communists were stronger than Stalin thought, and Chiang was weaker. As events developed, Chiang's forces collapsed in 1949, and he was driven out of mainland China.

Some people have said, "We lost China." It just happens that we never owned China. Whatever we had done in China over the years had had only a limited impact. And although it is unfortunate that a government friendly to us did not survive, we could not have involved ourselves in a major war at that time in China. President Truman, in spite of all the initiatives we had taken in other parts of the world, was wise enough to exercise restraint and not become involved in a civil war in mainland China.

So not all the postwar developments were favorable. Some of them did not go as well as we had hoped they might. . . .

President Kennedy handled the Cuban missile crisis with consummate skill and induced Khrushchev to take the offensive missiles out of Cuba. He was able to go on to an agreement with him on a limited test ban. The signing and ratification of the Limited Nuclear Test Ban Treaty marked a high water point in our relations with the Soviet Union. There were of course unsolved critical problems, particularly in regard to Germany and Southeast Asia. But the change in less than a year from the Cuban missile crisis to the test ban was so striking that I believe President Kennedy began to think seriously of a visit to the Soviet Union early in his second term should he be re-elected. But President Kennedy was assassinated three months later.

Within a year new personalities were to take over in Moscow. Khrushchev was removed from office, Brezhnev took his place as Secretary of the Party and Kosygin as Chairman of the Council of Ministers. . . .

QUESTIONS AND ANSWERS

Q—Do you believe that there is anything America could have done to assist Chiang, particularly in the latter period when we did withdraw our support?

A—I don't think so. I went to Chunking to talk with Chiang Kai-shek in January 1946. General Marshall was there at the time. Chiang had grave doubts about coming to an agreement for a coalition with the Communists, and he may have been justified in his fears. I asked him why he did not strengthen his government at once by bringing in the Democratic League, which included the leading Chinese intellectuals. They had recently participated in a Consultative Conference which had attempted to reconcile the contending parties. I also asked him why he didn't get rid of some of his warlords and some of the obviously corrupt people around him. He replied that they were the only ones he could count on for support if he brought the Communists into the government.

Perhaps the outcome might have been better if we had had quite a different approach. Looking at things from Moscow, my idea at the time was that we might better accept temporarily a divided China. If we could have prevented Chiang from sending his best troops into Manchuria where they were chewed up, he would have been far better off. It was hopeless for him to expect to take over the rule of Manchuria when he was having difficulty in controlling even the area where his forces were concentrated—southern China.

I also had grave doubts about the attempts to form a coalition government with the Communists. It seemed to me at the time that Chiang was too weak and the Communists too strong for him to have had much of a chance of survival.

In any event, General Marshall was sent out to attempt to mediate between the Nationalists and the Communists, and he did everything he could under his instructions. Despite General Marshall's patience and skill, the reluctance and suspicion of both sides and the inherent weakness of the Kuomintang made successful mediation impossible. . . .

Q—Mr. Ambassador, would you comment on the motivation of Soviet foreign policy? Do you think the motivation is primarily that of power politics and national power concerns, or of Communist ideology, or are they both equally determining factors?

A—It is a combination of both. Stalin had both. He was a Russian imperialist with ambitions similar to the Czars. He was also utterly determined to promote world Communist revolution with the oracle in Moscow. Since Stalin's death the world situation has changed, but the Kremlin still has both motivations. . . .

Q—If you could relive history, what changes would you make in the United States foreign policy during the wartime conferences and what effect that might have had on the future?

A—Well, I don't think much would have been different. You can argue about a lot of different things. People blame Eisenhower for not going to Berlin, but there had been a decision made in which the occupational zones of Germany were set. It was considered important that we should not meet and clash with the Russians, that we should decide in advance the zones each would occupy to avoid that possibility. The agreed zones were considered to be very favorable by our chiefs of staff at the time they were decided upon. They thought the Russians would be much further into Germany than they got and that we would not have gotten as far as we did. It didn't work out that way. I am not critical of them for this, as no one could have foreseen the military events.

Now if we had tried to do what Churchill proposed after V-E Day— stand on the Elbe until there was a political settlement about Eastern Europe—I don't think it would have done any good, and we would then have been held responsible for the cold war. Furthermore, our military plans required a redeployment of our forces in Europe to the Pacific. Churchill wanted to force a political settlement about the areas occupied by the Red Army before we withdrew from the Elbe. But even if we had gotten an agreement and free elections had been held, the governments elected would, in all probability, not have lasted. There was, in fact, a free election in Hungary in 1945 in which the Smallholders party (the small peasants' party) got over 50 per cent of the votes and the Communists only about 18 per cent. The government established after this election lasted only a short time, and the Communists—supported by the Red Army—took over and squeezed out the others.

There was no way we could have prevented any of these events in Eastern Europe without going to war with the Russians. There were a few military people who considered that. This wasn't De Gaulle, but a few French and American officers talked about going in and cleaning them up while we had such superiority in air power. It is perfectly absurd to think the American people would have stood for it, even if the President wanted to do it, which he didn't.

I think it was very important that Roosevelt and Churchill made the effort to come to an agreement with Stalin. One achievement was the establishment of the United Nations. With all the disappointments, it has been effective in many activities during the twenty-five years of its life, although handicapped by the differences that exist between the great powers. The fact that Stalin broke the agreements about Eastern Europe exposed his perfidy and aggressive designs. This aroused the suspicion of the West and eventually led to steps for mutual defense.

There is a group of historians who are now attempting to rewrite the history of that time. Arthur M. Schlesinger, Jr., has pointed out that such attempts to rewrite history have happened frequently in the past. These revisionists are creating myths about what happened and what our objectives were. Some of them take facts out of context and try to build up a case for imagined objectives. Some conveniently overlook Stalin's failure to cooperate, his violation of specific agreements and aggressive actions. Of course, I am not talking about those thoughtful analysts who, with the advantage of hindsight, point out more clearly the significance of events and perhaps mistakes than was possible at the time.

The military alternatives were perhaps more obvious than the political. At the time some people wanted us to go to Vienna, up the Ljubljana Gap, and get there before the Russians, instead of landing in the south of France as we did. Yet as things have turned out, Austria is free today anyway.

Churchill was always very much worried about attempting to cross the Channel. It turned out successfully. It would have been disastrous for the British if it hadn't. Churchill wanted to go at Hitler from the south—"the soft underbelly," as he called it. He didn't want to take the risk of crossing the Channel. Stalin, after having berated and even insulted us for two years for not establishing a second front in Europe by crossing the Channel, said to me after we had successfully landed, "The history of war has never witnessed such a grandiose operation." He added neither Napoleon nor Hitler had dared attempt it. Later, after he had received detailed reports, he spoke to me again about crossing the Channel, as "an unheard of achievement in the history of warfare." The number of men and the vast amount of equipment which had been thrown into France impressed him greatly. He added "the world had never seen an individual operation of such magnitude— an unbelievable accomplishment." He was unconcerned by the fact that he had previously minimized its difficulties and had accused us of cowardice in not having undertaken it before.

Undoubtedly mistakes were made, and undoubtedly many things might have been improved. Your question is an interesting one, and I have thought a lot about it. But the facts are that, although militarily unprepared, we fought a war successfully on two fronts. With our allies in Europe, we completely defeated Hitler, and almost alone we defeated Japan in the Pacific. That was an extraordinary achievement— and particularly as it was done in less than four years. As far as our relations with the Soviet Union since the end of the war are concerned, I doubt whether any different wartime military or political decisions would have had much effect.

The Cold War:
A Revisionist View

BARTON J. BERNSTEIN

*"There is no nation which has
attitudes so pure that they cannot
be bettered by self-examination."*
—John Foster Dulles (1946)

*"We are forced to act in the world
as it is, and not in the world as
we wish it were, or as we would
like it to become."*
—Henry L. Stimson (1947)

*Barton J. Bernstein is one of the "revisionists" whom Averell Harriman
criticizes for "creating myths about what happened [in the Cold War]
and what our objectives were." The revisionist position, expressed repeatedly during the 1960's, holds that Stalin was basically cautious
rather than aggressive in his actions immediately after World War II;
that the United States government, aiming to preserve American access
to a world trading empire, overlooked legitimate Soviet security needs;
and that, possessing preponderant power in the world, America refused
to cooperate with the Soviet Union, forcing the Kremlin into a hostile
posture in Eastern Europe to protect itself from future military threats.*

*Only a small proportion of American diplomatic historians has
totally accepted this analysis of American foreign policy, but the revisionist argument has influenced virtually every student in the field.
The central point of revisionist thinking, that the postwar power of
the United States gave it wider options than the Soviet Union ever had,
seems hard to question. Some theorists also maintain that American
and Soviet social and economic policies would eventually have con-
verged, and that such abrasive conflict between the two ideologies need
not have occurred at all. Yet we know so little of what Stalin was
thinking, and he gave so many contradictory signals that almost any
interpretation is possible. The experience of Vietnam, the breakdown
of monolithic power blocs, both East and West, and the emergence of
"détente" have all provided continuing stimulus for Cold War revisionism.*

Despite some dissents, most American scholars have reached a general consensus on the origins of the Cold War. As confirmed internationalists who believe that Russia constituted a threat to America and its European allies after World War II, they have endorsed their nation's acceptance of its obligations as a world power in the forties and its desire to establish a world order of peace and prosperity. Convinced that only American efforts prevented the Soviet Union from expanding past Eastern Europe, they have generally praised the containment policies of the Truman Doctrine, the Marshall Plan, and NATO as evidence of America's acceptance of world responsibility. While chiding or condemning those on the right who opposed international involvement (or had even urged preventive war), they have also been deeply critical of those on the left who have believed that the Cold War could have been avoided, or that the United States shared substantial responsibility for the Cold War.

Whether they are devotees of the new realism or open admirers of moralism and legalism in foreign policy, most scholars have agreed that the United States moved slowly and reluctantly, in response to Soviet provocation, away from President Franklin D. Roosevelt's conciliatory policy. The Truman administration, perhaps even belatedly, they suggest, abandoned its efforts to maintain the Grand Alliance and acknowledged that Russia menaced world peace. American leaders, according to this familiar interpretation, slowly cast off the shackles of innocence and moved to courageous and necessary policies.

Despite the widespread acceptance of this interpretation, there has long been substantial evidence (and more recently a body of scholarship) which suggests that American policy was neither so innocent nor so nonideological; that American leaders sought to promote their conceptions of national interest and their values even at the conscious risk of provoking Russia's fears about her security. In 1945 these leaders apparently believed that American power would be adequate for the task of reshaping much of the world according to America's needs and standards.

By overextending policy and power and refusing to accept Soviet interests, American policy-makers contributed to the Cold War. There was little understanding of any need to restrain American political efforts and desires. Though it cannot be proved that the United States could have achieved a *modus vivendi* with the Soviet Union in these years, there is evidence that Russian policies were reasonably cautious and conservative, and that there was at least a basis for accommodation.

The author wishes to express his gratitude for generous counsel to Gar Alperovitz, H. Stuart Hughes, Gabriel Kolko, Walter LaFeber, Lloyd Gardner, Allen J. Matusow, Thomas G. Paterson, Athan Theoharis, and Samuel Williamson. Research was conducted with the assistance of grants from the Rabinowitz Foundation, the American Philosophical Society, the Harry S. Truman Library Institute, the Charles Warren Center of Harvard University, and the Institute of American History at Stanford University. Portions of this paper were presented at the Warren Center in November 1967, at the John F. Kennedy Institute at Harvard in 1967–1968, and at the annual meeting of the Southern Historical Association in November 1968.

But this possibility slowly slipped away as President Harry S. Truman reversed Roosevelt's tactics of accommodation. As American demands for democratic governments in Eastern Europe became more vigorous, as the new administration delayed in providing economic assistance to Russia and in seeking international control of atomic energy, policy-makers met with increasing Soviet suspicion and antagonism. Concluding that Soviet-American cooperation was impossible, they came to believe that the Soviet state could be halted only by force or the threat of force.

The emerging revisionist interpretation, then, does not view American actions simply as the necessary response to Soviet challenges, but instead tries to understand American ideology and interests, mutual suspicions and misunderstandings, and to investigate the failures to seek and achieve accommodation.

I

During the war Allied relations were often marred by suspicions and doubts rooted in the hostility of earlier years. It was only a profound "accident"—the German attack upon the Soviet Union in 1941 —that thrust that leading anti-Bolshevik, Winston Churchill, and Marshal Josef Stalin into a common camp. This wartime alliance, its members realized, was not based upon trust but upon necessity; there was no deep sense of shared values or obvious similarity of interests, only opposition to a common enemy. "A coalition," as Herbert Feis has remarked, "is heir to the suppressed desires and maimed feelings of each of its members." Wartime needs and postwar aims often strained the uneasy alliance. In the early years when Russia was bearing the major burden of the Nazi onslaught, her allies postponed for two years a promised second front which would have diverted German armies. In December 1941, when Stalin requested recognition of 1941 Russian borders as they had been before the German attack (including the recently annexed Baltic states), the British were willing to agree, but Roosevelt rebuffed the proposals and aroused Soviet fears that her security needs would not be recognized and that her allies might later resume their anti-Bolshevik policies. So distrustful were the Allies that both camps feared the making of a separate peace with Germany, and Stalin's suspicions erupted into bitter accusations in March 1945, when he discovered (and Roosevelt denied) that British and American agents were participating in secret negotiations with the Germans. In anger Stalin decided not to send Vyacheslav Molotov, the Foreign Minister, to San Francisco for the April meeting on the founding of the United Nations Organization.

So suspicious were the Americans and British that they would not inform the Soviet Union that they were working on an atomic bomb. Some American leaders even hoped to use it in postwar negotiations with the Russians. In wartime, American opposition to communism had not disappeared, and many of Roosevelt's advisers were fearful of

Soviet intentions in Eastern Europe. In turn, Soviet leaders, recalling the prewar hostility of the Western democracies, feared a renewed attempt to establish a *cordon sanitaire* and resolved to establish a security zone in Eastern Europe.

Though Roosevelt's own strategy often seems ambiguous, his general tactics are clear: they were devised to avoid conflict. He operated often as a mediator between the British and Russians, and delayed many decisions that might have disrupted the wartime alliance. He may have been resting his hopes with the United Nations or on the exercise of America's postwar strength, or he may simply have been placing his faith in the future. Whatever future tactics he might have been planning, he concluded that America's welfare rested upon international peace, expanded trade, and open markets:

. . . it is our hope, not only in the interest of our own prosperity, but in the interest of the prosperity of the world, that trade and commerce and access to materials and markets may be freer after this war than ever before in the history of the world. . . . Only through a dynamic and soundly expanding world economy can the living standards of individual nations be advanced to levels which will permit a full realization of our hopes for the future.

His efforts on behalf of the postwar world generally reflected this understanding.

During the war Roosevelt wavered uneasily between emphasizing the postwar role of the great powers and minimizing their role and seeking to extend the principles of the Atlantic Charter. Though he often spoke of the need for an open postwar world, and he was reluctant to accept spheres of influence (beyond the Western hemisphere, where American influence was pre-eminent), his policies gradually acknowledged the pre-eminence of the great powers and yielded slowly to their demands. By late 1943 Roosevelt confided to Archbishop Francis Spellman (according to Spellman's notes) that "the world will be divided into spheres of influence: China gets the Far East; the U.S. the Pacific; Britain and Russia, Europe and Africa." The United States, he thought, would have little postwar influence on the continent, and Russia would probably "predominate in Europe," making Austria, Hungary, and Croatia "a sort of Russian protectorate." He acknowledged "that the European countries will have to undergo tremendous changes in order to adapt to Russia; but he hopes that in ten or twenty years the European influence would bring the Russians to become less barbarous."

In 1944 Roosevelt recognized the establishment of zones of influence in Europe. The Italian armistice of the year before had set the pattern for other wartime agreements on the control of affairs of liberated and defeated European nations. When Stalin requested the creation of a three-power Allied commission to deal with the problems of "countries falling away from Germany," Roosevelt and Churchill first rebuffed the Russian leader and then agreed to a joint commission for Italy which would be limited to information gathering. By excluding Russia from sharing in decision-making in Italy, the United States and Great Britain, later concluded William McNeill, "prepared the way for their own exclusion from any but a marginal share in the affairs of Eastern Europe."

When Roosevelt refused to participate in an Anglo-American invasion of southeastern Europe (which seemed to be the only way of restricting Russian influence in that area), Churchill sought other ways of dealing with Russian power and of protecting British interests in Greece. In May 1944 he proposed to Stalin that they recognize Greece as a British "zone of influence" and Rumania as a Russian zone; but Stalin insisted upon seeking Roosevelt's approval and refused the offer upon learning that the United States would not warmly endorse the terms. When the Soviets liberated Rumania in September they secured temporarily the advantages that Churchill had offered. They simply followed the British-American example in Italy, retained all effective power, and announced they were "acting in the interests of all the United Nations." From the Soviet Union, W. Averell Harriman, the American ambassador, cabled, "The Russians believe, I think, that we lived up to a tacit understanding that Rumania was an area of predominant Soviet interest in which we should not interfere. . . . The terms of the armistice give the Soviet command unlimited control of Rumania's economic life" and effective control over political organization.

With Russian armies sweeping through the Balkans and soon in a position to impose similar terms on Hungary and Bulgaria, Churchill renewed his efforts. "Winston," wrote an associate, "never talks of Hitler these days; he is always harping on the dangers of Communism. He dreams of the Red Army spreading like a cancer from one country to another. It has become an obsession, and he seems to think of little else." In October Churchill journeyed to Moscow to reach an agreement with Stalin. "Let us settle our affairs in the Balkans," Churchill told him. "Your armies are in Rumania and Bulgaria. We have interests, missions and agents there. Don't let us get at cross-purposes in small ways." Great Britain received "90 per cent influence" in Greece, and Russia "90 per cent influence" in Rumania, "80 per cent" in Bulgaria and Hungary, and "50 per cent" in Yugoslavia.

In the cases of Hungary and Bulgaria the terms were soon sanctioned by armistice agreements (approved by the United States) which left effective power with the Soviets. "The Russians took it for granted," Cordell Hull, then Secretary of State, wrote later, "that . . . Britain and the United States had assigned them a certain portion of the Balkans, including Rumania and Bulgaria, as their sphere of influence." In December Stalin even confirmed the agreement at a considerable price: he permitted British troops to put down a rebellion in Greece. "Stalin," wrote Churchill later, "adhered strictly and faithfully to our agreement . . . and during all the long weeks of fighting the communists in the streets of Athens, not one word of reproach came from *Pravda* or *Izvestia*."

At Yalta in February 1945 Roosevelt did not seem to challenge

Soviet dominance in east-central Europe, which had been established by the Churchill-Stalin agreement and confirmed by the armistices and by British action in Greece. What Roosevelt did seek and gain at Yalta was a weak "Declaration on Liberated Europe"—that the powers would consult "where in their judgment conditions require" assistance to maintain peace or to establish democratic governments. By requiring unanimity the declaration allowed any one power to veto any proposal that seemed to threaten that power's interests. In effect, then, the declaration, despite its statements about democratic governments, did not alter the situation in Eastern Europe. The operative phrases simply affirmed the principle that the three powers had already established: they could consult together when all agreed, and they could act together when all agreed. At Yalta the broadly phrased statement provoked little discussion—only a few pages in the official proceedings. Presumably the Russians did not consider it a repudiation of spheres of influence, only as rhetoric that Roosevelt wanted for home consumption. Despite later official American suggestions, the Yalta agreement was not a product of Roosevelt's misunderstanding of the Soviet meaning of "democracy" and "free elections." Rather, it ratified earlier agreements, and the State Department probably understood this.

While accepting the inevitable and acknowledging Russian influence in these areas, Roosevelt had not been tractable on the major issue confronting the three powers: the treatment of postwar Germany. All three leaders realized that the decisions on Germany would shape the future relations of Europe. A dismembered or permanently weakened Germany would leave Russia without challenge on the continent and would ease her fears of future invasion. As Anthony Eden, the British Foreign Minister explained, "Russia was determined on one thing above all others, that Germany would not again disturb the peace of Europe. . . . Stalin was determined to smash Germany so that it would never again be able to make war." A strong Germany, on the other hand, could be a partial counterweight to Russia and help restore the European balance of power on which Britain had traditionally depended for protection. Otherwise, as Henry Morgenthau once explained in summarizing Churchill's fears, there would be nothing between "the white snows of Russia and the white cliffs of Dover."

The Allied policy on Germany had been in flux for almost two years. At Teheran in 1943 the Allies had agreed in principle (despite Churchill's reluctance) that Germany should be dismembered, and in 1944 Roosevelt and a reluctant Churchill, much to the distress of Foreign Minister Anthony Eden, had agreed on a loosely phrased version of the Morgenthau Plan for the dismemberment and pastoralization of Germany. Not only would the plan have eliminated German military-industrial potential and thereby allayed Russian fears, but by stripping Germany it would also have provided the resources for Russian economic reconstruction. Churchill, despite his fear of Russia and his desire for Germany as a counterweight on the continent, had temporarily agreed to the plan because it seemed to be a prerequisite for increased American economic aid and promised to eliminate German industry as a postwar rival for the trade that the debt-ridden British economy would need. Many in the State and War Departments charged that the plan was economic madness, that it would leave not only Germany but also much of war-torn Western Europe (which would need postwar German production) without the means for economic reconstruction. (Secretary of the Treasury Morgenthau concluded after discussion with many officials that they wanted a strong Germany as a "bulwark against Bolshevism.") Yielding to the pleas of the War and State Departments, Roosevelt decided upon a plan for a stronger postwar Germany, and Churchill, under pressure from advisers, also backed away from his earlier endorsement of the Morgenthau Plan and again acted upon his fears of an unopposed Russia on the continent. At Yalta, he resisted any agreement on the dismemberment of Germany. Stalin, faced with Anglo-American solidarity on this issue, acceded. The final communiqué patched over this fundamental dispute by announcing that the three powers had pledged to "take such steps including the complete disarmament, demilitarization, and dismemberment of Germany as they deem requisite for future peace and security." The strategy of postponement had triumphed. Unable to reach a substantive agreement, the Big Three agreed to submit these problems (and the related, vital issues of reparations and boundaries) to three-power commissions.

Though Yalta has come to represent the triumph of the strategy of postponement, at the time it symbolized Allied accord. Stalin accepted a limitation of the veto power on certain quasi-judicial issues in the U.N. Security Council; Roosevelt conceded to Russia the return of the Kurile Islands, which stretched between Japan and Siberia, and special rights in Dairen and Port Arthur in Manchuria; Stalin promised to enter the Pacific war within three months of the end of the European conflict. "Stalin," as William McNeill explained, "had conceded something to the British in Yugoslavia; and Churchill had yielded a good deal in Poland."

II

Roosevelt's successor was less sympathetic to Russian aspirations and more responsive to those of Roosevelt's advisers, like Admiral William Leahy, Chief of Staff to the Commander in Chief; Harriman; James Forrestal, Secretary of the Navy; and James F. Byrnes, Truman's choice for Secretary of State, who had urged that he resist Soviet efforts in Eastern Europe. As an earlier self-proclaimed foe of Russian communism, Truman mistrusted Russia. ("If we see that Germany is winning the war," advised Senator Truman after the German attack upon Russia in 1941, "we ought to help Russia, and if Russia is winning we ought to help Germany and in that way kill as many as possible.") Upon entering the White House, he did not seek to follow Roosevelt's tactics of adjustment and accommodation. Only eleven days in the presidency and virtually on the eve of the United Nations conference,

Truman moved to a showdown with Russia on the issue of Poland.

Poland became the testing ground for American foreign policy, as Truman later said, "a symbol of the future development of our international relations." At Yalta the three powers had agreed that the Soviet-sponsored Lublin Committee (the temporary Polish government) should be "recognized on a broader democratic basis with the inclusion of democratic leaders from Poland itself and from Poland abroad." The general terms were broad: there was no specific formula for the distribution of power in the reorganized government, and the procedures required consultation and presumably unanimity from the representatives of the three powers. The agreement, remarked Admiral Leahy, was "so elastic that the Russians can stretch it all the way from Yalta to Washington without ever technically breaking it." ("I know, Bill—I know it. But it's the best I can do for Poland at this time," Roosevelt replied.)

For almost two months after Yalta the great powers haggled over Poland. The Lublin Committee objected to the Polish candidates proposed by the United States and Great Britain for consultation because these Poles had criticized the Yalta accord and refused to accept the Soviet annexation of Polish territory (moving the eastern boundary to the Curzon Line). In early April Stalin had offered a compromise— that about 80 per cent of the cabinet posts in the new government should be held by members of the Lublin Committee, and that he would urge the committee to accept the leading Western candidates if they would endorse the Yalta agreement (including the Curzon Line). By proposing a specific distribution of power, Stalin cut to the core of the issue that had disrupted negotiations for nearly three months, and sought to guarantee the victory he probably expected in Poland. Roosevelt died before replying, and it is not clear whether he would have accepted this 4 to 1 representation; but he had acknowledged that he was prepared to place "somewhat more emphasis on the Lublin Poles."

Now Truman was asked to acknowledge Soviet concern about countries on her borders and to assure her influence in many of these countries by granting her friendly (and probably non-democratic) governments, and even by letting her squelch anti-communist democrats in countries like Poland. To the President and his advisers the issue was (as Truman later expressed Harriman's argument) "the extension of Soviet control over neighboring states by independent action; we were faced with a barbarian invasion of Europe." The fear was not that the Soviets were about to threaten all of Europe but that they had designs on Eastern Europe, and that these designs conflicted with traditional American values of self-determination, democracy, and open markets.

Rushing back to Washington after Roosevelt's death, Harriman found most of FDR's advisers (now Truman's) sympathetic to a tougher approach. At a special White House meeting Harriman outlined what he thought were the Soviet Union's two policies—cooperation with the United States and Great Britain, and the creation of a unilateral security ring through domination of its border states. These policies, he contended, did not seem contradictory to Russian leaders, for "certain elements around Stalin" misinterpreted America's generosity and desire to cooperate as an indication of softness and concluded "that the Soviet Government could do anything that it wished without having any trouble with the United States." Before Roosevelt's death, Harriman had cabled: "It may be difficult . . . to believe, but it still may be true that Stalin and Molotov considered at Yalta that by our willingness to accept a general wording of the declaration on Poland and liberated Europe, by our recognition of the need of the Red Army for security behind its lines, and of the predominant interest of Russia in Poland as a friendly neighbor and as a corridor to Germany, we understood and were ready to accept Soviet policies already known to us."

Harriman wanted the American government to select a few test cases and make the Russians realize they could not continue their present policies. Such tactics, he advised, would place Russian-American relations on a more realistic basis and compel the Soviet Union to adhere to the American interpretation of the issues in dispute. Because the Soviet government "needed our [economic assistance] . . . in their reconstruction," and because Stalin did not wish to break with the United States, Harriman thought Truman "could stand on important issues without running serious risks." As early as January 1944 Harriman had emphasized that "the Soviet Government places the utmost importance on our cooperation" in providing economic assistance, and he had concluded: "it is a factor which should be integrated into the fabric of our overall relations." In early April Harriman had proposed that unless the United States were prepared "to live in a world dominated largely by Soviet influence, we must use our economic power to assist those countries that are naturally friendly to our concepts." In turn, he had recommended "tying our economic assistance directly into our political problems with the Soviet Union.

General George Marshall, the Army Chief of Staff, and Secretary of War Henry Stimson, however, recommended caution. Stimson observed "that the Russians perhaps were being more realistic than we were in regard to their own security," and he feared "that we would find ourselves breaking our relations with Russia on the most important and difficult question which we and Russia have gotten between us." Leahy, though supporting a firm policy, admitted that the Yalta agreement "was susceptible to two interpretations." Secretary of State Edward Stettinius read aloud the Yalta decision and concluded "that this was susceptible of only one interpretation."

Having heard his advisers' arguments, Truman resolved to force the Polish question: to impose his interpretation of the Yalta agreement even if it destroyed the United Nations. He later explained that this was the test of Russian cooperation. If Stalin would not abide by his agreements, the U.N. was doomed, and, anyway, there would not be enough enthusiasm among the American electorate to let the United States join the world body. "Our agreements with the Soviet Union so far . . . [have] been a one-way street." That could not continue, Truman told his advisers. "If the Russians did not wish to join us, they could go to hell." ("FDR's appeasement of Russia is over," joyously wrote Senator Arthur Vandenberg, the Republican leader on foreign policy.) Continuing in this spirit at a private conference with Molotov, the new President warned that economic aid would depend upon Russian behavior in fulfilling the Yalta agreement. Brushing aside the diplomat's contention that the Anglo-American interpretation of the Yalta agreement was wrong, the President accused the Russians of breaking agreements and scolded the Russian Foreign Minister. When Molotov replied, "I have never been talked to like that in my life," Truman warned him, "Carry out your agreement and you won't get talked to like that."

At the United Nations conference in San Francisco, when Anthony Eden, the British Foreign Minister, saw a copy of Truman's "blunt message" about Poland to Stalin, "he could scarcely believe his eyes . . . and cheered loudly," reported Vandenberg. But the policy of firmness was not immediately successful. American-Russian relations were further strained by the disputes at the meeting to create the U.N.—over the veto, the admission of fascist Argentina, and the persistent question of Poland. Despite Soviet objections and Roosevelt's promise at Yalta to exclude Argentina from the U.N., the United States supported the Latin American state's candidacy for membership. In committee Molotov, whom Stalin had sent to establish good will with the new President, tried to block the admission of Argentina until the Lublin Poles were also admitted, but his proposed bargain was overwhelmingly defeated. Later in the plenary session, when only three nations voted with Russia, the Soviets found additional evidence for their fears of an American bloc directed against their interests. The Truman administration's action also gave the Soviets more reason to doubt America's explanations that her interests in Poland were inspired simply by a desire to guarantee representative, democratic governments. Moreover, because of the American bloc and Soviet fears that the U.N. (like the League of Nations) might be used against her, Molotov was at first unwilling to accede to the demands of the United States and the smaller nations who wished to exclude procedural questions before the Security Council from the great power veto.

The Soviets were further embittered when the United States abruptly curtailed lend-lease six days after V-E Day. Though Truman later explained this termination as simply a "mistake," as policy-making by subordinates, his recollection was incomplete and wrong. Leo Crowley, the director of lend-lease, and Joseph Grew, the Under Secretary of State, the two subordinates most closely involved, had repeatedly warned the President of the likely impact of such action on relations with Russia, and the evidence suggests that the government, as Harriman had counseled, was seeking to use economic power to achieve diplomatic means. Termination of lend-lease, Truman later wrote, "should have been done on a gradual basis which would not have made it appear as if somebody had been deliberately snubbed." Yet, despite this later judgment, Truman had four days after signing the order in which to modify it before it was to be implemented and announced, and the lend-lease administrator (in the words of Grew) had made "sure that the President understands the situation." The administrator knew "that we would be having difficulty with the Russians and did not want them to be running all over town for help." After discussing the decision with Truman, Grew, presumably acting with the President's approval, had even contrived to guarantee that curtailment would be a dramatic shock. When the Soviet chargé d'affaires had telephoned Grew the day before the secret order was to become effective, the Under Secretary had falsely denied that lend-lease to Russia was being halted. Harriman, according to Grew's report to the Secretary of State, "said that we would be getting 'a good tough slashback' from the Russians but that we would have to face it."

Presumably to patch the alliance, Truman dispatched to Moscow Harry Hopkin's, Roosevelt's former adviser and a staunch advocate of Soviet-American friendship. Hopkins denied that Truman's action was an American effort to demonstrate economic power and coerce Russia ("pressure on the Russians to soften them up," as Stalin charged). Instead he emphasized that "Poland had become a symbol of our ability to work out our problems with the Soviet Union." Stalin acknowledged "the right of the United States as a world power to participate in the Polish question," but he stressed the importance of Poland to Soviet security. Within twenty-five years the "Germans had twice invaded Russia via Poland," he emphasized. "All the Soviet Union wanted was that Poland should not be in a position to open the gates to Germany," and that required a government friendly to Russia. There was "no intention," he promised, "to interfere in Poland's internal affairs" or to Sovietize Poland.

Through the Hopkins mission, Truman and Stalin reached a compromise: 70 per cent of the new Polish government (fourteen of twenty ministers) should be drawn from the Lublin Committee. At the time there was reason to believe that such heavy communist influence would not lead to Soviet control. Stalin had reaffirmed the pledge of free elections in Poland, and Stanislaw Mikolajczyk, former Prime Minister of the exile government in London and Deputy Prime Minister in the new coalition government, was optimistic. He hoped (in Harriman's words) that "a reasonable degree of freedom and independence can be preserved now and that in time after conditions in Europe can become more stable and [as] Russian turns her attention to her internal development, controls will be relaxed and Poland will be able to gain for herself her independence of life as a nation even though he freely accepts that Poland's security and foreign policy must follow the lead of Moscow."

Truman compromised and soon recognized the new Polish government, but he did not lose his hopes of rolling back the Soviets from their spheres of influence in Eastern Europe. Basing most of his case on the Yalta "Declaration on Liberated Europe" (for which he relied on State Department interpretations), Truman hoped to force Russia to permit representative governments in its zones, and expected that free elections would diminish, perhaps even remove, Soviet authority. Refusing to extend diplomatic recognition to Rumania and Bulgaria, he emphasized that these governments were "neither representative of nor responsive to the will of the people."

"The opportunities for the democratic elements in Rumania and Bulgaria are not less than, say, in Italy, with which the Governments of of the United States and the Soviet Union have already resumed diplomatic relations," replied Stalin, who was willing to exaggerate to emphasize his case. The Russians were demanding a *quid pro quo,* and they would not yield. At Potsdam, in late July, when Truman demanded "immediate reorganization" of the governments of Hungary and Bulgaria to "include representatives of all significant democratic elements" and three-power assistance in "holding . . . free and unfettered elections," Stalin pointed to Greece, again to remind Truman of the earlier agreements. The Russians were "not meddling in Greek affairs," he noted, adding that the Bulgarian and Rumanian governments were fulfilling the armistice agreements while in Greece "terrorism rages . . . against democratic elements." (One member of the American delegation later claimed that Stalin at one point made his position clear, stating that "any freely elected government [in Eastern Europe] would be anti-Soviet and that we cannot permit.") In effect, Stalin demanded that the United States abide by his construction of earlier agreements, and that Truman acknowledge what Roosevelt had accepted as the terms of the sphere-of-influence agreements—that democratic forms and anti-communist democrats of Eastern Europe be abandoned to the larger cause of Russian-American concord.

Though the Allies at Potsdam were not able to settle the dispute over influence in Eastern Europe, they did reach a limited agreement on other European issues. In a "package" deal the Soviets accepted Italy in the U.N. after a peace treaty could be arranged; the United States and Great Britain agreed to set the temporary western border of Poland at the Oder-Neisse line; and the Soviets settled for far less in reparations than they had expected. The decisions on Germany were the important settlements, and the provision on reparations, when linked with American avoidance of offering Russia economic aid, left Russia without the assistance she needed for the pressing task of economic reconstruction.

Russia had long been seeking substantial economic aid, and the American failure to offer it seemed to be part of a general strategy. Earlier Harriman had advised "that the development of friendly relations [with Russia] would depend upon a generous credit," and recommended "that the question of the credit should be tied into our overall diplomatic relations with the Soviet Union and at the appropriate time the Russians should be given to understand that our willingness to cooperate wholeheartedly with them in their vast reconstruction problem will depend upon their behavior in international matters." In January 1945 Roosevelt had decided not to discuss at Yalta the $6 billion credit to the Soviet Union, explaining privately, "I think it's very important that we hold this back and don't give them any promises until we get what we want." (Secretary Morgenthau, in vigorous disagreement, believed that both the President and Secretary of State Stettinius were wrong, and "that if they wanted to get the Russians to do something they should . . . do it nice. . . . Don't drive such a hard bargain that when you come through it does not taste good.") In future months American officials continued to delay, presumably using the prospect of a loan for political leverage. Shortly before Postdam, the administration had secured congressional approval for a $1 billion loan fund which could have been used to assist Russia, but the issue of "credits to the Soviet Union" apparently was never even discussed.

Shunting aside the loan, the United States also retreated from Roosevelt's implied agreement at Yalta that reparations would be about $20 billion (half of which the Soviets would receive); Truman's new Secretary of State, James F. Byrnes, pointed out that the figures were simply the "basis" for discussion. (He was technically correct, but obviously Roosevelt had intended it as a general promise and Stalin had so understood it. Had it not been so intended, why had Churchill refused to endorse this section of the Yalta agreement?) Because Byrnes was unwilling to yield, the final agreement on reparations was similar to the terms that would have prevailed if there had been no agreement: the Soviet Union would fill her claims largely by removals from her own zone. That was the substance of the Potsdam agreement. The Russians also surrendered any hopes of participating in control of the heavily industrialized Ruhr, and confirmed the earlier retreat from the policy of dismemberment of Germany. They settled for an agreement that they could trade food and raw materials from their zone for 15 per cent of such industrial capital equipment from the Western Zones "as is unnecessary for the German peace economy," and that the allies would transfer from the Western Zones "10 percent of such industrial capital equipment as is unnecessary for the German peace economy"—but the agreement left undefined what was necessary for the economy.

Potsdam, like Yalta, left many of the great questions unresolved. "One fact that stands out more clearly than others is that nothing is ever settled," wrote Lord Alanbrooke, Chief of the British Staff, in his diary. As he observed, neither the United States nor Russia had yielded significantly. Russia had refused to move from the areas that her armies occupied, and the United States had been vigorous in her efforts, but without offering economic assistance to gain concessions. Though the atomic bomb may not have greatly influenced Truman's actions in the months before Potsdam, the bomb certainly influenced his behavior at Potsdam. When he arrived he still wanted (and expected) Russian intervention in the Japanese war. During the conference he learned about the successful test at Alamogordo. With Russian intervention no longer necessary, Truman's position hardened noticeably. As sole possessor of the bomb, he had good reason to expect easier future dealings with Stalin. For months Stimson had been counseling that the bomb would be the "master card," and Truman, acting on Stimson's advice, even delayed the Potsdam Conference until a time when he would know about the bomb. On the eve of the conference the President had confided to an adviser, "If it explodes, as I think it will, I'll certainly have a hammer on those boys [the Russians]."

III

At Potsdam President Truman was "delighted" when Stimson brought him the news about the bomb on July 16. Upon learning more about the results of the test, Truman (according to Stimson) said "it gave him an entirely new feeling of confidence and he thanked me for having come to the conference and being present to help him in this way." The President's enthusiasm and new sense of power were soon apparent in his meetings with the other heads of state, for as Churchill notes (in Stimson's words), "Truman was evidently much fortified by something that had happened and . . . he stood up to the Russians in a most emphatic and decisive manner." After reading the full report on the Alamogordo explosion, Churchill said. "Now I know what happened to Truman yesterday. I couldn't understand it. When he got to the meeting after having read this report he was a changed man. He told the Russians just where they got off and generally bossed the whole meeting."

"From that moment [when we learned of the successful test] our outlook on the future was transformed," Churchill explained later. Forced earlier to concede parts of Eastern Europe to the Russians because Britain did not have the power to resist Soviet wishes and the United States had seemed to lack the desire, Churchill immediately savored the new possibilities. The Prime Minister (Lord Alanbrooke wrote in his diary about Churchill's enthusiasm) "was completely carried away . . . we now had something in our hands which would redress the balance with the Russians. The secret of this explosive and the power to use it would completely alter the diplomatic equilibrium. . . . Now we had a new value which redressed our position (pushing out his chin and scowling); now we could say, 'If you insist on doing this or that well . . . And then where were the Russians!'"

Stimson and Byrnes had long understood that the bomb could influence future relations with Russia, and, after the successful test, they knew that Russian entry was no longer necessary to end the Japanese war. Upon Truman's direction, Stimson conferred at Potsdam with General Marshall and reported to the President that Marshall no longer saw a need for Russian intervention. "It is quite clear," cabled Churchill from Potsdam, "that the United States do not at the present time desire Russian participation in the war against Japan."

"The new explosive alone was sufficient to settle matters," Churchill reported. The bomb had displaced the Russians in the calculations of American policy-makers. The combat use of the bomb, then, was not viewed as the only way to end the Far Eastern war promptly. In July there was ample evidence that there were other possible strategies—a noncombat demonstration, a warning, a blockade. Yet, before authorizing the use of the bomb at Hiroshima, Truman did not try *any* of the possible strategies, including the three most likely: guaranteeing the position of the Japanese Emperor (and hence making surrender conditional), seeking a Russian declaration of war (or announcement of intent), or waiting for Russian entry into the war.

As an invasion of the Japanese mainland was not scheduled until about November 1, and as Truman knew that the Japanese were sending out "peace feelers" and that the main obstacle to peace seemed to be the requirement of unconditional surrender (which threatened the position of the Emperor), he could wisely have revised the terms of surrender. At first Under Secretary of State Grew and then Stimson had urged Truman earlier to revise the terms in this way, and he had been sympathetic. But at Potsdam Stimson found that Truman and Byrnes had rejected his advice. As a result the proclamation issued from Potsdam by the United States, Great Britain. and China retained the demand for unconditional surrender when a guarantee of the Emperor's government might have removed the chief impediment to peace.

Nor was Truman willing to seek a Russian declaration of war (or even an announcement of intent). Even though American advisers had long believed that the *threat* of Russian entry might be sufficient to compel Japanese capitulation, Truman did not invite Stalin to sign the proclamation, which would have constituted a statement of Russian intent. There is even substantial evidence that Truman sought to delay Russian entry into the war.

Pledging to maintain the position of the Emperor, seeking a Russian declaration of war (or announcement of intent), awaiting Russian entry—each of these options, as well as others, had been proposed in the months before Hiroshima and Nagasaki. Each was available to Truman. Why did he not try one or more? No *definite* answer is possible. But it is clear that Truman was either incapable or unwilling to reexamine his earlier assumption (or decision) of using the bomb. Under the tutelage of Byrnes and Stimson, Truman had come to assume by July that the bomb should be used, and perhaps he was incapable of reconsidering this strategy because he found no compelling reason not to use the bomb. Or he may have consciously rejected the options because he wanted to use the bomb. Perhaps he was vindictive and wished to retaliate for Pearl Harbor and other atrocities. (In justifying the use of the bomb against the Japanese, he wrote a few days after Nagasaki, "The only language they seem to understand is the one we have been using to bombard them. When you have to deal with a beast you have to treat him as a beast.") Or, most likely, Truman agreed with Byrnes that using the bomb would advance other American policies: it would end the war before the Russians could gain a hold in Manchuria, it would permit the United States to exclude Russia from the occupation government of Japan, and it would make the Soviets more manageable in Eastern Europe. It would enable the United States to shape the peace according to its own standards.

At minimum, then, the use of the bomb reveals the moral insensitivity of the President—whether he used it because the moral implications did not compel a reexamination of assumptions, or because he sought retribution, or because he sought to keep Russia out of Manchuria and the occupation government of Japan, and to make her more manageable in Eastern Europe. In 1945 American foreign policy was not innocent, nor was it unconcerned about Russian power, nor did it assume that the United States lacked the power to impose its will on the Russian state, nor was it characterized by high moral purpose or consistent dedication to humanitarian principles.

IV

Both Secretary of War Stimson and Secretary of State Byrnes had foreseen the importance of the bomb to American foreign policy. To Stimson it had long promised to be the "master card" for diplomacy. After Hiroshima and Nagasaki Byrnes was eager to use the bomb as at least an "implied threat" in negotiations with Russia. and Truman seems to have agreed to a vigorous course in trying to roll back Russian influence in Eastern Europe.

Truman seemed to be rejecting Stimson's recommendations that international control of atomic energy be traded for important Russian concessions—"namely the settlement of the Polish, Rumanian, Yugo-slavian, and Manchurian problems." In his report on the Potsdam Conference the day after the second bomb, the President asserted that Rumania, Bulgaria, and Hungary "are not to be the spheres of influence of any one power" and at the same time proclaimed that the United States would be the "trustees" of the atomic bomb.

Following Truman's veiled threat, Byrnes continued his efforts to roll back the Soviet Union's influence. Assisted by a similar protest by the British, who clearly recognized the power of the bomb, he gained postponement of the Bulgarian election, charging that the government was not "adequately representative of important elements . . . of democratic opinion" and that its arrangements for elections "did not insure freedom from the fear of force or intimidation." In Hungary, Russia also acceded to similar Anglo-American demands and postponed the scheduled elections. It is not unreasonable to conclude that the bomb had made the Russians more tractable. "The significance of Hiroshima was not lost on the Russians," Alexander Werth, British correspondent in the Soviet Union, later reported. "It was clearly realized that this was a New Fact in the world's power politics, that the bomb constituted a threat to Russia. . . . Everybody . . . believed that although the two [atomic] bombs had killed or maimed [the] . . . Japanese, their real purpose was, first and foremost, to intimidate Russia."

Perhaps encouraged by his successes in Bulgaria and Hungary, Byrnes "wished to have the implied threat of the bomb in his pocket during the [September] conference" of foreign ministers in London. Stimson confided to his diary that Byrnes "was very much against any attempt to cooperate with Russia. His mind is full of his problems with the coming meeting . . . and he looks to having the presence of the bomb in his pocket . . . as a great weapon to get through the thing he has. He also told me of a number of acts of perfidy . . . of Stalin which they had encountered at Potsdam and felt in the light of those that we would not rely upon anything in the way of promises from them."

The London conference ended in deadlock, disbanding without even a joint communiqué. Despite American possession of the bomb, Molotov would not yield to American demands to reorganize the governments of Bulgaria and Rumania. In turn, he demanded for Russia a role in the occupation government of Japan, but Byrnes rebuffed the proposal. Unprepared for this issue, Byrnes was also unwilling or unable to understand Soviet anxieties about the security of their frontiers, and he pressed most vigorously for the reorganization of the Rumanian government. He would not acknowledge and perhaps could not understand the dilemma of his policy: that he was supporting free elections in areas (particularly in Rumania) where the resulting governments would probably be hostile to the Soviet Union, and yet he was arguing that democracy in Eastern Europe was compatible with Soviet demands for security. Unable to accept that Byrnes might be naive, Molotov questioned the Secretary's sincerity and charged that he wanted governments unfriendly to the Soviet Union. From this, Byrnes could only conclude later, "It seemed that the Soviet Union was determined to dominate Europe."

While the United States in the cases of these Eastern European nations chose to support traditional democratic principles and neither to acknowledge its earlier agreements on spheres of influence nor to respect Russian fears, Byrnes would not admit the similarity between Russian behavior in Rumania and British action in Greece. As part of the terms of his agreement with Churchill, Stalin had allowed the British to suppress a revolutionary force in Greece, and as a result the Greek government could not be accurately interpreted as broadly representative nor as a product of democratic procedures. Yet, as Molotov emphasized, the United States had not opposed British action in Greece or questioned the legitimacy of that government, nor was the United States making a reversal of British imperialism in Greece a condition for the large loan that Britain needed.

Some American observers, however, were aware of this double standard. In the northern Pacific and in Japan, America was to have the deciding voice, but in Eastern Europe, emphasized Walter Lippmann, "we invoke the principle that this is one world in which decisions must not be taken unilaterally." Most Americans did not see this paradox, and Byrnes probably expressed crystallizing national sentiment that autumn when he concluded that the dispute with Russia was a test of whether "we really believed in what we said about one world and our desire to build collective security, or whether we were willing to accept the Soviet preference for the simpler task of dividing the world into two spheres of influence."

Despite Byrnes's views, and although he could not secure a reorganization of the Rumanian government, communist influence was weakened in other parts of Eastern Europe. In Budapest free elections were held and the Communist party was routed; and early in November, just two days after the United States recognized Hungary, the Communists lost in the national elections there. In Bulgaria elections took place in "complete order and without disturbance," and despite American protests, a Communist-dominated single ticket (representing most of the political parties) triumphed.

While the Soviet Union would not generally permit in Eastern Europe conditions that conformed to Western ideals, Stalin was pursuing a cautious policy and seeking accommodation with the West. He was willing to allow capitalism but was suspicious of American efforts at economic penetration which could lead to political dominance. Though by the autumn of 1945 the governments in Russia's general area of influence were subservient in foreign policy, they varied in form and in degree of independence—democracy in Czechoslovakia (the only country in this area with a democratic tradition), free elections and the overthrow of the Communist party in Hungary, a Communist-formed coalition government in Bulgaria, a broadly based but Communist-dominated government in Poland, and a Soviet-imposed government in Rumania (the most anti-Russian of these nations). In all of these countries Communists controlled the ministries of interior (the police) and were able to suppress anti-Soviet groups, including anti-communist democrats.

Those who have attributed to Russia a policy of inexorable expansion have often neglected this immediate postwar period, or they have interpreted it simply as a necessary preliminary (a cunning strategy to allay American suspicions until the American Army demobilized and left the continent) to the consolidation and extension of power in east-central Europe, From this perspective, however, much of Stalin's behavior becomes strangely contradictory and potentially self-defeating. If he had planned to create puppets rather than an area of "friendly governments," why (as Isaac Deutscher asks) did Stalin "so stubbornly refuse to make any concessions to the Poles over their eastern frontiers?" Certainly, also, his demand for reparations from Hungary, Rumania, and Bulgaria would have been unnecessary if he had planned to take over these countries. (America's insistence upon using a loan to Russia to achieve political goals, and the nearly twenty-month delay after Russia first submitted a specific proposal for assistance, led Harriman to suggest in November that the loan policy "may have contributed to their [Russian] avaricious policies in the countries occupied or liberated by the Red Army.")

Russian sources are closed, so it is not possible to prove that Soviet intentions were conservative; nor for the same reason is it possible for those who adhere to the thesis of inexorable Soviet expansion to prove their theory. But the available evidence better supports the thesis that these years should be viewed not as a cunning preliminary to the harshness of 1947 and afterward, but as an attempt to establish a *modus vivendi* with the West and to protect "socialism in one country." This interpretation explains more adequately why the Russians delayed nearly three years before ending dissent and hardening policies in the countries behind their own military lines. It would also explain why the Communist parties in France and Italy were cooperating with the coalition governments until these parties were forced out of the coalitions in 1947. The American government had long hoped for the exclusion of these Communist parties, and in Italy, at least, American intimations of greater economic aid to a government without Communists was an effective lever. At the same time Stalin was seeking to prevent the revolution in Greece.

If the Russian policy was conservative and sought accommodation (as now seems likely), then its failure must be explained by looking beyond Russian actions. Historians must reexamine this period and reconsider American policies. Were they directed toward compromise? Can they be judged as having sought adjustment? Or did they demand acquiescence to the American world view, thus thwarting real negotiations?

There is considerable evidence that American actions clearly changed after Roosevelt's death. Slowly abandoning the tactics of accommodation, they became even more vigorous after Hiroshima. The insistence upon rolling back Soviet influence in Eastern Europe, the reluctance to grant a loan for Russian reconstruction, the inability to reach an agreement on Germany, the maintenance of the nuclear monopoly—all of these could have contributed to the sense of Russian insecurity. The point, then, is that in 1945 and 1946 there may still have been possibilities for negotiations and settlements, for accommodations and adjustments, if the United States had been willing to recognize Soviet fears, to accept Soviet power in her areas of influence, and to ease anxieties.

V

In October 1945 President Truman delivered what Washington officials called his "getting tough with the Russians" speech. Proclaiming that American policy was "based firmly on fundamental principles of righteousness and justice," he promised that the United States "shall not give our approval to any compromise with evil." In a veiled assault on Soviet actions in Eastern Europe, he declared, "We shall refuse to recognize any government imposed on any nation by the force of any foreign power." Tacitly opposing the bilateral trading practices of Russia, he asserted as a principle of American foreign policy the doctrine of the "open door"—all nations "should have access on equal terms to the trade and the raw materials of the world." At the same time, however, Truman disregarded the fact of American power in Latin America and emphasized that the Monroe Doctrine (in expanded form) remained a cherished part of American policy there: ". . . the sovereign states of the Western Hemisphere, without interference from outside the Western Hemisphere, must work together as good neighbors in the solution of their common economic problems."

"Soviet current policy," concluded a secret report by the Deputy Director of Naval Intelligence a few months later, "is to establish a Soviet Monroe Doctrine for the area under her shadow, primarily and urgently for security, secondarily to facilitate the eventual emergence of the USSR as a power which could not be menaced by any other world combination of powers." The report did not expect the Soviets ". . . to take any action during the next five years which might develop into hostilities with Anglo-Americans," but anticipated attempts to build up intelligence and potential sabotage networks, "encouragement of Communist parties in all countries potentially to weaken antagonists, and in colonial areas to pave the way for 'anti-imperialist' disorders and revolutions as a means of sapping the strength of . . . chief remaining European rivals, Britain and France." "Present Soviet maneuvers to control North Iran," the report explained, were conceived to "push . . . from their own oil . . . and closer to the enemy's oil." There was no need to fear military expansion beyond this security zone, suggested the report, for the Soviet Union was economically exhausted, its population undernourished and dislocated, its industry and transportation "in an advanced state of deterioration." Despite suggestions that Soviet policy was rather cautious, Truman was reaching a more militant conclusion. "Unless Russia is faced with an iron fist and strong language," asserted Truman to his Secretary of State in January, "another war is in the making. Only one language do they understand—'how many divisions have you' . . . I'm tired of babying the Soviets."

During the winter months Byrnes, Senator Vandenberg, and John Foster Dulles, a Republican adviser on foreign policy, publicly attacked Russian policies. Vandenberg warned "our Russian ally" that the United States could not ignore "a unilateral gnawing away at the status quo." After these attacks, Churchill, accompanied by the President, delivered at Fulton, Missouri, a speech that announced the opening of the Cold War. "From Stettin in the Baltic to Trieste in the Adriatic, an iron curtain has descended across the Continent," declared the former British war leader. Condemning the establishment of "police governments" in Eastern Europe and warning of "Communist fifth columns or . . . parties elsewhere," Churchill, with Truman's approval, called for an Anglo-American alliance to create "conditions of freedom and democracy as rapidly as possible in all [these] countries." The Soviet Union, he contended, did not want war, only "the fruits of war and the indefinite expansion of their power and doctrines." Such dangers could not be removed "by closing our eyes to them . . . nor will they be removed by a policy of appeasement." While he said that it was "not our duty *at this time* . . . to interfere forcibly in the internal affairs" of Eastern European countries, Churchill implied that intervention was advisable when Anglo-American forces were strengthened. His message was clear: ". . . the old doctrine of the balance of power is unsound. We cannot afford . . . to work on narrow margins, offering temptations to a trial of strength."

This was, as James Warburg later wrote, the early "idea of the containment doctrine . . . [and] the first public expression of the idea of a 'policy of liberation,'" which Dulles would later promulgate. Truman's presence on the platform at Fulton implied that Churchill's statement had official American endorsement, and though the President lamely denied afterward that he had known about the contents of the speech, he had actually discussed it with Churchill for two hours. Despite official denials and brief, widespread popular opposition to Churchill's message (according to public opinion polls), American policy was becoming clearly militant. It was not responding to a threat of immediate military danger; it was operating from the position of overwhelming power, and in the self-proclaimed conviction of righteousness.

Undoubtedly Truman also agreed with the former Prime Minister when Churchill said at Fulton:

It would . . . be wrong and imprudent to intrust the secret knowledge of experience of the atomic bomb, which the United States, Great Britain and Canada now share, to the world organization. . . . No one in any country has slept less well in their beds because this knowledge and the method and raw material to apply it are at present . . . in American hands. I do not believe that we should all have slept so soundly had the positions been reversed and some Communist or neo-Fascist state monopolized, for the time being, these dread agencies. . . . Ultimately, when the essential brotherhood of man is truly embodied and expressed in a world organization, these powers may be confided to it.

Here, in classic form, was a theme that would dominate the American dialogue on the Cold War—the assertion of the purity of Anglo-American intentions and the assumption that the opposing power was malevolent and had no justifiable interests, no justifiable fears, and should place its trust in a Pax Americana (or a Pax Anglo-Americana). Under Anglo-American power the world could be transformed, order maintained, and Anglo-American principles extended. Stalin characterized Churchill's message as, "Something in the nature of an ultimatum: 'Accept our rule voluntarily, and then all will be well: otherwise war is inevitable.'"

VI

Churchill's assurances notwithstanding, Russia had reason to fear the atomic bomb, particularly after Byrnes's efforts to use it as an "implied threat." For Byrnes the nuclear monopoly seemed to promise the possibility of creating on American terms a lasting structure of peace. Since this monopoly would last at least seven years, according to his estimates, America could achieve its objectives and presumably avoid an arms race. (A few days after Hiroshima, Byrnes instructed J. Robert Oppenheimer, the nuclear physicist, that "for the time being . . . international agreement was not practical and that he and the rest of the gang should pursue their work [on the hydrogen weapon] full force.")

Byrnes's strategy was briefly and unsuccessfully challenged by another member of the administration, Henry Stimson. Earlier Stimson had hoped that America's possession of the bomb could lead to the offer of a partnership with the Russians in return for a *quid pro quo—*

"the settlement of the Polish, Rumanian, Yugoslavian, and Manchurian problems," and the liberalization of the Soviet regime. Russia would have to roll back her curtain of secrecy and move toward an open society, reasoned Stimson, for "no permanently safe international relations can be established between two such fundamentally different national systems." The bomb, he believed, could not be shared until Russia liberalized her regime, and he hoped that the need for international controls would pry back the lid of secrecy. But his conversations with Harriman at Potsdam had made Stimson pessimistic about Russia's easing her restrictions, and after the bombing of Japan, as he watched Byrnes's strategy unfolding, he moved more strongly toward international cooperation. On September 5 the Secretary of War met with the President, explaining "that both my plan and Byrnes's plan contained chances which I outlined and I said that I thought that in my method there was less danger than in his and also we would be on the right path towards establishment of an international world, while on his plan we would be on the wrong path in that respect and would be tending to revert to power politics."

Rejecting his earlier idea of using possession of the bomb "as a direct lever" to produce "a change in Russian attitudes toward individual liberty," Stimson urged the President to invite the Soviet Union to share the secret "upon a basis of cooperation and trust."

It is true [he wrote to the President] if we approach them now, as I would propose, we may be gambling on their good faith and risk their getting into production of bombs sooner than they would otherwise. To put the matter concisely, I consider the problem of our satisfactory relations with Russia as not merely connected with but virtually dominated by the problem of the atomic bomb. Except for the problem of the control of that bomb, those relations, while vitally important, might not be immediately pressing. The establishment of relations of mutual confidence between her and us could afford to await the slow process of time. But with the discovery of the bomb, they become immediately emergent. *Those relations may be irretrievably embittered by the way in which we approach the solution of the bomb with Russia. For if we fail to approach them now and merely continue to negotiate with them, having this weapon rather ostentatiously on our hip, their suspicions and their distrust of our purposes and motives will increase.*

"The chief lesson I have learned in a long life," concluded Stimson, "is the only way you can make a man trustworthy is to trust him; and the surest way you can make a man untrustworthy is to distrust him and show your distrust." A week after learning that Byrnes planned to use the bomb as an "implied threat," Stimson warned Truman that a direct and forthright approach should be made before using "*express or implied threats* in our peace negotiations."

While Byrnes was at the unsuccessful London conference in mid-September, Stimson was lining up support for his new approach. The President seemed to approve of Stimson's memorandum. Truman "thought that we must take Russia into our confidence," wrote Stimson in his diary. Dean Acheson, the Under Secretary of State, also seemed "strongly on our side in the treatment of Russia," Stimson recorded. Robert P. Patterson, Stimson's Under Secretary who was scheduled to replace the Secretary upon his retirement later in the month, was convinced (in Stimson's words): "The safest way is not to try to keep the secret. It evidently cannot be kept . . . and that being so it is better to recognize it promptly and try to get on [better] terms with the Russians."

At a special cabinet meeting on September 21, Stimson outlined his proposal: "(1) that we should approach Russia at once with an opportunity to share on proper *quid pro quo* the bomb and (2) that this approach to Russia should be to her directly and not through the . . . [United Nations] or a similar conference of a number of states." He received support from Patterson, Robert Hannegan, the Postmaster General, Henry Wallace, the Secretary of Commerce, and Acheson, who was representing the State Department in Byrnes's absence. Explaining that he could not "conceive of a world in which we were hoarders of military secrets from our Allies, particularly this great Ally," Acheson (reported Forrestal) "saw no alternative except to give the full information to the Russians . . . for a *quid pro quo*."

Forrestal, Fred Vinson, the Secretary of the Treasury, Tom Clark, the Attorney General, and Clinton Anderson, the Secretary of Agriculture, opposed sharing the secret. Vinson compared it to the decision at the end of World War I to sink ships, and Anderson emphasized that the President must retain the confidence of the nation in his ability to "handle Russia." He warned that giving up information on atomic energy and the bomb would dangerously weaken that confidence. Forrestal, apparently the most vigorous opponent, objected to any attempt to "buy [Russian] understanding and sympathy. We tried that once with Hitler." Concluding that "trust had to be more than a one-way street," he recommended that the United States exercise "a trusteeship over the . . . bomb on behalf of the United Nations."

Twelve days later, on October 3, Truman publicly announced his decision: the United States would seek international control of atomic energy but would not share the secret of the bomb. Byrnes, who had just returned from the London conference, resisted even this plan: he opposed the sharing of any information with the Russians. Since he believed that his diplomacy had been frustrated by Russian secrecy and suspicions, he did not see how inspection could operate. Convinced that the United States should delay until it had achieved a "decent" peace, he urged the President to stall. He realized that the United States was relying more heavily on the bomb and sharply cutting back conventional forces, and he was unwilling to risk yielding nuclear mastery.

For more than two months the American government delayed even approaching the Russians. "The insistence by the inventors of mankind's most horrible weapon on withholding the secret from their ally has produced a most evident reaction in Moscow," reported the *New York Times*. It also led to Molotov's uneasy public boasting in November that Russia too would develop the bomb. ("We will have atomic energy and many other things too.") Finally, four months after Hiroshima, at the Moscow Conference of Foreign Ministers in late December, Byrnes invited Russia to join in recommending that the United Nations establish a commission on atomic energy.

During the next five months, while the Cold War intensified, the Truman administration organized to formulate a policy. In March it released a preliminary study (the Acheson-Lilienthal report) which sought to minimize the problems of inspection by recommending the establishment of an international Atomic Development Authority (ADA), which would control all significant nuclear activities. The ADA would be established in stages, and at each stage the United States would provide the necessary information, with the specific information on the bomb withheld until the final stage.

Probably this plan would have been unacceptable to the Russians. It would have left the secret of the bomb as an American trust for at least a few years, and it would have meant Russia's relinquishing possible control of a source of great economic potential to an international authority dominated by Western powers. In its emphasis, however, the report also conflicted with the desires of many American officials. It stressed generosity and negotiations when most were emphasizing fear and suspicion. It saw no need for punishment. A violation by any nation, under the proposed arrangements, would have been obvious and would have been a warning to other nations, and all would have returned at that point to big-power politics. The plan emphasized the necessity of international control and was willing to countenance small risks for world security when most emphasized the primacy of American security. ("We should not under any circumstances throw away our gun until we are sure that the rest of the world can't arm against us," asserted Truman.)

The final American plan was formulated and presented by Bernard Baruch, whom Truman had appointed as American representative to the U.N. Atomic Energy Commission. It emphasized "sanctions" and "condign punishments," and called for the elimination of the Security Council veto on matters of atomic energy. The issue of the veto was unnecessary; if any nation violated the treaty after the sharing of atomic energy, what action could be vetoed? In turn, until the nations reached the last stages of the plan, a violation, whatever the situation in the U.N., would lead to the withdrawal of other nations from the plan. Also, rather than following Stimson's advice and first approaching the Soviets privately on control of atomic energy, Baruch insisted upon negotiations in the public forum where positions could easily harden. Lacking the flexibility of the earlier plan but relying upon similar stages, the Baruch plan guaranteed the United States a nuclear monopoly for some years. Thus it left the United States with the option of using the bomb for leverage or even blackmail. While Byrnes and Truman may no longer have wanted to use the bomb as an "implied threat," its value was clear to the Joint Chiefs of Staff who had so counseled Baruch. The atomic bomb, "because of its decisive power is now an essential part of our military strength," explained General Carl

Spaatz, the Air Force Chief of Staff. "Our monopoly of the bomb, even though it is transitory, may well prove to be a critical factor in our efforts to achieve [peace]." Separately the military chiefs had outlined the strategy which the Baruch plan followed: "We should exploit [the nuclear monopoly] to assist in the early establishment of a satisfying peace. . . . It will be desirable for international agreements concerning the atomic bomb to follow the European peace treaties and definitely to precede the time when other countries would have atomic bombs."

Though the Western world generally viewed the plan as magnanimous and interpreted Russia's objections as further evidence of her refusal to negotiate sincerely, the Soviet criticisms were actually quite reasonable. The Baruch plan in its early stages *did* endanger Soviet security. Russia would have had to allow investigations of natural resources and mapping of the interior—thus surrendering a principal military advantage. The Baruch plan, charged Molotov, "proceeds from the desire to secure for the United States the monopolistic possession of the bomb." (Vandenberg had reportedly told Molotov privately, "We have the atomic bomb and we are not going to give it up. We are not going to compromise or trade with you. We are not going to give up our immortal souls.") American leaders, as the Soviets understood, were demanding absolute security for their own nation and refusing to trust Russia at the same time that they were demanding that the Soviets trust the United States and risk the possibility of having the American nuclear monopoly frozen.

The Russian plan, on the other hand, was clearly unacceptable to American leaders. It called for nuclear disarmament and the sharing of secrets first while delaying the establishment of controls. In effect it asked the United States to surrender its nuclear advantage and promised that the nations could thereafter wrestle with the problems of controls. For the Truman administration the Russian plan was further evidence of Soviet insincerity. American leaders could not understand objections to the suspension of the veto, nor, perhaps, why the Soviets feared a plan that could guarantee the American monopoly. Yet Baruch had been explicitly counseled earlier on the advantages of the monopoly, Byrnes had tried to exploit the monopoly, and presumably Truman had understood it. Perhaps because these men so thoroughly believed that their intentions were honorable, that their aim was to establish a just and lasting peace, and that the United States would never use the bomb first, they could not grant the validity of Soviet objections.

Truman and Foreign Policy: The Korean War

WALTER LA FEBER

Doubts about whether the United States should ever have intervened in Vietnam have inevitably encouraged reconsideration of our earlier intervention in Korea. There are certain—perhaps superficial—similarities between the two situations. Both were unpopular wars, demoralizing to the troops, misunderstood at home, and fought with a mixture of technical brilliance and gross miscalculation. When in Korea the aggressive American drive northward brought on the subsequent Chinese intervention, American officials, political and military, were caught as unprepared as they were later to be for the Tet offensive of early 1968. Exactly whom we were fighting—apart from the abstraction of communism—was almost as mysterious in Korea as in Vietnam. And the political repercussions of Korea—the McCarthy era at home—continue to haunt those who uneasily await the final reaction to Vietnam.

Unpopular as it was, the Korean war was relatively short and quickly forgotten. Americans were satisfied that they had taught the Communists a lesson—no longer would attempts to absorb (or snatch) territory go unchallenged. Only with the rise of Cold-War revisionism in the 1960s was the Korean conflict evaluated afresh. Walter LaFeber, whose careful study of the Cold War has probably gained a wider acceptance than any other work of revisionism, considers the Korean war in the context of a global design for an American-sponsored world order. He suggests that long-range objectives involving Europe, all of Asia, and the Pacific shaped American policy in Korea. The Communist adventure in Korea thus provided an opportunity for American policy-makers to define international power relations for a number of years thereafter.

In June 1950, Korea was a Cold War-wracked country which lacked everything except authoritarian governments, illiteracy, cholera epidemics, and poverty. For nearly a century, it had been a pawn in Far Eastern power plays. In 1905, Japan, after using force to stop a Russian thrust, had established a protectorate over Korea and in 1910 annexed that country. When the Japanese surrendered Korea in 1945, it became a testing ground in the renewed battle between Russia and the United States. After setting up dependent but Korean-led governments in zones seized from the Japanese, Russia and the United States evacuated their occupation armies in 1948 and 1949, respectively. In March 1949, North Korea and the Soviets signed an agreement for economic cooperation. Russian military advisers and aid strengthened a formidable 100,000-man army. American military advisers also remained in the south, but President Truman encountered difficulty sending large amounts of aid to Syngman Rhee's government. At the end of June 1950, about $60 million of an allotted $110 million in economic aid had been shipped. Military assistance had scarcely begun. As at the turn of the century, Korea was a prize in the struggle between Russia and countries to the West; and, as in 1904, China, although now a very different China, stood apart from the conflict. Mao's regime devoted itself to internal reconstruction and drawing up plans for a probable invasion of Formosa sometime during 1950.

Mao had little cause to linger over Korean problems; South Korea itself posed no threat to his new government or, apparently, to the remainder of the Communist bloc. MacArthur and Acheson had defined Korea as beyond the perimeter of American military defenses, although not outside the realm of United Nations responsibility. It seemed possible, moreover, that without either Chinese or Russian overt pressure, the South Korean government might crumble. South Korea suffered under Rhee's authoritarian government until the State Department publicly protested his disregard of constitutional rights in early 1950. In an election in May, President Rhee's party collected only forty-eight seats as opposed to one hundred and twenty seats for the other parties; this defeat occurred despite Rhee's arrest of thirty political opponents in "anti-communist" raids just before the election was held. The Korean President pieced together a coalition government that began what promised to be a precarious, perhaps short, struggle to hold power.

On June 7 the northern government of Kim Il Sung attempted to exploit Rhee's problems by initiating an all-out campaign for peaceful reunification of the country through general elections. Rhee attempted to stop the news of this offer from circulating in the South. With that encouragement, the northern government reiterated the proposal on June 19 and intensified its political offensive.

This North Korean initiative apparently fitted within a general strategy which Stalin was designing to counter two threats. In mid-May, Truman announced that discussions on a Japanese peace treaty would receive high priority. The negotiations would particularly consider Japanese independence and the establishment of American military bases on Japan's soil under long-term agreements. The talks, American officials observed, would not be burdened with Russian representation. For Stalin this announcement opened the unhappy prospect of unity between the two greatest industrial nations in the Pacific, perhaps even the extension of a NATO-like organization on the Asian periphery of the Soviet Union. The Sino-Soviet pact in February had singled out Japan as a potential threat to Asian Communism, and this had been followed by the Soviet press accusing Truman with attempting to "draw the Asiatic and Pacific countries into aggressive military blocs, to entangle those countries in the chains of some 'little' Marshall Plan for Asia." On May 30, the Japanese Communist party climaxed weeks of demonstrations with attacks on United States military personnel in Tokyo. If North Korea could unify the country, peacefully or otherwise, the threat of a militarized, western-oriented Japan would be blunted, perhaps neutralized.

The second threat might well have caused Stalin even more concern. Mao's success had not created but probably encouraged revolutions throughout Asia, particularly in Indochina, the Philippines, and Indonesia. The possibility that some of these revolutions might triumph, perhaps following the pattern set by Mao, could weaken Stalin's two-camp premise and loosen his direction over the world Communist bloc. Stalin's view of world matters had become so rigid that he could not accept the nationalist content of these revolts without wrecking his own doctrines and tempering his grip on Soviet and satellite affairs. Malenkov had added to these troubles with his November speech, but by the spring of 1950 (that is, after the Chinese had shown their obstinacy in the Sino-Soviet negotiations and the revolutionary situation had intensified in Asia), Malenkov came back into line. In a speech in March, he no longer talked about the "friendly" nations surrounding Russia, but about a Europe, and especially Germany, which "fascist and revanchist forces," led by the United States, planned to turn into "a military-strategic bridgehead of American aggression." A speech by Molotov the same month was equally aggressive. Stalin had confined the domestic debate; a short and successful war by a Russian-controlled North Korea could intimidate Japan and check the expansive aims and reputation of Mao. On June 25, large numbers of North Korean troops moved across the 38th parallel which divided the country. They followed Soviet-built tanks which had been shipped to Korea during the previous two months.

Attending to family business in Independence, Missouri, when the attack occurred, Truman immediately returned to Washington. He and Acheson assumed the invasion was Russian-directed, perhaps the beginning of an extensive Sino-Soviet thrust. Their initial reaction, however, was carefully measured. They ordered MacArthur in Tokyo to dispatch supplies to the South Korean troops. Then, moving to contain the action, Truman ordered the American Seventh Fleet to sail between China and Formosa, and sent additional assistance to counter-revolutionary forces in the Philippines and Indochina. In a hurriedly called session of the United Nations Security Council, an American resolution branding the North Koreans as aggressors, demanding a cessation of hostilities, and requesting a withdrawal behind the 38th parallel, passed 9–0 with Yugoslavia abstaining. The Soviet Union was not represented, for Yakov Malik continued his boycott to protest the exclusion of Red China. Two days later, as the military situation worsened, Truman ordered American air and naval units into action. That same day, the 27th, the United Nations passed a resolution recommending that its members aid South Korea in restoring peace. This passed 74–1, with Yugoslavia opposing and Egypt and India abstaining. Malik still had not appeared; the rapidity and extent of Truman's reaction had taken the Soviets by surprise.

The day after American units had been committed, the President conferred with Congressional leaders for the first time to inform them of his action. The only strong objection was voiced by Senator Taft who approved of Truman's action but disliked the sending of Americans to war without consulting Congress. Neither then nor later did the President discuss Taft's objection with the full Congress. Two days later, on June 30, Truman made the final commitment. The South Korean army of 65,000 men had suffered heavy losses in the first week of fighting. The President decided that only American ground units could stop the southward flood. In sending these troops Truman emphasized that the United States aimed only "to restore peace there and . . . restore the border." Supporting air attacks were similarly to be limited to the area around the 38th parallel.

Throughout the first week of the war the President carefully refrained from publicly linking the Russians to the attack. He hoped thereby to enable them to stop the aggression without loss of public face. On June 27 Truman dispatched a note to Moscow assuring Stalin that American objectives were limited; the President expressed the hope that the Soviets would help in quickly restoring the *status quo ante bellum*. Truman's immense concern about potential Russian involvement motivated the American statement on June 30 that the United Nations wanted only to restore the parallel as the dividing line, and also resulted in Truman countermanding Air Force directives of July 6 which ordered high-level photo reconnaissance over Russian ports. The Soviets initially responded to Truman's overtures by accusing South Korean forces of invading North Korea. Within ten days this view underwent considerable change. The war was a "civil war among the Koreans," Deputy Minister of Foreign Affairs Andrei Gromyko claimed on July 4. Under these circumstances, Gromyko concluded, the Soviet Union could take no action.

Privately in June and publicly during the late summer, the Truman Administration became less restrained in defining the Soviet role. "In Korea the Russians presented a check which was drawn on the bank account of collective security," Acheson claimed. "The Russians thought the check would bounce. . . . But to their great surprise, the teller paid it." The terms "collective security" and "U.N. action" became the catchwords which supposedly explained and justified Truman's decisions in late June. Both terms were misleading. The United States had no collective security pact in the Pacific in 1950. If the Japanese occupation served as an example of how collective security worked in the abstract, the American exclusion of Australia and Great Britain from control of Japan between 1945 and 1950 twisted collective security to mean unilateralism. As Acheson used the term "collective security," it meant the United States would both define the extent of the "collective" and unilaterally, if necessary, furnish the "security." Nor is there any indication that the President consulted his European or Asian allies before committing American air and naval units on the 27th. This was not the first nor would it be the last time the United States would take unilateral action in an explosive situation without consulting its Western European partners.

As for the sudden American concern to bolster the United Nations, this had not been apparent when the United States acted unilaterally or with some Western powers to establish the Truman Doctrine, the Rio Pact, the Marshall Plan, and NATO. American actions in Korea were consistent with this history, for the United States used the June 27th resolution to establish a military command in Korea that took orders not from the United Nations but from Washington. "The entire control of my command and everything I did came from our own Chiefs of Staff," MacArthur later recalled. "Even the reports which were normally made by me to the United Nations were subject to censorship by our State and Defense Departments. I had no direct connection with the United Nations whatsoever." Sixteen nations finally contributed to "United Nations" forces, but the United States provided 50 percent of the ground forces (with South Korea providing most of the remainder), 86 percent of the naval power, and 93 percent of the air power. In October during the Truman-MacArthur conference at Wake Island, a dozen American officials prepared plans for the reconstruction of *all* Korea without consulting anyone, not even the United Nations or Syngman Rhee.

The American attitude toward the United Nations was exemplified on November 3, 1950 when American delegate John Foster Dulles successfully pushed through the General Assembly a "Uniting for Peace" proposal giving the Assembly the right to make recommendations to United Nations members for collective security measures, including the use of force, if the use of the veto stopped the Security Council from taking action. The resolution also established a permanent "Peace Observation Commission" to report on trouble spots around the world and, finally, invited members to contribute troops that could be used in a United Nations force. This resolution transfigured the United Nations. The organization no longer rested on agreements among the great powers, without which neither the United Nations nor world peace could be viable. Instead power was thrown into a body where Costa Rica had voting power equal to that of the United States or the Soviet Union. Weakening the Soviet veto, the United States also weakened its own. Assuming, however, that it could control the General Assembly, the Administration had taken a calculated risk; it had, to paraphrase Acheson, issued a blank check on the future. After a decade of increased neutralist feelings among the multiplying underdeveloped nations, that check would appear increasingly rubberized.

The United States suffered 142,000 casualties in Korea not for the sake of "collective security" or the United Nations, but because the Executive branch of the government decided that the invasion signaled a direct threat to American interests in both Asia and Europe. Europe, indeed, remained uppermost in the minds of high State Department officials. As the fighting raged in Korea, Acheson devoted increasing amounts of time to the European situation. The State Department had long defined Europe as having first importance. Acheson, moreover, had gotten burned politically and diplomatically when the Korean attack raised questions about his January 12th speech which termed the Communist threat in Asia one of "subversion and penetration," and not "military." This was a rare, probably traumatic, departure from his usual reliance upon military "positions of strength," and he moved quickly to improve the military balance in Europe. . . .

[Meanwhile,] American forces were advancing to greater victories in Korea. What magnifying effects a series of battle losses would have on Republican power and McCarthyism, Democrats did not wish to contemplate. General MacArthur had apparently removed this possibility on September 15 with a brilliant landing at Inchon, back of the North Korean lines, while simultaneously launching a counterattack from the shallow perimeter at Pusan. Within two weeks the United Nations forces joined to cut off large sections of North Korean troops. The Administration's political goals developed accordingly. In late June, Truman reported that the main objective was the restoration of the 38th parallel; on September 1, he told the nation that the Koreans "have a right to be free, independent, and united"; ten days later he approved a National Security Council recommendation that MacArthur should drive the North Koreans north of the 38th and, if encountering no Chinese or Russian troops, to move north of the parallel and prepare for occupation; on September 27, Truman ordered MacArthur north of the parallel; and on October 7, the General Assembly cooperated by endorsing Truman's order 47–5. That day the lead troops of the United States First Cavalry Division crossed into North Korea.

All eyes now turned to China. Throughout July and August, the new Communist government had made little response to the conflict. Recovering from famine, a quarter century of war, and having as her top diplomatic objective the conquest of Formosa, China did not pose an immediate threat to the United Nations forces. In late August, Foreign Minister Chou En-lai made his first important move. At the United Nations, American delegate Warren Austin asked for the open door "within all parts of Korea," and later in the month, Secretary of Navy Francis Matthews applauded "a war to compel co-operation for peace." At this point, Chou reminded the world that "Korea is China's neighbor" and urged that the neighbor's problems be settled "peacefully." Mass anti-American rallies began to appear in Chinese cities. Ten days after the Inchon landing Peking warned India, which had become China's main link with the Western world, that it would not "sit back with folded hands and let the Americans come to the border." After the first remnants of the North Korean troops retreated behind the 38th, Chou formally told India in a dramatic midnight meeting on October 2 that China would attack if United Nations troops moved into North Korea. The United States discounted this threat, believing that it was aimed at influencing upcoming votes on the conflict in the United Nations. MacArthur responded by issuing an ultimatum for the complete surrender of North Korea. On October 7, as the first American troops crossed the border, Chinese troop concentrations on the Manchurian border just across the Yalu River from Korea increased from 180,000 to 320,000. On October 16, a few Chinese "volunteers" crossed the Yalu.

The Truman Administration remained convinced that China would not intervene. Emphasizing, as he had in earlier speeches, that China's immediate concern was with Russian penetration in the north, Acheson commented on national television on September 10, 1950, "I should think it would be sheer madness" for the Chinese to intervene, "and I see no advantage to them in doing it." Acheson later admitted that until late September, American intelligence considered Chinese intervention improbable. On October 9, the danger reached the boiling point when two American F-80 jets strafed a Soviet airfield only a few miles from Vladivostok, a major Russian city close to the Korean border. After the Soviets strongly protested, the United States apologized. Vexed that such a crisis could arise, and angered that he had to back down before Soviet protests just a month before national elections, Truman cancelled a trip to Independence, where he was to watch his sister installed as Worthy Matron in the Order of Eastern Star, and flew to Wake Island to check on MacArthur's policies. In the heavily-censored text of that meeting, little was implied about Russia, but the General assured the President, "We are no longer fearful of [Chinese] intervention. We no longer stand hat in hand." The Chinese, he informed Truman, possessed no air force. They might move 50,000 or 60,000 men across the Yalu, but if these troops attempted to move farther south without air cover, "there would be the greatest slaughter."

Eleven days later, on October 26, the first Chinese prisoner was captured, "so that you began to know, at that point," Acheson later commented, "that something was happening." This realization, however, made little apparent impact on American policies during the next four weeks. On November 21, advanced elements of American troops peered at Chinese sentries stationed several hundred yards across the Yalu. Three days later, MacArthur grandly announced the launching of the end-the-war offensive. At this point the United States government was still not certain whether, in Acheson's words, the Chinese "were committed to a full-scale offensive effort." Two days later, on November 26, the Chinese moved across the river in mass, trapping and destroying large numbers of United Nations troops, including 20,000 Americans and Koreans at the Chosin Reservoir; this outfit finally escaped with 4400 battle casualties and 7000 noncombat casualties, mostly severe cases of frostbite. Three weeks later the retreating United Nations forces once again fought below the 38th parallel, and now it was Chou En-lai who proclaimed his nation's intention of reunifying Korea. "They really fooled us when it comes right down to it; didn't they?" Senator Leverett Saltonstall once asked Acheson. "Yes, sir," the Secretary of State replied.

Throughout September and October the United States had continually assured Peking that Americans never wanted to fight Chinese or threaten in any way China's vital interests. All the Administration wanted, the Secretary of State remarked on November 29, was to "repel the aggressors and restore to the people of Korea their independence." The Chinese retaliated precisely because they interpreted "independence" and Austin's request for "full access" to all Korea to mean the stationing of American power on China's doorstep. From there the United States could exert pressure on both Mao's internal and external policies. China's intense hatred for the West, a hate nurtured by the just-concluded century of western exploitation of China, and Mao's determination to restore Chinese supremacy in Asia made impossible the acceptance of such an American presence. Although historically accustomed to hairsplitting on points of diplomacy, the Chinese failed to see the difference between American presence on the Yalu and American danger to Chinese industries and politics just across the Yalu.

Soviet thinking during November and December was more inscrutable than usual, but Stalin seems to have agreed with the Chinese that the United States could not be allowed to conquer all of Korea. Chinese intervention was a preferred preventive because it would not involve Russian men or large Soviet resources. Stalin meanwhile attempted to use the Chinese successes to pressure the West into reversing German rearmament policies.

In Washington, Administration officials were thoroughly frightened, and Truman's response to the intervention was considerably more explicit than Stalin's. The President reiterated that the United States had no "aggressive intentions toward China," and believed that the Chinese people opposed this sending of troops by their leaders. (This remark was in line with Truman's general theory that Communism anywhere never had popular support.) Because these people could not be heard, the President continued, the aggression must be crushed or "we can expect it to spread throughout Asia and Europe to this hemisphere." As in late June, however, Truman's response was measured. He countermanded MacArthur's order to bomb Chinese troops and supplies in Manchuria. The President finally allowed only the Korean halves of the bridges crossing the Yalu to be bombed, a compromise that infuriated MacArthur and told the Chinese exactly how restrained American retaliation to their intervention would be. In a news conference of November 30, Truman showed signs of losing this restraint. He intimated that the United States would use all the power it possessed to contain the Chinese, and he explicitly did not exclude using atomic bombs. This remark brought [British] Prime Minister Attlee flying to the United States on December 4.

Attlee was not without responsibility for the crises; his government had participated in the decision to send United Nations troops to the Yalu. He now worried that in the newly expanded war Truman would not be able to control the military, and particularly wondered at the spectacle of Truman flying 5000 miles to Wake Island to meet MacArthur who had flown 1900. ("I thought it a curious relationship between a Government and a general," Attlee commented later.) The Prime Minister received Truman's assurances that the United States was not planning to use the bomb. The two men then undertook a full, candid, and most revealing evaluation of the Asian tinderbox.

Both agreed that a general war must be averted and that the United Nations forces should not evacuate Korea unless forced out militarily. Then basic differences emerged. Attlee argued that China's admission to the United Nations could bring her into regular consultations leading to a cease-fire. Acheson doubted that in their present advantageous military position the Chinese would want a cease-fire; if they did and negotiations resulted, Mao would next demand a United Nations seat and concessions on Formosa. The United States had refused to discusss these two items before the intervention and Acheson now was in no mood to reward aggressors. Attlee countered that a cease-fire would make explicit the divisions between China and Russia: "I want them [the Chinese] to become a counterpoise to Russia in the Far East," Attlee argued. If "we just treat the Chinese as Soviet satellites, we are playing the Russian game."

Truman now hardened his earlier view of the Chinese. They were "Russian satellites," and if they succeeded in Korea "it would be Indo-China, then Hong Kong, then Malaya." Acheson interposed that he did not think it mattered whether China was a satellite or not, for she would act like Russia anyway. He believed the invasion into Korea "had design," and, like Truman, adopted the domino theory to warn that any compromise with the Chinese would have a "serious" effect on the Japanese and Philippine islands. Acheson recalled a "saying among State Department officials that with communistic regimes you could not bank good will; they balanced their books every night." Therefore, he argued, the West must develop great military power to stop "this sort of thing from happening in the future." Acheson and Truman also reminded Attlee that the United States could not be "internationalist" in Europe and "isolationist" in Asia; domestic political pressures made that impossible.

At that point Attlee questioned the basic American premise, the fundamental belief that underlay United States policy in Europe as well as Asia. He emphasized that the United Nations must be kept together even if this meant alienating important segments of American public opinion. Whatever the United States and Great Britain did would have to be done through the United Nations, Attlee argued, and this could not be accomplished by the efforts and votes of only the United States and the United Kingdom, "important as we are." Truman and Acheson disagreed; they believed the two nations were "important" enough. By controlling the United Nations forces and now, apparently, the United Nations itself through the "Uniting for Peace" resolution, American officials believed they could keep the American people united, prevent a bigger war in Asia, follow an "internationalist" policy in both Europe and Asia, punish China for moving into Korea by excluding her from the United Nations and Formosa, build up great military power throughout the world, and through it all keep the other United Nations members in agreement with American policies. It was a tall order, so demanding and inflexible that it fixed the American position on China for the next fifteen years.

American intelligence estimates reinforced Truman's and Acheson's views. A December 13 report stated that the Soviet Union hoped to use the war to move American power away from Korea and Formosa, establish China as the dominant power in the Far East and seat her in the United Nations, eliminate American power in Japan, and prevent German rearmament. The Administration expected little help from the United Nations in thwarting these Soviet drives. The most the United Nations could do was brand the Chinese as aggressors, which it did on February 1, 1951 by a vote of 44–7 with 9 abstentions. As the United Nations debated, its forces retreated from the South Korean capital of Seoul.

Although the military situation steadily eroded, not even the other nations in the Western Hemisphere would offer much assistance. The Latin Americans dutifully voted with the United States on resolutions in the United Nations and the Organization of American States, but in the early spring of 1951, when Truman personally appealed to Latin American Foreign Ministers to "establish the principle of sharing our burdens fairly," only Colombia responded with troops. Several other nations sent materiel, but Latin America as a whole failed to see the relevance of Korea to their own economic deprivation and political instability. Later in 1951 a shocked Administration attempted to woo its southern neighbors by extending to them the Mutual Security Program of military aid. Eight nations took the money in 1952 to protect themselves against Communist aggression; this both giver and receiver interpreted to mean preservation of the *status quo*. No other Latin American nation, however, sent men to Korea.

The United States would have to depend primarily upon its own resources in defending what Niebuhr had called "our far-flung lines." In December and January, the President requested emergency powers to expedite war mobilization. Closely following the guidelines suggested in NSC-68, he submitted a $50 billion defense budget; this contrasted with the $13.5 billion budget of six months before. The Administration doubled the number of air groups to ninety-five and obtained new bases in Morocco, Libya, and Saudi Arabia. Army personnel increased 50 percent to 3.5 million men. Truman thereby placed the nation on the Cold War footing on which it would remain, with few exceptions, during the 1950s and 1960s.

The President also embarked the United States upon another costly and momentous journey by committing it to developing and protecting the Western Pacific and Southeast Asia. The riches of the area made it a formidable prize: Burma, Thailand, and Indochina provided rice for much of Asia; Southeast Asia produced nearly 90 percent of the world's natural rubber, 60 percent of the world's tin, and the bulk of Asia's oil. Movements toward independence threw the area into turmoil immediately after the war, but with several exceptions (particularly Vietnam and the Philippines where an Un-Filipino Activities Committee tried to aid the Army in ferreting out the "Huk" rebels), a semblance of order appeared by 1950. Attempted Communist uprisings had been contained in most countries by nationalist elements.

Throughout Asia these anticolonial, nationalist movements had triumphed either peacefully or after short struggles. Vietnam was a tragic exception. There Ho Chi Minh had conducted anti-Japanese underground operations during the war and emerged in 1946 as the leading Communist and nationalist leader. Roosevelt had pressured the French to evacuate Indochina in early 1945. De Gaulle resisted that pressure until the Truman Administration reversed the American policy in order to obtain French cooperation in Europe. After a year of uneasy truce with the French, who were determined to reclaim their control over Indochina, full-scale war broke out in December 1946. The French army moved back into Vietnam carrying large numbers of American lend-lease weapons to eradicate Ho's forces. The Soviets, like the United States, refused to recognize Ho's Republic of Vietnam. Typically distrusting such revolutionaries, Stalin, like Truman, concentrated on European problems in 1946 and early 1947. By 1948 Ho was turning to the Communist Chinese for aid. He had not easily reached this decision, for the Indochinese had historically feared and distrusted their giant neighbor. On January 18, 1950, China recognized Ho's government. The Soviets followed thirteen days later.

After an intensive policy review, the United States fully committed itself to the French cause. On February 6, four and one-half months before the Korean war began, the United States recognized the Bao Dai government which had been established by the French. On June 12, an American military advisory mission prepared to aid the French forces. As early as May, Truman discussed large-scale aid for Bao Dai, and after the Korean conflict, began to pump in aid at the rate of half a billion dollars per year. When French General de Lattre de Tassigny visited Washington in September 1951, the State Department endorsed French war aims and methods.

Although involving itself in the French struggle long before June 1950, the Korean war provided a convenient background as the United States began explaining its commitments in Vietnam. A State Department pamphlet of 1951 defined United States interests as the "much-needed rice, rubber, and tin," but added, "perhaps even more important would be the psychological effect of the fall of Indochina. It would be taken by many as a sign that the force of communism is irresistible and would lead to an attitude of defeatism." The statement concluded that "Communist forces there must be decisively conquered down to the last pocket of resistance," to accomplish this, large amounts of American aid had been given. "Without this aid," the analysis concluded, ". . . it is doubtful whether [Bao Dai and the French] could hold their ground against the Communists."

After mid-1950, Congress began its first systematic aid program to Southeast Asia. The Administration coupled with this economic approach a program for overall military security. The linchpin would necessarily be Japan, the most highly industrialized Asian nation and the only one capable of providing a counterpoise to the Chinese. For three years Truman had failed to write the peace treaty which would cement an independent Japan to the West. The Soviets naturally opposed the pact Truman had in mind, but another intra-Administration dispute between the Defense and State Departments also retarded progress. Defense feared a pact would weaken its hold on Japanese military bases, but State argued that healthy political relations demanded a new agreement.

In March 1950, John Foster Dulles assumed control of the negotiations and almost single-handedly drove the treaty through to a successful conclusion in September 1951. It was a bravura performance. He silenced Defense Department critics by giving them a separate security pact assuring American bases in Japan. Russia was simply excluded from the early, decisive negotiations while Dulles talked only with Japan. When the Soviets finally were asked to participate, Dulles interpreted their proposal as an attempt to dominate the area around Japan; he read out the Russian resolution, one participant later recalled, demonstrated its effect on a map, "took this map dramatically and held it up like this . . . and then threw it on the floor with the utmost contempt. And that made a tremendous impression."

After shrewd parliamentary maneuvering by Dulles, who led the American delegation, and Acheson, who chaired the conference, the treaty was signed by fifty-one nations at a San Francisco conference on September 8, 1951. Russia was not one of the signatories. The treaty restored Japanese sovereignty over the home islands, but not over the Ryukyus (which included the large American base at Okinawa) or the Bonin Islands; these remained in American hands. The agreement allowed Japanese rearmament and "the stationing or retention of foreign armed forces on Japanese territory." In the security pact signed the same day, Japan allowed the stationing of American troops and planes on her soil, but not those of any third power.

The Administration hoped that the treaty would serve as the basis for a long-lasting anti-Communist alliance. For this reason Dulles rode roughshod over demands from American allies and neutrals in Asia who demanded reparations from Japan for her occupation of those countries during World War II. Dulles retained vivid memories of how the Versailles Peace Conference in 1919, in which he had participated as a young economic adviser, had blundered by fastening unreasonably high reparations on Germany. Now, he warned, he would brook no "Carthaginian peace" which would "lead to bitter animosity and in the end drive Japan into the orbit of Russia." Many allies in the Pacific area also urged reparations in order to weaken Japanese war potential; their memories of 1941–1945 matched the vividness of Dulles' recollection of 1919. Dulles solved this problem by negotiating a series of mutual defense treaties to insure the Philippines, Australia, and New Zealand against both reemerging Asian giants, Japan and China. Thirty months before, Acheson had assured Senator Lodge that other than NATO, the Administration contemplated no further regional arrangements. On September 1, 1951 the United States signed with Australia and New Zealand the so-called ANZUS treaty, pledging the security of these two nations and establishing a foreign ministers council for regular consultation.

Because Australia and New Zealand belonged to the British Commonwealth, Great Britain was conspicuous by its absence from ANZUS. As early as March 1914, Winston Churchill, then First Lord of the Admiralty, predicted that with British resources increasingly devoted to Europe, the "white men" in the Pacific would soon have to seek American protection. Thirty-seven years later the British were not as understanding. Angered because Dulles had informed it neither of prior arrangements on the Japanese treaty nor of the discussions of ANZUS, the London government argued that ANZUS derogated British prestige and left the vital British areas of Hong Kong, Malaya, and Burma outside its defensive perimeter. Dulles granted these arguments, but countered that if Britain came in, the French and Dutch would also and thereby transform ANZUS in the eyes of suspicious Asians into a colonial alliance. This argument effectively reduced British influence in the Pacific. "All roads in the Commonwealth lead to Washington," a Canadian official observed.

These negotiations in late 1950 and 1951 determined the geographical extent of the American commitment in the Pacific. During the spring of 1951, with drama and flourishes seldom seen in American history, the military extent of that commitment was decided. In late January, United Nations forces opened a successful drive back to the 38th parallel. As the battle stalemated along the former boundary line, State Department and Pentagon officials cautiously explored the possibility of negotiations with the Chinese on March 20. Three days later General MacArthur issued a personal statement urging that the Red military commanders "confer in the field" with him on surrender; China is "doomed to imminent military collapse," the General proclaimed. Not for the first time had MacArthur undercut his superiors in Washington.

As early as July 1950, he had shown reluctance to accept Truman's decision that Chiang Kai-shek should be contained on Formosa rather than unleashed on the mainland or allowed to ship troops to Korea. A month later, MacArthur sent a message to the annual convention of the Veterans of Foreign Wars, which labeled as "appeasement" any policy that would restrain Chiang. Truman angrily demanded that this message be recalled, and MacArthur complied although it had already been published. The Wake Island conference muted these differences, but the published minutes are embarrassing in their revelation of MacArthur's incredible condescension and Truman's tittering insecurity. Once the President was back in Washington, this insecurity disappeared. After MacArthur again recommended a naval blockade of China, air attacks to level Chinese military and industrial installations, and the use of 30,000 Formosan troops in Korea, Truman patiently explained on January 13 "the political factors" involved in the "world-wide threat" of the Soviet Union which made containment of the Korean war necessary. When MacArthur issued his March 23rd ultimatum, Truman's patience, never inexhaustible, evaporated.

Only the method and timing of relieving the General remained to be decided. On April 5, Representative Joe Martin, the leading Republican in the House, read a letter from MacArthur which charged that "here we fight Europe's war with arms while the diplomats there still fight it with words." "We must win," the letter emphasized. "There is no substitute for victory." The Joint Chiefs of Staff agreed with Truman that MacArthur would have to be relieved immediately; reports from the field indicated that the General was losing the confidence of his men and had already lost confidence in himself. On April 11, the President recalled MacArthur.

Truman knew the political dynamite in the decision. Less than two weeks earlier he had agreed with top advisors that an all-out speaking campaign would have to be undertaken by Cabinet-level officers because the Administration's " 'story' was not reaching the American public." The American people preferred quick victory to containment. This preference was dramatically demonstrated when the General returned to the greatest popular reception in American history. Senator McCarthy expressed the feelings toward Truman of not a few Americans when with characteristic restraint he told a press conference, "The son of a bitch ought to be impeached." Congress warmly received MacArthur's speech before a joint session, then in April and May settled down to investigate the case of the President versus the General.

In a battle of MacArthur versus Truman, the long-range issues tended to be overshadowed by the personalities involved. In Mac-Arthur's case this was not an advantage. Having last set foot in the United States fourteen years before, the General seemed unable or un-willing to grasp the political and social as well as the diplomatic views of his country. He revealed much describing the power he wielded in Japan between 1945 and 1950: "I had not only the normal executive authorities such as our own President has in this country, but I had legislative authority. I could by fiat issue directives." Although he had repeatedly advocated policies which contained the most somber world-wide ramifications, he now admitted having only a "superficial knowl-edge" of NATO and European affairs.

His basic message was curiously close to Truman's and Niebuhr's in 1948: because Communism posed a threat to all civilization, "you have got to hold every place." Or again, "What I advocate is that we defend every place, and I say that we have the capacity to do it. If you say that we haven't you admit defeat." Like Acheson, he insisted on not putting military power and politics into the intellectual equivalent of a cream separator; in time of war, however, MacArthur demanded the reversal of Acheson's priority: once involved in war, the General argued, the military commander must be supreme over all military and political affairs in his theater, "or otherwise you will have the system that the Soviet once employed of the political commissar, who would run the military as well as the politics of the country." Such a remark cut across the grain of traditional American policies of subordinating military to civilian officials unless the nation was involved in total war. This Mac-Arthur assumed to be the case. When he heard the suggestion of As-sistant Secretary of State Dean Rusk that war in Korea must not become a "general conflagration," MacArthur branded it "the concept of ap-peasement, the concept that when you use force, you can limit the force."

The General believed that by controlling the sea and air no one could "successfully launch an effort against us," but the United States could "largely neutralize China's capability to wage aggressive war and thus save Asia from the engulfment otherwise facing it." He expressed contempt for the Chinese Communists. "Never, in our day, will atomic weapons be turned out of China. They cannot turn out the ordinary weapons." Nor was there threat of Soviet intervention. Time, however, was short. If, as MacArthur once told Forrestal, Europe was a "dying system," and the Pacific would "determine the course of history in the next ten thousand years," victory must be won immediately. The "dreadful slaughter" had to end, MacArthur pleaded; American blood as well as dust is settling in Korea, and the "blood, to some extent" rests "on me." But now, he concluded emotionally, "There is no policy —there is nothing, I tell you, no plan, or anything."

The Administration had a plan, and Acheson outlined it in his testimony after MacArthur finished. Korea must be viewed as part of a "collective security system," Acheson argued. When so viewed two things readily became apparent. First, all-out war in Korea would suck in Russian force to aid Stalin's "largest and most important satellite." "I cannot accept the assumption that the Soviet Union will go its way regardless of what we do," the Secretary of State declared. If Russia did intervene, there could be "explosive possibilities not only for the Far East, but for the rest of the world as well." Unlike MacArthur, Acheson insisted on keeping the European picture uppermost in dealing with Korea. (Truman once added a variant on this: expansion of the war could "destroy the unity of the free nations," the President declared. "We cannot go it alone in Asia and go it with company in Europe.") Second, if Europe and the prevention of Russian entry in force did comprise the main objectives, American forces were not engaged in a "dreadful slaughter," or as Acheson remarked, "a pointless and inconclusive struggle," but had "scored a powerful victory" by dealing "Communist imperialist aims in Asia a severe setback" in preventing the armed conquest of all Korea.

MacArthur lost the argument. He lost it so decisively, moreover, that while negotiations to conclude a stalemated war fitfully began in Korea during the summer of 1951, Acheson accelerated the military buildup of Europe.

Harry Truman and the Fair Deal

ALONZO L. HAMBY

President Harry S Truman enunciated a program called the Fair Deal that was to be an extension of Franklin Roosevelt's New Deal. The rhetoric of Truman's speeches, especially his inaugural address of 1949, promised much, and Hamby argues that the Fair Deal definitely extended FDR's work. But Truman was by nature a moderate, a border-state politician whose very essence was compromise, and he operated in a period of rapprochement between government and business. Some centers of Democratic strength, notably the urban machines, seem to stand still rather than to grow in social awareness. Did local leaders urge the Truman administration to "go slow" because welfare laws jeopardized their organizations? One historian even asks whether "the Democratic coalition had ceased to be a 'have-not' coalition and had become interested chiefly in maintaining earlier gains." To question the possibilities of policies in the New Deal and Fair Deal is to ask about the possibilities of government today.

"Every segment of our population and every individual has a right to expect from our Government a fair deal," declared Harry S Truman in early 1949. In 1945 and 1946 the Truman administration had almost crumbled under the stresses of postwar reconversion; in 1947 and 1948 it had fought a frustrating, if politically rewarding, battle with the Republican Eightieth Congress. Buoyed by his remarkable victory of 1948 and given Democratic majorities in both houses of Congress, Truman hoped to achieve an impressive record of domestic reform. The president systematized his past proposals, added some new ones, and gave his program a name that would both connect his administration with the legacy of the New Deal and give it a distinct identity. The Fair Deal, while based solidly upon the New Deal tradition, differed from its predecessor in significant aspects of mood and detail. It reflected not only Truman's own aspirations but also a style of liberalism that had begun to move beyond the New Deal during World War II and had come to maturity during the early years of the cold war—"the vital center."

. . .

The legislative goals Truman announced for his administration, while not devised to meet the needs of an abstract theory, were well in tune with the vital-center approach: anti-inflation measures, a more progressive tax structure, repeal of the Taft-Hartley Act, a higher minimum wage, a farm program based on the concepts of abundant production and parity income, resource development and public power programs, expansion of social security, national medical insurance, federal aid to education, extensive housing legislation, and civil rights bills. The president's most controversial request was for authority to increase plant facilities in such basic industries as steel, preferably through federal financing of private enterprise but through outright government construction if necessary. Roundly condemned by right-wing opponents as "socialistic" and soon dropped by the administration, the proposal was actually intended to meet the demands of a prosperous, growing capitalist economy and emerged from the Fair Deal's search for the proper degree of government intervention to preserve the established American economic structure. "Between the reactionaries of the extreme left with their talk about revolution and class warfare, and the reactionaries of the extreme right with their hysterical cries of bankruptcy and despair, lies the way of progress," Truman declared in November 1949.

The Fair Deal was a conscious effort to continue the purpose of the New Deal but not necessarily its methods. Not forced to meet the emergencies of economic depression, given a solid point of departure by their predecessors, and led by a president more prone than FDR to demand programmatic coherence, the Fair Dealers made a systematic effort to discover techniques that would be at once more equitable and more practical in alleviating the problems of unequal wealth and opportunity. Thinking in terms of abundance rather than scarcity, they attempted to adapt the New Deal tradition to postwar prosperity. Seeking to go beyond the New Deal while preserving its objectives, the Truman administration advocated a more sweeping and better-ordered reform agenda. Yet in the quest for political means, Truman and the vital-center liberals could only fall back upon one of the oldest dreams of American reform—the Jacksonian-Populist vision of a union of producing classes, an invincible farmer-labor coalition. While superficially plausible, the Fair Deal's political strategy proved too weak to handle the burden thrust upon it.

The Fair Deal seemed to oscillate between militancy and moderation. New Dealers had frequently gloried in accusations of "liberalism" or "radicalism"; Fair Dealers tended to shrink from such labels. The New Dealers had often lusted for political combat; the Fair Dealers were generally more low keyed. Election campaigns demanded an aggressiveness that would arouse the Democratic presidential party, but the continued strength of the conservative coalition in Congress dictated accommodation in the post-election efforts to secure passage of legislative proposals. Such tactics reflected Truman's personal political experience and instincts, but they also developed naturally out of the climate of postwar America. The crisis of economic depression had produced one style of political rhetoric; the problems of prosperity and inflation brought forth another.

The Fair Deal mirrored Truman's policy preferences and approach to politics; it was no more the president's personal creation, however, than the New Deal had been Roosevelt's. Just as FDR's advisers had formulated much of the New Deal, a group of liberals developed much of the content and tactics of the Fair Deal. For the most part these were the men who had formed a liberal caucus within the administration in early 1947 shortly after the Republican triumph in the congressional elections of 1946, had worked to sway the president toward the left in his policy recommendations and campaign tactics, and had played a significant, if not an all-embracing, role in Truman's victory in 1948. Truman's special counsel, Clark M. Clifford, was perhaps the most prominent member of the group, but Clifford, although a shrewd political analyst, a persuasive advocate, and an extremely valuable administrative chief of staff, was neither the caucus's organizer nor a creative liberal thinker. Others gave the Fair Deal its substance as a program descending from the New Deal yet distinct from it.

.   .   .

The administration took the next step in April with the introduction in Congress of a new farm program, which had been drawn up under Brannan's direction. The Brannan Plan was difficult and complex in detail, but essentially it was an effort to maintain farm income at the record high level of the war and immediate postwar periods while letting market prices fall to a natural supply-demand level. Brannan thus proposed to continue the New Deal policy of subsidizing the farmers, but he broke dramatically with the New Deal technique of restricting production and marketing in order to achieve artificially high prices.

Many agrarian progressives, including Henry A. Wallace himself, had long been troubled by the price-support mechanisms and had sought methods of unleashing the productive capacity of the farms. Brannan seemed to show the way. He proposed the maintenance of farm income through direct payments to farmers rather than through crop restriction. In order to encourage and protect the family farm, moreover, he recommended supporting a maximum of about $26,100 worth of production per farm. To the consumer he promised milk at fifteen cents a quart, to the dairy farmer a sustained high income. To the Democratic party he offered an apparently ingenious device that would unite the interests of farmers and workers.

Liberals generally were enthusiastic over both the principles and the politics of the Brannan proposals. "The new plan lets growers grow and eaters eat, and that is good," commented Samuel Grafton. "If Brannan is right, the political miracle of 1948 will become a habit as farmers, labor and consumers find common political goals," wrote agricultural columnist Angus MacDonald. James Patton called the Brannan Plan "a milestone in the history of American agriculture," and the *Nation* asserted that the average consumer should devote all his spare time to support of the program.

The plan immediately ran into the opposition of the conservatives who dominated Congress. Republicans feared that the political coalition Brannan was trying to build would entrench the Democrats in power. Large producers, most effectively represented by the powerful Farm Bureau Federation, regarded the plan as discriminatory, and many Democrats with ties to the Farm Bureau refused to support it, among them Senate majority leader Scott Lucas and Clinton Anderson, now the freshman senator from New Mexico. By June it was obvious to most political analysts that the Brannan Plan had no chance of passage in

1949. The administration and most liberals nevertheless remained optimistic. The issue seemed good, the alignment of interests logical and compelling: enough political education and campaigning could revive the scheme and revolutionize American politics.

Both the CIO and the Farmers Union undertook campaigns to spread the message of farmer-labor unity. An article in the *National Union Farmer* typified the effort:

Workers today are in a tough spot. just like farmers. Production has been steadily declining, and that means fewer jobs and lower wages. And that means smaller markets for farm products. This worries everybody but Big Business, but these advocates of scarcity still rule the roost. Monopoly wants less production, less employment, lower wages, fewer family farmers, less collective bargaining, lower farm prices and less competition except for jobs. . . . There is little basic difference between the labor fight against the Taft-Hartley law, and our fight against attempts to tax cooperatives out of existence. . . . Labor's strong objections to 40¢ an hour as a minimum is no different than our equally strong objections to 60% of parity.

Brannan campaigned extensively for his program. "Farm income equals jobs for millions of American workers," he told a labor gathering in a typical effort. "Together, let workers and farmers unite in achieving a full employment, full production economy." The administration sponsored regional farmer-labor conferences around the country. The one attracting the most attention was held in June at Des Moines, Iowa, and featured prominent labor leaders, important Democratic congressmen, and Vice-President Alben Barkley. Other such grass-roots meetings were organized as far east as upstate New York, and the Democratic National Committee prepared a pamphlet on the Brannan Plan for mass distribution. On Labor Day the president devoted two major appearances, one in Pittsburgh and the other in Des Moines, to the Brannan Plan and to farmer-labor unity. "Those who are trying to set these two great groups against each other just have axes of their own to grind," he warned his Pittsburgh audience. "Price supports must . . . give consumers the benefit of our abundant farm production," he told his Des Moines listeners.

Many liberals and Democratic politicians remained convinced that they had an overwhelming political strategy. "In 1950 and '52, the Brannan Plan will be the great issue in the doubtful states," wrote journalist A. G. Mezerik. "After that, Congress will enact a new farm bill—one which is based on low prices for consumers and a high standard of living for family farmers." In early 1950 the Brannan Plan seemed to be gaining popular support. Liberals inside and outside the administration continued to hope for vindication at the polls in November. They could not, of course, foresee the Korean War and the ways in which it would change the shape of American politics.

Even without the Korean War, however, even without the disruptive impact of McCarthyism, it is doubtful that the Brannan Plan would have worked the miracles expected of it. The liberals inside and outside the administration who had created or worked for it assumed that urban and rural groups could be united simply on grounds of mutual self-interest. They failed to understand that these groups were not deeply concerned with *mutual* self-interest; both sides had practiced with some success methods that had taken care of their own self-interest. The rhetoric about urban-rural interdependence was extremely superficial, talked but not deeply felt. Most farm and labor leaders, even those progressive in their outlook, hardly had a basis for communication. The ADA conference of February 1949 included some of the best-informed figures from the unions and the farms. Yet one of the labor leaders had to ask for an explanation "in simple language" of the concept of parity. One of the farm leaders then admitted that he had no idea what the dues check-off was or how it worked. The farm leaders also frankly commented that their constitutents were strongly against such things as a minimum wage applied to farm workers, the extension of social security to cover farm labor and farmers in general, and especially the re-establishment of any sort of price controls. The situation at Des Moines seems to have been much the same. Even some of the Farmers Union officials at the conference were annoyed by the presence of the labor people. "Some farmers wondered if they wern't being sucked in to help the forces of labor fight the Taft-Hartley Act," reported journalist Lauren Soth. Such ideas, of course, were not entirely fanciful. Most of the observers at Des Moines sensed the artificiality of the whole affair, but they continued to hope that further contacts would consummate the union of city and country.

The farm leaders harbored a provincial suspicion of labor, while the reverse was true in the cities. "While labor has given general support to the Brannan plan, I have had the suggestion made, almost ironically, that labor might be given a guaranteed income if such were to be granted to farmers," remarked Jim Loeb in November 1949. Many liberals felt that, as proposed by the administration, the Brannan Plan was too generous. The Chicago *Sun-Times* and the *Nation* agreed that the principles and machinery of the Brannan system were excellent, but both dissented from Brannan's proposal to support farm income at record heights. "The country as a whole should not undertake to support farm income at a higher level than is fair and just," warned the *Sun-Times,* adding that it would always be easier to raise supports than to lower them. Chester Bowles went a step further when he proposed that the whole matter of agricultural subsidies should be tied to urban employment with no supports at all during periods of full employment. Such ideas were hardly the current of a new urban-rural coalition.

Many urban liberals found the plan itself difficult to grasp and could not work up much enthusiasm about it. "Most of us do not understand it completely," admitted Jim Loeb a month and a half after its introduction. A group of ADA leaders had a cordial meeting with Brannan in June 1949 and pledged their support. Actually, however, the ADA did little to promote the program. In the spring of 1950 a Philadelphia liberal wrote to the organization asking for information on the issue, but Violet Gunther, the legislative director, replied that the ADA had published nothing other than an endorsement in the platform, nor could she think of any group other than the Farmers Union that might have something available. The *Nation* and the *New Republic* gave only occasional mention to the plan. Most liberals could heartily endorse and even get excited about Brannan's political objectives, but understanding and identifying with the scheme itself was quite a different matter.

For a time in early 1950 declining farm prices seemed to generate a surge of support for the Brannan Plan. At the beginning of June, Albert Loveland, the undersecretary of agriculture, won the Iowa Democratic senatorial primary on a pro-Brannan platform and thereby encouraged the administration to believe that the Midwest was moving in its direction. Just a few weeks later, however, the Korean War began, creating situations and pressures that doomed most of the Fair Deal.

Even if the Brannan Plan had become law, it is far from certain that it would have created the dream farmer-liberal coalition. Most leading agricultural economists, including those of a progressive outlook, were convinced that the proposal would be unworkable and prohibitively expensive. Some liberal economists condemned its failure to give the rural poor at least as much aid as the middle-class family farm. Even assuming that the economists were wrong, there is no guarantee that a smoothly functioning Brannan program could have performed the neat trick of uniting the very different cultures of urban liberalism and rural insurgency; such a feat probably would have required more than mutual economic benefits. The down-to-earth, church-social ethos of the Farmers Union would not automatically homogenize with the sophisticated, intellectual progressivism of the city liberals or the wage-and-hour, union-shop, reformism of labor.

During 1949 and early 1950 the Truman administration managed a record of substantial legislative accomplishment, but it consisted almost entirely of additions to such New Deal programs as the minimum wage, social security, and public power. The Housing Act of 1949, with its provisions for large-scale public housing, appeared to be a breakthrough, but weak administration, local opposition, and inadequate financing subsequently vitiated hopes that it would help the poor. Acting on his executive authority, Truman took an important step by forcing the army to agree to a policy of desegregation. The heart of the Fair Deal, however—repeal of the Taft-Hartley Act, civil rights legislation, aid to education, national medical insurance, and the Brannan Plan—failed in Congress. Given the power of the well-entrenched conservative coalition and a wide-spread mood of public apathy about big new reforms, Truman could only enlarge upon the record of his predecessor.

Democratic strategists hoped for a mandate in the congressional elections of 1950. In the spring Truman made a successful whistle-stop tour of the West and Midwest, rousing party enthusiasm and apparently demonstrating a solid personal popularity. Loveland's victory provided further encouragement, and in California the aggressive Fair

Dealer Helen Gahagan Douglas won the Democratic nomination for the Senate by a thumping margin. Two incumbent Fair Deal supporters— Frank Graham of North Carolina and Claude Pepper of Florida—lost their senatorial primaries, but, as Southerners who had run afoul of the race issue, they did not seem to be indictors of national trends. Nevertheless, the hope of cutting into the strength of the conservative opposition ran counter to the historical pattern of mid-term elections. The beginning of the Korean War at the end of June destroyed any chances of success.

The most immediate impact of Korea was to refuel an anti-Communist extremism that might otherwise have sputtered out. Senator Joseph R. McCarthy had begun his rise to prominence in February 1950, but he had failed to prove any of his multiple allegations and seemed definitively discredited by the investigations of a special Senate committee headed by Millard Tydings. McCarthy, it is true, was a talented demagogue who should have been taken more seriously by the liberals and the Truman administration in early 1950, but it seems probable that his appeal would have waned more quickly if the cold war with communism had not suddenly become hot. As it was, many of his Senate colleagues rushed to emulate him. In September 1950 Congress passed the McCarran Internal Security Act; only a handful of congressional liberals dared dissent from the overwhelming vote in favor. Truman's subsequent veto was intelligent and courageous, but was issued more for the history books than with any real hope of success. In the subsequent campaign, liberal Democrats, whether they had voted for the McCarran Act or not, found themselves facing charges of softness toward communism.

The war hurt the administration in other ways. It touched off a brief but serious inflation, which caused widespread consumer irritation. By stimulating demand for agricultural products it brought most farm prices up to parity levels and thereby undercut whatever attractiveness the Brannan Plan had developed in rural areas. Finally it removed the Democratic party's most effective spokesman—the president —from active participation in the campaign. Forced to play the role of war leader, Truman allowed himself only one major partisan speech, delivered in St. Louis on the eve of the balloting.

The Fair Deal might have been a winning issue in a nation oriented toward domestic concerns and recovering from an economic recession; it had much less appeal in a country obsessed with Communist aggression and experiencing an inflationary war boom. The reaction against the administration was especially strong in the Midwest. Indiana's Democratic aspirant for the Senate asked Oscar Ewing to stay out of the state. In Iowa, Loveland desperately attempted to reverse his identification with the Brannan Plan. In Missouri the managers of senatorial candidate Thomas C. Hennings, Jr. privately asked White House aides to make Truman's St. Louis speech a foreign policy address that would skip lightly over Fair Deal issues. A few days before the election the columnist Stewart Alsop returned from a Midwestern trip convinced that the region had never been more conservative. Nevertheless, Truman's political advisers, and probably Truman himself, felt that the Fair Deal still had appeal. Given the basic strength of the economy and the victories in Korea that followed the Inchon landing, the White House believed that the Democrats could easily rebut generalized charges of fumbling or softness toward communism. In mid-October the Democratic National Committee and many local leaders were so confident of success that their main concern was simply to get out the vote.

The November results, however, showed a Democratic loss of twenty-eight seats in the House of Representatives and five seats in the Senate. Truman seized every opportunity to remind all who would listen that the numbers were small by traditional mid-term standards. Liberal political analysts, including Kenneth Hechler, a White House staffer, and Gus Tyler of the International Ladies Garment Workers Union, subjected the returns to close scrutiny and all but pronounced a Democratic victory. All the same, most of the Democrats who went under had been staunch Fair Dealers. Republican candidates, including John Marshall Butler in Maryland, Richard M. Nixon in California, Everett McKinley Dirksen in Illinois, and Robert A. Taft in Ohio, scored some of the most spectacular GOP victories by blending right-wing conservatism with McCarthyism. The Midwestern losses were especially disappointing. Hechler argued that the corn-belt vote primarily reflected urban defections and that the Democrats had done comparatively well among farmers. Perhaps so, but for all practical purposes the results put an end to the Brannan strategy of constructing a farmer-labor coalition. Truman was probably more accurate than Hechler when, with characteristic overstatement, he privately expressed his disappointment: "The main trouble with the farmers is that they hate labor so badly that they will not vote for their own interests."

Thereafer, with the Chinese intervention transforming the Korean War into a more serious conflict and with the dismissal of General Douglas MacArthur in April 1951, Truman faced a tough attack from a Republican opposition determined to capitalize upon the frustrations of Korea. Finding it necessary to place party unity above all else, he quietly shelved most of his domestic legislative program and sought to bring the conservative wing of his party behind his military and defense policies. He secretly asked Richard B. Russell of Georgia, the kingpin of the Southern conservatives, to assume the Democratic leadership in the Senate. Russell, content with the substance of power, declined and gave his nod to Ernest W. McFarland of Arizona, an amiable tool of the Southern bloc; Truman made no effort to prevent McFarland's selection as Senate majority leader. The president's State of the Union message was devoted almost entirely to foreign policy and defense mobilization and mentioned social welfare programs only as an afterthought. Subsequently Truman told a press conference that while he supported the Fair Deal as much as ever, "first things come first, and our defense programs must have top priority."

Truman's success in achieving a minimum degree of party unity became apparent in the weeks of investigation and accusation that followed General MacArthur's return to America. Russell, playing the role of parliamentarian-statesman to the hilt and cashing in on his great prestige with senators of both parties, chaired the Senate committee that looked into the MacArthur incident, and he saw to it that the administration was able to deliver a thorough rebuttal to the general. The Northern liberal, Brien McMahon of Connecticut, relentlessly grilled hostile witnesses. The Western representative of oil and gas interests, Robert S. Kerr of Oklahoma, lashed out at MacArthur himself with a vehemence and effectiveness that no other Democrat could match. The tandem efforts of Russell, McMahon, and Kerr demonstrated the new party solidarity, but in terms of the Fair Deal the price was high.

In July 1951 the Federal Power Commission renounced the authority to regulate "independent" (non-pipeline-owning) natural gas producers. The ruling amounted to an adminstrative enactment of a bill, sponsored by Kerr, which Truman had vetoed a year earlier; Truman's close friend and most recent appointee to the Federal Power Commission, Mon Wallgren, cast the deciding vote. Although he talked like a militant liberal in a private conversation with ADA leaders, the president stalled throughout 1951 on repeated demands for the establishment of a Korean War Fair Employment Practices Committee. In December the administration established an ineffective Committee on Government Contract Compliance. Other domestic programs were soft-pedaled to near-invisibility.

Yet even the Korean War was not entirely inimical to reform. Its exigencies forced the army to transform its policy of integration into practice. Korea also provided a test for one of the basic underpinnings of the Fair Deal—Leon Keyserling's philosophy of economic expansion. Truman did not in the end fully embrace Keyserling's policies, but in the main he followed the guidance of his chief economic adviser. The Korean War years demonstrated the extent to which Keyserling's economics diverged from conventional New Deal–World War II Keynesianism and revealed both the strengths and weaknesses of his approach.

From the outbreak of the fighting, most liberals favored either immediate strong economic controls akin to those that had held down inflation in World War II or at least the establishment of stand-by machinery that could impose them rapidly. Truman disliked such measures on the basis of both principle and politics. He and his diplomatic advisers also wanted to signal the Soviet Union that the United States regarded the North Korean attack as a limited challange meriting a limited response. Keyserling's expansionary economics provided an attractive alternative to the liberal clamor for controls. Convinced that extensive controls would put the economy in a strait jacket and retard the expansion necessary to meet both consumer and defense needs and assuming a North Korean defeat in a few months, the administration decided to accept a short-term, war-scare inflation (probably unavoidable in any case) and concentrate on economic growth, which would be underwritten in large measure by tax incentives for business. An expanding economy would be the best long-term answer to inflation:

growth policies could fit a small war into the economy, avoid the social and political strains accompanying wartime controls, and reduce inflationary pressures to a level at which fiscal and monetary policies could contain them. Liberals outside the administration watched with alarm as prices went up, but Truman and Keyserling continued to gamble on a quick end to the war and the development of an economy capable of producing both guns and butter.

Their plan might have worked fairly well had the United States not overreached itself militarily in Korea. The Chinese intervention of November 1950 wrecked hopes of a quick recovery, set off another round of scare buying, and intensified war demands upon the economy. The administration quickly threw up a price-wage control structure, but by the end of February 1951, eight months after the beginning of the Korean conflict, the consumer price index had risen eight per cent (an annual rate of twelve per cent). Keyserling agreed that the new situation necessitated controls, but he accepted them with reluctance and sought to keep them as simple as possible, even at the risk of benefiting profiteers. "We'll never be able to out-control the Russians," he told a Senate committee, "but we can out-produce them." Speaking to an ADA economic conference, he asserted that many liberals, in their opposition to tax breaks for large business and in their demands for stronger controls, were confusing the Korean War with World War II and "engaging merely in hackneyed slogans out of the past."

Most liberals disagreed with Keyserling's emphases. As production was his first imperative, an end to the wage-price spiral was theirs. "Unless we are willing seriously to endanger the basis of existence of the American middle class, we must stop prices from rising," wrote Hans Landsberg in the *Reporter*. The liberals assumed that economic expansion was possible within a framework of rigid, tightly administered controls. Chester Bowles observed that the controlled economy of World War II had turned out a twofold increase in industrial production. John Kenneth Galbraith rejected the idea that Keyserling's expansionary policies could outrun the inflationary pressures they themselves created. The bulk of liberals regarded the administration approach as dangerous, the product of political expediency rather than sound economic analysis.

Neither Keyserling nor the more conventional liberals won a complete victory. Truman, who understood all too well the political dangers of a prolonged inflation, made substantial concessions to the controllers, led by Michael V. DiSalle, head of the Office of Price Stabilization. In the interest of fairness Truman approved a more complex system of price controls than Keyserling thought desirable, giving DiSalle considerable leeway to roll back some prices while approving advances in other areas. By March 1951 inflation was under control; during the final ten months of the year the cost-of-living index increased by less than two and one-half per cent. The waves of scare buying that followed the North Korean attack and the Chinese intervention had subsided. Higher taxes and restraints on credit were beginning to affect consumer buying. The Federal Reserve System, despite opposition from the administration, initiated a stringent monetary policy. Tax breaks for businesses expanding plant facilities presaged increased productive capacity. All these factors, along with the government stabilization program, discouraged an inflationary psychology.

At the time, however, it appeared to most economic observers that the lull was only temporary. Many of the administration's liberal critics refused even to admit the existence of a lull and called for tougher controls as if prices were still skyrocketing. More moderate analysts feared that the impact of large government defense orders would set off another inflationary spiral in the fall. Influenced by such expectations, Truman ostentatiously mounted an anti-inflation crusade, demanding that Congress not only extend his control authority, due to expire on June 30, but actually strengthen it. In fact the Defense Production Act of 1951 weakened the president's powers considerably. Truman signed it reluctantly, comparing it to "a bulldozer, crashing aimlessly through existing pricing formulas, leaving havoc in its wake." A subsequent tax bill failed to meet administration revenue requests and increased the danger of serious inflation.

Yet price stability persisted through 1952, in large measure because defense production, hampered by multiple shortages and bottlenecks, lagged far behind its timetable. In late 1951 these problems and the fear of renewed inflation led Truman to decide in favor of a "stretch-out" of defense production schedules; in doing so he overrode Keyserling's urgings for an all-out effort to break the bottlenecks and concentrate relentlessly upon expansion. Given the serious problems in defense industry, the stretch-out decision may have seemed necessary to Truman, but it also carried the dividend of economic stability.

The president had steered a course between the orthodox liberal obsession with inflation and Keyserling's easy disregard of its perils; perhaps as a result the economy failed to expand at the rate Keyserling had hoped. On balance, however, Truman's approach to the political economy of the Korean War was closer to Keyserling's, and the conflict produced a dramatic economic growth. Before the war the peak gross national product had been $285 billion in 1948; by the end of 1952 the GNP (measured in constant dollar values) had reached a rate of $350 billion. The production index of durable manufactured goods had averaged 237 in 1950; by the last quarter of 1952 it had reached 313. The expansion, even if less than Keyserling had wanted, was breathtaking. Moreover, aside from the probably unavoidable inflation that accompanied the early months of the war, this remarkable growth had occurred in a climate of economic stability. Using a somewhat more orthodox approach than Keyserling preferred, the administration had achieved one of the central goals of the Fair Deal.

In its efforts to carry on with the reforming impulse of the New Deal the Truman administration faced nearly insuperable obstacles. A loosely knit but nonetheless effective conservative coalition had controlled Congress since 1939, successfully defying Franklin Roosevelt long before it had to deal with Truman. Postwar prosperity muted economic liberalism and encouraged a mood of apathy toward new reform breakthroughs, although Truman's victory in 1948 indicated that most of the elements of the old Roosevelt coalition were determined to preserve the gains of the New Deal. The cold war probably made it more difficult to focus public attention upon reform and dealt severe blows to civil liberties. It did, however, give impetus to the movement for Negro equality.

The Fair Deal attempted to adapt liberalism to the new conditions. Under the intellectual leadership of Leon Keyserling it formulated policies that sought to transcend the conflicts of the New Deal era by encouraging an economic growth that could provide abundance for all Americans. With Charles Brannan pointing the way, the Truman administration tried to translate abundance into a political coalition that could provide the votes for its social welfare policies. The political strategy, ambitious but unrealistic, collapsed under the weight of the Korean War. Keyserling's economics, on the other hand, received a lift from Korea; in a period of adversity the Fair Deal was able to achieve at least one of its objectives.

PART TWO

1952-1959

The age of Eisenhower—that era of placidity and order that has already become an object of nostalgia—was shorter than we remember. Eisenhower became President, the Korean war ended, and Joseph Stalin died —all in 1953. But Joseph McCarthy was still a power in the land and the economy sagged immediately after Korea, so that placidity scarcely developed before about 1954. And by 1957 and 1958, beneath the Eisenhower consensus, anxiety stirred over Russian spacecrafts, colonial revolutions, civil-rights disorder, and muckraking journalism—all harbingers of the decade to come.

This short and welcome respite from the strains of war did not bring long-term social stability. In the interchangeable suburbs, Americans were learning new styles of living, new attitudes toward money and family behavior. An economy increasingly based on consumer credit undermined old habits. Meanwhile, the great flux was obscured by public assurances of rooted values and by political stalemate. Yet the decade of the 1950's moved rapidly toward a rendezvous with the new world it was creating. Blacks were increasingly angry; the right wing more sour and disillusioned; the dispirited and invisible poor rising into view of the liberal middle class; adolescents in high school and college finding their own voices (and musical sounds).

Before the decade's end, a fresh spirit of criticism was abroad. The Supreme Court had spoken in a historic school segregation case, and blacks had already discovered the techniques that could force change. Martin Luther King demonstrated their resolve to an uneasy nation at Montgomery in 1955. In John Kennedy, liberals had found a practical hero and the Right a vulnerable enemy. An era of muckraking, which began late in the decade with the writings of C. Wright Mills, John Kenneth Galbraith, Michael Harrington, and others, revealed areas of national shame and failure. The nation would soon come to noisy confrontation over the changes the 1950's had quietly wrought.

Nixon Agonistes:
The Checkers Speech

GARRY WILLS

Nixon-watching, like Johnson-watching and Kennedy-watching, has become a minor national pastime. Men who get to be President usually are highly complex people, and political success at any level often requires a certain amount of evasion, what Richard Nixon himself has called being "devious . . . in the best sense." However understandable evasiveness may be, it is ironic that a large amount of the unflattering reputation for deviousness that has accompanied Nixon throughout his political career comes from his famous "Checkers" speech of 1952— a talk given in defense against charges that the candidate had spent campaign funds on personal needs. ("Checkers" was the Nixons' cocker spaniel, an irrelevant animal Nixon dragged into the speech along with his wife's "cloth" coat.) As Garry Wills shows, this was in many ways the most open moment of Nixon's career, an occasion when he was forced to tear aside the veil of privacy which has been his primary way of handling the ferocious demands of public life. Unlike Lyndon Johnson, Richard Nixon is not comfortable before the crowds.

The Checkers speech ushered in the age of television politics. Estes Kefauver, investigating criminals in 1950, had made himself a household name in a series of nationally televised hearings, but he had not tailored the medium to his ends. Nixon was the first politician to realize the immense possibilities of television and to exploit every subtle popular response the new medium could evoke. Intellectuals have always held the Checkers speech in bad odor, seeing in it a disgusting exhibition of bathos and an unvarnished attempt to manipulate public emotions. But Wills details the tensions and political infighting which surged around the vice-presidential candidate during the week preceding the speech. He argues persuasively that the Checkers speech was both Nixon's only chance to save his career and also a direct confrontation with the presidential candidate, Dwight D. Eisenhower.

One other thing I probably should tell you, because if I don't they'll probably be saying this about me too, we did get something—a gift—after the election. A man down in Texas heard Pat on the radio mention the fact that our two youngsters would like to have a dog. And, believe it or not, the day before we left on this campaign trip we got a message from Union Station in Baltimore saying that they had a package for us. We went down to get it. You know what it was? It was a little cocker spaniel dog in a crate that he sent all the way from Texas. Black and white spotted. And our little girl— Tricia, the six-year-old—named it Checkers. And you know the kids love that dog and I just want to say this right now, that regardless of what they say about it, we're going to keep it.—The Checkers Speech

Riding in the staff bus during Nixon's 1968 campaign, I talked with one of his speech writers about the convention in Miami. Nixon's wooing of Strom Thurmond had been much criticized. But Nixon's man now said the acceptance speech eclipsed everything that went before: "That was so clearly the major event of the convention—a brilliant job. To talk about that convention is, simply, to talk about that speech. What did *you* think of it?" I answered that it reminded me of the Checkers speech. The comment seemed to horrify my interlocutor; and Professor Martin Anderson, traveling with Nixon as an adviser on urban matters, turned around in the seat before us to object: "People forget that the Checkers speech was a political master stroke, an act of political genius!" But I had not forgotten: that was, I assured him, my point.

Professor Anderson's defensiveness was understandable. Nixon has often been sneered at, over the years, for his television speech in the campaign of 1952. The very term "Checkers speech," reducing the whole broadcast to its saccharine doggy-passage, is a judgment in itself. But that broadcast saved Nixon's career, and made history. By the beginning of the 1968 campaign, sixteen years later, it was a journalistic commonplace that Nixon did not appear to advantage on television. His wan first TV encounter with John Kennedy had dimmed the public's earlier impression. But Nixon only risked that debate with Kennedy because he had such a record of success on the TV screen: in the history of that medium, his 1952 speech was probably a greater milestone than the presidential debate that came eight years later. Nixon first demonstrated the political uses and impact of television. In one half hour Nixon converted himself from a liability, breathing his last, to one of the few people who could add to Eisenhower's preternatural appeal— who could gild the lily. For the first time, people saw a living political drama on their TV sets—a man fighting for his whole career and future —and they judged him under that strain. It was an even greater achievement than it seemed. He had only a short time to prepare for it. The show, forced on him, was meant as a form of political euthanasia. He came into the studio still reeling from distractions and new demoralizing blows.

Nixon, naturally, puts the Checkers speech, along with the whole "fund crisis," among the six crises he survived with credit. It belongs there. He probably displayed more sheer nerve in that crisis than in any of the others. As a freshman in Congress, he did not stand to lose so much by the Hiss investigation. He had, moreover, an unsuspected hoard of evidence in that encounter; and he was backed by dedicated men like Father Cronin, while backing another dedicated man, Whittaker Chambers. In the crises he deals with after 1952, he was a Vice-President, in some way speaking for the nation, buoyed by its resources, defending it as much as himself; never totally without dignity. But at the time when he went onto the TV screen in 1952, he was hunted and alone. Nine years later he would write of that ordeal, "This speech was to be the most important of my life. I felt now that it was my battle alone. I had been deserted by so many I had thought were friends but who panicked in battle when the first shot was fired." It was, without exaggeration, "the most searing personal crisis of my life." It was also the experience that took the glitter out of politics for Mrs. Nixon. . . .

The first news story broke on Thursday, September 18. There had been warnings in the Nixon camp all the four preceding days. A newsman in Washington asked Nixon about the fund on Sunday. Monday, three other reporters checked facts with Dana Smith, the administrator of the fund. By Wednesday, Jim Bassett, Nixon's press secretary, heard something was brewing from his old reporter friends. The candidate had just begun his first major tour—a whistlestop north through California; when the train stopped for water around midnight, a worried staff man waited with more rumors. Thursday, it broke: the New York *Post* had a story with the headline, SECRET RICH MEN'S TRUST FUND KEEPS NIXON IN STYLE FAR BEYOND HIS SALARY. The story did not justify that sensational summary, and neither did subsequent investigation. The fund was public, independently audited, earmarked for campaign expenses, and collected in small donations over two years by known Nixon campaign backers. It was neither illegal nor unethical. And the press soon discovered that the Democratic nominee, Adlai Stevenson, had similar funds, only larger in their amount and looser in their administration. Why, then, was so much made of Nixon's fund, and so little of Stevenson's?

Nixon's official explanation, at the time, was his standard charge: the commies were behind it all. By Friday morning, the day after the charge was published, there were hecklers at his train stops to shout "Tell us about the sixteen thousand!" At a town called Marysville, he did tell them. His own version of that speech, included in his book, is more moderate than some others; but even his excerpts seem gamy enough: "You folks know the work that I did investigating Communists in the United States. Ever since I have done that work the Communists and the left-wingers have been fighting me with every possible smear. When I received the nomination for the Vice Presidency I was warned that if I continued to attack the Communists in this government they would continue to smear me. And believe me, you can expect that they will continue to do so. They started it yesterday. They have tried to say that I had taken $16,000 for my personal use." The *they* is conveniently vague throughout. They—i.e., the New York *Post* and other papers—published the charge. Go far enough back up the paragraph, through intervening "theys," and you find that the antecedent is, more immediately, "the Communists in this Government," and, in the first place, "Communists and [broad sweep here] left-wingers." The explanation is beautifully lucid and inclusive (if a little unspecific about the machinery that makes the nation's press perform the communists' bidding): since the publicizing or nonpublicizing of fund scandals is at the disposal of communists, who were (naturally) supporting Adlai Stevenson, the Stevenson fund got (naturally) no publicity like that accorded to Nixon.

Behind this funny explanation, there are scattered but clear indications, in his book, of the true story, a sad one. At one point Nixon asks why his own statement of the "basic facts" about the fund received so little attention from the press. His answer ignores the conspiratorial explanation given eight pages earlier, and supplies four reasons, two of them technical (denials never get as big a play as accusations in the press, news travels east to west and he was in California), and two more substantive: reporters are mainly Democrats (though Nixon admits that publishers are mainly Republicans, which makes for some balance), and "the big-name, influential Washington reporters cover the presidential candidates while the less-known reporters are assigned to the vice presidential candidates." The last reason, the real one, looks like another point of newspaper mechanics—the mere logistics of press assignment; until we ask why that should matter. The answer, in Nixon's own words, is that his own press release "got lost in the welter of news and speculation over whether General Eisenhower would or would not choose to find a new running mate." *That* was the news on Eisenhower's train—because Ike's advisers were known to be searching for a way to dump Nixon, and Ike was a man who at this stage followed his advisers almost blindly. In short, the Nixon fund was a big story because Eisenhower, by his silence and hints and uneasiness, made it one. For no other reason.

It was natural for Eisenhower to acquiesce in a staff decision to drop Nixon. That staff had presented him with Nixon in the first place. (Ike's knowledge of his running mate was very slim—he thought, for instance, he was forty-two rather than thirty-nine.) The General had, in fact, learned of Nixon's choice at exactly the same time Nixon did. When Herb Brownell asked Ike what he thought of Nixon, the presidential nominee expressed surprise that the decision was his to make. He said he would leave the matter to Brownell, provided the latter consulted "the collective judgment of the leaders of the party" (the top man, in military politics, protects himself by putting a subordinate in charge of the operation, under staff scrutiny). So Brownell called a meeting of the party's leaders, and went through the form of considering Taft and others. But then Dewey got up, to speak for the winning camp. Nixon he said, and Nixon it was. That decision made, Brownell went to the phone, dialed Nixon, and had him listen in while, on another phone, he told Eisenhower that the choice had been made.

As the fund story broke, Nixon wondered where Ike stood. Thursday went by, and Friday. No word from the General—to the public, or to Nixon. But the Establishment was at work: the very thing that had made Nixon good "for balance" made him unpalatable in himself, seen through Establishment eyes. He was there to draw in the yokels. If there was any doubt about his ability to do that, no one would feel compunction at his loss: Ike was too valuable a property to be risked with anyone who might hurt him. This was the attitude on Eisenhower's train, and it spread to Nixon's as newsmen jumped over from the main tour to watch the death throes in the smaller one. The machinery of execution made itself visible Saturday morning, when the New York *Herald Tribune*—the voice of the Eastern Establishment—asked for Nixon's resignation from the ticket. It was, Nixon realized, an order. The same voice that had summoned him was now dismissing him. A waiting game had been played for three days to see if he would go without having to be ordered, and Nixon had not gone. The Saturday editorial (written Friday), following so close on the *Post*'s revelation, appearing before Nixon had conferred with Eisenhower, was the first of several "hints" that he was not wanted. Despite his studied deference toward Eisenhower, Nixon makes it clear he was not dense: "The publishers and other top officials of the *Tribune* had very close relations with Eisenhower and" (for which read, *I mean*) "with some of his most influential supporters. I assumed that the *Tribune* would not have taken this position editorially unless it also represented the thinking of the people around Eisenhower. And, as I thought more about it, it occurred to me" (the little light bulb above a cartoon character's head—Nixon must play this role straight) "that this might well be read as" (*obviously had to be*) "the view of Eisenhower himself, for I had not heard from him since the trouble began two days before."

At ten o'clock Friday night a reporter told him the next day's *Herald Tribune* would ask him to resign. Nixon, who had not heard this, was stunned. He summoned his closest advisers, Chotiner and Bill Rogers (who would, after more of Nixon's crises, at last be his Secretary of State). These two had received the editorial an hour and a half earlier, but they were not going to tell him about it till morning—afraid he would lose sleep if he saw it (a judgment events confirmed). He asked for the editorial and read: "The proper course of Senator Nixon in the circumstances is to make a formal offer of withdrawal from the ticket." So that was it. Nixon is quite candid here: "I knew now the fat was in the fire. That sounded like the official word from Eisenhower himself." He spent four hours discussing his options with Chotiner and Rogers. Then, at two in the morning, he told his wife, and went through the whole discussion again with her.

The next day, Saturday, three days after the story broke, with newsmen plaguing him for his decision, he had to brace himself for defiance of the Establishment. It was an all-day job. He asked Chotiner and Rogers to get the ultimatum spelled out, if they could, from Ike's inner circle—Chotiner tried to reach Dewey, Rogers called Fred Seaton. They got no direct answer. But the indirect command was growing more insistent; sharper and sharper "hints" were thrown to the public (and, by this roundabout path, to Nixon). Sherman Adams had summoned a man all the way from Hawaii to join the Eisenhower train, and the man was all too obviously a second-string Nixon: Bill Knowland, tough anticommunist and Californian. Eisenhower had finally spoken too, off the record. The newsmen on his train had taken a poll that came out forty-to-two for dumping Nixon; news of this was passed along to Ike's press secretary (Dewey's press man in the last campaign, Jim Hagerty), along with the newsmen's opinion that Ike might be stalling to arrange a whitewash job for Nixon. Ike did not like such talk; it questioned not only Nixon's honesty, but his. He invited the newsmen into his compartment for a talk off the record—but the main part of it was soon made public. "I don't care if you fellows are forty-to-two against me, but I'm taking my time on this. Nothing's decided, contrary to your idea that this is all a setup for a whitewash of Nixon. Nixon has got to be clean as a hound's tooth." Again, Nixon got the point: "Our little group was somewhat[!] dismayed by reports of Eisenhower's attitude.

I must admit it made me feel like the little boy caught with jam on his face."

By Saturday night, then, the issue was clear: knuckle under, or defy the closest thing modern America has had to a political saint. Nixon, here as in all his crises, claims the decision was made on purely selfless grounds: he was thinking of Ike's own welfare—switching men in mid-campaign might make the General unpopular. (This is like worrying that the Milky Way might go out.) Not that Nixon is insincere in his claim. Politicians are very deft at persuading themselves that the world's best interests just happen to coincide with the advancement of their own careers. He says he put the question to his four advisers (Chotiner, Rogers, Bassett, and Congressman Pat Hillings) this way: "Forget about me. If my staying on the ticket would lead to Eisenhower's defeat, I would never forgive myself. If my getting off the ticket is necessary to assure his victory, it would be worth it, as far as any personal embarrassment to me is concerned. Looking at it this way—should I take the initiative and resign from the ticket at this time?"

But Nixon does not feel obliged to present his friends as men crippled by nobility. Chotiner, for instance, plays straight man here, saying all the "natural" things Nixon is too lofty for: "How stupid can they be? If these damned amateurs around Eisenhower just had the sense they were born with they would recognize that this is a purely political attack . . . This whole story has been blown up out of all proportion because of the delay and indecision of the amateurs around Eisenhower." Not even good old Murray, though, blunt fellow as he is, can be described in this book as attacking the Big Man himself—just the little men around him. When Nixon's friends start criticizing Eisenhower, the veil of anonymity must be lowered over them: "But now, some were beginning to blame Eisenhower, for not making a decision one way or the other." Nixon himself would never dream of questioning his leader: "What had happened during the past week had not shaken my faith in Eisenhower. If, as some of my associates thought, he appeared to be indecisive, I put the blame not on him but on his lack of experience in political warfare and on the fact that he was relying on several equally inexperienced associates. I could see his dilemma."

The decision to be made at this session was simple: obey the order relayed by the *Herald Tribune,* or risk disobedience. But, after a full day of campaigning through Oregon, he sat up with his inner circle, in Portland, debating the matter till three in the morning. Then, left alone, he went over the whole thing in his mind for two more hours. By five o'clock Sunday morning, he had set himself on a course he meant never to abandon: he would not resign. Sunday brought blow on blow meant to shake that resolution. First, there was a long telegram from Harold Stassen, still trying to clear some path for himself. He recommended, for Nixon's own good ("it will strengthen you and aid your career"), that a resignation be sent right off to Ike. Then, that afternoon, Dewey called to give Nixon the decision of "all the fellows here in New York." Dewey had a plan for breaking the stalemate caused by Nixon's refusal to resign and Eisenhower's refusal to back him: Nixon must plead his cause before the people. If the response was big enough, he could stay. And when Dewey said big enough, he meant the impossible—near-unanimity. Nixon reports the ultimatum this way: "You will probably get over a million replies, and that will give you three or four days to think it over. At the end of that time, if it is sixty percent for you and forty percent against you, say you are getting out, as that is not enough of a majority. If it is ninety to ten, stay on." It is no wonder Nixon—or, rather, "some of the members of my staff"—felt wary of this offer: "They feared a concerted campaign might be put under way to stack the replies against me." The whole plan was stacked against him. It started with the presumption that Nixon was through, and with feigned generosity gave him a chance to climb back onto the ticket. If Nixon took the offer and (as was expected) lost, then he must abide by the consequences. It was a brilliant way of forcing resignation on a man who was determined not to resign.

Nixon said he would consider it. Chotiner got in touch with Party Chairman Arthur Summerfield, to find out how the broadcast would be handled. Summerfield said they had offers from some TV sponsors to give Nixon one of their spots. Chotiner naturally protested: Nixon could hardly go on the air to defend himself against the charge of being a messenger boy for California businessmen, and explain this on time given him by some large corporation! He told Summerfield the National Committee would have to buy the time, if they expected any show at all. (Money had already been set aside for two half-hour appearances by the vice-presidential candidate. But now Summerfield was in the unfortunate position of not knowing who would be the candidate: if he gave one of the periods to Nixon, and Nixon failed, that left only one spot for his successor. At $75,000 a throw, these were not shows to be granted easily.)

Nixon had to deliver a scheduled speech that night (Sunday) at the Portland Temple Club. He was still considering the TV broadcast when he came back to his hotel. He knew this contest was not what it appeared—Nixon against the press, or the Democrats, or the people. It was Nixon against Ike—a contest that, as Stevenson would learn twice over, no one can expect to win. Candidates simply do not get 90 percent victories in America—and Nixon was being told to produce that figure or get lost. He was asked to do it in circumstances that told against him. Eisenhower had been presented by his managers as the voice of a purgative honesty meant to remedy corruption. The very fact that this arbiter of morals was silent, that Nixon was sent out to argue on his own, was an implied judgment on him. He would be guilty until proved innocent, and he could not call on the one character witness who, in this set of circumstances, mattered.

Meanwhile, the Eisenhower camp had received no answer to its "offer." Now was the time to turn the screw. No escape was to be left him. The phone rang in Portland. Ike. For the first and last time during the crisis. Giving the ultimatum all his personal weight: "I think you ought to go on a nationwide television program and tell them everything there is to tell, everything you can remember since the day you entered public life. Tell them about any money you have ever received." The public self-revelation for which Nixon would be blamed in later years was being forced on him, against all his own inclinations, personal and political. By temperament and conditioning, Nixon is reserved, with Quaker insistence on the right of privacy. Nixon's mother, a woman of tremendous self-control, later said of the Checkers speech: "At the point when he gave that itemized account of his personal expenditures, I didn't think I could take it."

Nixon asked Eisenhower if he meant to endorse him. The response was put in a particularly galling way: "If I issue a statement now backing you up, in effect people will accuse me of condoning wrongdoing." Ike knew, and Nixon knew he knew, that the results of a vast survey of Nixon's affairs would be available in a matter of hours. This study had been going on for three days; Sherman Adams, at the outset of the scandal, called Paul Hoffman, one of the architects of Eisenhower's candidacy, and ordered a thorough inquest into Nixon's finances. Hoffman went to the best. He put Price Waterhouse to work checking Nixon's accounts, and the law firm of Gibson, Dunn and Crutcher went over all legal aspects of the matter. Fifty lawyers and accountants worked on a round-the-clock basis. The results of this scrutiny were being compiled Sunday night. No wrongdoing would be found. The objective moral evidence would soon be in Eisenhower's hands. But he refused to make his own judgment based on this evidence. He wanted the people, who could not know as much as he did, to decide whether Nixon was honest, and he would follow them. The people, meanwhile, were waiting to hear Ike's decision so they could follow *him*. Nixon was caught between two juries, each of which was waiting for the other to reach a verdict before it would move.

He tried to strike a bargain: if Eisenhower was satisfied with the TV broadcast, would he *at that point* make a decision to endorse Nixon? (If he did not, then a victory scored on the TV screen would be subject to attrition, as lingering or renewed doubts worked on a situation inexplicably unresolved.) But Ike was not making bargains: he said he would need three or four days (the same period Dewey had mentioned) for the popular reaction to be accurately gauged—during which time, Nixon would presumably be stalled in Los Angeles waiting for the response, his campaign tour all too noticeably suspended. Nixon finally blew: "There comes a time when you have to piss or get off the pot!" But Seraphim piss not, neither Cherubim. The great Cherub sat blithely there, enthroned on his high pot. Nixon sculpts and prettifies the unyielding refusal: "One of Eisenhower's most notable characteristics is that he is not a man to be rushed on important decisions."

There was nothing he could do now but go ahead with the show. And if so, the sooner the better. Chotiner was back on the phone getting clearance for the $75,000. Sherman Adams and Arthur Summerfield finally yielded that point around midnight. The press corps had been alerted, an hour before, that there would be an announcement. It was one o'clock in the morning when Nixon came down; newsmen thought this must be it—his resignation. He deliberately built up suspense by saying he was breaking off—tense pause—his campaign tour. To make a statement over television. Two days from now. Tuesday night. He let them think it might still be his resignation he would announce. The more interest he could generate in the next two days, the bigger his audience on Tuesday night.

That was Monday morning. He got little sleep before he boarded a plane for Los Angeles that afternoon; during the flight, he drafted the first of a series of outlines for his talk. In Los Angeles, he got the reports from Price Waterhouse and Gibson, Dunn in time to put their findings in presentable summary. After midnight, he called his old English and history teachers at Whittier College, with a request that they find some suitable Lincoln quotes for the speech. They phoned two quotes to him by ten o'clock that morning—one witty and one maudlin (he used the latter). Nixon walked the streets with Bill Rogers, discussing approaches he might take. He was keyed up, and thought he just might bring it off.

And then the last blow fell. Tuesday, after a mere four hours of sleep, he kept at his outline resolution, as is his way. He did not go to El Capitan Theater to check the TV set or props or lighting; he wanted every minute for his preparation—it was a pattern familiar to those who have watched Nixon key himself up for a crisis by mood-setting spiritual exercises. And then, with less than an hour before he must leave for the studio, the cruel blow came, shattering his schedule, his carefully programmed psychological countdown. It was Dewey on the phone again, with a last demand: "There has been a meeting of all of Eisenhower's top advisers. They have asked me to tell you that it is their opinion that at the conclusion of the broadcast tonight you should submit your resignation to Eisenhower." The Establishment was taking no chances that its scheme might misfire. Nixon asked if that was the word from the General's own mouth. Dewey answered that the men he spoke of would not have commissioned him to make such a call at such an hour unless they were speaking for the master. (But, as usual, Ike was protected: afterward he could write, "Just before the broadcast Governor Dewey telephoned him from New York reporting the conviction of some of my supporters there"—two can play at that "some of the staff" game—"that he should resign, which the young Senator later said he had feared represented my views." Poor Senator, so fearful, so young, so avuncularly cared for in this retrospective benediction. Those who have called Nixon a master of duplicity should contrast his account of the fund crisis with the smoothed-over version in Eisenhower's book, which does not even mention the "hound's tooth" remark.)

Nixon stalled on the line to Dewey, stalled and wriggled. He said it was too late to change his prepared speech. Dewey said he could, of course, deliver his personal defense and accounting; all he had to do was tack on, at the end, a formal resignation offered to Ike. Nixon said he had to leave for the studio. Dewey: "Can I say you have accepted?" Nixon: "You will have to watch the show to see—and tell them I know something about politics too!"

Nixon had a half hour to tell his staff of this new lightning bolt, get their reaction, shower, shave, dress for the show, making meanwhile his own decision—and trying to collect his wits and memory over the notes for his talk. It had been five days full of pressure, sleeplessness, betrayal, ultimatums—climaxed with the most unsettling demand of all, made when he was at a poise of tension and could be knocked off balance so easily. A whole series of crises. Thursday: answer the charges? Friday: dodge newsmen, or face them; rely on the formal answer or return to the defense again and again; stall or throw oneself upon Ike's mercy? Saturday: heed the *Trib* and resign? Sunday: do the TV show? Monday: what to say on the show? And now, at the last minute, Tuesday: defy Dewey (and, through him, Ike)? Already the strain had shown in Nixon. Sunday in Portland, when Hillings brought a wire from Nixon's mother with the Quaker understated promise of prayers WE ARE THINK-ING OF YOU, Nixon broke down and cried. "I thought I had better leave the room," Hillings said, "and give him time to compose himself." Chotiner, busy calling party people to get money for the show, remembered "I was more worried about Dick's state of mind than about the Party. He was edgy and irritable."

Even the inner circle could not tell for sure whether Nixon would stand up to the pressure, or give in while he spoke. After reporting Dewey's call, he was silent, his mind working desperately at the problem. During the twenty-five-minute ride to the studio, he went over his notes (on debater-type cards). He had withdrawn to his last ditch, to make an entirely lone stand there. The one thing he demanded in studio arrangements was that even Chotiner and Rogers be kept out. Only his wife would be present, within camera range, visible to Nixon. It is as if he were dramatizing, to himself more than others, the isolation he stood in at this dying moment of defiance.

One of the criticisms made of Nixon's television speech is that the hoarse voice and hurt face, hovering on the edge of tears, were either histrionic or (if unfeigned) disproportionate and "tasteless." But no one who knows the full story can suspect Nixon of acting, or blame him for the tension he felt and conveyed—it would be like blaming a recently flayed man for "indecent exposure." Nixon was deserted, in more ways than he could tell. And he was fighting back with more nerve than any-body knew. Besides concentrating fiercely on his appeal to the audience, which had to succeed if anything else were to follow, he was reaching out across their heads to touch swords in a secret duel with Ike.

And Eisenhower understood. Stewart Alsop, in his useful little book *Nixon and Rockefeller,* quotes from an interview with one who watched Eisenhower's reactions throughout the TV show. The General had to give a speech in Cleveland as soon as Nixon went off the air; the audi-ence for that talk was watching a large screen in the auditorium, while Eisenhower and thirty of his people clustered by the TV set in a back-stage office. Even this entourage, predominantly opposed to Nixon, was touched as the show progressed; some wept openly. But Eisenhower was calm, tapping a yellow pad with his pencil, ready to jot down com-ments on the speech. He took no notes while the talk was in progress, though the tapping stopped twice. Nixon, forced to act like a criminal who must clear himself, deftly made his actions look like those of a man with nothing to fear. And he issued a challenge: the *other* candidates must have something to fear, unless they followed his example. He devoted much of his half hour to this challenge, dictating terms to his accusers. (It is this part of the speech—moving onto the offensive—that so pleased Chotiner.)

Now I'm going to suggest some courses of conduct.

First of all, you have read in the papers about other funds. Now, Mr. Stevenson, apparently, had a couple—one of them in which a group of business people paid and helped to supplement the salaries of state employees. Here is where the money went directly into their pockets.

I think what Mr. Stevenson should do is come before the American people, as I have, and give the names of the people who have contributed to that fund, and give the names of the people who put this money into their pockets at the same time they were receiving money from their state government, and see what favors, if any, they gave out for that.

I don't condemn Mr. Stevenson for what he did. But, until the facts are in there, a doubt will be raised.

As far as Mr. Sparkman is concerned, I would suggest the same thing. He's had his wife on the payroll. I don't condemn him for that. But I think he should come before the American people and indicate what outside sources of income he has had.

I would suggest that under the circumstances both Mr. Sparkman and Mr. Stevenson should come before the American people, as I have, and make a complete statement as to their financial history. If they don't it will be an admission that they have something to hide. And I think you will agree with me.

Because, remember, a man who's to be President and a man who's to be Vice President must have the confidence of all the people. That's why I'm doing what I'm doing, and that's what I suggest that Mr. Stevenson and Mr. Sparkman, since they are under attack, should be doing.

Eisenhower stopped tapping with his pencil—jabbed it, instead, down into the yellow pad—when Nixon said any candidate who did not reveal his finances must have something to hide. Of course, Nixon did not mention Eisenhower, and his phrase about other candidates joining him "since they are under attack" left a loophole for the General. But the overall force of the passage could not be missed. All candidates, he was arguing, should act as he had. That meant *Eisenhower*, too—as Ike realized, and events were to prove. After this all the candidates did make their statements.

There were reasons why it was inconvenient for Eisenhower to make his books public—e.g., the special tax decision on earnings of his *Crusade in Europe*. Besides, as Alsop delicately puts it, "the military rarely get into the habit of making charitable contributions . . ." More important, Nixon was turning the tables on Ike. Eisenhower had brought him to this revelation. Nixon would force the same hard medicine down his mentor's throat.

Yet an even defter stroke followed. Dewey had been vague on how the speech should be judged. He told Nixon to have telegrams addressed to Los Angeles, and measure the talk's impact by their content. This arrangement, besides tying Nixon down for several days, still left the matter with Eisenhower. The real decision would be made by the General, assessing news reaction. Nixon would be left to play games with his switchboard and his mail, unable to vindicate himself if Eisenhower decided the show had not cleared him.

But when it came time for Nixon to mention the sending of telegrams, he said: "I am submitting to *the Republican National Committee* tonight, through this television broadcast, the decision *it is theirs to make* . . . Wire and write *the Republican National Committee* whether you think I should stay or whether I should get off; and whatever *their decision* is, I will abide by it." (Italics added.) The General stabbed again, pencil into pad, a sword struck down as he fenced that image on the screen, and lost. Nixon has always been a party man; his strength lay there. Karl Mundt and Robert Humphreys, manning the Washington headquarters of the National Committee while Chairman Arthur Summerfield traveled with Ike, had routinely issued statements backing Nixon from the very first day of his troubles. Now, by a cool disarming maneuver, Nixon was taking the matter away from the Eastern Establishment and putting it in the hands of men sympathetic to the regulars, to grassroots workers—people who respond in a partisan way to partisan attacks upon one of their own, people most vulnerable to the planned schmaltz and hominess of the Checkers reference, people with small debts of their own and Republican cloth coats. If the decision was theirs to make, then—the real point of the broadcast as Nixon had reshaped it—*it was not Ike's.* It is no wonder that, while others in Cleveland wept, the man who had directed OVERLORD, the largest military operation in the world's history, the *General,* made an angry stab. He knew enough about maneuver to see he was outflanked. Alsop's informant said: "Before that, I'd always liked and admired Ike, of course, but I'd often wondered how smart he really was. After that, I knew Ike got what Dick was getting at right away."

The importance of that decision, redirecting the appeal to the National Committee, explains Nixon's breakdown when he saw he had gone off the air. Under the pressure of the performance, undertaken without rehearsal, using sketchy notes, he had done something rare for him—missed the countdown toward sign-off by a minute or two: "Time had run out. I was cut off just as I intended to say where the National Committee was located and where the telegrams and letters should be sent." He had based everything on this point; he needed every wire that would reach Washington. What if the telegrams were diffused ineffectually about the country, sent to him, to Ike, to TV channels and local campaign offices? He needed a crushing weight of response all directed to one point, and now (he thought) he would not get it. (The wires in fact did go everywhere, but in such breathtaking numbers that all doubt was swept before them.) He threw his cards to the floor in a spasm, told Pat he had failed; when Chotiner came into the studio, elated by the skilled performance, Nixon just shook his head and claimed, "I was an utter flop." Outside the theater, as his car pulled away, an Irish setter friskily rocked alongside barking: Nixon turned,

Bill Rogers would remember, and twisted out a bitter, "At least I won the dog vote tonight." The end, he thought, of the Checkers speech. He was touching bottom. That night he would finally, after all his earlier resistance, resign.

But it took more kicks and blows to bring him to it. During the first hours after his broadcast, others were jubilant and support poured in; but no call came from the General (a wire had been sent off, but was stuck in the traffic-jam of them at Nixon's hotel switchboard—no one called from the Cleveland camp to give Nixon its message). The first notice he had of the telegram came over the news wires—and it brought word of still another ultimatum. Eisenhower did not often lose wars of attrition. They were his kind of battle.

The crowd waiting for Ike in Cleveland was hoarse with shouts and praise for the TV show they had witnessed. Eisenhower's own first comment was to Chairman Summerfield, about the $75,000: "Well, Arthur, you got your money's worth." Hagerty came back from the auditorium and told Eisenhower he could not deliver his prepared talk on inflation with this crowd. He would have to speak to the Nixon issue. The General knew. He had already chosen his strategy. He fashioned its main lines on the yellow pad, and tried it on his advisers. First, a sop to the crowd: "I like courage . . . Tonight I saw an example of courage . . . I have never seen anyone come through in such a fashion as Senator Nixon did tonight . . . When I get in a fight, I would rather have a courageous and honest man by my side than a whole boxcar full of pussyfooters."

All the praise was a cover, though. Eisenhower was a master of the basics—supply, firepower, and retention of position. After praising Nixon for courage, Ike added that he had not made his mind up on the main subject—whether Nixon would remain on the ticket: "It is obvious that I have to have something more than one single presentation, necessarily limited to thirty minutes, the time allowed Senator Nixon." But if Eisenhower, who had chosen him as his running mate, who had access to the research of the lawyers and accountants, to the advice of top politicians in the party, could not make up his mind after watching the TV show, then how could anyone in the public do so? There is only one explanation for this performance: Ike was determined not to let Nixon take the decision out of his hands. "I am not going to be swayed by my idea of what will get most votes . . . I am going to say: Do I myself believe this man is the kind of man America would like to have for its Vice President?" That is, at one minute he will not be swayed by what the people want and would vote for, and the next minute he is accepting the sacred pledge of finding out what the public wants and will vote for!

Then Eisenhower read them his telegram to Nixon, which shows the real thrust of his remarks: "While technically no decision rests with me, you and I know the realities of the situation require a pronouncement which the public considers decisive." (Or: Get your National Committee support, and see how far it carries you without me.) "My personal decision is going to be based on personal conclusions." (Or: I won't

judge you by reaction to your talk—which is what he had promised he
would do.) "I would most appreciate it if you can fly to see me at once."
(Or: Here, Rover.) "Tomorrow evening I will be at Wheeling, W. Va."
(Or: Tomorrow *you* will be at Wheeling, W. Va.) Not only was Eisenhower reasserting the personal jurisdiction Nixon had challenged; he
wanted a public dramatization of the lines of authority. Having cleared
himself with the public, Nixon must appear before a superior tribunal,
summoned there to make his defense again, in greater detail, while
judgment was pointedly suspended.

Nixon could not submit; yet, once the demand was made public,
he could not go further in public defiance, either. He gave in. Rose
Woods took down his dictated telegram of resignation.

But he would get in one last blow of his own. The wire was not
directed toward Eisenhower, as Dewey had insisted it should be. He
addressed it to the National Committee! As Rose Woods went out of
the room to send the message, Chotiner followed her and tore off the
top sheet of her pad. Rose said she could not have sent it anyway.
Nixon is, by his own admission, subject to sharp lapses and lowering of
his guard in the emotional depletion that follows on conflict. In four
of his book's six crises he finds an example of that pattern: and the
example for the fund crisis is his telegram to the National Committee.
His loss of grip began the minute the show went off the air and he
threw his cards to the floor. " 'What more can he possibly want from
me?' I asked . . . I didn't believe I could take any more of the suspense
and tension of the past week." Chotiner went to work on him, however,
and persuaded him that he could avoid both of the unpalatable things
being forced on him—resignation, or compliance with Eisenhower's summons. If he just resumed his interrupted campaign-schedule (next step,
Missoula, Montana), the General would have to back down. The wave
of public response was already seismic. Nixon reports Chotiner's counsel
this way: "Chotiner, particularly, insisted that I not allow myself to be
put in the position of going to Eisenhower like a little boy to be taken
to the woodshed, properly punished, and then restored to a place of
dignity." At this point, there was a call from Ike's camp. Arthur Summerfield, pleased that things had turned out well, was asking for Chotiner—who soon dashed his spirits. Murray said Nixon had just dictated
his resignation; he admitted, when Summerfield gasped, that the telegram was torn up—"but I'm not so sure how long it's going to stay
torn." Summerfield said things could be smoothed over when Dick
reached Wheeling. But Dick was not going to Wheeling: "We're flying
to Missoula tonight." Summerfield wanted to know how to head off this
disaster—so Chotiner set terms: Nixon will not come unless he is sure
of a welcoming endorsement, without further inquisition. This was, of
course, a demand that Eisenhower back down on the stated purpose of
the summons, which was to go into greater detail than thirty minutes
would allow.

Eisenhower, realistic about cutting his losses, saw when this news
reached him that the idea of further investigation could not be sustained. He let Summerfield give Nixon's camp the proper assurances.

But Nixon would still be answering a humiliating public call. Just before the plane took off for Missoula, Bert Andrews, who had worked with Nixon all through the Hiss affair, called from the Eisenhower press room in Cleveland: Ike would have no choice now but to receive Nixon warmly; Nixon would have to lose a little face in order to avoid flouting the General's summons. Nixon agreed, and let his staff arrange a flight to Wheeling after the stop at Missoula. Ike was at the airport, to throw his arm around him and call him "my boy"—looking gracious, kind, generous, as if supporting an embattled man rather than picking up strength from a victorious one. The only thing that could resolve the crisis—Ike's blue-eyed smile of benediction—had been bestowed.

But they did not forget the night when they touched swords. There would never be any trust between them. And Nixon had begun a tutelage that would gall him and breed resentment through years of friction and slights.

The Underestimation
of Dwight D. Eisenhower

MURRAY KEMPTON

Dwight Eisenhower was surely among the most beloved of American Presidents. Yet his case is unusual for he was clearly a man loved for what he was rather than for what he did in the White House. And voter affection for the former General did not apparently extend to his adopted party: for six of his eight years in office, Eisenhower faced a Congress in which the Republicans constituted a minority. As Rexford Tugwell has pointed out, he was "the least partisan President" since George Washington. He stood above the political battle—where the people apparently wanted him to stand. And of course this rendered the battle beneath—the world of such men as Vice President Richard Nixon and Senate Majority leader Lyndon Johnson—that much less interesting. Depression and war had meant a generation of political excitement and conflict. After 1952 the pendulum swung, and Americans enjoyed respite from turbulence, sat back, and left things to Ike.

Eisenhower's accomplishments as President were limited but real. He stabilized the Cold War around a potentially disastrous strategy of "massive retaliation" which he had no intention of invoking except in speeches. And he stabilized the New Deal, neither extending it nor cutting it back, therefore making it part of the mainstream of American politics. And he did cool off the sour tensions accumulating over a generation of political stress. What he did not do, the problems that he simply kept in the cooler, nevertheless began to emerge during his second administration. A long list of national needs (that were to define the accomplishments and the failures of the tumultuous sixties) was already pressing for action when Dwight Eisenhower bid his farewell with a prescient warning about the "military-industrial complex" that had grown over-mighty during his own administration. Whether Eisenhower's record deserved the criticism it drew from liberals during the 1950's or whether his presidency merits the encomiums that they are bestowing on him in the war-weary present is the question posed in these readings by Murray Kempton and Richard H. Rovere.

He was a far more complex and devious man than most people realized, and in the best sense of those words.—Richard Nixon, *Six Crises*

The full moment of revelation about the great captains may be possible only for one of the casualties they leave behind them. Richard Nixon was writing in hospital: just once, the resentment whose suppression is the great discipline of his life breaks through and is taken back with that saving clause about the best sense of the word, of course. Yea, though He slay me yet must I depend on Him.

Dwight Eisenhower was as indifferent as Calvin Coolidge, as absolute as Abraham Lincoln, more contained than John Kennedy, more serpentine than Lyndon Johnson, as hard to work for as Andrew Johnson. Historians seem to accept most of these qualities as necessary for greatness; certainly none of them diminish it. But, then, most are accounted sinister by the great mass of civilians, and to confuse civilians and to keep them off his back is the soldier's art. Eisenhower, who understood everything, seems to have decided very early that life is nothing unless it is convenient; to show the living flesh of greatness to one's contemporaries means to show one's face in combat and to be argued about; the only convenient greatness is to appear as a monument.

The most precise description of Eisenhower was rendered in another connection by Edward Lear:

> On the top of the Crumpetty Tree
>   The Quangle Wangle sat,
> But his face you could not see,
>   On account of his Beaver Hat
> For his Hat was a hundred and
>   two feet wide,
>   With ribbons and bibbons on
>   every side
> And bells, and buttons, and loops,
>   and lace.
> So that nobody ever could see the face
>   Of the Quangle Wangle Quee.

Innocence was Eisenhower's beaver hat, and the ribbons grew longer and more numerous until his true lines were almost invisible. It took a very long watch indeed to catch the smallest glimpse.

"He told Nixon and others, including myself, that he was well aware that somebody had to do the hard-hitting infighting,[1] and he had no objections to it as long as no one expected *him* to do it," Sherman Adams says.

It was the purpose of his existence never to be seen in what he did. When he fired Sherman Adams, his chief of staff, as a political liability in 1958, Adams thought it was Nixon's doing. While he was coldly measuring the gain or loss from dropping Nixon as his 1952 Vice-Presidential candidate, Nixon thought it was Tom Dewey's doing.

When this gesture proved insufficient, Eisenhower accommodated to what was inevitable, if transient, and even offered himself up as battle trophy for Goldwater's brief triumph at the San Francisco convention. It was a situation where, the surreptitiously neat having failed, the heroically messy could hardly succeed. The useless employment of further resources would have been an affront to that superb sense of economy which made Eisenhower a soldier successful just being so immune to notions of glory and to pleasurable anticipations of bleeding.

"He is the most immoral man I have ever known," one of Nelson

---

1. *Definable to the Democrats as the dirty work.*

Rockefeller's captains said not long ago. He was probably wrong; there is always the danger of going overboard in moments when the watcher thinks he has found Eisenhower out. To be absolutely immoral is a perilous excess; being moderate in all things means, after all, being moderate in the expenditure of morality.

No thought was to be uttered undisguised; the face had as many ranges, indeed as many roles as there are sins to commit, because it was an instrument for hinting without ever quite saying. Even the syntax was an instrument. When things were at their stickiest in the Formosa Strait, James Hagerty, his Press Secretary, told the President that the best course would be to refuse to answer any questions at all on the subject if it came up at his press conference.

" 'Don't worry, Jim,' I told him as we went out the door. 'If that question comes up, I'll just confuse them.' "

Those press conferences, his highest achievements as craftsman in masks, seem certain to be half the sport and half the despair of historians; they will give up, one has to assume, and settle for the judgment that he was a man hopelessly confused, it being so difficult to confess that anyone, across so many years, could still so superbly confuse you. The mask he contrived for his comfort has already become the reputation. Generals like MacArthur and Montgomery, as proud of their intelligence as he was appalled by their weakness for theatre, seem to have thought him stupid, as he certainly thought them a little dippy. The other Presidents already evoked most often for comparison with him are General Grant and James Buchanan. But still there abides the mystery of why he never left the country ruined by his laziness, as Buchanan did, or himself ruined by his friends, as Grant did.

The difference in both cases was partly Eisenhower's intelligence, partly his appreciation of those occasions when self-indulgence can produce worse inconveniences, partly that chilliness of his nature which protected him from ever indulging others.

"I could understand it if he played golf all the time with old Army friends, but no man is less loyal to his old friends than Eisenhower," John Kennedy observed when he was a Senator. "He is a terribly cold man. All his golfing pals are rich men he has met since 1945."

"In the evenings when he had no official engagements or on weekends," says Adams, "the President liked to spend his time with old friends whose faces were often seen at Gettysburg—Bill Robinson, the entertaining George Allen, Cliff Roberts, Pete Jones, Bob Woodruff, Al Gruenther, Slats Slater, Freeman Gosden ['Amos' of the famous radio team of Amos and Andy], Sig Larmon."

These Sigs and Petes and Slatses could hardly have been more stimulating than his old Army comrades—of whose intelligence he *does* seem to have entertained the lowest opinion—and, when one member of a salon is granted special distinction as "entertaining," his fellow inmates must be dreary indeed.

But the Sigs and Petes had one substantial advantage; they earned his affection as Casanova made *his* conquests: they were men who paid.

Once, Eisenhower remembers, he had a few days' rest in Scotland on a state trip; and someone, thinking he might be lonely, suggested that he call a few friends to fly over for golf and bridge.

"The idea," he says, "struck me as intriguing, in certain respects the brighest I had heard during the entire trip. Forgetting the time differential, I picked up the telephone and within minutes was talking to Bill Robinson in New York. My call got him out of bed; in New York it was two o'clock in the morning. Without a moment's hesitation he accepted my invitation and a few hours later he and 'Pete' Jones were on their way. I was indeed fortunate to have friends who were such light sleepers."

He lived among strangers; his protective coloration was the appearance of being amiable and innocent. Very seldom does he give himself away: once he said that, when he was President of Columbia, he never went for a walk at night without carrying his service revolver with him. There is surprising hauteur in this image of the most eminent neighbor at large in Morningside Heights; but there is also the grandeur of a man whose dedication it was never to experience a moment on confrontation without the proper weight of means; to him all life was a matter of logistics.

He is revealed best, if only occasionally, in the vast and dreary acreage of his memoirs of the White House years. There he could feel safe in an occasional lapse of guard. For one thing, political history is the opiate of Democrats and he had spent eight years grandly erasing any suggestion from the minds of anyone else that anything he might ever say could be remotely interesting. He had concealed his marvelous intelligence from admirer and critic alike; by now, there was little danger of its being noticed even if confessed; he could be as secure in his memoirs as in his private diary.

The Eisenhower who emerges here intermittently free from his habitual veils is the President most superbly equipped for truly consequential decision we may ever have had, a mind neither rash nor hesitant, free of the slightest concern for how things might look, indifferent to any sentiment, as calm when he was demonstrating the wisdom of leaving a bad situation alone as when he was moving to meet it on those occasions when he absolutely had to.

Of course, we think: That is the way he wants us to see him; he is still trying to fool us; but he won't get away with it this time. And so he has fooled us again, for the Eisenhower who tells us that he never makes an important mistake is telling us for the first time about the real Eisenhower.

There is the sound of trumpets, the fog of rhetoric, then for just a moment the focus of the cold intelligence.

The President-elect goes to Korea.

We used light airplanes to fly along the front and were impressed by the rapidity with which wounded were being brought back for treatment; evacuation was almost completely by helicopter since there were no landing fields for conventional planes in the mountains. Except for sporadic artillery fire and sniping there was little action at the moment, *but in view of the strength of the positions the enemy had developed, it was obvious that any frontal attack would present great difficulties.*

All else would be conversation; one look had decided Eisenhower to fold the war.

Iraq's monarchy has been overthrown, Lebanon's government is collapsing, the British are otherwise committed; President Eisenhower will have to send the Marines.

The basic mission of United States forces in Lebanon was not primarily to fight. Every effort was made to have our landing be as much of a garrison move as possible. In my address I had been careful to use the term 'stationed in' Lebanon. . . . If it had been prudent, I would have preferred that the first battalion ashore disembark at a dock rather than across the beaches. However, the attitude of the Lebanese army was at that moment unknown, and it was obviously wise to disembark in deployed formation ready for any emergency. As it turned out, there was no resistance; the Lebanese along the beaches welcomed our troops. The geographic objectives of the landings included only the city of Beirut and the adjoining airfield.

And, thereunder, he appends this note of explanation:

The decision to occupy only the airfield and capital was a political one which I adhered to over the recommendations of some of the military. If the Lebanese army were unable to subdue the rebels when we had secured their capital and protected their government, I felt, we were backing up a government with so little popular support that we probably should not be there.

There was French Indochina, now of course Vietnam, and this cold intelligence looks upon the French with all the remote distance it would always feel from the romantic poetry of war:

The President is told that the French propose to put 10,000 troops in Dien Bien Phu.

. . . I said, "You cannot do this."

"This will bring the enemy into the open," he said. "We cannot find them in the jungle, and this will draw them out where we can then win."

"The French know military history," I said. "They are smart enough to know the outcome of becoming firmly emplaced and then besieged in an exposed position with poor means of supply and reinforcements."

Never thereafter could he contemplate the war in Indochina except in the frozen tones of a War College report on a maneuver by officers who can henceforth abandon all hope of promotion. The French, he instructs Foster Dulles, have committed the classic military blunder. In Geneva, Dulles is said to have hinted that the United States might use the atom bomb to save the French; there is no evidence that he would have dared transmit that suggestion to a President who plainly would not have trusted him with a stick of dynamite to blow up a fishpond.

Dulles, unhopefully, does transmit a French plea for United States bomber support of the Dien Bien Phu garrison; Eisenhower does not even seem to have noticed it. He had already made up his mind about that:

There were grave doubts in my mind about the effectiveness of such air strikes on deployed troops where good cover was plentiful. Employment of air strikes alone to support French troops in the jungle would create a double jeopardy: *it would comprise an act of war and would also entail the risk of having intervened and lost.*

Sitting with Under Secretary of State Bedell Smith, "I remarked that, if the United States were, unilaterally, to permit its forces to be drawn into conflict in Indochina, and in a succession of Asian wars, the end result would be to drain off our resources and to weaken our overall defensive position."

The French went down; Eisenhower blamed them and the British, who, of course, blamed Dulles.

Then, in his utmost refinement, there is the Eisenhower who supervised the C.I.A.'s U-2 reconnaissance flights over the Soviet Union:

A final important characteristic of the plane was its fragile construction. This led to the assumption (insisted upon by the C.I.A. and the Joint Chiefs) that in the event of mishap the plane would virtually distintegrate. It would be impossible, if things should go wrong, they said, for the Soviets to come into possession of the equipment intact—or, unfortunately, of a live pilot. This was a cruel assumption, but I was assured that the young pilots undertaking these missions were doing so with their eyes wide open and motivated by a high degree of patriotism, a swashbuckling bravado, and certain material inducements.[2]

Then Francis Powers' U-2 was shot down, and Eisenhower, of course, ordered the announcement of the "previously designed 'cover story.'"

Upon which, "Mr. Khrushchev, appearing before the Supreme Soviet once more, announced what to me was unbelievable. The uninjured pilot of our reconnaissance plane, along with much of his equipment intact, was in Soviet hands."

The State Department was still lamely adhering to the cover story. That seemed totally irrational to Eisenhower, who at once ordered a

2. One of the confusions making difficult the full appreciation of Eisenhower's subtlety is the condition that he seems to explain himself in anticlimactic series. For example: "As president of Columbia, I became deeply interested in the educational, financial and public relations aspects of the job." Normally one would expect a college president to be more interested in education than in public relations, and the succession seems anticlimactic. But, with a little thought, one understands that Eisenhower knew he was at Columbia as a public-relations man. In the same way, normal rhetoric would assign the climactic role in the readiness of a soldier to sacrifice his life to "high degree of patriotism"; Eisenhower, with perfect understanding, gives the emphasis to "certain material inducements."

full confession, altering its draft "to eliminate any phrase that seemed to me to be defensive in tone.

"In the diplomatic field," he explained, "it was routine practice to deny responsibility for an embarrassing occurrence when there is even a one percent chance of being believed, but when the world can entertain not the slightest doubt of the facts, there is no point in trying to evade the issue."

And there we have, in Dwight Eisenhower of all unexpected persons, the model of that perfect statesman of Voltaire's ironic dream, the one who could learn nothing from Machiavelli except to denounce Machiavelli.

The precepts are plain to see:

1) Always pretend to be stupid; then when you have to show yourself smart, the display has the additional effect of surprise.

2) Taking the blame is a function of servants. When the orange is squeezed, throw it away.

3) When a situation is hopeless, never listen to counsels of hope. Fold the enterprise.

4) Do nothing unless you know exactly what you will do if it turns out to have been the wrong thing. Walk not one inch forward onto ground which has not been painfully tested by someone else.

5) Never forget the conversation you had with Zhukov about how the Russian army clears minefields. "We march through them," Zhukov had said. It is a useful instruction if applied with the proper economy. Keep Nixon and Dulles around for marching through minefields.

6) Always give an enemy an exit.

7) Never give an ally his head.

8) Assume that your enemies are just as sensible as you are. ("Personally I had always discounted the probability of the Soviets doing anything as 'reaction.' Communists do little on impulse; rather their aggressive moves are invariably the result of deliberate decision.")

9) Lie whenever it seems useful, but stop lying the moment ninety-nine percent of the audience ceases to believe you.

10) Respond only when there is some gain besides honor in meeting the challenge or some serious loss from disregarding it. For example, when Eisenhower was the first candidate for President in memory who indicated that he was unable to pronounce the word "injunction" when discussing the labor problem, I suggested to one of his admirers that he seemed extraordinarily dumb.

"If he's so dumb," was the reply, "why is he such a good bridge player?"

Like all defenses of Dwight Eisenhower, it seemed silly at first; but, with thought one understood its force. Eisenhower spent the Twenties as an officer in garrison; his friends were civilians in towns like Leavenworth, Kansas. He learned to play bridge well because his pay did not cover losing money to civilians. He is equipped to respond to any challenge which seems to him sensible.

He was the great tortoise upon whose back the world sat for eight years. We laughed at him; we talked wistfully about moving; and all the while we never knew the cunning beneath the shell.

I talked to him just once. He was in Denver, getting ready for the 1952 campaign when he would have to run with Republicans like Senator Jenner who had called General Marshall, the chief agent of Eisenhower's promotion, "a living lie." I had thought that anyone so innocent as Eisenhower would be embarrassed by this comradeship and proposed to ask what he thought about what Jenner had said. It seemed cruel to spring any such trap to anyone this innocent, so I told Hagerty that I intended to ask the question.

The time came and I asked, "General, what do you think of those people who call General Marshall a living lie?"

He leaped to his feet and contrived the purpling of his face. How dare anyone say that about the greatest man who walks in America? He shook his finger in marvelous counterfeit of the palsy of outrage.

He would die for General Marshall. He could barely stand to be in the room with anyone who would utter such a profanation. The moment passed when the enlisted man in garrison endures his ordeal as example to the rest of the troops; and suddenly I realized that, in his magnificent rage at me, he had been careful not to mention Senator Jenner at all.

Afterward Hagerty took me over and the General offered the sunshine of his smile; there was not the slightest indication that he was thinking that there was anything for him to forgive or me either. It had simply been the appointed ceremony. I was too dumb to understand him then. It would be ten years before I looked at his picture and realized that the smile was always a grin.

Eisenhower Revisited—
A Political Genius?
A Brilliant Man?

RICHARD H. ROVERE

It has been slightly more than a decade since Robert Frost greeted the dawn of a "next Augustan age . . . of poetry and power" and Dwight D. Eisenhower, ex-President, left Washington for Gettysburg—still an immensely popular figure who, had the law permitted and the spirit and the flesh been willing, could easily have been the man taking the oath of office on January 20, 1961, thus deferring the Augustan age for at least four more years. Eisenhower was held in high esteem for the rest of his life, but throughout most of the sixties those amateurs who sit in more or less professional judgment on Presidents—other politicians, historians, journalists—came more and more into agreement that his eight years in the White House had been a period of meager accomplishment and lackadaisical leadership. The greatest failure, the consensus seemed to be, was one of anticipation. What a prescient statesman could have foreseen in the fifties, the argument runs, was that the ship of state was headed for a sea of troubles, and this the 34th President conspicuously failed to perceive. He lacked foresight and imagination and thus bore considerable responsibility for the difficulties of the three men who succeeded him in the sixties.

Many of those who judged him most harshly until only a few years ago are now having second and third thoughts about the man and his Presidency—thoughts that should ring most agreeably in the ears of those whose faith had never never wavered. Such nay-sayers on the left as Murray Kempton and I. F. Stone are finding virtues in him they failed to detect while he served, and others are making claims for him that not even his partisans made when he sought office or held it. Garry Wills, the eminent Nixonologist, advises us in "Nixon Agonistes" that Eisenhower was "a political genius." Walter Cronkite, who first knew Eisenhower in France during the war and saw him often in subsequent years, recently said that he never thought highly of Eisenhower "either as a general or a President" but that in the post-White House years he discovered that Eisenhower was in actuality a "brilliant" man—indeed, "more brilliant than many brilliant men I have met."

A political genius? A brilliant man? Who ever said or thought that about Eisenhower in his own time? Certainly not Eisenhower himself. It was not that he was lacking in vanity; he had his share, but there is no evidence that he ever thought of himself as possessing a great talent for politics or a towering intellect, and the aspect of his "genius" that Wills calls "realism" would have deterred him from this kind of self-appraisal. He was, and we can be sure that he knew he was, no slouch politically (had he been below average in this respect, he would not have risen in the Army), and he was certainly not lacking in intelligence. But his real strengths lay elsewhere, and the Wills and Cronkite superlatives seem, one has to say, silly.

In the case of Garry Wills, the judgment supports a theory. Wills maintains that Eisenhower all along saw Richard Nixon in the light in which Wills today sees him. In Cronkite's case, the delayed but nonetheless dazzling illumination appeared in the course of many meetings he had with Eisenhower while taping some television interviews in the mid-sixties. He asserts his discovery of the ex-President's "brilliance" but does not tell us how it was made manifest.

For my part, I think the revisionist phenomenon as a whole can be rather easily accounted for—though I do not wish to suggest that new judgments are erroneous simply because they are new or, at least, as I see it, obvious in their origins. Seen from 1971, the most important single thing about Dwight D. Eisenhower was that, through luck or good management or some combination of both, *we did not go to war* while he was President. To be sure, we came close on occasion, and his Secretary of State practiced a brand of cold-war diplomacy in which what was called "brinkmanship" at the time—risking war, including nuclear war—was an indispensable strategy. It can also be argued that Dulles's and Eisenhower's Indochina policy made Kennedy's and Johnson's and Nixon's all but inevitable and that, had Eisenhower held office for a third term, he would have found himself at war in Vietnam. The contrary can also be argued, but it does not matter, we were at war when he came to office, and six months later we were out of it, and we did not enter another war during his tenure. Eight years of Eisenhower: seven and a half years of peace. Ten years of Kennedy, Johnson, Nixon: almost ten solid years of war.

What else is there to celebrate about the Eisenhower years? I can think of a few things, but they are of far less consequence and, moreover, they are not blessings of the sort that can be appreciated only in hindsight—unless one chooses to include among them such engineering projects as the St. Lawrence Seaway and the interstate highway system. Though I have myself altered some of my views about Eisenhower over the years, I have felt since 1958 or thereabouts that the country benefited from his first term but would have been better off if he had not had a second. I think I can defend this view in 1971. By 1953 we had made our point in Korea—the expulsion of the invading armies—and it was time for a settlement. It required a Republican President (not necessarily Eisenhower, though of course it helped that he was a successful military man) to end that war on terms short of the "victory" for which Gen. Douglas MacArthur said there was "no substitute." As Harry Truman was to say, he or any other Democrat would have been "lynched" for agreeing to the settlement Eisenhower so cheerfully accepted. It also required a Republican in the White House (though, again, not necessarily Eisenhower) to bring about the downfall of Senator Joe McCarthy.

Eisenhower, to be sure, never took the initiative against McCarthy. He declined to "get into the gutter" with the demagogue, and he tolerated, for a while, a certain amount of high-level appeasement. But the fact remains that 15 months after Eisenhower took office McCarthy was done for. With an active, militant President, the job might have been done somewhat sooner and with less loss of dignity all around. However, a Republican President did not have to be an activist to draw McCarthy's fire. Though nominally a Republican, McCarthy was bound by the nature of his mission in American political life to attack any administration, and when in time he attacked his own party's stewardship of affairs, resistance was bound to be offered. It tends now to be forgotten that McCarthy scored most of his triumphs when the Democrats controlled both the White House and Congress, and he would probably have been more difficult to deal with had they remained in control. It has always seemed to me that the election of Adlai Stevenson in 1952, however desirable it might have been in certain respects, would have prolonged both the Korean war and McCarthyism, and I have reason to think that, in later years, Stevenson believed this, too. The country was bitterly divided in 1952, and 20 years of Democratic governance was one of the causes of disunity.

Putting Eisenhower in the White House seemed a way of promoting national unity, which, though hardly the highest of political values, is not one to be disregarded. But by 1956 Eisenhower had achieved just about all that it was in his power to achieve. The war was over, McCarthy was a spent force and the President had, at the Geneva Summit Conference of 1955, helped negotiate a limited but nonetheless helpful *détente* in the cold war.

The second term was anticlimax almost all the way. It was also rather melancholy and at times squalid. The President was not a well man. The Democrats, growing in power in the Congress and knowing that no one would ever again ride Eisenhower's coattails, were openly seeking to embarrass him and passing bills he felt he had to veto. In midterm, he lost the two men he had relied on most heavily. John Foster Dulles left office and soon died, and Sherman Adams, who was general manager at the White House, had to retire because of a clear conflict of interest. Eisenhower began on his own to practice some of Dulles's peripatetic diplomacy, but it didn't work. In 1960, he started for another summit meeting, in Paris, but Nikita Khrushchev refused to make the final ascent because of the unpleasantness over the U-2 affair. Eisenhower set out for Japan, but for security reasons (rioting anti-American students, etc.) was advised to turn around and go home.

There is more to being a President than entering or ending wars— and more than instituting or failing to institute political and social change. Style and character are important and closely related aspects of leadership. Eisenhowever came to us as a hero—not in the old sense of a man who had displayed great valor but in the newer sense of having been an organizer of victory. His style, though, was anything but heroic. It was in part fatherly, in larger part avuncular. He was not an exhorter —except now and then in campaigns—and as a counselor his performance was as a rule inadequate. He had difficulties with language, particularly when he extemporized. Readers of press-conference texts found his syntax all but impenetrable and often concluded that his thinking was as muddled as the verbatim transcripts. Actually, he was seldom as unclear as he appeared to be when encountered in cold type. Those who listened and watched as he talked were rarely in doubt as to what he was saying. Inflection and expression conveyed much of what seemed missing or mixed up in print. But he was never, to put it mildly, eloquent, never a forceful persuader. He never influenced, or sought to influence, American thought.

Eulogizing Eisenhower in April, 1969, President Nixon said of his late mentor: "For more than a quarter of a century, he spoke with a moral authority seldom equaled in American public life." Nixon did not explain how, when or where the impact of this "moral authority" was felt. Eisenhower was an upright man, a believer in the Protestant ethic he seemed to embody. But the man he twice defeated was no less honorable, and Stevenson had a moral vision that seemed somewhat broader, deeper and less simplistic than Eisenhower's. Do any survivors recall the Eisenhower years as a period notable for elevated standards of morality in public life or elsewhere? In our public life, there were two issues full of "moral" content—McCarthyism and race. On neither did the President personally exercise any of the kind of authority Nixon attributed to him. He was not a McCarthyite or a racist, but he conspicuously failed to engage his personal prestige or that of his office in the struggles against demagogy and racial injustice.

A President can also provide leadership by improving the quality of public life—the quality of the people he appoints and associates himself with, the quality of the acts he and they perform, the quality of the ideas his administration espouses. If in the future, the brief Presidency of Eisenhower's successor is well regarded, it will be largely because of his quest for "excellence." Kennedy brought many first-rate people to Washington, and if one of the lessons they taught us is that first-rate people can sometimes mess things up as badly as third-raters or fourth-raters, it is nevertheless true that some of them performed brilliantly and should continue to serve the Republic for some years to come. No such praise, so far as I am aware, accrues to Eisenhower—except in the case of one institution, the Supreme Court.

He appointed a Chief Justice and four Associate Justices, and all but one of the five (Charles Whittaker, who sat only briefly) served with high distinction. In this respect, Eisenhower's record may be as good as any in history. There was about it, though, a kind of inadvertent quality—as if some architect had achieved splendor while seeking only mediocrity. The President was surprised and in some cases hugely disappointed by the performance of the institution he had created.

In the executive branch, mediocrity was the rule. The one Cabinet member of stature was John Foster Dulles, an imposing man in many ways but also a stiff, self-righteous Calvinist who intensified the cold war as an ideological conflict and sometimes seemed bent on making it a theological one as well—making, as he put it, "the moral force of Christendom . . . felt in the conduct of nations." Nevertheless, Dulles was a man of some intellectual prowess, and nothing of the sort could be said for anyone else in the upper echelons. Eisenhower's measure of expertise in any field was that of the Bitch Goddess: success, usually financial success. Especially in the early days, it was a businessman's administration—to a degree that bred misgivings even in the mind of the first Senator Robert Taft of Ohio, who made no bones about being a spokesman for business but said, when he heard of the first appointments, "I don't know of any reasons why success in business should mean success in public service. . . . Anyone who thinks he can just transfer business methods to government is going to have to learn that it isn't so." Eisenhower's appointments were uninspired and uninspiring; one cannot think of any major office holder whose example might have led any young man or young woman to feel that public life might be a high calling. On the White House staff, there were from time to time highly gifted younger men—Maxwell Rabb, Emmet Hughes, Malcolm Moos—but for the most part they lacked power and visibility, though Moos exerted an influence of a kind when he wrote the line about the "military-industrial complex" into Eisenhower's farewell address.

Still and all, who in 1971 wouldn't exchange a trainload of mediocrities, incompetents and even pickpockets for a speedy end to the war in Vietnam and to the rancor and discord it has created? There may be some survivors of the better-dead-than-Red set, but even a number of these, one suspects, no longer see the conflict in Vietnam as one that compels a choice between extinction and the surrender of American independence. There was peace under Eisenhower, and the question of historical interest to those of us who survived the ensuing decade is whether this indisputable fact is to be ascribed to his stewardship or to luck or to some combination of both. I lean toward the combination theory, with perhaps a heavier emphasis on luck than others might care to make.

The opportunities for military involvement during his tenure were fully as numerous as those of the Kennedy, Johnson and Nixon years. In Asia, there were Korea, the Formosa Strait and Indochina; in Europe, Germany and Hungary; in the Middle East, Suez and Lebanon, and in our own hemisphere, Cuba. In some of these troubled areas, intervention was seriously contemplated; in others, it seemed out of the question from the start. In the Suez crisis of 1956, our policy from the onset was to stay out militarily: we made our disapproval so clear to the British and the French that we were not consulted in the planning stages. Nor was there ever much likelihood of our doing anything about Hungary, which erupted just after Suez in the closing days of the Presidential campaign; the Dulles line on Eastern Europe was always that we stood ready to help in the task of "liberation," but it was never much more than a line, and in moments of crisis behind the Iron Curtain—except when there was trouble in Berlin—we looked the other way. In 1958 in Lebanon, we did, at the request of its beleaguered President, land combat-ready Marine and Army units, but there was no combat and the troops spent their time girl-watching on the beaches they had stormed.

But elsewhere the risks were large. Even before his inauguration, Eisenhower went to Korea in search of peace, and in a matter of months a welcome (though far from satisfactory) settlement was made. Politically, in this country, the credit was all his, and if the whole truth is ever known—it will probably never be—it might turn out that he deserves it all. From what is currently known, his principal strategy seems to have been nuclear blackmail—a threat conveyed to our adversaries that if they dragged their feet much longer in the truce talks while pressing on with the war, this country would not consider itself bound to a reliance on conventional weapons. (Eisenhower was never opposed to the use of atomic weapons on moral grounds. He regarded them simply as explosives, suitable for some demolition jobs and not for others. His later assertions about general war's being "unthinkable" in the atomic age were based not on a moral judgment but a military one. He saw no point in a war no one would survive. But tactical "nukes" were another matter.) Maybe that did it, and maybe not. The truth could only come from the other side, and about all we now have on any other factor is Khrushchev's memory of Chou En-lai later explaining that the Chinese losses in Korea had become militarily insupportable. In any case, with all due respect for and gratitude to Eisenhower, one is compelled to wonder what would have happened—what could have happened—if the Communists had said that they weren't afraid of our bombs and intended to carry on with the war. Did he have a fallback position? If so, was it credible? Or did he, as seems so out of character, stake everything on a wildly dangerous threat of holocaust? These are questions that await answers that may never come. We know only that the war was terminated the following summer.

In Formosa we have what is perhaps the clearest case of prudent management during the Eisenhower Presidency. The danger was that we would be suckered into at least an air and sea war against Communist China, which was, as it still is, insisting on the rightness of its claim to sovereignty over Formosa and all the islands between it and the mainland. Eisenhower was, in 1954 and 1955, under enormous pressure from his own military and diplomatic advisers, among them Dulles, from Congressional Republicans and from many prominent Americans who had supported his candidacy (Henry Luce, for example) to give Chiang Kai-shek every form of assistance he asked for and to help in the defense of every rock in the Formosa Strait—not only to help keep the Generalissimo in his fortress but to aid in preparations for a return to the mainland by the Nationalist armies that had been driven out half a decade earlier. Eisenhower quite clearly had no taste for the entire enterprise. He knew that Chiang alone could never dislodge the Communists, no matter how much materiel we gave him, and he knew, too, that Mao Tse-tung's forces, no matter how many shells they lobbed at the close-in islands, were unequipped for an amphibious invasion of Formosa. So he jollied Chiang with hardware and money and high-level visitors, meanwhile protecting himself with a Congressional resolution and a treaty that pledged direct military assistance to Chiang only if we—not he—determined that Peking's maneuvers in the Formosa Strait were unmistakably preparatory to an assault on Formosa itself.

Had Admiral Radford, then Chairman of the Joint Chiefs, been in control, he might have made that fateful determination a dozen times over. Eisenhower read the cables and studied the maps and found no occasion for invoking those parts of the agreements that could have led to war. His methods were in certain ways dubious—there were questions about the constitutionality of the treaty and the resolution—but at least in the perspective of the present he found a way of averting a war that could have been far costlier than the one we have been in for most of the last decade. There can be little doubt that this was his will and his doing, for, as far as Communist China was concerned, he was the only "dove" in his administration.

Indochina—as always, it is the most complicated of matters. Eisenhower did not get involved militarily, but he may, by his patronage of his Secretary of State and by other words and acts, have made subsequent intervention all but unavoidable. It was Eisenhower who articulated the "domino theory" for Southeast Asia, and we know from his memoirs that on several occasions he seriously considered intervention and was deterred not primarily by political or moral considerations but by military and, to some extent, diplomatic ones. An obvious restraint was our lack of troops and weapons suitable for fighting the kind of war he quite correctly judged it to be. He gave thought to the use of nuclear weapons, and two carriers whose planes had nuclear bombs were in the Tonkin Gulf. But, as Earl Ravenal writes in Foreign Affairs, he "could not identify an appropriate enemy or target to fit the massive nuclear response [and] narrowly declined to intervene."

He considered using ground troops to aid the French but stipulated that under no circumstances would he go it alone—that is, without Asian and European allies. Dulles looked for suitable allies but found none. Had Eisenhower found either the appropriate targets for nuclear retaliation or willing partners in intervention, he might still have come up with an excuse for staying out, for nonintervention seemed almost always his preference; his distaste for war was general and a consistent factor in his reasoning. But it was indisputably under Eisenhower that we made heavy commitments to the powers that were and were to be in Saigon, and it was with Eisenhower's blessing that Dulles set up the Southeast Asia Treaty Organization, at once a political joke and a political disaster.

During his time, Eisenhower was not called upon to make good on any of Dulles's commitments in the region. I think it quite conceivable, however, that had he held office in the early sixties he might have found himself a prisoner of his own past and of then-current events and have followed pretty much the course of his successors. One advantage he had over his successors, though, was confidence in his own military judgment, and this might have saved him, us and the Vietnamese from the horrors that were soon to come.

Eisenhower's two terms fell between the two great Berlin crises—the one brought on by the blockade of the Western Sector in 1948 and the one brought on by the Berlin Wall 10 years ago. There was continuous tension over Germany throughout the fifties, but the dangers of war lessened as NATO, whose supreme command he had left to seek the

Presidency, grew in strength and as circumspection seemed increasingly to prevail in the Kremlin. These were the early days of the world of two nuclear superpowers, and the "balance of terror" would probably have held under any leadership save that of a madman. Though in Europe Dulles made a good many enemies for himself and for his Government, his European diplomacy was always more traditional and more prudent, as witness the Austrian treaty, than his diplomacy elsewhere in the world, and it would, I think, be rather difficult to fault Eisenhower for his handling of American policy in Germany.

In his memoirs, Eisenhower wrote of the Bay of Pigs as a "fiasco" for which "indecision and untimely counterorders" were "apparently responsible." He did not elaborate. But whatever he meant by Kennedy's "indecision," the original conclusion that we should sponsor an invasion came out of the Eisenhower, not the Kennedy, Administration. As he acknowledged, his military and intelligence people had, with his encouragement, armed and trained the forces in exile and, as we learned in the aftermath, completion of the scheme was urged on the new President by such holdovers as Allen Dulles of the C.I.A. and Gen. Lyman Lemnitzer, Chairman of the Joint Chiefs of Staff. Kennedy took responsibility for the bad show of which Eisenhower was the original producer. Eisenhower was lucky enough to be out of office when the rehearsals were over and the performers were ready for the opening. We can only conjecture as to whether he would have called off the whole business or gone about it in some other way. But he surely bears some responsibility for the policy and for the crucial failure of intelligence which led the executors of the policy to believe that the Cuban people would welcome the invaders as liberators and would take up arms to join them.

I have been somewhat surprised in thinking and writing about the Eisenhower years a decade later to discover that we know a good deal less about the Eisenhower Administration than about most recent ones. The historians haven't got around to it yet, and the few memoirists it produced haven't revealed very much except about themselves. Eisenhower's two large volumes were put together mainly with scissors and paste. Richard Nixon's "Six Crises" is all about Richard Nixon. Sherman Adams's "First-Hand Report" is not first-hand at all but second- and third-hand—dealing extensively with large events, such as Indochina and Formosa, about which he knew little and, despite his closeness to the President, was seldom if ever consulted. Robert Murphy's "Diplomat Among Warriors" is a stiff-necked but instructive work, only part of which bears on the Eisenhower period. Emmet Hughes's "Ordeal of Power" is a thoughtful, critical work, but Hughes's experience was limited to two brief tours in the White House as a speechwriter and political consultant. A few journalists—notably Robert J. Donovan in "Eisenhower: The Inside Story"—produced creditable works, more useful on the whole than the memoirs, but the literature by and large is thin.

"The President of the United States," Alfred Kazin wrote in reviewing the first volume of Eisenhower's memoirs, "had to look up the public record that most of us more or less knew in order to find out what happened during his Adminstration." This, I think, comes close to the heart of the matter about Eisenhower. For eight years as President, he presided in the most literal dictionary sense—he occupied the seat of authority. But he exercised authority only when there was no other choice. He headed an administration but he rarely administered. In foreign affairs, he stepped in only on certain European questions and when, as Commander in Chief, he was required to make command decisions. In domestic affairs his temperament was in line with his economics—laissez-faire. Whenever possible, he let the Government run itself—and it was possible a good part of the time.

In fairness, though, it must be recalled that Eisenhower never offered himself as an activist. He never pledged innovation or any sort of basic reform. One cannot quite contend that he was the product of a political "draft," but, at least as much as any chief executive in this century, he had the office thrust upon him. His style was well known to those who engineered his nomination and to those who elected and reelected him. Whatever else may be said in dispraise, he did not betray his trust. He construed it rather narrowly, but in doing so he embodied a long tradition and a specifically Republican tradition.

His command decisions seem, in retrospect, to have been generally wise. He was clear about the hazards of intervention in Asia. However, he deputized Dulles to contract military alliances all over the place—confident, perhaps, that in crises he could prevail as he had in Korea. He deputized much to the other Dulles, Allen, too—and it was under him that the C.I.A. became a force in world affairs and undertook such missions as the overturn of Governments in Iran and Guatemala. Eisenhower was anything but an empire builder—he was by almost any definition an anti-imperialist—but it was while he presided that this country began, if not to acquire new holdings overseas, to use its power in an imperial manner far beyond the Americas.

Domestically, he and we marked time. In the first few years, this was more or less defensible. The country might not have sustained him if he had tried to remake it. Once the Korean war was over and McCarthy's fangs had been drawn, complacency was the dominant American mood, and very few Americans were aware of the large structural faults in many of our institutions. In 1954, the Supreme Court ruled that if we were to be true to ourselves and our pretensions, racism had to be deinstitutionalized, but this was about the only blow to complacency until, in the second term, sputnik went aloft and made some Americans wonder about our educational system. With hindsight, we can see that practically all the problems that bedeviled us in the sixties had been worsening in the fifties. It can be said, to be sure, that nearly all of them predated the fifties by decades, even centuries, and that Eisenhower was no more to blame in such matters than most of his predecessors. And this is only just. He was not a cause of any of our present domestic disorders. Neither, though, did he perceive them or heed the prophets of his time—and there were several—who did perceive them.

What Eisenhower clearly lacked—and this was due as much to the education and experience that had been his lot as a servant of his country as to any deficiency of mind or spirit—was the kind of knowledge of the American condition he might have gained if his background had been in politics rather than in the military. He went through most of the fifties and on into the sixties with an image of this country formed in Kansas *circa* 1910. Nowhere is this so dismayingly clear as in the closing words of the second volume of his memoirs, which was published in a dreadful year for this country, 1965—after his successor had met violent death in Dallas, at a time when violence increasingly characterized our race relations, when the generation gap was widening alongside the credibility gap, when our sons were marching by the tens of thousands into the Vietnam quagmire. In that year, he could bring himself to this apostrophe:

I have unshakable faith that the ideals and the way of life that Western civilization has cherished . . . will flourish everywhere to the infinite benefit of mankind . . . At home . . . our level of education constantly rises . . . opportunity for the properly ambitious boy or girl increases daily. Prospects for the good life were never better, provided only that each continues to feel that he, himself, must earn and deserve these advantages.

Imbued with sense and spirit we will select future leaders [who will] keep a firm, sure hand on the rudder of this splendid ship of state, guiding her through future generations to the great destiny for which she was created.

A good man? Of course. A "brilliant" man? Hardly. "A political genius"? If so, the evidence remains concealed. A good President? Better than average, perhaps, and very useful in his early years. But by and large not what the times required.

The Army-McCarthy Hearings

America's painful adjustment to the Cold War will be forever memorialized by the era to which Joseph McCarthy gave his name. When people do not understand what is happening or what is required of them, when their best instincts and their worst fears are somehow tangled together, then men like Joseph McCarthy have their chance. In the early 1950's there was such a thing as subversion; the problem of disloyalty was real if limited; some spies were discovered in government (although not by Senator McCarthy). But a limited security problem in the hands of an oily demagogue proved to have virtually unlimited political use. McCarthy became a prime agent in the Republican drive to oust the Democrats from a 20-year hold on the federal government. Through accusation or insinuation he retired men from public careers and damaged the reputation of many innocent men in private lives.

Buoyed by these successes, McCarthy took on establishment institutions such as the church and—the case before you—the army.

McCarthy should have selected his victims with more care. Six months after his bout with the army he had been censured by his colleagues in the Senate and his national influence was over. McCarthy had believed that he represented a massive national sentiment which could do battle with every constituted power; and many commentators and politicians, liberal and conservative, had taken him at his word. They were all wrong: when powerful men decided to stop him, he was quickly demolished, and with few political aftereffects.

The Army-McCarthy hearings were on television for 188 hours during their 36-day run from April 22 to June 16, 1954. In David T. Bazelon's description it was "in a fabulously exact sense, the greatest political show on earth." Amid the welter of names, the confusion of charges and countercharges, the points of order and other interruptions, millions of viewers nevertheless got the message. As the Checkers speech showed the way television could save a political career, these hearings showed how it could pitilessly destroy one. The show was unforgettable. McCarthy's sarcasm and disparaging tone of voice lost their customary effectiveness; he went from fame to an alcoholic's death. His flinty adversary, Joseph E. Welch, whose capacity for wit as well as for righteous indignation had thrilled 20 million viewers, was able in his retirement to play a star role as a movie lawyer. The age of television politics was upon us.

Cast of principal characters:

Robert T. Stevens   Secretary of the Army

Senator Joseph R. McCarthy   U.S. Senator, Wisconsin (Rep.)
                                       Chairman, Senate subcommittee

John G. Adams	Counselor for the Army
Joseph N. Welch	Special Counsel for the Army
Senator Karl E. Mundt	U.S. Senator, Kansas (Rep.) Chairman of hearings
Ray H. Jenkins	Chief Counsel, Senate subcommittee
John L. McClellan	U.S. Senator, Arkansas (Dem.) Subcommittee member
Stuart Symington	U.S. Senator, Missouri (Dem.) Subcommittee member
Pvt. G. David Schine	U.S. Army private and former McCarthy aide
Roy M. Cohn	Chief Counsel for Sen. McCarthy

. . .

Secretary STEVENS. Gentlemen of the committee, I am here today at the request of this committee. You have my assurance of the fullest cooperation.

In order that we may all be quite clear as to just why this hearing has come about, it is necessary for me to refer at the outset to Pvt. G. David Schine, a former consultant of this committee. David Schine was eligible for the draft. Efforts were made by the chairman of this committee, Senator Joseph R. McCarthy, and the subcommittee's chief counsel, Mr. Roy M. Cohn, to secure a commission for him. Mr. Schine was not qualified, and he was not commissioned. Selective service then drafted him. Subsequent efforts were made to seek preferential treatment for him after he was inducted.

. . .

Before getting into the Schine story I want to make two general comments.

First, it is my responsibility to speak for the Army. The Army is about a million and a half men and women, in posts across this country and around the world, on active duty and in the National Guard and Organized Reserves, plus hundreds of thousands of loyal and faithful civil servants.

Senator McCARTHY. Mr. Chairman, a point of order.

Senator MUNDT. Senator McCarthy has a point of order.

Senator McCARTHY. Mr. Stevens is not speaking for the Army. He is speaking for Mr. Stevens, for Mr. Adams, and Mr. Hensel. The committee did not make the Army a party to this controversy, and I think it is highly improper to try to make the Army a party. Mr. Stevens can only speak for himself. . . .

May I say that, regardless of what the Chair and Mr. McClellan decided, when Mr. Stevens says, "It is my responsibility to speak for the Army," he is not speaking for the Army here. All we were investigating has been some Communists in the Army, a very small percentage, I would say much less than 1 percent. And when the Secretary says that, in effect "I am speaking for the Army," he is putting the 99.9 percent of good, honorable, loyal men in the Army into the position of trying to oppose the exposure of Communists in the Army.

I think it should be made clear at the outset, so we need not waste time on it, hour after hour, that Mr. Stevens is speaking for Mr. Stevens and those who are speaking through him; when Mr. Adams speaks, he is speaking for Mr. Adams and those who are speaking through him, and likewise Mr. Hensel.

I may say I resent very, very much this attempt to connect the great American Army with this attempt to sabotage the efforts of this committee's investigation into communism.

Mr. JENKINS. I again say, Mr. Chairman, there is nothing in this statement from which an inference can be drawn that the Army has become a party in interest to this controversy. We are in accord with the Senator, that the parties in interest are Mr. Stevens, Mr. Adams, and Mr. Hensel.

Senator McCARTHY. If that is understood, then I have no objection. . . .

I speak for the Army today out of a pride and confidence that grows greater every day I spend on the job. There are personal reasons, too, for my pride in the Army and for my resentment of any slur against it or any of the armed services. The 2 oldest of our 4 sons enlisted in the Navy during World War II. Our third son enlisted in 1952 as a private and is now a corporal with the Seventh Army in Europe. He has been overseas 21 months.

Second, I want to affirm here my full belief in the right of Congress to investigate—and that means scrutinizing the activities of the Army or any other department of the executive branch of the Government. The conscientious exercise of this obligation is one of the checks, contemplated by the Constitution, against the possibility of unlimited executive authority by the executive branch of the Government.

As a member of the executive branch, it is my duty to do everything I properly can to help this and other committees of Congress. I have such a profound regard for elective office in this country that it comes very easily for me to cooperate with the Senators, the Representatives, and the committees of Congress.

Let me now turn to the point at issue and first summarize the Schine story. I have been informed that—

1. From mid-July of last year until March 1 of this year, David Schine was discussed between one branch or other of the Department of the Army and Senator McCarthy or members of his staff in more than 65 telephone calls.

2. During the same period, this matter was discussed at approxi-

mately 19 meetings between Army personnel and Senator McCarthy or members of his staff.

3. Requests made on Schine's behalf ranged from several for a direct commission before he was inducted into the Army to many for special assignments, relief from routine duties such as KP, extra time off, and special visitor privileges.

4. From November 10, 1953, to January 16, 1954, Schine, by then a private in the Army, obtained 15 passes from the post. By way of comparison, the majority of other newly inducted personnel obtained three passes during the same period. . . .

About that time these two friends left, and because I wanted Senator McCarthy to restate before Mr. Cohn what he had told me on the courthouse steps, I said, "Let's talk about Schine."

That started a chain of events, an experience similar to none which I have had in my life.

Mr. Cohn became extremely agitated, became extremely abusive. He cursed me and then Senator McCarthy. The abuse went in waves. He would be very abusive and then it would kind of abate and things would be friendly for a few moments. Everybody would eat a little bit more, and then it would start in again. It just kept on.

I was trying to catch a 1:30 train, but Mr. Cohn was so violent by then that I felt I had better not do it and leave him that angry with me and that angry with Senator McCarthy because of a remark I had made. So I stayed and missed my 1:30 train. I thought surely I would be able to get out of there by 2:30. The luncheon concluded——

Mr. JENKINS. You say you were afraid to leave Senator McCarthy alone there with him? Mr. Adams, what did he say? You say he was very abusive.

Mr. ADAMS. He was extremely abusive.

Mr. JENKINS. Was or not any obscene language used?

Mr. ADAMS. Yes.

Mr. JENKINS. Just omit that and tell what he did say which constituted abuse, in your opinion.

Mr. ADAMS. I have stated before, sir, the tone of voice has as much to do with abuse as words. I do not remember the phrases, I do not remember the sentences, but I do remember the violence.

Mr. JENKINS. Do you remember the subject?

Mr. ADAMS. The subject was Schine. The subject was the fact—the thing that Cohn was angry about, the thing that he was so violent about, was the fact that, (1), the Army was not agreeing to an assignment for Schine and, (2), that Senator McCarthy was not supporting his staff in its efforts to get Schine assigned to New York. So his abuse was directed partly to me and partly to Senator McCarthy.

As I say, it kind of came in waves. There would be a period of extreme abuse, and then there would be a period where it would get almost back to normal, and ice cream would be ordered, and then about halfway through that a little more of the same. I missed the 2:30 train, also.

This violence continued. It was a remarkable thing. At first Senator McCarthy seemed to be trying to conciliate. He seemed to be trying to conciliate Cohn and not to state anything contrary to what he had stated to me in the morning. But then he more or less lapsed into silence. Finally, at about 3 o'clock or 10 minutes to 3 we left the restaurant and got in Cohn's car, which was directly in front of the restaurant. Mr. Cohn stated that he was going to give me a ride to the station, which is directly uptown from the courthouse. I had proposed going by subway, but he said, "No, I can get you there quicker."

So we began riding up Fourth Avenue in New York and Cohn's anger erupted again. As it erupted it was directed more on this occasion toward Senator McCarthy than it was to me. As we were riding uptown Senator McCarthy turned around to me and on 2 or 3 occasions during the ride uptown, which took about 15 minutes, he asked me if I could not when I got back to Washington talk to Mr. Stevens and arrange an assignment in New York for Schine.

When we got to 34th Street, which is where———

Mr. JENKINS. What was your reply to that request of the Senator, Mr. Adams?

Mr. ADAMS. My recollection is that I made no reply. I didn't say much on the ride uptown. It was a little difficult.

Mr. JENKINS. You mean that both you and the Senator had been completely subdued?

Mr. ADAMS. I had been.

Mr. JENKINS. All right. You were riding uptown in Mr. Cohn's car, being driven by Mr. Cohn, as a matter of fact?

Mr. ADAMS. Yes sir.

Mr. JENKINS. You were being taken to the station?

Mr. ADAMS. That is right.

Mr. JENKINS. I will ask you to tell the committee the events of that trip.

Mr. ADAMS. As I stated, Senator McCarthy said to me 2 or 3 times, or asked me on 2 or 3 occasions if I wouldn't go back to Washington and ask Mr. Stevens to arrange for Schine's assignment in New York. When we got to 34th Street, which is where the turn must be made if you are going to go over to Penn Station, which is on 7th Avenue, we attempted a left turn which was not permitted and a policeman would not permit it and ordered us to go on ahead, which took us under a long tunnel, the tunnel which goes under the Grand Central Station, and we came out about 45th Street or thereabouts going away from the station and I had then 10 or 12 minutes to make the 3:30 train. I complained to Mr. Cohn. I said, "You are just taking me away from the station," and in a final fit of violence he stopped the car in the middle of four lanes of traffic and said, "Get there however you can." So I climbed out of the car in the middle of four lanes of traffic between 46th and 47th Street on Park Avenue, ran across the street and jumped into a cab to try to make the 3:30 train.

Mr. JENKINS. Senator Potter directs me to ask you whether or not you made the train. [Laughter.]

Mr. ADAMS. The 3:30 train was 10 minutes late, so I made it.

Mr. Carr told me a few days later that he didn't think that I should feel badly about the way I was put out of the car because he said I should have been there to see the way Senator McCarthy left the car a few blocks later.

. . .

Mr. JENKINS. Mr. Adams, when did you finally tell Mr. Cohn, if you did so, that Schine in all probability was scheduled for overseas duty?

Mr. ADAMS. On January 13. I was at the Capitol with Mr. Stevens. He was coming up on another appointment. I often use that means of talking to him. He is a very busy man. I jump in his car and ride to his appointment with him. I did it on this occasion. When I got here to the Senate Office Building, instead of going back to the Pentagon as I had originally planned, I told Mr. Stevens that I thought I would go down and see if I could not get back in good with Mr. Cohn and conciliate him because we had been having so much difficulty over Schine.

So I went down to room 101. Mr. Cohn was there and Mr. Carr was there. As I remember, we lunched together in the Senate cafeteria, and everything was peaceful. When we returned to room 101, toward the latter part of the conversation I asked Cohn—I knew that 90 percent of all inductees ultimately face overseas duty and I knew that one day we were going to face that problem with Mr. Cohn as to Schine.

So I thought I would lay a little groundwork for future trouble I guess. I asked him what would happen if Schine got overseas duty.

Mr. JENKINS. You mean you were breaking the news gently, Mr. Adams?

Mr. ADAMS. Yes, sir; that is right. I asked him what would happen if Schine got overseas duty. He responded with vigor and force, "Stevens is through as Secretary of the Army."

I said, "Oh, Roy," something to this effect, "Oh, Roy, don't say that. Come on. Really, what is going to happen if Schine gets overseas duty?"

He responded with even more force, "We will wreck the Army."

Then he said, "The first thing we are going to do is get General Ryan for the way he has treated Dave at Fort Dix. Dave gets through at Fort Dix tomorrow or this week, and as soon as he is gone we are going to get General Ryan for the obscene way in which he has permitted Schine to be treated up there."

He said, "We are not going to do it ourselves. We have another committee of the Congress interested in it."

Then he said, "I wouldn't put it past you to do this. We will start investigations. We have enough stuff on the Army to keep investigations going indefinitely, and if anything like such-and-such double-cross occurs, that is what we will do."

This remark was not to be taken lightly in the context in which it it was given to me. . . .

Senator SYMINGTON. Have you the written instructions that you were going to deliver to the committee?

Mr. ADAMS. It is a letter to the Secretary of Defense from the President of the United States.

This is a letter signed Dwight D. Eisenhower addressed the Honorable, the Secretary of Defense, Washington, D. C.:

DEAR MR. SECRETARY: It has long been recognized that to assist the Congress in achieving its legislative purposes every Executive Department or Agency must, upon the request of a Congressional Committee, expeditiously furnish information relating to any matter within the jurisdiction of the Committee, with certain historical exceptions—some of which are pointed out in the attached memorandum from the Attorney General. This Administration has been and will continue to be diligent in following the principle. However, it is essential for the successful working of our system that the persons entrusted with power over any one of the three great branches of Government shall not encroach upon the authority confided to the others. The ultimate responsibility for the conduct of the Executive Branch rests with the President.

Within this Constitutional framework each branch should cooperate fully with each other for the common good. However, throughout our history the President has withheld information whenever he found that what was sought was confidential or its disclosure would be incompatible with the public interest or jeopardize the safety of the Nation.

Because it is essential to efficient and effective administration that employees of the Executive Branch be in a position to be completely candid in advising with each other on official matters, and because it is not in the public interest that any of their conversations or communications, or any documents or reproductions, concerning such advice be disclosed, you will instruct employees of your Department that in all of their appearances before the Subcommittee of the Senate Committee on Government Operations regarding the inquiry now before it they are not to testify to any such conversations or communications or to produce any such documents or reproductions. This principle must be maintained regardless of who would benefit by such disclosures.

I direct this action so as to maintain the proper separation of powers between the Executive and Legislative Branches of the Government in accordance with my responsibilities and duties under the Constitution. This separation is vital to preclude the exercise of arbitrary power by any branch of the Government. By this action I am not in any way restricting the testimony of such witnesses to what occurred regarding any matters where the communication was directly between any of the principals in the controversy within the Executive Branch on the one hand and a member of the Subcommittee or its staff on the other.

Sincerely,

/s/ DWIGHT D. EISENHOWER

To the letter, sir, is attached a 10-page memorandum from the Attorney General to the President. . . .

Senator MCCARTHY. Mr. Chairman, I must admit that I am somewhat at a loss as to know what to do at the moment. One of the subjects of this inquiry is to find out who was responsible for succeeding and calling off the hearing of Communist infiltration in Government.

That the hearings have been called off, no one can question. I fear that maybe in my mind I was doing an injustice, possibly, to Mr. Adams and Mr. Hensel.

I strongly felt all along that they were the men responsible for it. At this point, I find out there is no way of ever getting at the truth, because we do find that the charges were conceived, instigated, at a meeting which was testified to by Mr. Adams.

Now for some fantastically strange reason, the iron curtain is pulled down so we can't tell what happened at that meeting. I don't think the President is responsible for this. I don't think his judgment is that bad, Mr. Chairman.

There is no reason why any one should be afraid of the facts, of the truth, that came out of that meeting. It is a very important meeting. It doesn't have to do with security matters. It doesn't have to do with national security. It merely has to do with why these charges were filed. . . .

The question is how far can—I am not talking about the present occupant in the White House. But we have a tremendously important question here, Mr. Chairman. That is, how far can the President go? Who all can he order not to testify? If he can order the Ambassador to the U. N. not to testify about something having nothing to do with the U. N., but a deliberate smear against my staff, then any President—and we don't know who will be President in 1956, 1960, 1964—but any President [laughter]—I won't repeat that. Any President can, by an Executive order, keep the facts from the American people. . . .

Now we are getting down to the meat of the case, Mr. Chairman, and that is, who was responsible for the issuance of the smear that has held this committee up for weeks and weeks and weeks, and has allowed Communists to continue in our defense plants, Mr. Chairman, handling top-secret material, as I said before, with a razor poised over the jugular vein of this Nation? Who is responsible for keeping all these Army officers down here and all the Senators tied up while the world is going up in flames?

I do think, Mr. Chairman, that we should go into executive session. I must have a ruling as to what will be behind an iron curtain and what facts we can bring out before I can intelligently question the witnesses. I do think that someone, for his own benefit, should contact the President immediately and point out to him, perhaps, that he and I and many of us campaigned and promised the American people that if they would remove our Democrat friends from the control of this Government, then we would no longer engage in Government by secrecy, whitewash and coverup.

Mr. Jenkins. You will recall, Mr. Cohn, that he testified that you said that if Schine went overseas, Stevens was through as Secretary of the Army?

Mr. Cohn. I heard him say that, sir.

Mr. Jenkins. Did you or not?

Mr. Cohn. No, sir.

Mr. Jenkins. Did you say anything like that, Mr. Cohn?

Mr. COHN. No, sir, and my recollection is that I did not. I have talked to Mr. Carr who was sitting there the whole time, and he says I did not. . . .

Mr. JENKINS. All right, now you are saying you did not say it, Mr. Cohn?

Mr. COHN. Yes, sir. I am saying I am sure I did not make that statement, and I am sure that Mr. Adams and anybody else with any sense, and Mr. Adams has a lot of sense, could ever believe that I was threatening to wreck the Army or that I could wreck the Army. I say, sir, that the statement is ridiculous.

Mr. JENKINS. I am talking about Stevens being through as Secretary of the Army.

Mr. COHN. That is equally ridiculous, sir.

Mr. JENKINS. And untrue?

Mr. COHN. Yes, sir, equally ridiculous and untrue, I could not cause the President of the United States to remove Stevens as Secretary of the Army.

. . .

Senator McCARTHY. Let me ask you this, Mr. Cohn: Had you something to do with the Hiss case, I believe, also; is that right?

Mr. COHN. I had. What I had to do with the Hiss case is not important enough to mention here, sir.

Senator McCARTHY. Enough to do with it so that you are aware of the facts in the case. Let me ask you this: Are you convinced if it had not been for a congressional committee having exposed the facts in the Hiss case, that Alger Hiss today would be free?

Mr. COHN. Yes, sir. . . .

Senator McCARTHY. Just this one question: Mr. Cohn, do you agree with me that, No. 1, the administration is certainly heading in the right direction so far as getting rid of Communists are concerned, and, No. 2, that it is ridiculous, a complete waste of time to have these exchanges of statements between the White House and this committee, that there is no reason on earth why there should be any contest between the executive department and this committee insofar as exposing Communists, graft, and corruption is concerned, that we all should be heading the same way, there should be none of this silly bickering, fighting about this exposure, that we should be getting the complete cooperation from the executive and that should be flowing both ways, of course?

Senator MUNDT. The Senator's time has expired. You can answer the question.

Senator McCARTHY. Let me finish the question. And if that could be accomplished, a great service could be performed for the country?

Mr. COHN. I am sure of that, sir.

Senator MUNDT. Mr. Welch, you have 10 minutes. After your 10 minutes, we will recess.

Mr. WELCH. Mr. Chairman, ordinarily, with the clock as late as it is I would call attention to it, but not tonight.

Mr. Cohn, what is the exact number of Communists or subversives that are loose today in these defense plants?

Mr. COHN. The exact number that is loose, sir?

Mr. WELCH. Yes, sir.

Mr. COHN. I don't know.

Mr. WELCH. Roughly how many?

Mr. COHN. I can only tell you, sir, what we know about it.

Mr. WELCH. That is 130, is that right?

Mr. COHN. Yes, sir. I am going to try to particularize for you, if I can.

Mr. WELCH. I am in a hurry. I don't want the sun to go down while they are still in there, if we can get them out.

Mr. COHN. I am afraid we won't be able to work that fast, sir.

Mr. WELCH. I have a suggestion about it, sir. How many are there?

Mr. COHN. I believe the figure is approximately 130.

Mr. WELCH. Approximately one-two-three?

Mr. COHN. Yes, sir. Those are people, Mr. Welch——

Mr. WELCH. I don't care. You told us who they are. In how many plants are they?

Mr. COHN. How many plants?

Mr. WELCH. How many plants.

Mr. COHN. Yes, sir; just 1 minute, sir. I see 16 offhand, sir.

Mr. WELCH. Sixteen plants?

Mr. COHN. Yes, sir.

Mr. WELCH. Where are they, sir?

Mr. COHN. Senator McCarthy——

Mr. WELCH. Reel off the cities.

Mr. COHN. Would you stop me if I am going too far?

Mr. WELCH. You can't go too far revealing Communists, Mr. Cohn. Reel off the cities for us.

Mr. COHN. Schenectady, N .Y.; Syracuse, N. Y.; Rome, N. Y.; Quincy, Mass.; Fitchburg, Mass.; Buffalo, N. Y.; Dunkirk, N. Y.; another at Buffalo, N. Y.; Cambridge, Mass.; New Bedford, Mass.; Boston, Mass.; Quincy, Mass.; Lynn, Mass.; Pittsfield, Mass.; Boston, Mass.

Mr. WELCH. Mr. Cohn, you not only frighten me, you make me ashamed when there are so many in Massachusetts. [Laughter.] This is not a laughing matter, believe me. Are you alarmed at that situation, Mr. Cohn?

Mr. COHN. Yes, sir; I am.

Mr. WELCH. Nothing could be more alarming, could it?

Mr. COHN. It certainly is a very alarming thing.

Mr. WELCH. Will you not, before the sun goes down, give those names to the FBI and at least have those men put under surveillance.

Mr. COHN. Mr. Welch, the FBI——

Senator McCARTHY. Mr. Chairman.

Mr. WELCH. That is a fair question.

Senator McCARTHY. Mr. Chairman, let's not be ridiculous. Mr. Welch knows, as I have told him a dozen times, that the FBI has all of this information. The defense plants have the information. The only thing we can do is to try and publicly expose these individuals and hope that they will be gotten rid of. And you know that, Mr. Welch.

Mr. WELCH. I do not know that.

Mr. Cohn, do you mean to tell us that J. Edgar Hoover and the FBI know the names of these men and are doing nothing about them?

Mr. COHN. No, sir. I mean to say—

Mr. WELCH. Do you mean to tell us they are doing something about them?

Mr. COHN. Yes, sir.

Mr. WELCH. What are they doing about them?

Mr. COHN. Here is what they do about them. They notify the Defense Department and the appropriate security——

Mr. WELCH. Don't they put them under surveillance?

Mr. COHN. Appropriate security agencies involved. The FBI gives them full information. It is then up to them, the places where the information goes, to decide whether or not they will act on the FBI information. All the FBI can do is give the information. Their power ends right there.

Mr. WELCH. Cannot the FBI put these 130 men under surveillance before sundown tomorrow?

Mr. COHN. Sir, if there is need for surveillance in the case of espionage or anything like that, I can well assure you that Mr. John Edgar Hoover and his men know a lot better than I, and I quite respectfully suggest, sir, than probably a lot of us, just who should be put under surveillance. I do not propose to tell the FBI how to run its shop. It does it very well.

Mr. WELCH. And they do it, don't they, Mr. Cohn?

Mr. COHN. When the need arises, of course.

Mr. WELCH. And will you tell them tonight, Mr. Cohn, that here is a case where the need has arisen, so that it can be done by sundown tomorrow night?

Mr. COHN. No, sir; there is no need for my telling the FBI what to do about this or anything else.

Mr. WELCH. Are you sure they know every one of them?

Mr. COHN. I would take an oath on it, sir. I think the FBI has complete information about the Communist movement in this country and that would include information about these people.

Mr. WELCH. That being true, Mr. Cohn, can you and I both rest easy tonight?

Mr. COHN. Sir, I certainly agree with you, it is a very disturbing situation.

Mr. WELCH. Well, if the FBI has got a firm grasp on these 130 men, I will go to sleep.

Do you assure me that is so?

Mr. COHN. Sir, I am sure that the FBI does its job well, that it knows all about these people, that it has told the appropriate agencies about these people, and that the failure to act goes elsewhere than in the hands of the FBI.

Mr. WELCH. Just for the purpose of safety, for fear something could be missed somewhere, would you mind, as a patriotic American citizen, sending the 130 names over to the FBI tonight?

Let's be sure we are not taking any chances.

Mr. COHN. I wouldn't mind it at all, sir.

Mr. WELCH. Would you do it, sir?

Senator McCARTHY. Would you yield?

Mr. WELCH. No; I won't yield. I want to find out if he will do it and if he won't, will you do it?

Senator McCARTHY. You asked a question. Will you let me answer it?

Mr. WELCH. I asked it of the witness, sir.

Senator McCARTHY. I want you to know that the FBI has complete access to any files we have, any information we have, at any time.

Mr. Welch knows, I am sure you do, Mr. Welch, that the FBI has no power to order anyone fired. You know that, for example, in the Alger Hiss case, the FBI had furnished all the information and he still rose to be a top man in the State Department. You know, Mr. Welch, that the FBI furnished all the information on the spy Harry Dexter White. You know that despite that fact, Mr. Welch, despite the fact that the FBI had given all of the information, and sent over reports day after day after day, Harry Dexter White, the Communist spy, got to be a top Treasury official. So let's not deceive the American people by blaming the FBI for Communists being in defense plants. . . .

Mr. WELCH. Well, Mr. Chairman, my confidence in the FBI is simply limitless, and I think Mr. Cohn's confidence is similar; is that right, sir?

Mr. COHN. Yes, sir; that is right.

Mr. WELCH. All I am suggesting is that we just nudge them a little and be sure they are busy on these 130.

Would you mind helping nudge them?

Mr. COHN. Sir, you do not have to nudge the FBI about this or about anything else.

Mr. WELCH. Then they have got the whole 130, have they, Mr. Cohn?

Mr. COHN. I am sure of it, sir, and a lot more.

. . .

Mr. WELCH. Then, as a second line of defense, let's send the 130 names to the Department of Defense tonight. Would you mind doing that?

Mr. COHN. Whatever the committee directs on that, sir.

Mr. WELCH. I wish the committee would direct that all the names be sent both to the FBI and to the Department of Defense with extreme suddenness.

Mr. WELCH. Mr. Cohn, tell me once more: Every time you learn of a Communist or a spy anywhere, is it your policy to get them out as fast as possible?

Mr. COHN. Surely, we want them out as fast as possible, sir.

Mr. WELCH. And whenever you learn of one from now on, Mr. Cohn, I beg of you, will you tell somebody about them quick?

Mr. COHN. Mr. Welch, with great respect, I work for the committee here. They know how we go about handling situations of Communist infiltration and failure to act on FBI information about Communist infiltration. If they are displeased with the speed with which I and the group of men who work with me proceed, if they are displeased with the order in which we move, I am sure they will give me appropriate instructions along those lines, and I will follow any which they give me.

Mr. WELCH. May I add my small voice, sir, and say whenever you know about a subversive or a Communist spy, please hurry. Will you remember those words?

Senator McCARTHY. Mr. Chairman.

Mr. COHN. Mr. Welch, I can assure you, sir, as far as I am concerned, and certainly as far as the chairman of this committee and the members, and the members of the staff, are concerned, we are a small group, but we proceed as expeditiously as is humanly possible to get out Communists and traitors and to bring to light the mechanism by which they have been permitted to remain where they were for so long a period of time.

Senator McCARTHY. Mr. Chairman, in view of that question——

Senator MUNDT. Have you a point of order?

Senator McCARTHY. Not exactly, Mr. Chairman, but in view of Mr. Welch's request that the information be given once we know of anyone who might be performing any work for the Communist Party, I think we should tell him that he has in his law firm a young man named Fisher whom he recommended, incidentally, to do work on this committee, who has been for a number of years a member of an organization which was named, oh, years and years ago, as the legal bulwark of the Communist Party, an organization which always swings to the defense of anyone who dares to expose Communists. I certainly assume that Mr. Welch did not know of this young man at the time he recommended him as the assistant counsel for this committee, but he has such terror and such a great desire to know where anyone is located who may be serving the Communist cause, Mr. Welch, that I thought we should just call to your attention the fact that your Mr. Fisher, who is still in your law firm today, whom you asked to have down here looking over the secret and classified material, is a member of an organization, not named by me but named by various committees, named by the Attorney General, as I recall, and I think I quote this verbatim, as "the legal bulwark of the Communist Party." He belonged to that for a sizable number of years, according to his own admission, and he belonged to it long after it had been exposed as the legal arm of the Communist Party.

Knowing that, Mr. Welch, I just felt that I had a duty to respond to your urgent request that before sundown, when we know of anyone serving the Communist cause, we let the agency know. We are now letting you know that your man did belong to this organization for either 3 or 4 years, belonged to it long after he was out of law school.

I don't think you can find anyplace, anywhere, an organization which has done more to defend Communists—I am again quoting the report—to defend Communists, to defend espionage agents, and to aid the Communist cause, than the man whom you originally wanted down here at your right hand instead of Mr. St. Clair.

I have hesitated bringing that up, but I have been rather bored with your phony requests to Mr. Cohn here that he personally get every Communist out of government before sundown. Therefore, we will give you information about the young man in your own organization.

I am not asking you at this time to explain why you tried to foist him on this committee. Whether you knew he was a member of that Communist organization or not, I don't know. I assume you did not, Mr. Welch, because I get the impression that, while you are quite an actor, you play for a laugh, I don't think you have any conception of the danger of the Communist Party. I don't think you yourself would ever knowingly aid the Communist cause. I think you are unknowingly aiding it when you try to burlesque this hearing in which we are attempting to bring out the facts, however.

Mr. WELCH. Mr. Chairman.

Senator MUNDT. Mr. Welch, the Chair should say he has no recognition or no memory of Mr. Welch's recommending either Mr. Fisher or anybody else as counsel for this committee.

I will recognize Mr. Welch.

Senator McCARTHY. Mr. Chairman, I will give you the news story on that.

Mr. WELCH. Mr. Chairman, under these circumstances I must have something approaching a personal privilege.

Senator MUNDT. You may have it, sir. It will not be taken out of your time.

Mr. WELCH. Senator McCarthy, I did not know—Senator, sometimes you say "May I have your attention?"

Senator McCARTHY. I am listening to you. I can listen with one ear.

Mr. WELCH. This time I want you to listen with both.

Senator McCARTHY. Yes.

Mr. WELCH. Senator McCarthy, I think until this moment——

Senator McCARTHY. Jim, will you get the news story to the effect that this man belonged to this Communist-front organization? Will you get the citations showing that this was the legal arm of the Communist Party, and the length of time that he belonged, and the fact that he was recommended by Mr. Welch? I think that should be in the record.

Mr. WELCH. You won't need anything in the record when I have finished telling you this.

Until this moment, Senator, I think I never really gaged your cruelty or your recklessness. Fred Fisher is a young man who went to the Harvard Law School and came into my firm and is starting what looks to be a brilliant career with us.

When I decided to work for this committee I asked Jim St. Clair, who sits on my right, to be my first assistant. I said to Jim, "Pick somebody in the firm who works under you that you would like." He chose Fred Fisher and they came down on an afternoon plane. That night, when he had taken a little stab at trying to see what the case was about, Fred Fisher and Jim St. Clair and I went to dinner together. I then said to these two young men, "Boys, I don't know anything about you except I have always liked you, but if there is anything funny in the life of either one of you that would hurt anybody in this case you speak up quick."

Fred Fisher said, "Mr. Welch, when I was in law school and for a period of months after, I belonged to the Lawyers Guild," as you have suggested, Senator. He went on to say, "I am secretary of the Young Republicans League in Newton with the son of Massachusetts' Governor, and I have the respect and admiration of the 25 lawyers or so in Hale & Dorr."

I said, "Fred, I just don't think I am going to ask you to work on the case. If I do, one of these days that will come out and go over national television and it will just hurt like the dickens."

So, Senator, I asked him to go back to Boston.

Little did I dream you could be so reckless and so cruel as to do an injury to that lad. It is true he is still with Hale & Dorr. It is true that he will continue to be with Hale & Dorr. It is, I regret to say, equally true that I fear he shall always bear a scar needlessly inflicted by you. If it were in my power to forgive you for your reckless cruelty, I will do so. I like to think I am a gentleman, but your forgiveness will have to come from someone other than me.

Senator McCarthy. Mr. Chairman.

Senator Mundt. Senator McCarthy?

Senator McCarthy. May I say that Mr. Welch talks about this being cruel and reckless. He was just baiting; he has been baiting Mr. Cohn here for hours, requesting that Mr. Cohn, before sundown, get out of any department of Government anyone who is serving the Communist cause.

I just give this man's record, and I want to say, Mr. Welch, that it has been labeled long before he became a member, as early as 1944——

Mr. Welch. Senator, may we not drop this? We know he belonged to the Lawyers Guild, and Mr. Cohn nods his head at me. I did you, I think, no personal injury, Mr. Cohn.

Mr. Cohn. No, sir.

Mr. Welch. I meant to do you no personal injury, and if I did, I beg your pardon.

Let us not assassinate this lad further, Senator. You have done enough. Have you no sense of decency sir, at long last? Have you left no sense of decency?

Senator McCarthy. I know this hurts you, Mr. Welch. But I may say, Mr. Chairman, on a point of personal privilege, and I would like to finish it——

Mr. Welch. Senator, I think it hurts you, too, sir.

Senator McCarthy. I would like to finish this.

Mr. Welch has been filibustering this hearing, he has been talking day after day about how he wants to get anyone tainted with communism out before sundown. I know Mr. Cohn would rather not have me go into this. I intend to, however, Mr. Welch talks about any sense of decency. If I say anything which is not the truth, then I would like to know about it.

The foremost legal bulwark of the Communist Party, its front organizations, and controlled unions, and which, since its inception, has never failed to rally to the legal defense of the Communist Party, and individual members thereof, including known espionage agents.

Now, that is not the language of Senator McCarthy. That is the language of the Un-American Activities Committee. And I can go on with many more citations. It seems that Mr. Welch is pained so deeply he thinks it is improper for me to give the record, the Communist-front record, of the man whom he wanted to foist upon this committee. But it doesn't pain him at all—there is no pain in his chest about the unfounded charges against Mr. Frank Carr; there is no pain there about the attempt to destroy the reputation and take the jobs away from the young men who were working in my committee.

And, Mr. Welch, if I have said anything here which is untrue, then tell me. I have heard you and every one else talk so much about laying the truth upon the table that when I hear—and it is completely phony, Mr. Welch, I have listened to you for a long time—when you say "Now, before sundown, you must get these people out of Government," I want to have it very clear, very clear that you were not so serious about that when you tried to recommend this man for this committee.

And may I say, Mr. Welch, in fairness to you, I have reason to believe that you did not know about his Communist-front record at the time you recommended him. I don't think you would have recommended him to the committee, if you knew that.

I think it is entirely possible you learned that after you recommended him.

Senator MUNDT. The Chair would like to say again that he does not believe that Mr. Welch recommended Mr. Fisher as counsel for this committee, because he has through his office all the recommendations that were made. He does not recall any that came from Mr. Welch, and that would include Mr. Fisher.

Senator McCARTHY. Let me ask Mr. Welch. You brought him down, did you not, to act as your assistant?

Mr. WELCH. Mr. McCarthy, I will not discuss this with you further. You have sat within 6 feet of me, and could have asked me about Fred Fisher. You have brought it out. If there is a God in heaven, it will do neither you nor your cause any good. I will not discuss it further. I will not ask Mr. Cohn any more questions. You, Mr. Chairman, may, if you will, call the next witness.

Senator MUNDT. Are there any questions?

Mr. JENKINS. No further questions, Mr. Chairman.

Mr. JENKINS. Senator McCarthy, how do you regard the communistic threat to our Government as compared with other threats with which it is confronted?

.   .   .

Mr. Jenkins, the thing that I think we must remember is that this is a war which a brutalitarian force has won to a greater extent than any brutalitarian force has won a war in the history of the world before.

For example, Christianity, which has been in existence for 2,000 years, has not converted, convinced nearly as many people as this Communist brutalitarianism has enslaved in 106 years, and they are not going to stop.

I know that many of my good friends seem to feel that this is a sort of a game you can play, that you can talk about communism as though it is something 10,000 miles away.

Mr. Jenkins, in answer to your question, let me say it is right here with us now. Unless we make sure that there is no infiltration of our Government, then just as certain as you sit there, in the period of our lives you will see a red world. There is no question about that, Mr. Jenkins. . . .

The Affluent Society

JOHN KENNETH GALBRAITH

John Kenneth Galbraith's The Affluent Society *was one of those rare books whose title gave a name to an era. Rarer still, the book also directly influenced public policy and national opinion. Galbraith enunciated what was called at the time a theory of "qualitative liberalism," the idea that domestic policy had to shift from virtually total emphasis on increasing wealth to a new concern for the quality of life. Galbraith argued that increased production did not automatically translate into progress. Unless care was taken, more goods could mean greater inequality of wealth as well as deterioration of the natural and human environment. For example, if one produced more food but failed to finance adequate sanitation facilities, the result would be more filth, a deteriorating environment, and declining public health.*

Galbraith's ideas were tested in the reform decade of the 1960's as major investment in the public sector—investment in public health, environmental improvement, a revival of state and local government —sought to provide improved services to correct the "social balance" between an individualistic consumer culture and public needs. Public higher education flourished as did improved recreational and cultural facilities, increases in social welfare, and a variety of important public health services. Then, as could have been predicted from Galbraith's own theory, rising inflation began to wipe out gains, with public services suffering and urban blight spreading outward from the center cities to envelop the suburbs in which the majority of the American population now resided. Although Galbraith's analysis was written in the 1950's, it remains worthy of consideration even for the present.

The final problem of the productive society is what it produces. This manifests itself in an implacable tendency to provide an opulent supply of some things and a niggardly yield of others. This disparity carries to the point where it is a cause of social discomfort and social unhealth. The line which divides our area of wealth from our area of poverty is roughly that which divides privately produced and marketed goods and services from publicly rendered services. Our wealth in the first is not only in startling contrast with the meagerness of the latter, but our wealth in privately produced goods is, to a marked degree, the cause of crisis in the supply of public services. For we have failed to see the importance, indeed the urgent need, of maintaining a balance between the two.

This disparity between our flow of private and public goods and services is no matter of subjective judgment. On the contrary, it is the source of the most extensive comment which only stops short of the

119

direct contrast being made here. In the years following World War II, the papers of any major city—those of New York were an excellent example—told daily of the shortages and shortcomings in the elementary municipal and metropolitan services. The schools were old and overcrowded. The police force was under strength and underpaid. The parks and playgrounds were insufficient. Streets and empty lots were filthy, and the sanitation staff was underequipped and in need of men. Access to the city by those who work there was uncertain and painful and becoming more so. Internal transportation was overcrowded, unhealthful, and dirty. So was the air. Parking on the streets had to be prohibited, and there was no space elsewhere. These deficiencies were not in new and novel services but in old and established ones. Cities have long swept their streets, helped their people move around, educated them, kept order, and provided horse rails for vehicles which sought to pause. That their residents should have a nontoxic supply of air suggests no revolutionary dalliance with socialism.

The discussion of this public poverty competed, on the whole successfully, with the stories of ever-increasing opulence in privately produced goods. The Gross National Product was rising. So were retail sales. So was personal income. Labor productivity had also advanced. The automobiles that could not be parked were being produced at an expanded rate. The children, though without schools, subject in the playgrounds to the affectionate interest of adults with odd tastes, and disposed to increasingly imaginative forms of delinquency, were admirably equipped with television sets. We had difficulty finding storage space for the great surpluses of food despite a national disposition to obesity. Food was grown and packaged under private auspices. The care and refreshment of the mind, in contrast with the stomach, was principally in the public domain. Our colleges and universities were severely overcrowded and underprovided, and the same was true of the mental hospitals.

The contrast was and remains evident not alone to those who read. The family which takes its mauve and cerise, air-conditioned, power-steered, and power-braked automobile out for a tour passes through cities that are badly paved, made hideous by litter, blighted buildings, billboards, and posts for wires that should long since have been put underground. They pass on into a countryside that has been rendered largely invisible by commercial art. (The goods which the latter advertise have an absolute priority in our value system. Such aesthetic considerations as a view of the countryside accordingly come second. On such matters we are consistent.) They picnic on exquisitely packaged food from a portable icebox by a polluted stream and go on to spend the night at a park which is a menace to public health and morals. Just before dozing off on an air mattress, beneath a nylon tent, amid the stench of decaying refuse, they may reflect vaguely on the curious unevenness of their blessings. Is this, indeed, the American genius?

In the production of goods within the private economy it has long been recognized that a tolerably close relationship must be maintained between the production of various kinds of products. The output of steel and oil and machine tools is related to the production of automobiles. Investment in transportation must keep abreast of the output of goods to be transported. The supply of power must be abreast of the growth of industries requiring it. The existence of these relationships—coefficients to the economist—has made possible the construction of the input-output table which shows how changes in the production in one industry will increase or diminish the demands on other industries. To this table, and more especially to its ingenious author, Professor Wassily Leontief, the world is indebted for one of its most important of modern insights into economic relationships. If expansion in one part of the economy were not matched by the requisite expansion in other parts—were the need for balance not respected—then bottlenecks and shortages, speculative hoarding of scarce supplies, and sharply increasing costs would ensue. Fortunately in peacetime the market system operates easily and effectively to maintain this balance, and this together with the existence of stocks and some flexibility in the coefficients as a result of substitution, insures that no serious difficulties will arise. We are reminded of the existence of the problem only by noticing how serious it is for those countries—Poland or, in a somewhat different form, India—which seek to solve the problem by planned measures and with a much smaller supply of resources.

Just as there must be balance in what a community produces, so there must also be balance in what the community consumes. An increase in the use of one product creates, ineluctably, a requirement for others. If we are to consume more automobiles, we must have more gasoline. There must be more insurance as well as more space on which to operate them. Beyond a certain point more and better food appears to mean increased need for medical services. This is the certain result of the increased consumption of tobacco and alcohol. More vacations require more hotels and more fishing rods. And so forth. With rare exceptions—shortages of doctors are an exception which suggests the rule—this balance is also maintained quite effortlessly so far as goods for private sale and consumption are concerned. The price system plus a rounded condition of opulence is again the agency.

However, the relationships we are here discussing are not confined to the private economy. They operate comprehensively over the whole span of private and public services. As surely as an increase in the output of automobiles puts new demands on the steel industry so, also, it places new demands on public services. Similarly, every increase in the consumption of private goods will normally mean some facilitating or protective step by the state. In all cases if these services are not forthcoming, the consequences will be in some degree ill. It will be convenient to have a term which suggests a satisfactory relationship between the supply of privately produced goods and services and those of the state, and we may call it social balance.

The problem of social balance is ubiquitous, and frequently it is obtrusive. As noted, an increase in the consumption of automobiles requires a facilitating supply of streets, highways, traffic control, and parking space. The protective services of the police and the highway patrols must also be available, as must those of the hospitals. Although the need for balance here is extraordinarily clear, our use of privately produced vehicles has, on occasion, got far out of line with the supply of the related public services. The result has been hideous road congestion, an annual massacre of impressive proportions, and chronic colitis in the cities. As on the ground, so also in the air. Planes collide with disquieting consequences for those within when the public provision for air traffic control fails to keep pace with private use of the airways.

But the auto and the airplane, versus the space to use them, are merely an exceptionally visible example of a requirement that is pervasive. The more goods people procure, the more packages they discard and the more trash that must be carried away. If the appropriate sanitation services are not provided, the counterpart of increasing opulence will be deepening filth. The greater the wealth the thicker will be the dirt. This indubitably describes a tendency of our time. As more goods are produced and owned, the greater are the opportunities for fraud and the more property that must be protected. If the provision of public law enforcement services do not keep pace, the counterpart of increased well-being will, we may be certain, be increased crime.

The city of Los Angeles, in modern times, is a near-classic study in the problem of social balance. Magnificently efficient factories and oil refineries, a lavish supply of automobiles, a vast consumption of handsomely packaged products, coupled with the absence of a municipal trash collection service which forced the use of home incinerators, made the air nearly unbreathable for an appreciable part of each year. Air pollution could be controlled only by a complex and highly developed set of public services—by better knowledge stemming from more research, better policing, a municipal trash collection service, and possibly the assertion of the priority of clean air over the production of goods. These were long in coming. The agony of a city without usable air was the result.

The issue of social balance can be identified in many other current problems. Thus an aspect of increasing private production is the appearance of an extraordinary number of things which lay claim to the interest of the young. Motion pictures, television, automobiles, and the vast opportunities which go with the mobility, together with such less enchanting merchandise as narcotics, comic books, and pornographia, are all included in an advancing gross national product. The child of a less opulent as well as a technologically more primitive age had far fewer such diversions. The red schoolhouse is remembered mainly because it had a paramount position in the lives of those who attended it that no modern school can hope to attain.

In a well-run and well-regulated community, with a sound school system, good recreational opportunities, and a good police force—in short a community where public services have kept pace with private production—the diversionary forces operating on the modern juvenile may do no great damage. Television and the violent mores of Hollywood and Madison Avenue must contend with the intellectual discipline of the school. The social, athletic, dramatic, and like attractions of the school also claim the attention of the child. These, together with the other recreational opportunities of the community, minimize the tendency to delinquency. Experiments with violence and immorality are checked by an effective law enforcement system before they become epidemic.

In a community where public services have failed to keep abreast of private consumption things are very different. Here, in an atmosphere of private opulence and public squalor, the private goods have full sway. Schools do not compete with television and the movies. The dubious heroes of the latter, not Miss Jones, become the idols of the young. The hot rod and the wild ride take the place of more sedentary sports for which there are inadequate facilities or provision. Comic books, alcohol, narcotics, and switchblade knives are, as noted, part of the increased flow of goods, and there is nothing to dispute their enjoyment. There is an ample supply of private wealth to be appropriated and not much to be feared from the police. An austere community is free from temptation. It can be austere in its public services. Not so a rich one.

Moreover, in a society which sets large store by production, and which has highly effective machinery for synthesizing private wants, there are strong pressures to have as many wage earners in the family as possible. As always all social behavior is part of a piece. If both parents are engaged in private production, the burden on the public services is further increased. Children, in effect, become the charge of the community for an appreciable part of the time. If the services of the community do not keep pace, this will be another source of disorder.

Residential housing also illustrates the problem of the social balance, although in a somewhat complex form. Few would wish to contend that, in the lower or even the middle income brackets, Americans are munificently supplied with housing. A great many families would like better located or merely more houseroom, and no advertising is necessary to persuade them of their wish. And the provision of housing is in the private domain. At first glance at least, the line we draw between private and public seems not to be preventing a satisfactory allocation of resources to housing.

On closer examination, however, the problem turns out to be not greatly different from that of education. It is improbable that the housing industry is greatly more incompetent or inefficient in the United States than in those countries—Scandinavia, Holland, or (for the most part) England—where slums have been largely eliminated and where *minimum* standards of cleanliness and comfort are well above our own. As the experience of these countries shows, and as we have also been learning, the housing industry functions well only in combination with a large, complex, and costly array of public services. These include land purchase and clearance for redevelopment; good neighborhood and city planning, and effective and well-enforced zoning; a variety of financing and other aids to the housebuilder and owner; publicly supported research and architectural services for an industry which, by its nature, is equipped to do little on its own; and a considerable amount of direct or assisted public construction for families in the lowest income brackets. The quality of the housing depends not on the industry, which is given, but on what is invested in these supplements and supports.

The case for social balance has, so far, been put negatively. Failure to keep public services in minimal relation to private production and use of goods is a cause of social disorder or impairs economic performance. The matter may now be put affirmatively. By failing to exploit the opportunity to expand public production we are missing opportunities for enjoyment which otherwise we might have had. Presumably a community can be as well rewarded by buying better schools or better parks as by buying bigger automobiles. By concentrating on the latter rather than the former it is failing to maximize its satisfactions. As with schools in the community, so with public services over the country at large. It is scarcely sensible that we should satisfy our wants in private goods with reckless abundance, while in the case of public goods, on the evidence of the eye, we practice extreme self-denial. So, far from systematically exploiting the opportunities to derive use and pleasure from these services, we do not supply what would keep us out of trouble.

The conventional wisdom holds that the community, large or small, makes a decision as to how much it will devote to its public services. This decision is arrived at by democratic process. Subject to the imperfections and uncertainties of democracy, people decide how much of their private income and goods they will surrender in order to have public services of which they are in greater need. Thus there is a balance, however rough, in the enjoyments to be had from private goods and services and those rendered by public authority.

It will be obvious, however, that this view depends on the notion of independently determined consumer wants. In such a world one could with some reason defend the doctrine that the consumer, as a voter, makes an independent choice between public and private goods. But given the dependence effect—given that consumer wants are created by the process by which they are satisfied—the consumer makes no such choice. He is subject to the forces of advertising and emulation by which production creates its own demand. Advertising operates exclusively, and emulation mainly, on behalf of privately produced goods and services. Since management and emulative effects operate on behalf of private production, public services will have an inherent tendency to lag behind. Automobile demand which is expensively synthesized will inevitably have a much larger claim on income than parks or public health or even roads where no such influence operates. The engines of mass communication, in their highest state of development, assail the eyes and ears of the community on behalf of more beer but not of more schools. Even in the conventional wisdom it will scarcely be contended that this leads to an equal choice between the two.

The competition is especially unequal for new products and services. Every corner of the public psyche is canvassed by some of the nation's most talented citizens to see if the desire for some merchantable product can be cultivated. No similar process operates on behalf of the nonmerchantable services of the state. Indeed, while we take the cultivation of new private wants for granted we would be measurably shocked to see it applied to public services. The scientist or engineer or advertising man who devotes himself to developing a new carburetor, cleanser, or depilatory for which the public recognizes no need and will feel none until an advertising campaign arouses it, is one of the valued members of our society. A politician or a public servant who dreams up a new public service is a wastrel. Few public offenses are more reprehensible.

So much for the influences which operate on the decision between public and private production. The calm decision between public and private consumption pictured by the conventional wisdom is, in fact, a remarkable example of the error which arises from viewing social behavior out of context. The inherent tendency will always be for public services to fall behind private production. We have here the first of the causes of social imbalance.

Social balance is also the victim of two further features of our society—the truce on inequality and the tendency to inflation. Since these are now part of our context, their effect comes quickly into view.

With rare exceptions such as the post office, public services do not carry a price ticket to be paid for by the individual user. By their nature they must, ordinarily, be available to all. As a result, when they are improved or new services are initiated, there is the ancient and troublesome question of who is to pay. This, in turn, provokes to life the collateral but irrelevant debate over inequality. As with the use of taxation as an instrument of fiscal policy, the truce on inequality is broken. Liberals are obliged to argue that the services be paid for by progressive taxation which will reduce inequality. Committed as they are to the urgency of goods (and also, as we shall see, . . . to a somewhat mechanical view of the way in which the level of output can be kept most secure) they must oppose sales and excise taxes. Conservatives rally to the defense of inequality—although without ever quite committing themselves in such uncouth terms—and oppose the use of income taxes. They, in effect, oppose the expenditure not on the merits of the service but on the demerits of the tax system. Since the debate over inequality cannot be resolved, the money is frequently not appropriated and the service not performed. It is a casualty of the economic goals of both liberals and conservatives for both of whom the questions of social balance are subordinate to those of production and, when it is evoked, of inequality.

In practice matters are better as well as worse than this statement of the basic forces suggests. Given the tax structure, the revenues of all levels of government grow with the growth of the economy. Services can be maintained and sometimes even improved out of this automatic accretion.

However, this effect is highly unequal. The revenues of the federal government, because of its heavy reliance on income taxes, increase more than proportionately with private economic growth. In addition, although the conventional wisdom greatly deplores the fact, federal appropriations have only an indirect bearing on taxation. Public services are considered and voted on in accordance with their seeming urgency. Initiation or improvement of a particular service is rarely, except for purposes of oratory, set against the specific effect on taxes. Tax policy, in turn, is decided on the basis of the level of economic activity, the resulting revenues, expediency, and other considerations. Among these the total of the thousands of individually considered appropriations is but one factor. In this process the ultimate tax consequence of any individual appropriation is *de minimus,* and the tendency to ignore it reflects the simple mathematics of the situation. Thus it is possible for the Congress to make decisions affecting the social balance without invoking the question of inequality.

Things are made worse, however, by the fact that a large proportion of the federal revenues are pre-empted by defense. The increase in defense costs has also tended to absorb a large share of the normal increase in tax revenues. The position of the federal government for improving the social balance has also been weakened since World War II by the strong, although receding, conviction that its taxes were at artificial wartime levels and that a tacit commitment exists to reduce taxes at the earliest opportunity.

In the states and localities the problem of social balance is much more severe. Here tax revenues—this is especially true of the General Property Tax—increase less than proportionately with increased private production. Budgeting too is far more closely circumscribed than in the case of the federal government—only the monetary authority enjoys the pleasant privilege of underwriting its own loans. Because of this, increased services for states and localities regularly pose the question of more revenues and more taxes. And here, with great regularity, the question of social balance is lost in the debate over equality and social equity.

Thus we currently find by far the most serious social imbalance in the services performed by local governments. The F.B.I. comes much more easily by funds than the city police force. The Department of Agriculture can more easily keep its pest control abreast of expanding agricultural output than the average city health service can keep up with the needs of an expanding industrial population. One consequence is that the federal government remains under constant pressure to use its superior revenue position to help redress the balance at the lower levels of government.

Finally, social imbalance is the natural offspring of persistent inflation. Inflation by its nature strikes different individuals and groups with highly discriminatory effect. The most nearly unrelieved victims, apart from those living on pensions or other fixed provision for personal security, are those who work for the state. In the private economy the firm which sells goods has, in general, an immediate accommodation to the inflationary movement. Its price increases are the inflation. The incomes of its owners and proprietors are automatically accommodated to the upward movement. To the extent that wage increases are part of the inflationary process, this is also true of organized industrial workers. Even unorganized white collar workers are in a milieu where prices and incomes are moving up. The adaption of their incomes, if less rapid than that of the industrial workers, is still reasonably prompt.

The position of the public employee is at the other extreme. His pay scales are highly formalized, and traditionally they have been subject to revision only at lengthy intervals. In states and localities inflation does not automatically bring added revenues to pay higher salaries and incomes. Pay revision for all public workers is subject to the temptation to wait and see if the inflation isn't coming to an end. There will be some fear—this seems to have been more of a factor in England than in the United States—that advances in public wages will set a bad example for private employers and unions.

Inflation means that employment is pressing on the labor supply and that private wage and salary incomes are rising. Thus the opportunities for moving from public to private employment are especially favorable. Public employment, moreover, once had as a principal attraction a high measure of social security. Industrial workers were subject to the formidable threat of unemployment during depression. Public employees were comparatively secure, and this security was worth an adverse salary differential. But with improving economic security in general this advantage has diminished. Private employment thus has come to provide better protection against inflation and little worse protection against other hazards. Though the dedicated may stay in public posts, the alert go.

The deterioration of the public services in the years of inflation has not gone unremarked. However, there has been a strong tendency to regard it as an adventitious misfortune—something which, like a nasty shower at a picnic, happened to blight a generally good time. Salaries were allowed to lag, which was a pity. This is a very inadequate view. Discrimination against the public services is an organic feature of inflation. Nothing so weakens government as persistent inflation. The public administration of France for many years, of Italy until recent times, and of other European and numerous South American countries have been deeply sapped and eroded by the effects of long-continued inflation. Social imbalance reflects itself in inability to enforce laws, including significantly those which protect and advance basic social justice, and in failure to maintain and improve essential services. One outgrowth of the resulting imbalance has been frustration and pervasive discontent. Over much of the world there is a rough and not entirely accidental correlation between the strength of indigenous communist parties or the frequency of revolutions and the persistence of inflation.

A feature of the years immediately following World War II was a remarkable attack on the notion of expanding and improving public services. During the depression years such services had been elaborated and improved partly in order to fill some small part of the vacuum left by the shrinkage of private production. During the war years the role of government was vastly expanded. After that came the reaction. Much of it, unquestionably, was motivated by a desire to rehabilitate the prestige of private production and therewith of producers. No doubt some who joined the attack hoped, at least tacitly, that it might be possible to sidestep the truce on taxation vis-à-vis equality by having less taxation of all kinds. For a time the notion that our public services had somehow become inflated and excessive was all but axiomatic. Even liberal politicians did not seriously protest. They found it necessary to aver that they were in favor of public economy too.

In this discussion a certain mystique was attributed to the satisfaction of privately supplied wants. A community decision to have a new school means that the individual surrenders the necessary amount, willy-nilly, in his taxes. But if he is left with that income, he is a free man. He can decide between a better car or a television set. This was advanced with some solemnity as an argument for the TV set. The difficulty is that this argument leaves the community with no way of preferring the school. All private wants, where the individual can choose, are inherently superior to all public desires which must be paid for by taxation and with an inevitable component of compulsion.

The cost of public services was also held to be a desolating burden on private production, although this was at a time when the private production was burgeoning. Urgent warnings were issued of the unfavorable effects of taxation on investment—"I don't know of a surer way of killing off the incentive to invest than by imposing taxes which are regarded by people as punitive." This was at a time when the inflationary effect of a very high level of investment was causing concern. The same individuals who were warning about the inimical effects of taxes were strongly advocating a monetary policy designed to reduce investment. However, an understanding of our economic discourse requires an appreciation of one of its basic rules: men of high position are allowed, by a special act of grace, to accommodate their reasoning to the answer they need. Logic is only required in those of lesser rank.

Finally it was argued, with no little vigor, that expanding government posed a grave threat to individual liberties. "Where distinction and rank is achieved almost exclusively by becoming a civil servant of the state . . . it is too much to expect that many will long prefer freedom to security."

With time this attack on public services has somewhat subsided. The disorder associated with social imbalance has become visible even if the need for balance between private and public services is still imperfectly appreciated.

Freedom also seemed to be surviving. Perhaps it was realized that all organized activity requires concessions by the individual to the group. This is true of the policeman who joins the police force, the teacher who gets a job at the high school, and the executive who makes his way up the hierarchy of Du Pont. If there are differences between public and private organization, they are of kind rather than of degree. As this is written the pendulum has in fact swung back. Our liberties are now menaced by the conformity exacted by the large corporation and its impulse to create, for its own purposes, the organization man. This danger we may also survive.

Nonetheless, the postwar onslaught on the public services left a lasting imprint. To suggest that we canvass our public wants to see where happiness can be improved by more and better services has a sharply radical tone. Even public services to avoid disorder must be defended. By contrast the man who devises a nostrum for a nonexistent need and then successfully promotes both remains one of nature's noblemen.

Pilgrimage to Nonviolence

MARTIN LUTHER KING, JR.

A major source of the civil rights movement of the late 1950s and early 1960s was the revival of interest in religion that took place in the United States after World War II. The Reverend Martin Luther King, Jr.'s discussion of the origins of the tactic of nonviolence indicates the depth of religious searching that prepared him for the role he assumed in the Montgomery, Alabama, bus boycott in 1955 and continued until his assassination in 1968. The terms in which King viewed the world, essentially those of a sophisticated Protestant evangelism, gave him a ready communication with white leaders who were responding to a similar intellectual milieu. These common themes made it easier for white churchmen and leaders of public opinion to understand the radically different social experience of black Americans that, combined with such a body of ideas, set the tone of a great social movement for more than a decade after the mid-1950's.

In my senior year in theological seminary, I engaged in the exciting reading of various theological theories. Having been raised in a rather strict fundamentalist tradition, I was occasionally shocked when my intellectual journey carried me through new and sometimes complex doctrinal lands, but the pilgrimage was always stimulating, gave me a new appreciation for objective appraisal, and critical analysis, and knocked me out of my dogmatic slumber.

Liberalism provided me with an intellectual satisfaction that I had never found in fundamentalism. I became so enamored of the insights of liberalism that I almost fell into the trap of accepting uncritically everything it encompassed. I was absolutely convinced of the natural goodness of man and the natural power of human reason.

A basic change in my thinking came when I began to question some of the theories that had been associated with so-called liberal theology. Of course, there are aspects of liberalism that I hope to cherish always: its devotion to the search for truth, its insistence on an open and analytical mind, and its refusal to abandon the best lights of reason. The contribution of liberalism to the philological-historical criticism of biblical literature has been of immeasurable value and should be defended with religious and scientific passion.

But I began to question the liberal doctrine of man. The more I observed the tragedies of history and man's shameful inclination to choose the low road, the more I came to see the depths and strength of sin. My reading of the works of Reinhold Niebuhr made me aware of the complexity of human motives and the reality of sin on every level of man's existence. Moreover, I came to recognize the complexity

130

Helen Corbitt's
APRICOT SHERBET

4 cups apricot nectar
1 cup water-packed apricots, chopped
1 3-ounce package lemon gelatin
Juice of 1 lemon
Artificial sugar (if necessary)

Mix and freeze in ice cream freezer, 6 parts of ice to 1 of ice cream salt. Or freeze in your deep freeze and whip when partially frozen in your electric mixer and return to freezer.
(1½ quarts) Calories per half cup — 34.

vement and the glaring reality of collective evil.
alism had been all too sentimental concerning
nat it leaned toward a false idealism.

e that the superficial optimism of liberalism con-
overlooked the fact that reason is darkened by
ht about human nature, the more I saw how our
sin encourages us to rationalize our actions.
now that reason by itself is little more than an
an's defensive ways of thinking. Reason, devoid
of faith, can never free itself from distortions

some aspects of liberalism, I never came to an
eo-orthodoxy. While I saw neo-orthodoxy as a
sentimental liberalism, I felt that it did not
swer to basic questions. If liberalism was too
man nature, neo-orthodoxy was too pessimistic.
n of man, but also on other vital issues, the
went too far. In its attempt to preserve the
ce of God, which had been neglected by an overstress of
his immanence in liberalism, neo-orthodoxy went to the extreme of
stressing a God who was hidden, unknown, and "wholly other." In its
revolt against overemphasis on the power of reason in liberalism, neo-
orthodoxy fell into a mood of antirationalism and semifundamentalism,
stressing a narrow uncritical biblicism. This approach, I felt, was inadequate both for the church and for personal life.

So although liberalism left me unsatisfied on the question of the
nature of man, I found no refuge in neo-orthodoxy. I am now convinced that the truth about man is found neither in liberalism nor in
neo-orthodoxy. Each represents a partial truth. A large segment of Protestant liberalism defined man only in terms of his essential nature,
his capacity for good; neo-orthodoxy tended to define man only in
terms of his existential nature, his capacity for evil. An adequate understanding of man is found neither in the thesis of liberalism nor in
the antithesis of neo-orthodoxy, but in a synthesis which reconciles the
truths of both.

During the intervening years I have gained a new appreciation
for the philosophy of existentialism. My first contact with this philosophy came through my reading of Kierkegaard and Nietzsche. Later
I turned to a study of Jaspers, Heidegger, and Sartre. These thinkers
stimulated my thinking; while questioning each, I nevertheless learned
a great deal through a study of them. When I finally engaged in a
serious study of the writings of Paul Tillich, I became convinced that
existentialism, in spite of the fact that it had become all too fashion-
able, had grasped certain basic truths about man and his condition
that could not be permanently overlooked.

An understanding of the "finite freedom" of man is one of the
permanent contributions of existentialism, and its perception of the
anxiety and conflict produced in man's personal and social life by the
perilous and ambiguous structure of existence is especially meaningful

for our time. A common denominator in atheistic or theistic existentialism is that man's existential situation is estranged from his essential nature. In their revolt against Hegel's essentialism, all existentialists contend that the world is fragmented. History is a series of unreconciled conflicts, and man's existence is filled with anxiety and threatened with meaninglessness. While the ultimate Christian answer is not found in any of these existential assertions, there is much here by which the theologian may describe the true state of man's existence.

Although most of my formal study has been in systematic theology and philosophy, I have become more and more interested in social ethics. During my early teens I was deeply concerned by the problem of racial injustice. I considered segregation both rationally inexplicable and morally unjustifiable. I could never accept my having to sit in the back of a bus or in the segregated section of a train. The first time that I was seated behind a curtain in a dining car I felt as though the curtain had been dropped on my selfhood. I also learned that the inseparable twin of racial unjustice is economic injustice. I saw how the systems of segregation exploited both the Negro and the poor whites. These early experiences made me deeply conscious of the varieties of injustice in our society.

Not until I entered theological seminary, however, did I begin a serious intellectual quest for a method that would eliminate social evil. I was immediately influenced by the social gospel. In the early 1950s I read Walter Rauschenbusch's *Christianity and the Social Crisis,* a book which left an indelible imprint on my thinking. Of course, there were points at which I differed with Rauschenbusch. I felt that he was a victim of the nineteenth-century "cult of inevitable progress," which led him to an unwarranted optimism concerning human nature. Moreover, he came perilously close to identifying the Kingdom of God with a particular social and economic system, a temptation to which the church must never surrender. But in spite of these shortcomings, Rauschenbusch gave to American Protestantism a sense of social responsibility that it should never lose. The gospel at its best deals with the whole man, not only his soul but also his body, not only his spiritual well-being but also his material well-being. A religion that professes a concern for the souls of men and is not equally concerned about the slums that damn them, the economic conditions that strangle them, and the social conditions that cripple them, is a spiritually moribund religion.

After reading Rauschenbusch, I turned to a serious study of the social and ethical theories of the great philosophers. During this period I had almost despaired of the power of love to solve social problems. The turn-the-other-cheek and the love-your-enemies philosophies are valid, I felt, only when individuals are in conflict with other individuals; when racial groups and nations are in conflict, a more realistic approach is necessary.

Then I was introduced to the life and teachings of Mahatma Gandhi. As I read his works I became deeply fascinated by his campaigns of nonviolent resistance. The whole Gandhian concept of *satya-graha* (*satya* is truth which equals love and *graha* is force; *satyagraha* thus means truth-force or love-force) was profoundly significant to me. As I delved deeper into the philosophy of Gandhi, my skepticism concerning the power of love gradually diminshed, and I came to see for the first time that the Christian doctrine of love, operating through the Gandhian method of nonviolence, is one of the most potent weapons available to an oppressed people in their struggle for freedom. At that time, however, I acquired only an intellectual understanding and appreciation of the position, and I had no firm determination to organize it in a socially effective situation.

When I went to Montgomery, Alabama, as a pastor in 1954, I had not the slightest idea that I would later become involved in a crisis in which nonviolent resistance would be applicable. After I had lived in the community about a year, the bus boycott began. The Negro people of Montgomery, exhausted by the humiliating experiences that they had constantly faced on the buses, expressed in a massive act of nonco-operation their determination to be free. They came to see that it was ultimately more honorable to walk the streets in dignity than to ride the buses in humiliation. At the beginning of the protest, the people called on me to serve as their spokesman. In accepting this responsibility, my mind, consciously or unconsciously, was driven back to the Sermon on the Mount and the Gandhian method of nonviolent resistance. This principle became the guiding light of our movement. Christ furnished the spirit and motivation and Gandhi furnished the method.

The experience in Montgomery did more to clarify my thinking in regard to the question of nonviolence than all of the books that I had read. As the days unfolded, I became more and more convinced of the power of nonviolence. Nonviolence became more than a method to which I gave intellectual assent; it became a commitment to a way of life. Many issues I had not cleared up intellectually concerning nonviolence were now resolved within the sphere of practical action.

My privilege of traveling to India had a great impact on me personally, for it was invigorating to see firsthand the amazing results of a nonviolent struggle to achieve independence. The aftermath of hatred and bitterness that usually follows a violent campaign was found nowhere in India, and a mutual friendship, based on complete equality, existed between the Indian and British people within the Commonwealth.

I would not wish to give the impression that nonviolence will accomplish miracles overnight. Men are not easily moved from their mental ruts or purged of their prejudiced and irrational feelings. When the underprivileged demand freedom, the privileged at first react with bitterness and resistance. Even when the demands are couched in nonviolent terms, the initial response is substantially the same. I am sure that many of our white brothers in Montgomery and throughout the South are still bitter toward the Negro leaders, even though these leaders have sought to follow a way of love and nonviolence. But the nonviolent approach does something to the hearts and souls of those committed to it. It gives them new self-respect. It calls up resources of strength and courage that they did not know they had. Finally, it so stirs the conscience of the opponent that reconciliation becomes a reality.

More recently I have come to see the need for the method of nonviolence in international relations. Although I was not yet convinced of its efficacy in conflicts between nations, I felt that while war could never be a positive good, it could serve as a negative good by preventing the spread and growth of an evil force. War, horrible as it is, might be preferable to surrender to a totalitarian system. But I now believe that the potential destructiveness of modern weapons totally rules out the possibility of war ever again achieving a negative good. If we assume that mankind has a right to survive, then we must find an alternative to war and destruction. In our day of space vehicles and guided ballistic missiles, the choice is either nonviolence or nonexistence.

I am no doctrinaire pacifist, but I have tried to embrace a realistic pacifism which finds the pacifist position as the lesser evil in the circumstances. I do not claim to be free from the moral dilemmas that the Christian nonpacifist confronts, but I am convinced that the church cannot be silent while mankind faces the threat of nuclear annihilation. If the church is true to her mission, she must call for an end to the arms race.

Some of my personal sufferings over the last few years have also served to shape my thinking. I always hesitate to mention these experiences for fear of conveying the wrong impression. A person who constantly calls attention to his trials and sufferings is in danger of developing a martyr complex and impressing others that he is consciously seeking sympathy. It is possible for one to be self-centered in his self-sacrifice. So I am always reluctant to refer to my personal sacrifices. But I feel somewhat justified in mentioning them in this essay because of the influence they have had upon my thought.

Due to my involvement in the struggle for the freedom of my people, I have known very few quiet days in the last few years. I have been imprisoned in Alabama and Georgia jails twelve times. My home has been bombed twice. A day seldom passes that my family and I are not the recipients of threats of death. I have been the victim of a near-fatal stabbing. So in a real sense I have been battered by the storms of persecution. I must admit that at times I have felt that I could no longer bear such a heavy burden, and have been tempted to retreat to a more quiet and serene life. But every time such a temptation appeared, something came to strengthen and sustain my determination. I have learned now that the Master's burden is light precisely when we take his yoke upon us.

My personal trials have also taught me the value of unmerited suffering. As my sufferings mounted I soon realized that there were two ways in which I could respond to my situation—either to react with bitterness or seek to transform the suffering into a creative force. I decided to follow the latter course. Recognizing the necessity for suffering, I have tried to make of it a virtue. If only to save myself from bitterness, I have attempted to see my personal ordeals as an opportunity to transfigure myself and heal the people involved in the tragic situation which now obtains. I have lived these last few years with the conviction that unearned suffering is redemptive. There are some who still find the Cross a stumbling block, others consider it foolishness, but I am more convinced than ever before that it is the power of God unto social and individual salvation. So like the Apostle Paul I can now humbly, yet proudly, say, "I bear in my body the marks of the Lord Jesus."

The agonizing moments through which I have passed during the last few years have also drawn me closer to God. More than ever before I am convinced of the reality of a personal God. True, I have always believed in the personality of God. But in the past the idea of a personal God was little more than a metaphysical category that I found theologically and philosophically satisfying. Now it is a living reality that has been validated in the experiences of everyday life. God has been profoundly real to me in recent years. In the midst of outer dangers I have felt an inner calm. In the midst of lonely days and dreary nights I have heard an inner voice saying, "Lo, I will be with you." When the chains of fear and the manacles of frustration have all but stymied my efforts, I have felt the power of God transforming the fatigue of despair into the buoyancy of hope. I am convinced that the universe is under the control of a loving purpose, and that in the struggle for righteousness man has cosmic companionship. Behind the harsh appearances of the world there is a benign power. To say that this God is personal is not to make him a finite object besides other objects or attribute to him the limitations of human personality; it is to take what is finest and noblest in our consciousness and affirm its perfect existence in him. It is certainly true that human personality is limited, but personality as such involves no necessary limitations. It means simply self-consciousness and self-direction. So in the truest sense of the word, God is a living God. In him there is feeling and will, responsive to the deepest yearnings of the human heart: *this* God both evokes and answers prayer.

The past decade has been a most exciting one. In spite of the tensions and uncertainties of this period something profoundly meaningful is taking place. Old systems of exploitation and oppression are passing away; new systems of justice and equality are being born. In a real sense this is a great time to be alive. Therefore, I am not yet discouraged about the future. Granted that the easygoing optimism of yesterday is impossible. Granted that we face a world crisis which leaves us standing so often amid the surging murmur of life's restless sea. But every crisis has both its dangers and its opportunities. It can spell either salvation or doom. In a dark, confused world the Kingdom of God may yet reign in the hearts of men.

The Texture of Poverty

MICHAEL HARRINGTON

The poor, Michael Harrington urges us, "need an American Dickens to record the smell and texture and quality of their lives." Yet his own brilliant mixture of reporting and social analysis served the essential purpose of encouraging a compassionate view of the poor, which meant first forcing people to see them. The book remains curiously stirring— what we might expect from a novel, but not from a book which constantly quotes the findings of empirical social science.

The Other America, from which this excerpt by Harrington is taken, was one of several muckraking social-science works that forced a new perspective on poverty in modern America. John Kenneth Galbraith in The Affluent Society *had pointed to the persistence of poverty amid affluence and questioned whether economic growth alone would eradicate it. Robert Lampman and Gabriel Kolko demonstrated that the New Deal had not significantly changed the distribution of wealth. All these writers cleave the path for a new liberal program that, ironically, undermined the claims of older liberals that the New Deal had reformed the economy in the interest of poorer Americans.*

Harrington's book continues to be the most vital of the many polemics that muckraked American society in the late fifties and the sixties. It was an important book because it helped launch a war on poverty which, for all its shortcomings, has made a real difference. For one thing the poor are no longer so invisible or politically powerless. They make themselves known despite official efforts to eliminate the word "poverty" from the national vocabulary. This is not to say that they may never become "invisible" again: The job that Harrington did in the early sixties (like Dickens' a century before) will clearly need constant redoing.

I

There are perennial reasons that make the other America an invisible land.

Poverty is often off the beaten track. It always has been. The ordinary tourist never left the main highway, and today he rides interstate turnpikes. He does not go into the valleys of Pennsylvania where the towns look like movie sets of Wales in the thirties. He does not see the company houses in rows, the rutted roads (the poor always have bad roads whether they live in the city, in towns, or on farms), and everything is black and dirty. And even if he were to pass through such a place by accident, the tourist would not meet the unemployed men in the bar or the women coming home from a runaway sweatshop.

Then, too, beauty and myths are perennial masks of poverty. The traveler comes to the Appalachians in the lovely season. He sees the hills, the streams, the foliage—but not the poor. Or perhaps he looks at a run-down mountain house and, remembering Rousseau rather than seeing with his eyes, decides that "those people" are truly fortunate to be living the way they are and that they are lucky to be exempt from the strains and tensions of the middle class. The only problem is that "those people," the quaint inhabitants of those hills, are undereducated, underprivileged, lack medical care, and are in the process of being forced from the land into a life in the cities, where they are misfits.

These are normal and obvious causes of the invisibility of the poor. They operated a generation ago; they will be functioning a generation hence. It is more important to understand that the very development of American society is creating a new kind of blindness about poverty. The poor are increasingly slipping out of the very experience and consciousness of the nation.

If the middle class never did like ugliness and poverty, it was at least aware of them. "Across the tracks" was not a very long way to go. There were forays into the slums at Christmas time; there were charitable organizations that brought contact with the poor. Occasionally, almost everyone passed through the Negro ghetto or the blocks of tenements, if only to get downtown to work or to entertainment.

Now the American city has been transformed. The poor still inhabit the miserable housing in the central area, but they are increasingly isolated from contact with, or sight of, anybody else. Middle-class women coming in from Suburbia on a rare trip may catch the merest glimpse of the other America on the way to an evening at the theater, but their children are segregated in suburban schools. The business or professional man may drive along the fringes of slums in a car or bus, but it is not an important experience to him. The failures, the unskilled, the disabled, the aged, and the minorities are right there, across the tracks, where they have always been. But hardly anyone else is.

In short, the very development of the American city has removed poverty from the living, emotional experience of millions upon millions of middle-class Americans. Living out in the suburbs it is easy to assume that ours is, indeed, an affluent society.

This new segregation of poverty is compounded by a well-meaning ignorance. A good many concerned and sympathetic Americans are aware that there is much discussion of urban renewal. Suddenly, driving through the city, they notice that a familiar slum has been torn down and that there are towering, modern buildings where once there had been tenements or hovels. There is a warm feeling of satisfaction, of pride in the way things are working out: the poor, it is obvious, are being taken care of.

The irony in this . . . is that the truth is nearly the exact opposite to the impression. The total impact of the various housing programs in postwar America has been to squeeze more and more people into existing slums. More often than not, the modern apartment in a towering building rents at $40 a room or more. For, during the past decade and a half, there has been more subsidization of middle- and upper-income housing than there has been of housing for the poor.

Clothes make the poor invisible too: America has the best-dressed poverty the world has ever known. For a variety of reasons, the benefits of mass production have been spread much more evenly in this area than in many others. It is much easier in the United States to be decently dressed than it is to be decently housed, fed, or doctored. Even people with terribly depressed incomes can look prosperous.

This is an extremely important factor in defining our emotional and existential ignorance of poverty. In Detroit the existence of social classes became much more difficult to discern the day the companies put lockers in the plants. From that moment on, one did not see men in work clothes on the way to the factory, but citizens in slacks and white shirts. This process has been magnified with the poor throughout the country. There are tens of thousands of Americans in the big cities who are wearing shoes, perhaps even a stylishly cut suit or dress, and yet are hungry. It is not a matter of planning, though it almost seems as if the affluent society had given out costumes to the poor so that they would not offend the rest of society with the sight of rags.

Then, many of the poor are the wrong age to be seen. A good number of them (over 8,000,000) are sixty-five years of age or better; an even larger number are under eighteen. The aged members of the other America are often sick, and they cannot move. Another group of them live out their lives in loneliness and frustration: they sit in rented rooms, or else they stay close to a house in a neighborhood that has completely changed from the old days. Indeed, one of the worst aspects of poverty among the aged is that these people are out of sight and out of mind, and alone.

The young are somewhat more visible, yet they too stay close to their neighborhoods. Sometimes they advertise their poverty through a lurid tabloid story about a gang killing. But generally they do not disturb the quiet streets of the middle class.

And finally, the poor are politically invisible. It is one of the cruelest ironies of social life in advanced countries that the dispossessed at the bottom of society are unable to speak for themselves. The people of the other America do not, by far and large, belong to unions, to fraternal organizations, or to political parties. They are without lobbies of their own; they put forward no legislative program. As a group, they are atomized. They have no face; they have no voice. . . .

II

Out of the thirties came the welfare state. Its creation had been stimulated by mass impoverishment and misery, yet it helped the poor least of all. Laws like unemployment compensation, the Wagner Act, the various farm programs, all these were designed for the middle third in the cities, for the organized workers, and for the upper third in the country, for the big market farmers. If a man works in an extremely low-paying job, he may not even be covered by social security or other welfare programs. If he receives unemployment compensation, the payment is scaled down according to his low earnings.

One of the major laws that was designed to cover everyone, rich and poor, was social security. But even here the other Americans suffered discrimination. Over the years social security payments have not even provided a subsistence level of life. The middle third have been able to supplement the Federal pension through private plans negotiated by unions, through joining medical insurance schemes like Blue Cross, and so on. The poor have not been able to do so. They lead a bitter life, and then have to pay for that fact in old age.

Indeed, the paradox that the welfare state benefits those least who need help most is but a single instance of a persistent irony in the other America. Even when the money finally trickles down, even when a school is built in a poor neighborhood, for instance, the poor are still deprived. Their entire environment, their life, their values, do not prepare them to take advantage of the new opportunity. The parents are anxious for the children to go to work; the pupils are pent up, waiting for the moment when their education has complied with the law.

Today's poor, in short, missed the political and social gains of the thirties. They are, as Galbraith rightly points out, the first minority poor in history, the first poor not to be seen, the first poor whom the politicians could leave alone.

The first step toward the new poverty was taken when millions of people proved immune to progress. When that happened, the failure was not individual and personal, but a social product. But once the historic accident takes place, it begins to become a personal fate.

The new poor of the other America saw the rest of society move ahead. They went on living in depressed areas, and often they tended to become depressed human beings. In some of the West Virginia towns, for instance, an entire community will become shabby and defeated. The young and the adventurous go to the city, leaving behind those who cannot move and those who lack the will to do so. The entire area becomes permeated with failure, and that is one more reason the big corporations shy away.

Indeed, one of the most important things about the new poverty is that it cannot be defined in simple, statistical terms. Throughout this book a crucial term is used: aspiration. If a group has internal vitality, a will—if it has aspiration—it may live in dilapidated housing, it may eat an inadequate diet, and it may suffer poverty, but it is not impoverished. So it was in those ethnic slums of the immigrants that played such a dramatic role in the unfolding of the American dream. The people found themselves in slums, but they were not slum dwellers.

But the new poverty is constructed so as to destroy aspiration; it is a system designed to be impervious to hope. The other America does not contain the adventurous seeking a new life and land. It is populated by the failures, by those driven from the land and bewildered by the city, by old people suddenly confronted with the torments of loneliness and poverty, and by minorities facing a wall of prejudice.

In the past, when poverty was general in the unskilled and semiskilled work force, the poor were all mixed together. The bright and the dull, those who were going to escape into the great society and those who were to stay behind, all of them lived on the same street. When the middle third rose, this community was destroyed. And the entire invisible land of the other Americans became a ghetto, a modern poor farm for the rejects of society and of the economy.

It is a blow to reform and the political hopes of the poor that the middle class no longer understands that poverty exists. But, perhaps more important, the poor are losing their links with the great world. If statistics and sociology can measure a feeling as delicate as loneliness (and some of the attempts to do so will be cited later on), the other America is becoming increasingly populated by those who do not belong to anybody or anything. They are no longer participants in an ethnic culture from the old country; they are less and less religious; they do not belong to unions or clubs. They are not seen, and because of that they themselves cannot see. Their horizon has become more and more restricted; they see one another, and that means they see little reason to hope.

Galbraith was one of the first writers to begin to describe the newness of contemporary poverty, and that is to his credit. Yet because even he underestimates the problem, it is important to put his definition into perspective.

For Galbraith, there are two main components of the new poverty: case poverty and insular poverty. Case poverty is the plight of those who suffer from some physical or mental disability that is personal and individual and excludes them from the general advance. Insular poverty exists in areas like the Appalachians or the West Virginia coal fields, where an entire section of the country becomes economically obsolete.

Physical and mental disabilities are, to be sure, an important part of poverty in America. The poor are sick in body and in spirit. But this is not an isolated fact about them, an individual "case," a stroke of bad luck. Disease, alcoholism, low IQ's, these express a whole way of life. They are, in the main, the effects of an environment, not the biographies of unlucky individuals. Because of this, the new poverty is something that cannot be dealt with by first aid. If there is to be a lasting assault on the shame of the other America, it must seek to root out of this society an entire environment, and not just the relief of individuals.

But perhaps the idea of "insular" poverty is even more dangerous. To speak of "islands" of the poor (or, in the more popular term, of "pockets of poverty") is to imply that one is confronted by a serious, but relatively minor, problem. This is hardly a description of a misery that extends to 40,000,000 or 50,000,000 people in the United States. They have remained impoverished in spite of increasing productivity and the creation of a welfare state. That fact alone should suggest the dimensions of a serious and basic situation.

And yet, even given these disagreements with Galbraith, his achievement is considerable. He was one of the first to understand that there are enough poor people in the United States to constitute a subculture of misery, but not enough of them to challenge the conscience and the imagination of the nation.

Finally, one might summarize the newness of contemporary poverty by saying: These are the people who are immune to progress. But then the facts are even more cruel. The other Americans are the victims of the very inventions and machines that have provided a higher living standard for the rest of the society. They are upside-down in the economy, and for them greater productivity often means worse jobs; agricultural advance becomes hunger.

In the optimistic theory, technology is an undisguised blessing. A general increase in productivity, the argument goes, generates a higher standard of living for the whole people. And indeed, this has been true for the middle and upper thirds of American society, the people who made such striking gains in the last two decades. It tends to overstate the automatic character of the process, to omit the role of human struggle. (The CIO was organized by men in conflict, not by economic trends.) Yet it states a certain truth—for those who are lucky enough to participate in it.

But the poor, if they were given to theory, might argue the exact opposite. They might say: Progress is misery.

As the society became more technological, more skilled, those who learn to work the machines, who get the expanding education, move up. Those who miss out at the very start find themselves at a new disadvantage. A generation ago in American life, the majority of the working people did not have high-school educations. But at that time industry was organized on a lower level of skill and competence. And there was a sort of continuum in the shop: the youth who left school at sixteen could begin as a laborer, and gradually pick up skill as he went along.

Today the situation is quite different. The good jobs require much more academic preparation, much more skill from the very outset. Those who lack a high-school education tend to be condemned to the economic underworld—to low-paying service industries, to backward factories, to sweeping and janitorial duties. If the fathers and mothers of the contemporary poor were penalized a generation ago for their lack of schooling, their children will suffer all the more. The very rise in productivity that created more money and better working conditions for the rest of the society can be a menace to the poor.

But then this technological revolution might have an even more disastrous consequence: it could increase the ranks of the poor as well as intensify the disabilities of poverty. At this point it is too early to make any final judgment, yet there are obvious danger signals. There are millions of Americans who live just the other side of poverty. When a recession comes, they are pushed onto the relief rolls. (Welfare payments in New York respond almost immediately to any economic decline.) If automation continues to inflict more and more penalties on the unskilled and the semiskilled, it could have the impact of permanently increasing the population of the other America.

Even more explosive is the possibility that people who participated in the gains of the thirties and the forties will be pulled back down into poverty. Today the mass-production industries where unionization made such a difference are contracting. Jobs are being destroyed. In the process, workers who had achieved a certain level of wages, who had won working conditions in the shop, are suddenly confronted with impoverishment. This is particularly true for anyone over forty years of age and for members of minority groups. Once their job is abolished, their chances of ever getting similar work are very slim.

It is too early to say whether or not this phenomenon is temporary, or whether it represents a massive retrogression that will swell the numbers of the poor. To a large extent, the answer to this question will be determined by the political response of the United States in the sixties. If serious and massive action is not undertaken, it may be necessary for statisticians to add some old-fashioned, pre-welfare-state poverty to the misery of the other America.

Poverty in the 1960's is invisible and it is new, and both these factors make it more tenacious. It is more isolated and politically powerless than ever before. It is laced with ironies, not the least of which is that many of the poor view progress upside-down, as a menace and a threat to their lives. And if the nation does not measure up to the challenge of automation, poverty in the 1960's might be on the increase.

There are mighty historical and economic forces that keep the poor down; and there are human beings who help out in this grim business, many of them unwittingly. There are sociological and political reasons why poverty is not seen; and there are misconceptions and prejudices that literally blind the eyes. The latter must be understood if anyone is to make the necessary act of intellect and will so that the poor can be noticed.

Here is the most familiar version of social blindness: "The poor are that way because they are afraid of work. And anyway they all have big cars. If they were like me (or my father or my grandfather), they could pay their own way. But they prefer to live on the dole and cheat the taxpayers."

This theory, usually thought of as a virtuous and moral statement, is one of the means of making it impossible for the poor ever to pay their way. There are, one must assume, citizens of the other America who choose impoverishment out of fear of work (though, writing it down, I really do not believe it). But the real explanation of why the poor are where they are is that they made the mistake of being born to the wrong parents, in the wrong section of the country, in the wrong industry, or in the wrong racial or ethnic group. Once that mistake has been made, they could have been paragons of will and morality, but most of them would never even have had a chance to get out of the other America.

There are two important ways of saying this: The poor are caught in a vicious circle; or, The poor live in a culture of poverty.

In a sense, one might define the contemporary poor in the United States as those who, for reasons beyond their control, cannot help themselves. All the most decisive factors making for opportunity and advance are against them. They are born going downward, and most of them stay down. They are victims whose lives are endlessly blown round and round the other America.

Here is one of the most familiar forms of the vicious circle of poverty. The poor get sick more than anyone else in the society. That is because they live in slums, jammed together under unhygienic conditions; they have inadequate diets, and cannot get decent medical care. When they become sick, they are sick longer than any other group in the society. Because they are sick more often and longer than anyone else, they lose wages and work, and find it difficult to hold a steady job. And because of this, they cannot pay for good housing, for a nutritious diet, for doctors. At any given point in the circle, particularly when there is a major illness, their prospect is to move to an even lower level and to begin the cycle, round and round, toward even more suffering.

This is only one example of the vicious circle. Each group in the other America has its own particular version of the experience, and these will be detailed throughout this book. But the pattern, whatever its variations, is basic to the other America.

The individual cannot usually break out of this vicious circle. Neither can the group, for it lacks the social energy and political strength to turn its misery into a cause. Only the larger society, with its help and resources, can really make it possible for these people to help themselves. Yet those who could make the difference too often refuse to act because of their ignorant, smug moralisms. They view the effects of poverty—above all, the warping of the will and spirit that is a consequence of being poor—as choices. Understanding the vicious circle is an important step in breaking down this prejudice.

There is an even richer way of describing this same, general idea: Poverty in the United States is a culture, an institution, a way of life.

There is a famous anecdote about Ernest Hemingway and F. Scott Fitzgerald. Fitzgerald is reported to have remarked to Hemingway, "The rich are different." And Hemingway replied, "Yes, they have money." Fitzgerald had much the better of the exchange. He understood that being rich was not a simple fact, like a large bank account, but a way of looking at reality, a series of attitudes, a special type of life. If this is true of the rich, it is ten times truer of the poor. Everything about them, from the condition of their teeth to the way in which they love, is suffused and permeated by the fact of their poverty. And this is sometimes a hard idea for a Hemingway-like middle-class America to comprehend.

The family structure of the poor, for instance, is different from that of the rest of the society. There are more homes without a father, there are less marriage, more early pregnancy and if Kinsey's statistical findings can be used, markedly different attitudes toward sex. As a result of this, to take but one consequence of the fact, hundreds of thousands, and perhaps millions, of children in the other America never know stability and "normal" affection.

Or perhaps the policeman is an even better example. For the middle class, the police protect property, give directions, and help old ladies. For the urban poor, the police are those who arrest you. In almost any slum there is a vast conspiracy against the forces of law and order. If someone approaches asking for a person, no one there will have heard of him, even if he lives next door. The outsider is "cop," bill collector, investigator (and, in the Negro ghetto, most dramatically, he is "the Man").

While writing this book, I was arrested for participation in a civil-rights demonstration. A brief experience of a night in a cell made an abstraction personal and immediate: the city jail is one of the basic institutions of the other America. Almost everyone whom I encountered in the "tank" was poor: skid-row whites, Negroes, Puerto Ricans. Their poverty was an incitement to arrest in the first place. (A policeman will be much more careful with a well-dressed, obviously educated man who might have political connections than he will with someone who is poor.) They did not have money for bail or for lawyers. And, perhaps most important, they waited their arraignment with stolidity, in a mood of passive acceptance. They expected the worst, and they probably got it.

There is, in short, a language of the poor, a psychology of the poor, a world view of the poor. To be impoverished is to be an internal alien, to grow up in a culture that is radically different from the one that dominates the society. The poor can be described statistically; they can be analyzed as a group. But they need a novelist as well as a sociologist if we are to see them. They need an American Dickens to record the smell and texture and quality of their lives. The cycles and trends, the massive forces, must be seen as affecting persons who talk and think differently.

I am not that novelist. Yet in this book I have attempted to describe the faces behind the statistics, to tell a little of the "thickness" of personal life in the other America. Of necessity, I have begun with large groups: the dispossessed workers, the minorities, the farm poor, and the aged. Then, there are three cases of less massive types of poverty, including the only single humorous component in the other America. And finally, there are the slums, and the psychology of the poor.

Throughout, I work on an assumption that cannot be proved by Government figures or even documented by impressions of the other America. It is an ethical proposition, and it can be simply stated: In a nation with a technology that could provide every citizen with a decent life, it is an outrage and a scandal that there should be such social misery. Only if one begins with this assumption is it possible to pierce through the invisibility of 40,000,000 to 50,000,000 human beings and to see the other America. We must perceive passionately, if this blindness is to be lifted from us. . . .

III

There are few people in the United States who accept Rousseau's image of the "noble savage," of primitive, untutored man as being more natural than, and superior to, his civilized descendants. Such an idea could hardly survive in a society that has made technological progress one of its most central values. There are occasional daydreams about "getting away from it all," of going to an idyllic countryside, but these are usually passing fancies.

Yet, there is a really important remnant of Rousseau's myth. It is the conviction that, as far as emotional disturbance and mental disease go, the poor are noble savages and the rich are the prime victims of tension and conflict.

There are the literature of the harried executive, the tales of suburban neurosis, the theme of the danger of wealth and leisure. It is not so much that anyone says that the poor are healthy in spirit because they are deprived of material things. Rather, the poor are just forgotten, as usual. The novels and the popular sociology are written by the middle class about the middle class, and there is more than a little strain of self-pity. The result is an image in which personal maladjustment flourishes at the top of the society, the price the well-off pay for their power. As you go down the income scale, this theory implies, life becomes more tedious and humdrum, if less upset. (However, it should be noted that the white-collar strata have the chronicler of their quiet desperation in Paddy Chayevsky.)

The truth is almost exactly opposite to the myth. The poor are subject to more mental illness than anyone else in the society, and their disturbances tend to be more serious than those of any other class. This conclusion has emerged from a series of studies made over the past few decades. There is still considerable controversy and disagreement with regard to the reasons behind this situation. But the fact itself would seem to be beyond dispute.

Indeed, if there is any point in American society where one can see poverty as a culture, as a way of life, it is here. There is, in a sense, a personality of poverty, a type of human being produced by the grinding, wearing life of the slums. The other Americans feel differently than the rest of the nation. They tend to be hopeless and passive, yet prone to bursts of violence; they are lonely and isolated, often rigid and hostile. To be poor is not simply to be deprived of the material things of this world. It is to enter a fatal, futile universe, an America within America with a twisted spirit.

Perhaps the most classic (but still controversial) study of this subject is the book *Social Class and Mental Illness* by August B. Hollingshead and F. C. Redlich. Published in 1958, it summarizes a careful research project in New Haven, Connecticut. It is an academic, scholarly work, yet its statistics are the description of an abyss.

Hollingshead and Redlich divided New Haven into five social classes. At the top (Class I) were the rich, usually aristocrats of family as well as of money. Next came the executives and professionals more newly arrived to prestige and power. Then, the middle class, and beneath them, the workers with decent paying jobs. Class V, the bottom class, was made up of the poor. About half of its members were semiskilled, about half unskilled. The men had less than six years of education, the women less than eight.

As it turned out, this five-level breakdown was more revealing than the usual three-class image of American society (upper, middle, and

lower). For it showed a sharp break between Class V at the bottom
and Class IV just above it. In a dramatic psychological sense, the skilled
unionized worker lived much, much closer to the middle class than he
did to the world of the poor. Between Class IV and Class V, Hollingshead and Redlich found a chasm. This represents the gulf between
working America, which may be up against it from time to time but
which has a certain sense of security and dignity, and the other America
of the poor.

Perhaps the most shocking and decisive statistic that Hollingshead
and Redlich found was the one that tabulated the rate of treated
psychiatric illness per 100,000 people in New Haven. These are their
results:

Classes I and II	556 per 100,000
Class III	538
Class IV	642
Class V	1,659

From the top of society down to the organized workers, there are differences, but relatively small ones. But suddenly, when one crosses the
line from Class IV to Class V, there is a huge leap, with the poor showing a rate of treated psychiatric illness of almost three times the magnitude of any other class.

But the mental suffering of the poor in these figures is not simply
expressed in gross numbers. It is a matter of quality as well. In Classes
I and II, 65 percent of the treated psychiatric illness is for neurotic
problems, and only 35 percent for the much graver disturbances of
psychoses. But at the bottom, in Class V, 90 percent of the treated illness is for psychosis, and only 10 percent for neurosis. In short, not only
the rate but also the intensity of mental illness is much greater for
the poor.

One of the standard professional criticisms of Hollingshead and
Redlich is that their figures are for treated illness (those who actually
got to a doctor or clinic) and do not indicate the "true prevalence" of
mental illness in the population. Whatever merits this argument has in
relation to other parts of the study, it points up that these particular
figures are an understatement of the problem. The higher up the class
scale one is, the more likely that there will be recognition of mental
illness as a problem and that help will be sought. At the bottom of
society, referral to psychiatric treatment usually comes from the courts.
Thus, if anything, there is even more mental illness among the poor
than the figures of Hollingshead and Redlich indicate.

The one place where this criticism might have some validity is
with regard to the intensity of emotional disturbance. Only 10 percent
of the poor who received treatment are neurotics, yet the poor neurotic
is the least likely person in the society to show up for treatment. He
can function, if only in an impaired and maimed way. If there were
something done about this situation, it is quite possible that one would

find more neurosis in the other America at the same time as one discovered more mental illness generally.

However, it is not necessary to juggle with statistics and explanations in order to corroborate the main drift of the New Haven figures. During the fifties the Cornell University Department of Psychiatry undertook an ambitious study of "Midtown," a residential area in New York City. The research dealt with a population of 170,000 from every social class, 99 percent of them white. (By leaving out the Negroes, there probably was a tendency to underestimate the problem of poverty generally, and the particular disabilities of a discriminated minority in particular.) The goal of the study was to discover "true prevalence," and there was interviewing in depth.

The Cornell scholars developed a measure of "mental health risk." They used a model of three classes, and consequently their figures are not so dramatic as those tabulated in New Haven. Yet they bear out the essential point: the lowest class had a mental health risk almost 40 percent greater than the highest class. Once again the world of poverty was given definition as a spiritual and emotional reality.

The huge brute fact of emotional illness in the other America is fairly well substantiated. The reasons behind the fact are the subject of considerable controversy. There is no neat and simple summary that can be given at the present time, yet some of the analyses are provocative for an understanding of the culture of poverty even if they must be taken tentatively.

One of the most interesting speculations came from the Cornell study of "Midtown" in New York City. The researchers developed a series of "stress factors" that might be related to an individual's mental health risk. In childhood, these were poor mental health on the part of the parents, poor physical health for the parents, economic deprivation, broken homes, a negative attitude on the part of the child toward his parents, a quarrelsome home, and sharp disagreements with parents during adolescence. In adult life, the stress factors were poor health, work worries, money worries, a lack of neighbors and friends, marital worries, and parental worries.

The Cornell team then tested to see if there was any relationship between these factors and mental health. They discovered a marked correlation. The person who had been subjected to thirteen of these stress factors was three times more likely to be mentally disturbed than the person who had felt none of them. Indeed, the researchers were led to conclude that the sheer number of stress factors was more important than the quality of stresses. Those who had experienced any three factors were of a higher mental risk than those who had experienced two.

If the Cornell conclusions are validated in further research, they will constitute an important revision of some widely held ideas about mental health. The Freudian theory has emphasized the earliest years and the decisive trauma in the development of mental illness (for example, the death of a parent). This new theory would suggest a more cumulative conception of mental illness: as stress piles upon stress over a period of time, there is a greater tendency toward disturbance. It would be an important supplement to the Freudian ideas.

But if this theory is right, there is a fairly obvious reason for the emotional torment of the other America. The stress factors listed by the Cornell study are the very stuff of the life of the poor: physical illness, broken homes, worries about work and money, and all the rest. The slum, with its vibrant, dense life hammers away at the individual. And because of the sheer, grinding, dirty experience of being poor, the personality, the spirit, is impaired. It is as if human beings dilapidate along with the tenements in which they live.

However, some scholars have attempted to soften the grimness of this picture with a theory about "drift." The poor, they argue, have a high percentage of disturbed people, not because of the conditions of life in the urban and rural slums, but because this is the group that gets all the outcasts of society from the rest of the classes. If this thesis were true, then one would expect to find failures from the higher classes as a significant group in the culture of the poor.

Hollingshead and Redlich tested this theory in New Haven and did not find any confirmation for it. The mentally impaired poor had been, for the most part, born poor. Their sickness was a product of poverty, instead of their poverty being a product of sickness. Similarly, in the Midtown study, no evidence was turned up to indicate that the disturbed poor were the rejects from other classes. There are some exceptions to this rule: alcoholics, as noted before, often tend to fall from a high position into the bitterest poverty. Still, current research points to a direct relationship between the experience of poverty and emotional disturbance.

And yet, an ironic point turned up in the Midtown research. It was discovered that a certain kind of neurosis was useful to a minority of poor people. The obsessive-compulsive neurotic often got ahead; his very sickness was a means of advancement out of the other America and into the great world. And yet, this might only prepare for a later crisis. On the lower and middle rungs of business society, hard work, attention to detail, and the like are enough to guarantee individual progress. But if such a person moves across the line, and is placed in a position where he must make decisions, there is the very real possibility of breakdown.

IV

Someone in trouble, someone in sorrow, a fight between neighbors, a coffin carried from a house, were things that coloured their lives and shook down fiery blossoms where they walked.—Sean O'Casey

The feelings, the emotions, the attitudes of the poor are different. But different from what? In this question there is an important problem of dealing with the chaotic in the world of poverty.

The definition makers, the social scientists, and the moralists come from the middle class. Their values do not include "a fight between neighbors" as a "fiery blossom." Yet that is the fact in the other America. (O'Casey was talking about Ireland; he might as well have been describing any slum in the United States.) Before going on and exploring the emotional torment of the poor, it would be well to understand this point.

Take the gangs. They are violent, and by middle-class standards they are antisocial and disturbed. But within a slum, violence and disturbance are often norms, everyday facts of life. From the inside of the other America, joining a "bopping" gang may well not seem like deviant behavior. It could be a necessity for dealing with a hostile world. (Once, in a slum school in St. Louis, a teacher stopped a fight between two little girls. "Nice girls don't fight," she told them. "Yeah," one of them replied, "you should have seen my old lady at the tavern last night.")

Indeed, one of the most depressing pieces of research I have ever read touches on this point. H. Warren Dunham carefully studied forty catatonic schizophrenics in Chicago in the early forties. He found that none of them had belonged to gangs or had engaged in the kind of activity the middle class regards as abnormal. They had, as a matter of fact, tried to live up to the standards of the larger society, rather than conforming to the values of the slum. "The catatonic young man can be described as a good boy and one who has all the desirable traits which all the social agencies would like to inculcate in the young men of the community."

The middle class does not understand the narrowness of its judgments. And worse, it acts upon them as if they were universal and accepted by everyone. In New Haven, Hollingshead and Redlich found two girls with an almost identical problem. Both of them were extremely promiscuous, so much so that they eventually had a run-in with the police. When the girl from Class I was arrested, she was provided with bail at once, newspaper stories were quashed, and she was taken care of through private psychotherapy. The girl from Class V was sentenced to reform school. She was paroled in two years, but was soon arrested again and sent to the state reformatory.

James Baldwin made a brilliant and perceptive application of this point to the problem of the Negro in a speech I heard not long ago. The white, he said, cannot imagine what it is like to be Negro: the danger, the lack of horizon, the necessity of always being on guard and watching. For that matter, Baldwin went on, the Negro problem is really the white problem. It is not the Negro who sets dark skin and kinky hair aside as something fearful, but the white. And the resolution of the racial agony in America requires a deep introspection on the part of the whites. They must discover themselves even more than the Negro.

This is true of all the juvenile delinquents, all the disturbed people, in the other America. One can put it baldly: their sickness is often a means of relating to a diseased environment. Until this is understood, the emotionally disturbed poor person will probably go on hurting himself until he becomes a police case. When he is finally given treatment, it will be at public expense, and it will be inferior to that given the rich. (In New Haven, according to Hollingshead and Redlich, the poor are five times more likely to get organic therapy—including shock treatment—rather than protracted, individual professional care.)

For that matter, some of the researchers in the field believe that sheer ignorance is one of the main causes of the high rate of disturbance among the poor. In the slum, conduct that would shock a middle-class neighborhood and lead to treatment is often considered normal. Even if someone is constantly and violently drunk, or beats his wife brutally, people will say of such a person, "Well, he's a little odd." Higher up on the class scale an individual with such a problem would probably realize that something was wrong (or his family would). He will have the knowledge and the money to get help.

One of the researchers in the field who puts great stress on the "basic universals" of the Freudian pattern (mother figure, father figure, siblings) looks upon this factor of ignorance as crucial. He is Dr. Lawrence Kubie. For Dr. Kubie, the fundamental determinants of mental health and illness are the same in every social class. But culture and income and education account for whether the individual will handle his problem; whether he understands himself as sick; whether he seeks help, and so on. This theory leaves the basic assumptions of traditional psychoanalysis intact, but, like any attempt to deal with the poor, it recognizes that something is different.

For the rich, then, and perhaps even for the better-paid worker, breakdowns, neurosis, and psychosis appear as illness and are increasingly treated as such. But the poor do not simply suffer these disturbances; they suffer them blindly. To them it does not appear that they are mentally sick; to them it appears that they are trapped in a fate.

PART THREE

The 1960's

When John F. Kennedy was inaugurated in 1961, the second youngest man ever elected President replaced the oldest man ever to serve in the office. The generation that came of age in the era of World War I was giving way to a breed shaped by World War II—men like Richard Nixon, Robert McNamara, William Westmoreland, Norman Mailer, Barry Goldwater. Kennedy's young administration stirred the nation far beyond what any of his policies would have suggested. A new generation may not always have fresh perspectives, but it is bound to have a new style, and even that is exciting.

But that generation paced a hard path. Assassinations, disorders, disastrous foreign adventures, and an accidental President obscured its record before its policies had a chance to bear fruit. Many of Kennedy's ideas resulted in legislation only after his death when Lyndon Johnson pushed his program for a "Great Society" through Congress. By then a generation even younger than the Kennedy administration had burst upon the national political scene, before anyone had even adjusted to the hard brilliance of the men who swept in early in the decade. The 1960's were years of extraordinary self-consciousness. The awareness of self was so sharp—my people, my generation, my "thing"—that the nation became almost ungovernable in traditional ways. Everyone had to be met directly (the process of "confrontation"), had to be self-directed (black power, women's liberation, student power), yet had to fit into a more crowded and interdependent nation (computerized data banks, tax records, the desire for law and order).

Americans—to their credit—have never been an easy people to govern. This old, near anarchic virtue asserted itself more strongly than ever in the 1960's, and strongest of all among the newest generation. The decade ended with accomplishments that would have astonished men of a generation before: the abolition of legal segregation, widespread government-financed medical and educational services, the longest economic boom in our history, men on the moon. Yet it also finished amidst potential chaos with the legitimacy of nearly every major institution—political parties, churches, universities, corporations, the government itself—deeply eroded.

The year 1968 was the climax of this history, a turning point that did not turn. The youngest generation fell back in disarray, the men who depended for inspiration largely on the New Deal vanished from the national scene, and an administration that described itself as conservative came to power. But whatever they called themselves, the new Nixon bureaucrats were another group of the hard young men—now growing old—who had come out of World War II; on many issues their conservatism reached farther forward than had the Kennedy liberalism of 1960—to which they often turned for their rhetoric.

The Feminine Mystique

BETTY FRIEDAN

Women have always been a majority treated like a minority: discriminated against in politics, in schools, and on the job, condescended to in nearly every social relationship, scoffed at for almost every aspiration. It is true that certain benefits have accompanied this second-class citizenship. Millions of women enjoyed the advantage of being discounted as a force in society, took the pleasures of prosperity and apparently paid few of the tangible costs in meaningless work or early death. But women as a group have suffered from a remarkably consistent discrimination, and throughout the industrialized countries they have fought back, winning a place for themselves in the economic, cultural, and political worlds.

But something went wrong in the United States in the twentieth century; while women in other countries increasingly found satisfying careers outside the home, American women seemed to be retreating. More of them worked, but at less demanding or rewarding jobs. And they had more children than their peers in other countries. Safely ensconced in the growing suburbs after World War II, apparently uninterested in politics or a career, they seemed calm and safe—the envy, one assumed, of the world. But they had one problem. "The Problem," Betty Friedan called it, "that has no name": more and more of them were miserable. The bored housewife syndrome became a national parlor game, broadcast through the mass media, discussed in countless living rooms and doubtless in as many bedrooms. Betty Friedan brought the problem into the open in her influential The Feminine Mystique *(1963), a book that heralded a new assertiveness on the part of American women such as had not been seen since the women's suffrage movement.*

In part, this new militancy reflects the general climate of political activism in the 1960's; in part it grows from new opportunities open to women. But clearly much of it is a direct and understandable response to the peculiar circumstances of the postwar era, whose attitude toward woman's role Betty Friedan has captured in vigorous polemic.

In the early 1960's *McCall's* has been the fastest growing of the women's magazines. Its contents are a fairly accurate representation of the image of the American woman presented, and in part created, by the large-circulation magazines. Here are the complete editorial contents of a typical issue of *McCall's* (July, 1960):

1. A lead article on "increasing baldness in women," caused by too much brushing and dyeing.
2. A long poem in primer-size type about a child, called "A Boy Is A Boy."

153

3. A short story about how a teenager who doesn't go to college gets a man away from a bright college girl.

4. A short story about the minute sensations of a baby throwing his bottle out of the crib.

5. The first of a two-part intimate "up-to-date" account by the Duke of Windsor on "How the Duchess and I now live and spend our time. The influence of clothes on me and vice versa."

6. A short story about a nineteen-year-old girl sent to a charm school to learn how to bat her eyelashes and lose at tennis. ("You're nineteen, and by normal American standards, I now am entitled to have you taken off my hands, legally and financially, by some beardless youth who will spirit you away to a one-and-a-half-room apartment in the Village while he learns the chicanery of selling bonds. And no beardless youth is going to do that as long as you volley to his backhand.")

7. The story of a honeymoon couple commuting between separate bedrooms after an argument over gambling at Las Vegas.

8. An article on "how to overcome an inferiority complex."

9. A story called "Wedding Day."

10. The story of a teenager's mother who learns how to dance rock-and-roll.

11. Six pages of glamorous pictures of models in maternity clothes.

12. Four glamorous pages on "reduce the way the models do."

13. An article on airline delays.

14. Patterns for home sewing.

15. Patterns with which to make "Folding Screens—Bewitching Magic."

16. An article called "An Encyclopedic Approach to Finding a Second Husband."

17. A "barbecue bonanza," dedicated "to the Great American Mister who stands, chef's cap on head, fork in hand, on terrace or back porch, in patio or backyard anywhere in the land, watching his roast turning on the spit. And to his wife without whom (sometimes) the barbecue could never be the smashing summer success it undoubtedly is . . ."

There were also the regular front-of-the-book "service" columns on new drug and medicine developments, child-care facts, columns by Clare Luce and by Eleanor Roosevelt, and "Pots and Pans," a column of readers' letters.

The image of woman that emerges from this big, pretty magazine is young and frivolous, almost childlike; fluffy and feminine; passive; gaily content in a world of bedroom and kitchen, sex, babies, and home. The magazine surely does not leave out sex; the only passion, the only pursuit, the only goal a woman is permitted is the pursuit of a man. It is crammed full of food, clothing, cosmetics, furniture, and the physical bodies of young women, but where is the world of thought and ideas, the life of the mind and spirit? In the magazine image, women do no work except housework and work to keep their bodies beautiful and to get and keep a man.

This was the image of the American woman in the year Castro led a revolution in Cuba and men were trained to travel into outer space; the year that the African continent brought forth new nations, and a plane whose speed is greater than the speed of sound broke up a Summit Conference; the year artists picketed a great museum in protest against the hegemony of abstract art; physicists explored the concept of anti-matter; astronomers, because of new radio telescopes, had to alter their concepts of the expanding universe; biologists made a breakthrough in the fundamental chemistry of life; and Negro youth in Southern schools forced the United States, for the first time since the Civil War, to face a moment of democratic truth. But this magazine, published for over 5,000,000 American women, almost all of whom have been through high school and nearly half to college, contained almost no mention of the world beyond the home. In the second half of the twentieth century in America, woman's world was confined to her own body and beauty, the charming of man, the bearing of babies, and the physical care and serving of husband, children, and home. And this was no anomaly of a single issue of a single women's magazine.

I sat one night at a meeting of magazine writers, mostly men, who work for all kinds of magazines, including women's magazines. The main speaker was a leader of the desegregation battle. Before he spoke, another man outlined the needs of the large women's magazine he edited:

Our readers are housewives, full time. They're not interested in the broad public issues of the day. They are not interested in national or international affairs. They are only interested in the family and the home. They aren't interested in politics, unless it's related to an immediate need in the home, like the price of coffee. Humor? Has to be gentle, they don't get satire. Travel? We have almost completely dropped it. Education? That's a problem. Their own education level is going up. They've generally all had a high-school education and many, college. They're tremendously interested in education for their children—fourth-grade arithmetic. You just can't write about ideas or broad issues of the day for women. That's why we're publishing 90 per cent service now and 10 per cent general interest.

Another editor agreed, adding plaintively: "Can't you give us something else besides 'there's death in your medicine cabinet'? Can't any of you dream up a new crisis for women? We're always interested in sex, of course."

At this point, the writers and editors spent an hour listening to Thurgood Marshall on the inside story of the desegregation battle, and its possible effect on the presidential election. "Too bad I can't run that story," one editor said. "But you just can't link it to woman's world."

As I listened to them, a German phrase echoed in my mind—
"*Kinder, Kuche, Kirche,*" the slogan by which the Nazis decreed that

women must once again be confined to their biological role. But this was not Nazi Germany. This was America. The whole world lies open to American women. Why, then, does the image deny the world? Why does it limit women to "one position, one role, one occupation"? Not long ago, women dreamed and fought for equality, their own place in the world. What happened to their dreams; when did women decide to give up the world and go back home?

A geologist brings up a core of mud from the bottom of the ocean and sees layers of sediment as sharp as a razor blade deposited over the years—clues to changes in the geological evolution of the earth so vast that they would go unnoticed during the lifespan of a single man. I sat for many days in the New York Public Library, going back through bound volumes of American women's magazines for the last twenty years. I found a change in the image of the American woman, and in the boundaries of the woman's world, as sharp and puzzling as the changes revealed in cores of ocean sediment.

In 1939, the heroines of women's magazine stories were not always young, but in a certain sense they were younger than their fictional counterparts today. They were young in the same way that the American hero has always been young: they were New Women, creating with a gay determined spirit a new identity for women—a life of their own. There was an aura about them of becoming, of moving into a future that was going to be different from the past. The majority of heroines in the four major women's magazines (then *Ladies' Home Journal, McCall's, Good Housekeeping, Woman's Home Companion*) were career women—happily, proudly, adventurously, attractively career women —who loved and were loved by men. And the spirit, courage, independence, determination—the strength of character they showed in their work as nurses, teachers, artists, actresses, copywriters, saleswomen— were part of their charm. There was a definite aura that their individuality was something to be admired, not unattractive to men, that men were drawn to them as much for their spirit and character as for their looks.

These were the mass women's magazines—in their heyday. The stories were conventional: girl-meets-boy or girl-gets-boy. But very often this was not the major theme of the story. These heroines were usually marching toward some goal or vision of their own, struggling with some problem of work or the world, when they found their man. And this New Woman, less fluffily feminine, so independent and determined to find a new life of her own, was the heroine of a different kind of love story. She was less aggressive in pursuit of a man. Her passionate involvement with the world, her own sense of herself as an individual, her self-reliance, gave a different flavor to her relationship with the man. The heroine and hero of one of these stories meet and fall in love at an ad agency where they both work. "I don't want to put you in a garden behind a wall," the hero says. "I want you to walk with me hand in hand, and together we could accomplish whatever we wanted to" ("A Dream to Share," *Redbook,* January, 1939).

These New Women were almost never housewives; in fact, the stories usually ended before they had children. They were young because the future was open. But they seemed, in another sense, much older, more mature than the childlike, kittenish young housewife heroines today. One, for example, is a nurse ("Mother-in-Law," *Ladies' Home Journal,* June, 1939). "She was, he thought, very lovely. She hadn't an ounce of picture book prettiness, but there was strength in her hands, pride in her carriage and nobility in the lift of her chin, in her blue eyes. She had been on her own ever since she left training, nine years ago. She had earned her way, she need consider nothing but her heart."

One heroine runs away from home when her mother insists she must make her debut instead of going on an expedition as a geologist. Her passionate determination to live her own life does not keep this New Woman from loving a man, but it makes her rebel from her parents; just as the young hero often must leave home to grow up. "You've got more courage than any girl I ever saw. You have what it takes," says the boy who helps her get away ("Have a Good Time, Dear," *Ladies' Home Journal,* May 1939).

Often, there was a conflict between some commitment to her work and the man. But the moral, in 1939, was that if she kept her commitment to herself, she did not lose the man, if he was the right man. A young widow ("Between the Dark and the Daylight," *Ladies' Home Journal,* February, 1939) sits in her office, debating whether to stay and correct the important mistake she has made on the job, or keep her date with a man. She thinks back on her marriage, her baby, her husband's death . . . "the time afterward which held the struggle for clear judgment, not being afraid of new and better jobs, of having confidence in one's decisions." How can the boss expect her to give up her date! But she stays on the job. "They'd put their life's blood into this campaign. She couldn't let him down." She finds her man, too—the boss!

These stories may not have been great literature. But the identity of their heroines seemed to say something about the housewives who, then as now, read the women's magazines. These magazines were not written for career women. The New Woman heroines were the ideal of yesterday's housewives; they reflected the dreams, mirrored the yearning for identity and the sense of possibility that existed for women then. And if women could not have these dreams for themselves, they wanted their daughters to have them. They wanted their daughters to be more than housewives, to go out in the world that had been denied them.

It is like remembering a long-forgotten dream, to recapture the memory of what a career meant to women before "career woman" became a dirty word in America. Jobs meant money, of course, at the end of the depression. But the readers of these magazines were not the women who got the jobs; career meant more than job. It seemed to mean doing something, being somebody yourself, not just existing in and through others.

I found the last clear note of the passionate search for individual identity that a career seems to have symbolized in the pre-1950 decades in a story called "Sarah and the Seaplane," (*Ladies' Home Journal,* February, 1949). Sarah, who for nineteen years has played the part of docile daughter, is secretly learning to fly. She misses her flying lesson to accompany her mother on a round of social calls. An elderly doctor houseguest says: "My dear Sarah, every day, all the time, you are committing suicide. It's a greater crime than not pleasing others, not doing justice to yourself." Sensing some secret, he asks if she is in love. "She found it difficult to answer. In love? In love with the good-natured, the beautiful Henry [the flying teacher]? In love with the flashing water and the lift of wings at the instant of freedom, and the vision of the smiling, limitless world? 'Yes,' she answered, 'I think I am.' "

The next morning, Sarah solos. Henry "stepped away, slamming the cabin door shut, and swung the ship about for her. She was alone. There was a heady moment when everything she had learned left her, when she had to adjust herself to be alone, entirely alone in the familiar cabin. Then she drew a deep breath and suddenly a wonderful sense of competence made her sit erect and smiling. She was alone! She was answerable to herself alone, and she was sufficient.

" 'I can do it!' she told herself aloud. . . . The wind blew back from the floats in glittering streaks, and then effortlessly the ship lifted itself free and soared." Even her mother can't stop her now from getting her flying license. She is not "afraid of discovering my own way of life." In bed that night she smiles sleepily, remembering how Henry had said, "You're my girl."

"Henry's girl! She smiled. No, she was not Henry's girl. She was Sarah. And that was sufficient. And with such a late start it would be some time before she got to know herself. Half in a dream now, she wondered if at the end of that time she would need someone else and who it would be."

And then suddenly the image blurs. The New Woman, soaring free, hesitates in midflight, shivers in all that blue sunlight and rushes back to the cozy walls of home. In the same year that Sarah soloed, the *Ladies' Home Journal* printed the prototype of the innumerable paeans to "Ocupation: Housewife" that started to appear in the women's magazines, paeans that resounded throughout the fifties. They usually begin with a woman complaining that when she has to write "housewife" on the census blank, she gets an inferiority complex. ("When I write it I realize that here I am, a middle-aged woman, with a university education, and I've never made anything out of my life. I'm just a housewife.") Then the author of the paean, who somehow never is a housewife (in this case, Dorothy Thompson, newspaper woman, foreign correspondent, famous columnist, in *Ladies' Home Journal*, March, 1949), roars with laughter. The trouble with you, she scolds, is you don't realize you are expert in a dozen careers, simultaneously. "You might write: business manager, cook, nurse, chauffeur, dressmaker, interior decorator, accountant, caterer, teacher, private secretary—or just put down philanthropist. . . . All your life you have been giving away your energies, your skills, your talents, your services, for love." But still, the housewife complains, I'm nearly fifty and I've never done what I hoped to do in my youth—music—I've wasted my college education.

Ho-ho, laughs Miss Thompson, aren't your children musical because of you, and all those struggling years while your husband was finishing his great work, didn't you keep a charming home on $3,000 a year, and make all your children's clothes and your own, and paper the living room yourself, and watch the markets like a hawk for bargains? And in time off, didn't you type and proofread your husband's manuscripts, plan festivals to make up the church deficit, play piano duets with the children to make practicing more fun, read their books in highschool to follow their study? "But all this vicarious living—through others," the housewife sighs. "As vicarious as Napoleon Bonaparte," Miss Thompson scoffs, "or a Queen. I simply refuse to share your self-pity. You are one of the most successful women I know."

As for not earning any money, the argument goes, let the housewife compute the cost of her services. Women can save more money by their managerial talents inside the home than they can bring into it by outside work. As for woman's spirit being broken by the boredom of household tasks, maybe the genius of some women has been thwarted, but "a world full of feminine genius, but poor in children, would come rapidly to an end. . . . Great men have great mothers."

And the American housewife is reminded that Catholic countries in the Middle Ages "elevated the gentle and inconspicuous Mary into the Queen of Heaven, and built their loveliest cathedrals to 'Notre Dame—Our Lady.' . . . The homemaker, the nurturer, the creator of children's environment is the constant recreator of culture, civilization, and virtue. Assuming that she is doing well that great managerial task and creative activity, let her write her occupation proudly: 'housewife.' "

In 1949, the *Ladies' Home Journal* also ran Margaret Mead's *Male and Female*. All the magazines were echoing Farnham and Lundberg's *Modern Woman: The Lost Sex*, which came out in 1942, with its warning that careers and higher education were leading to the "masculinization of women with enormously dangerous consequences to the home, the children dependent on it and to the ability of the woman, as well as her husband, to obtain sexual gratification."

And so the feminine mystique began to spread through the land, grafted onto old prejudices and comfortable conventions which so easily give the past a stranglehold on the future. Behind the new mystique were concepts and theories deceptive in their sophistication and their assumption of accepted truth. These theories were supposedly so complex that they were inaccessible to all but a few initiates, and therefore irrefutable. It will be necessary to break through this wall of mystery and look more closely at these complex concepts, these accepted truths, to understand fully what has happened to American women.

The feminine mystique says that the highest value and the only commitment for women is the fulfillment of their own femininity. It says that the great mistake of Western culture, through most of its history, has been the undervaluation of this femininity. It says this femininity is so mysterious and intuitive and close to the creation and

origin of life that man-made science may never be able to understand it.
But however special and different, it is in no way inferior to the nature
of man; it may even in certain respects be superior. The mistake, says
the mystique, the root of women's troubles in the past is that women
envied men, women tried to be like men, instead of accepting their own
nature, which can find fulfillment only in sexual passivity, male domination, and nurturing maternal love.

But the new image this mystique gives to American women is
the old image: "Occupation: housewife." The new mystique makes the
housewife-mothers, who never had a chance to be anything else, the
model for all women; it presupposes that history has reached a final
and glorious end in the here and now, as far as women are concerned.
Beneath the sophisticated trappings, it simply makes certain concrete,
finite, domestic aspects of feminine existence—as it was lived by women
whose lives were confined, by necessity, to cooking, cleaning, washing,
bearing children—into a religion, a pattern by which all women must
now live or deny their femininity.

Fulfillment as a woman had only one definition for American
women after 1949—the housewife-mother. As swiftly as in a dream, the
image of the American woman as a changing, growing individual in a
changing world was shattered. Her solo flight to find her own identity
was forgotten in the rush for the security of togetherness. Her limitless
world shrunk to the cozy walls of home.

The transformation, reflected in the pages of the women's maga-
zines, was sharply visible in 1949 and progressive through the fifties.
"Femininity Begins at Home," "It's a Man's World Maybe," "Have
Babies While You're Young," "How to Snare a Male," "Should I Stop
Work When We Marry?" "Are You Training Your Daughter to be a
Wife?" "Careers at Home," "Do Women Have to Talk So Much?"
"Why GI's Prefer Those German Girls," "What Women Can Learn
from Mother Eve," "Really a Man's World, Politics," "How to Hold
On to a Happy Marriage," "Don't Be Afraid to Marry Young," "The
Doctor Talks about Breast-Feeding," "Our Baby Was Born at Home,"
"Cooking to Me is Poetry," "The Business of Running a Home."

By the end of 1949, only one out of three heroines in the women's
magazines was a career woman—and she was shown in the act of re-
nouncing her career and discovering that what she really wanted to be
was a housewife. In 1958, and again in 1959, I went through issue after
issue of the three major women's magazines (the fourth, *Woman's
Home Companion,* had died) without finding a single heroine who had
a career, a commitment to any work, art, profession, or mission in the
world, other than "Occupation: housewife." Only one in a hundred
heroines had a job; even the young unmarried heroines no longer
worked except at snaring a husband.

These new happy housewife heroines seem strangely younger than
the spirited career girls of the thirties and forties. They seem to get
younger all the time—in looks, and a childlike kind of dependence.
They have no vision of the future, except to have a baby. The only

active growing figure in their world is the child. The housewife heroines are forever young, because their own image *ends* in childbirth. Like Peter Pan, they must remain young, while their children grow up with the world. They must keep on having babies, because the feminine mystique says there is no other way for a woman to be a heroine. Here is a typical specimen from a story called "The Sandwich Maker" (*Ladies' Home Journal*, April, 1959). She took home economics in college, learned how to cook, never held a job, and still plays the child bride, though she now has three children of her own. Her problem is money. "Oh, nothing boring, like taxes or reciprocal trade agreements, or foreign aid programs. I leave all that economic jazz to my constitutionally elected representative in Washington, heaven help him."

The problem is her $42.10 allowance. She hates having to ask her husband for money every time she needs a pair of shoes, but he won't trust her with a charge account. "Oh, how I yearned for a little money of my own! Not much, really. A few hundred a year would have done it. Just enough to meet a friend for lunch occasionally, to indulge in extravagantly colored stockings, a few small items, without having to appeal to Charley. But, alas, Charley was right. I had never earned a dollar in my life, and had no idea how money was made. So all I did for a long time was brood, as I continued with my cooking, cleaning, cooking, washing, ironing, cooking."

At last the solution comes—she will take orders for sandwiches from other men at her husband's plant. She earns $52.50 a week, except that she forgets to count costs, and she doesn't remember what a gross is so she has to hide 8,640 sandwich bags behind the furnace. Charley says she's making the sandwiches too fancy. She explains: "If it's only ham on rye, then I'm just a sandwich maker, and I'm not interested. But the extras, the special touches—well, they make it sort of creative." So she chops, wraps, peels, seals, spreads bread, starting at dawn and never finished, for $9.00 net, until she is disgusted by the smell of food, and finally staggers downstairs after a sleepless night to slice a salami for the eight gaping lunch boxes. "It was too much. Charley came down just then, and after one quick look at me, ran for a glass of water." She realizes that she is going to have another baby.

"Charley's first coherent words were 'I'll cancel your lunch orders. You're a mother. That's your job. You don't have to earn money, too.' It was all so beautifully simple! 'Yes, boss,' I murmured obediently, frankly relieved." That night he brings her home a checkbook; he will trust her with a joint account. So she decides just to keep quiet about the 8,640 sandwich bags. Anyhow, she'll have used them up, making sandwiches for four children to take to school, by the time the youngest is ready for college.

The road from Sarah and the seaplane to the sandwich maker was traveled in only ten years. In those ten years, the image of American woman seems to have suffered a schizophrenic split. And the split in the image goes much further than the savage obliteration of career from women's dreams.

In an earlier time, the image of woman was also split in two—the good, pure woman on the pedestal, and the whore of the desires of the flesh. The split in the new image opens a different fissure—the feminine woman, whose goodness includes the desires of the flesh, and the career woman whose evil includes every desire of the separate self. The new feminine morality story is the exorcising of the forbidden career dream, the heroine's victory over Mephistopheles: the devil, first in the form of a career woman, who threatens to take away the heroine's husband or child, and finally, the devil inside the heroine herself, the dream of independence, the discontent of spirit, and even the feeling of a separate identity that must be exorcised to win or keep the love of husband and child.

In a story in *Redbook* ("A Man Who Acted Like a Husband," November, 1957) the child-bride heroine, "a little freckle-faced brunette" whose nickname is "Junior," is visited by her old college roommate. The roommate Kay is "a man's girl, really, with a good head for business . . . she wore her polished mahogany hair in a high chignon, speared with two chopstick affairs." Kay is not only divorced, but she has also left her child with his grandmother while she works in television. This career-woman-devil tempts Junior with the lure of a job to keep her from breast-feeding her baby. She even restrains the young mother from going to her baby when he cries at 2 A.M. But she gets her comeuppance when George, the husband, discovers the crying baby uncovered, in a freezing wind from an open window, with blood running down its cheek. Kay, reformed and repentant, plays hookey from her job to go get her own child and start life anew. And Junior, gloating at the 2 A.M. feeding—"I'm glad, glad, glad I'm just a housewife" starts to dream about the baby, growing up to be a housewife, too.

With the career woman out of the way, the housewife with interests in the community becomes the devil to be exorcised. Even PTA takes on a suspect connotation, not to mention interest in some international cause (see "Almost a Love Affair," *McCall's*, November, 1955). The housewife who simply has a mind of her own is the next to go. The heroine of "I Didn't Want to Tell You" (*McCall's*, January, 1958) is shown balancing the checkbook by herself and arguing with her husband about a small domestic detail. It develops that she is losing her husband to a "helpless little widow" whose main appeal is that she can't "think straight" about an insurance policy or mortgage. The betrayed wife says: "She must have sex appeal and what weapon has a wife against that?" But her best friend tells her: "You're making this too simple. You're forgetting how helpless Tania can be, and how grateful to the man who helps her . . ."

"I couldn't be a clinging vine if I tried," the wife says. "I had a better than average job after I left college and I was always a pretty independent person. I'm not a helpless little woman and I can't pretend to be." But she learns, that night. She hears a noise that might be a burglar; even though she knows it's only a mouse, she calls helplessly to her husband, and wins him back. As he comforts her pretended panic, she murmurs that, of course, he was right in their argument that morning. "She lay still in the soft bed, smiling sweet, secret satisfaction, scarcely touched with guilt."

The end of the road, in an almost literal sense, is the disappearance of the heroine altogether, as a separate self and the subject of her own story. The end of the road is togetherness, where the woman has no independent self to hide even in guilt; she exists only for and through her husband and children.

Coined by the publishers of *McCall's* in 1954, the concept "togetherness" was seized upon avidly as a movement of spiritual significance by advertisers, ministers, newspaper editors. For a time, it was elevated into virtually a national purpose. But very quickly there was sharp social criticism, and bitter jokes about "togetherness" as a substitute for larger human goals—for men. Women were taken to task for making their husbands do housework, instead of letting them pioneer in the nation and the world. Why, it was asked, should men with the capacities of statesmen, anthropologists, physicists, poets, have to wash dishes and diaper babies on weekday evenings or Saturday mornings when they might use those extra hours to fulfill larger commitments to their society?

Significantly, critics resented only that men were being asked to share "woman's world." Few questioned the boundaries of this world for women. No one seemed to remember that women were once thought to have the capacity and vision of statesmen, poets, and physicists. Few saw the big lie of togetherness for women.

Consider the Easter 1954 issue of *McCall's* which announced the new era of togetherness, sounding the requiem for the days when women fought for and won political equality, and the women's magazines "helped you to carve out large areas of living formerly forbidden to your sex." The new way of life in which "men and women in ever-increasing numbers are marrying at an earlier age, having children at an earlier age, rearing larger families and gaining their deepest satisfaction" from their own homes, is one which "men, women and children are achieving together . . . not as women alone, or men alone, isolated from one another, but as a family, sharing a common experience."

The picture essay detailing that way of life is called "a man's place is in the home." It describes, as the new image and ideal, a New Jersey couple with three children in a gray-shingle split-level house. Ed and Carol have "centered their lives almost completely around their children and their home." They are shown shopping at the supermarket, carpentering, dressing the children, making breakfast together. "Then Ed joins the members of his car pool and heads for the office."

Ed, the husband, chooses the color scheme for the house and makes the major decorating decisions. The chores Ed likes are listed: putter around the house, make things, paint, select furniture, rugs and draperies, dry dishes, read to the children and put them to bed, work in the garden, feed and dress and bathe the children, attend PTA meetings, cook, buy clothes for his wife, buy groceries.

Ed doesn't like these chores: dusting, vacuuming, finishing jobs he's started, hanging draperies, washing pots and pans and dishes, picking up after the children, shoveling snow or mowing the lawn, changing diapers, taking the baby-sitter home, doing the laundry, ironing. Ed, of course, does not do these chores.

For the sake of every member of the family, the family needs a head. This means Father, not Mother. . . . Children of both sexes need to learn, recognize and respect the abilities and functions of each sex. . . . He is not just a substitute mother, even though he's ready and willing to do his share of bathing, feeding, comforting, playing. He is a link with the outside world he works in. If in that world he is interested, courageous, tolerant, constructive, he will pass on these values to his children.

There were many agonized editorial sessions, in those days at *McCall's.* "Suddenly, everybody was looking for this spiritual significance in togetherness, expecting us to make some mysterious religious movement out of the life everyone had been leading for the last five years—crawling into the home, turning their backs on the world—but we never could find a way of showing it that wasn't a monstrosity of dullness," a former *McCall's* editor reminisces. "It always boiled down to, goody, goody, goody, Daddy is out there in the garden barbecuing. We put men in the fashion pictures and the food pictures, and even the perfume pictures. But we were stifled by it editorially.

"We had articles by psychiatrists that we couldn't use because they would have blown it wide open: all those couples propping their whole weight on their kids but what else could you do with togetherness but child care? We were pathetically grateful to find anything else where we could show father photographed with mother. Sometimes, we used to wonder what would happen to women, with men taking over the decorating, child care, cooking, all the things that used to be hers alone. But we couldn't show women getting out of the home and having a career. The irony is, what we meant to do was to stop editing for women as women, and edit for the men and women together. We wanted to edit for people, not women."

But forbidden to join man in the world, can women be people? Forbidden independence, they finally are swallowed in an image of such passive dependence that they want men to make the decisions, even in the home. The frantic illusion that togetherness can impart a spiritual content to the dullness of domestic routine, the need for a religious movement to make up for the lack of identity, betrays the measure of women's loss and the emptiness of the image. Could making men share the housework compensate women for their loss of the world? Could vacuuming the living-room floor together give the housewife some mysterious new purpose in life?

In 1956, at the peak of togetherness, the bored editors of *McCall's* ran a little article called "The Mother Who Ran Away." To their amazement, it brought the highest readership of any article they had ever run. "It was our moment of truth," said a former editor. "We suddenly realized that all those women at home with their three and a half children were miserably unhappy."

But by then the new image of American woman, "Occupation:

housewife," had hardened into a mystique, unquestioned and permitting no questions, shaping the very reality is distorted.

By the time I started writing for women's magazines, in the fifties, it was simply taken for granted by editors, and accepted as an immutable fact of life by writers, that women were not interested in politics, life outside the United States, national issues, art, science, ideas, adventure, education, or even their own communities, except where they could be sold through their emotions as wives and mothers.

Politics, for women, became Mamie's clothes and the Nixons' home life. Out of conscience, a sense of duty, the *Ladies' Home Journal* might run a series like "Political Pilgrim's Progress," showing women trying to improve their children's schools and playgrounds. But even approaching politics through mother love did not really interest women, it was thought in the trade. Everyone knew those readership percentages. An editor of *Redbook* ingeniously tried to bring the bomb down to the feminine level by showing the emotions of a wife whose husband sailed into a contaminated area.

"Women can't take an idea, an issue, pure," men who edited the mass women's magazines agreed. "It had to be translated in terms they can understand as women." This was so well understood by those who wrote for women's magazines that a natural childbirth expert submitted an article to a leading woman's magazine called "How to Have a Baby in a Atom Bomb Shelter." "The article was not well written," an editor told me, "or we might have bought it." According to the mystique, women, in their mysterious femininity, might be interested in the concrete biological details of having a baby in a bomb shelter, but never in the abstract idea of the bomb's power to destroy the human race.

Such a belief, of course, becomes a self-fulfilling prophecy. In 1960, a perceptive social psychologist showed me some sad statistics which seemed to prove unmistakably that American women under thirty-five are not interested in politics. "They may have the vote, but they don't dream about running for office," he told me. "If you write a political piece, they won't read it. You have to translate it into issues they can understand—romance, pregnancy, nursing, home furnishings, clothes. Run an article on the economy, or the race question, civil rights, and you'd think that women had never heard of them."

Maybe they hadn't heard of them. Ideas are not like instincts of the blood that spring into the mind intact. They are communicated by education, by the printed word. The new young housewives, who leave high school or college to marry, do not read books, the psychological surveys say. They only read magazines. Magazines today assume women are not interested in ideas. But going back to the bound volumes in the library, I found in the thirties and forties that the mass-circulation magazines like *Ladies' Home Journal* carried hundreds of articles about the world outside the home. "The first inside story of American diplomatic relations preceding declared war"; "Can the U.S. Have Peace After This War?" by Walter Lippmann; "Stalin at Midnight," by Harold Stassen; "General Stilwell Reports on China"; articles about the last days of Czechoslovakia by Vincent Sheean; the persecution of Jews in Germany; the New Deal; Carl Sandburg's account of Lincoln's assassination; Faulkner's stories of Mississippi, and Margaret Sanger's battle for birth control.

In the 1950's they printed virtually no articles except those that serviced women as housewives, or described women as housewives, or permitted a purely feminine identification like the Duchess of Windsor or Princess Margaret. "If we get an article about a woman who does anything adventurous, out of the way, something by herself, you know, we figure she must be terribly aggressive, neurotic," a *Ladies' Home Journal* editor told me. Margaret Sanger would never get in today.

In 1960, I saw statistics that showed that women under thirty-five could not identify with a spirited heroine of a story who worked in an ad agency and persuaded the boy to stay and fight for his principles in the big city instead of running home to the security of a family business. Nor could these new young housewives identify with a young minister, acting on his belief in defiance of convention. But they had no trouble at all identifying with a young man paralyzed at eighteen. ("I regained consciousness to discover that I could not move or even speak. I could wiggle only one finger of one hand." With help from faith and a psychiatrist, "I am now finding reasons to live as fully as possible.")

Does it say something about the new housewife readers that, as any editor can testify, they can identify completely with the victims of blindness, deafness, physical maiming, cerebral palsy, paralysis, cancer, or approaching death? Such articles about people who cannot see or speak or move have been an enduring staple of the women's magazines in the era of "Occupation: housewife." They are told with infinitely realistic detail over and over again, replacing the articles about the nation, the world, ideas, issues, art and science; replacing the stories about adventurous spirited women. And whether the victim is man, woman or child, whether the living death is incurable cancer or creeping paralysis, the housewife reader can identify. . . .

A baked potato is not as big as the world, and vacuuming the living room floor—with or without makeup—is not work that takes enough thought or energy to challenge any woman's full capacity. Women are human beings, not stuffed dolls, not animals. Down through the ages man has known that he was set apart from other animals by his mind's power to have an idea, a vision, and shape the future to it. He shares a need for food and sex with other animals, but when he loves, he loves as a man, and when he discovers and creates and shapes a future different from his past, he is a man, a human being.

This is the real mystery: why did so many American women, with the ability and education to discover and create, go back home again, to look for "something more" in housework and rearing children? For, paradoxically, in the same fifteen years in which the spirited New Woman was replaced by the Happy Housewife, the boundaries of the human world have widened, the pace of world change has quickened, and the very nature of human reality has become increasingly free from biological and material necessity. Does the mystique keep American woman from growing with the world? Does it force her to deny reality, as a woman in a mental hospital must deny reality to believe she is a queen? Does it doom women to be displaced persons, if not virtual schizophrenics, in our complex, changing world?

It is more than a strange paradox that as all professions are finally open to women in America, "career woman" has become a dirty word; that as higher education becomes available to any woman with the capacity for it, education for women has become so suspect that more and more drop out of high school and college to marry and have babies; that as so many roles in modern society become theirs for the taking, women so insistently confine themselves to one role. Why, with the removal of all the legal, political, economic, and educational barriers that once kept woman from being man's equal, a person in her own right, an individual free to develop her own potential, should she accept this new image which insists she is not a person but a "woman," by definition barred from the freedom of human existence and a voice in human destiny?

The feminine mystique is so powerful that women grow up no longer knowing that they have the desires and capacities the mystique forbids. But such a mystique does not fasten itself on a whole nation in a few short years, reversing the trends of a century, without cause. What gives the mystique its power? Why did women go home again?

The Kennedy Nation

DAVID BURNER and THOMAS R. WEST

John Fitzgerald Kennedy was one of the most attractive men ever to be President of the United States. He was, Norman Mailer once wrote, "our leading man." His confidence that he could "get the nation moving again," his handsome and stylish wife, photogenic children, and appealing and able associates touched chords in American society that his predecessor Eisenhower, for all the love and respect the General generated, would not have tried to reach. Especially Kennedy was the hero of the new men and women—in the professions, the universities, business and government—who were reaching positions of leadership, a new generation "born in this century."

The discussion here of Kennedy and his presidential term recognizes this elan and its vital—if intangible—effect on American culture. Nevertheless, the account is no part of the hagiography that began to appear after his assassination. While the authors have an admiration for Kennedy, this version of his administration is sharply aware of its failings as well as its successes. A president who both stalled and spurred civil rights, who both eased and intensified the Cold War, who tended to allow events to move to a crisis but then responded to the emergency, JFK is not easy to evaluate.

The Kennedy dynasty is of a different time and character from that of the Adams family, the New England Lodges, the New York Hamilton Fishes, or the presidential Roosevelts. It, too, has its connections and continuities—a strong sense of family purpose, a loyalty to a church, a story of immigrant ancestors and a fortune built by succeeding generations, but unlike the other dynastic American families, the Kennedy family gives an impression of being unsettled and undefined, in the midst of defining and fulfilling itself through political activity. Joseph Kennedy, Sr., used money and power to establish the family in national politics. Each of his three presidential-contender sons acquired a separate political personality, each expressing an energy and buoyancy that in part explain the family's tonic effect on American political life.

Having lost much of what it once possessed in stable private institutions and a confident public life, the United States today may have use for a conscious rediscovery of politics as a unifying and inventive force. But political partisanship, the American practice that made a citizen a lifelong Democrat, an unbending Republican, or a sturdy Eugene Debs Socialist, and fixed a party to a set of clear and disputatious principles, is among the institutional certainties that have been lost. A politician capable of returning vitality to public life must do so in the terms now available, which involve not the assertion of some traditional party principle but a quick, intelligent, competent response to issues and a sensitivity to the uses and effects of the media.

For a moment in the 1960's, much of the country was close to achieving a shared public experience such as it had not enjoyed for years. Some political observers believed that foreign policy had become a series of adroit confrontations of crises at innumerable points around the globe. The crises were met with firmness, without the near hysterias of the early Cold War period. The country was prosperous enough to begin to support an expanding federal social program that Lyndon Johnson would carry further. A brilliant technology had the space programs as its most visibly daring expression, and as its most pressing demand a renovation of American schools; and its virtues of intellectual imagination and precise workmanship could speak promisingly of the national character. The civil rights movement promised a moral reformation. The distinctive events of the early 1960's—the civil rights demonstrations, the manned space explorations, and the missile crisis—appeared to test and affirm the national will, and through television they immediately became collective public events.

Americans may remember that time with some embarrassment. The optimism and self-confidence had an element of contrivance, of being the product of politics by mass media and of the pieties of advertising. Here we can particularly recall the enthusiasm for culture and the arts that seized on these things as though a poem by Robert Frost could be a national accomplishment and embellishment like a space satellite. The Bay of Pigs was a commentary on the foreign policy of the period, and historians still like to trace the connections between the Kennedy years and the war in Vietnam. But we owe it to the spirit of those years to remember for contrast the atrophy of national will and purpose that has been more recently the dominant condition of American politics and to acknowledge as well that the partially contrived political mood of the early 1960's was ultimately productive of some of the finest social legislation of the twentieth century.

Within a few years of John Kennedy's presidency, the elements of the public experience that he had symbolized were flying apart. Technology, as the horrors of its performance in Vietnam came to light and as worry over the American environment increased, became among liberals an object of mistrust. The respect for educated self-cultivation that was a mark of the 1960's may have in the present-day cults of therapeutic selfishness its corrupt descendants. The increasingly beneficent economy of the Kennedy and the early Johnson years has passed over into an uncontrolled inflation. Yet in better days these were the components of a precariously successful cooperative public that deserves careful understanding.

In a world in which qualities of differing value can have an irritating way of going together, we have in the case of the Kennedys a political aggressiveness that translates into energetic and, in recent years, progressive public leadership—or, more specifically, into public image making. Americans are right, of course, to be suspicious of image making. Images are manipulative, and they are meaningless unless social realities underlie them. But political images, rhetoric, and gestures can fix our attention on certain national realities or possibilities and bring them into greater focus. A military parade can do this; so did the Selma march and the antiwar demonstrations. We do not claim that John Kennedy had much to do with formulating the liberal policies of the 1960s, although he was important to beginning a reconsideration of Cold War premises. But he did manage to represent in his crisp person both the trained competencies of American life—he was singularly appropriate to the early days of the space program—and the new political hopefulness. It is a property of the American people, a property that the imperatives of modern technology enforce, to express and define themselves not only in the traditional, the repetitive, and the local, as other and perhaps richer cultures do, but also in acts of making or willing, which can include the remaking of character. The adage "this country will be a great place when we get it finished" says something about the worthiness, as well as the naivete, of American civilization. The deliberate invoking of a public mood of moral endeavor is a legitimately American act—an act, to be sure, that needs the check of a close critical scrutiny. It is near to what Theodore Roosevelt had in mind when he called the presidency a bully pulpit.

The Kennedy administration began on a chill January morning in Washington, D.C. There was also a chill on the words that echo from that time and place. First came the poetry of Robert Frost, his white hair gleaming in the sunlight. The bright light marred his vision as he was reading his poem:

> It makes the prophet in us all presage
> The glory of a next Augustan age
> Of a power leading from its strength and
>   pride,
> Of young ambition eager to be tried,
> Firm in our free beliefs without dismay,
> In any game the nations want to play.
> A golden age of poetry and power
> Of which this noonday's the beginning
>   hour.

The inaugural address, attributable in part to Theodore Sorenson, set the tone for a presidential administration as few such addresses have ever done. It committed a free people to "pay any price, bear any burden, meet any hardship." It recalled the "graves of young Americans who answered the call to service" around the globe. There was a chill in the words of the inaugural address: beneath the inevitable conventional commitments to strength and freedom and peace lay a curiously solemn call to action at a moment that, in fact, was no grimmer than any other in the Cold War. The address stands as a remarkable piece, not for any specific declaration of policy, but for a mood that seems in retrospect to accord with that biting cold January morning.

John Kennedy was a foreign policy president. It has been common for presidencies in this century to receive much of their definition from the global events that have impinged so dramatically upon them, but the peculiar circumstances of Kennedy's times conspired with his personality and interests to bring about a presidential style of vigorous engagement in diplomatic and military affairs.

By the 1960's, the vocabulary available for the public discussion of foreign affairs and of the Cold War in particular differed in unspectacular but important ways from the rhetoric that had prevailed a decade earlier. There was less of the primitive anticommunism that had expressed itself in the witch hunts of the early years of the Cold War and in the implicit assumption, which commentators and statesmen had once shared with the public, that communists throughout the world had a common ideological commitment that was unmodified by national culture or national interests. Along with this altering of perception had come a subtle alteration in the definition of the virtues appropriate to the conflict. The new stress was on patience, coolness, skilled response to military and diplomatic crises. It was as if the technological intelligence needed for maintaining the economies and the weaponries of the great powers now was to lend its sober competence to world politics as well. The exigencies of the Cold War period, which did not permit decisive and satisfying encounters, had played a large part in this shift in mentality. It was a triumph of the argument that the liberal architects of the Cold War had sustained against the right-wingers who wanted some simple and immediate means of crushing international communism. A generation familiar with the conviction that the very premises of the Cold War were simplistic may find it hard to realize that from the time of Dean Acheson's State Department during the Truman administration through the days of the presidential campaign of 1964, the most insistent attacks on the nation's foreign policies came not from the left but from the right, and they called forth from liberal cold warriors a rhetoric emphasizing diplomatic maneuver, measured action, the necessity of alliance, the limits of possibility. The concern for sophistication in foreign policy came also from the involvement of academics in the Cold War administrations.

John Kennedy read Ian Fleming's James Bond novels. That went well with his special temperamental relationship to the Cold War mentality of his day. Fleming's fictional character James Bond is more than an arrogant practitioner of secret warfare. The extraordinary violence of the stories should not keep us from recognizing that they were among the early efforts in a spy genre that looked beyond the simple conflict between the West and some monolithic communist bloc to picture instead a multiplicity of interests and intrigues. James Bond, moreover, is armed with light, precise, futuristic gadgets that remind the reader of the increasingly sophisticated technological world of the Cold War itself. And it is that same revision in the understanding of international politics that found a spokesman in a war hero, the skipper of a small, swift craft, who wanted a defter, more mobile, more expert military force capable of fighting in limited wars. Kennedy took the same position that Generals Maxwell Taylor and Matthew Ridgeway had taken when they spoke against the view that Americans should rely on the nuclear deterrent. Taylor, who had retired in 1959 in protest against Eisenhower's policies, returned in 1961 as an important adviser and in 1962 became Chief of Staff. Kennedy's propensity for identifying military elan with technical expertise is in full conformity with the idea of the Peace Corps, those warriors for peace. They were an American presence abroad whose strength was supposed to lie not merely in their goodwill but in their knowledge and skill. It happens that the most spectacular moment of Kennedy's administration was the Cuban missile crisis, but in any event he seemed more passive toward domestic issues, the moved rather than the mover. The genuine debt that domestic liberalism owes to Kennedy is in large part a debt to a style and energy that received their clearer and more consistent articulation in international events.

Many voters in 1960 had preferred the style of Nixon to Kennedy's terse rhetoric. The new president immediately took steps to draw the nation together. He met with Nixon in Florida after the election. He retained such staple figures of government as J. Edgar Hoover of the FBI and Allen Dulles of the Central Intelligence Agency. This meant not only that he wanted continuity in government but also that he had patience with symbols of the past. In January he forced through Congress a change in the size of the House Rules Committee, which meant that it could be packed with his supporters, but the closeness of that victory led to a caution about domestic issues.

Kennedy's cabinet selections suggest the character of his foreign policy. For secretary of state, he passed over such independent minds as William Fulbright of Arkansas, chairman of the Senate Foreign Relations Committee, and Adlai Stevenson, who as early as the mid-1950's had called for an end to nuclear testing. Instead, following the advice of foreign policy expert Robert Lovett and former Secretary of State Dean Acheson, Kennedy turned to the State Department bureaucracy for Dean Rusk, a strong-willed man who favored the goals of the Cold War, if not its customary techniques. Robert McNamara brought a degree of efficiency to the Defense Department, but rarely disagreed on policy with the Joint Chiefs of Staff.

Some of the mentality Kennedy brought to office quickly took concrete form in the Bay of Pigs fiasco. Under the Eisenhower administration, the Central Intelligence Agency had prepared an invasion force to spark a general uprising against Fidel Castro in Cuba. On a coffee plantation in a mountainous region of Guatemala, more than a thousand Cuban refugee guerrillas awaited orders to invade. To cancel the planned invasion, Kennedy reasoned, would make the new administration look weak. So in April 1961 he gave the signal. The landing spot the CIA chose was in fact well fortified and allowed the rebels no opportunity to retreat to the mountains. The motley force put large quantities of radio equipment and munitions in a single boat, which was blown up; air cover was wholly inadequate; and Kennedy had the self-restraint not to launch an all-out attack. Castro easily destroyed the invaders. The CIA apparently advised Kennedy that the well-entrenched Castro could be overthrown without the cooperation of the armed forces of the United States. Perhaps the anticommunist traditions of his family and church, and the memory of congressional resolutions calling for the liberation of Eastern Europe, had engendered in him a naive assumption that people who lived under any form of communism yearned for freedom and would revolt if given an opportunity, and that since communism was evil, it could not succeed. It is possible also that Kennedy's competitiveness had driven him to seek a crisis. In his inaugural address, he had declared, "Before my term has ended, we shall have to test anew whether a nation organized and governed such as ours can endure."

One of Kennedy's responses to the failure in Cuba, which was, after all, an act of aggression by one sovereign state against another, was to press for the Alliance for Progress, a $10 billion, decade-long program of economic aid to Latin America. Also, in 1961 the Development Loan Fund was established; it was to provide over a billion American dollars in aid to underdeveloped nations. The Bay of Pigs, which lifted Kennedy's standing in public opinion polls, made him more rather than less belligerent. He pushed harder for increased military spending, and in 1961 Congress responded with a 15 percent increase. Kennedy discounted the argument that building up an arsenal of new weapons would provoke the Soviet Union into a like response. The Russians did nevertheless respond with a similar increase in their defense expenditures.

In June 1961 Kennedy and Khrushchev met in Vienna. Kennedy's object was to maintain the existing balance of power between the two blocs; the West desired a stable world open to western economic expansion. Khrushchev was against any global arrangement that would hinder the revolutionary process, and at Vienna he stood for the right of rebellion against reactionary governments. Khrushchev's threat to sign a separate peace treaty with East Germany gave the United States the prospect, at best, of being forced to negotiate with a government it had not recognized or, at worst, of facing a ban on entering Berlin.

The encounter discouraged Kennedy, who perceived Khrushchev as intransigently committed to upsetting international order. Upon returning home, he increased draft quotas, called up reserves, demanded a crash civil defense program that led to a popular stir about bomb shelters, and asked for estimates on casualties in the event of nuclear war. Dean Acheson urged a hard line on Berlin, calling the crisis a "simple contest of wills." He recommended sending a division of American troops on the autobahn through East Germany to Berlin, and urged Kennedy to make it clear that Americans would fight a nuclear war if necessary. Since there was nothing to negotiate, a willingness to go to the conference table would be taken as a sign of weakness. Kennedy seemed momentarily to agree with Acheson. In an address on July 25, 1961, he said: "We do not want to fight, but we have fought before."

In August when Khrushchev acted on the construction of the Berlin Wall, sealing off the eastern sector from the western sector, Kennedy remained on edge, remarking that there was one chance in five of a nuclear exchange. He sent 1,500 troops from West Germany into West Berlin, and Vice President Lyndon Johnson went there to pledge American lives to the defense of the city.

The Wall, in denying East Berliners freedom to cross to the West, was an outrage. But with regard to the objective of establishing a separate East German nation so that the Soviet Union would never have to face an armed and hostile united Germany in league with western powers, Khrushchev had compromised. He had withdrawn from the deadline of January 1, 1962, for western assent to a separate East Germany as a condition for continuing to enjoy access to West Berlin. When it eventually became clear to Washington that the wall was essentially a defensive measure, some members of Congress charged that the administration had overreacted on Berlin, that Kennedy had created a pseudocrisis.

In September 1961 the Soviet Union began to detonate nuclear bombs of enormous power; the United States followed in the spring of 1962. The older policy of massive retaliation that the Eisenhower administration had pursued now existed perilously alongside a new Kennedy policy of reliance on conventional arms and an indicated willingness to use them in any part of the world. Events in the Third World threatened to upset the delicate balance and precipitate the ultimate conflict between the Soviet Union and the United States.

In distant Southeast Asia, indigenous communist forces endangered the existing regimes in Laos and South Vietnam. In Laos the president, remembering the Bay of Pigs, avoided direct intervention. He also sensed that the United States, as he had expressed it in a speech at the University of Washington in November 1961, "cannot impose [its] will upon the other 94 percent of mankind. . . . We cannot right every wrong or reverse each adversity. . . . There cannot be an American solution to every world problem." Kennedy eventually compromised by abandoning a right-wing faction in Laos and supporting a "neutral and independent" government. Perhaps the president had after all made some headway with Khrushchev in Vienna. The Russians also exercised their influence in behalf of Laotian neutrality. In 1962 the parties agreed on a "troika" coalition government, which approved a genuine cease-fire. In Africa the communist powers failed to increase their influence. The United Nations put down a separatist movement, friendly to the West, that would have weakened the new nation of the Congo. Kennedy issued an order that prohibited the sale by Americans of arms to South Africa as long as that country continued its policy of harsh racial separation.

In the late spring of 1962, several months after the United States had stopped altogether the importation of Cuban sugar, Castro decided to allow the Russians to set up intermediate-range missiles in Cuba. For the first time, the Soviet Union was placing missiles outside its own national boundaries. Our air surveillance revealed the sites as their construction neared completion. Although emplacement of the missiles was quite compatible with international law, and no strong addition to the military threat the missiles in the Soviet Union itself already posed to the United States, the weapons were a blatant challenge to the visible status quo. (The United States had years before placed its missiles in friendly countries along the periphery of the Soviet Union.) Khrushchev had evidently decided to test American intentions. His justification was the protection of Cuba against a United States invasion—a possibility that, even in the opinion of the allies of the United States, Kennedy's Bay of Pigs attempt had made believable.

Both the president's military consultants and Dean Acheson recommended an immediate air strike, which would have wiped out Russian advisers along with the missiles. But Robert McNamara and Robert Kennedy disagreed. The attorney general argued that it was not in the American character to launch an air attack against a small island unable to retaliate. America would be faithless to its past if it attacked Cuba much as the Japanese had attacked Pearl Harbor.

Kennedy decided on a less drastic course of action. Appearing on television to announce the presence of the missiles and inform the public of his response, he instituted a naval blockade against Soviet ships bringing additional missile equipment to Cuba. He set the barrier as close to Cuba as he dared, hoping that Khrushchev would decide not to risk an incident. The United States permitted a harmless tanker to enter the quarantine area, but then, as millions watched, the first ship carrying technical equipment turned back. Khrushchev announced that he was removing the missiles from Cuba. Some critics blamed Kennedy for unnecessarily bringing the world close to nuclear war when he could have brought about an exchange: the president, determined not to be weak, had declined Khrushchev's offer to give up the missile sites if the United States would relinquish some useless bases in Turkey. Khrushchev, it was argued, had displayed greater maturity than Kennedy by refusing to risk war. But Kennedy, too, had exercised some restraint in the face of a Soviet provocation, and he did promise not to attempt aggression against Cuba. To his country Kennedy now appeared to be a courageous and mature statesman. His talk on television, and the events of the week that unfolded before the nation, made for a peculiar experience: a country at war but not in combat, a people at once involved and spectators. Since the crisis occurred just before the midterm elections, it probably helped the Democrats to gain four seats in the Senate and to hold their losses in the House to two—an excellent performance for a party in power at midterm.

After the missile crisis, confrontations between the Soviet Union and the United States shifted to the Third World, where there would be less risk of war between them. Direct relations between the two superpowers, in fact, improved. A "hot line" between Moscow and the White House insured instant communication in an emergency. Kennedy, in a speech at American University in June 1963, heralded a new era of cooperation between the two countries. It is said that he was here at odds with Secretary Rusk's hawkish ideas. In this same year the Soviets rejected Chinese militancy, insisting on the need for peaceful coexistence and the avoidance of nuclear war. The Test Ban Treaty of 1963 outlawed atmospheric testing of nuclear weapons. This was the only enduring accomplishment of Kennedy's foreign policy. Two powers close to achieving a nuclear capacity, France and Communist China, refused to sign.

After the Vietnam war had proved its futility, some Kennedy partisans argued that despite his escalation of the war, he had been ready by late 1963 to pull out after the 1964 election. The evidence for this claim is weak. It consists mostly of the president's own conflicting statements on the war and the testimony of a few friends, notably Kenneth O'Donnell and Senator Mike Mansfield. Kennedy's most trusted war counselors knew nothing of his alleged doubts. His own words reflect the sophisticated but flawed argument that the real enemy in Vietnam was China, and that this necessitated continued commitment. Asked in a television interview on September 9, 1963, whether he still believed in the domino theory, Kennedy replied:

I believe it . . . China is so large, looms so high just beyond the frontiers, that if South Vietnam went, it would not only give them [the Chinese] an approved geographic location for guerrilla assault on Malaysia, but would also give the impression that the wave of the future in Southeast Asia was China and the Communists. . . . What I am concerned about is that Americans will get impatient and say because they don't like events in Southeast Asia or they don't like the government in Saigon, that we should withdraw. That only makes it easy for the Communists. I think we should stay. . . .

It was Kennedy people, in fact, who conceived and for several years carried on the war in Vietnam. In much the same way that civil rights and medicare legislation was shepherded hurriedly through Congress, Lyndon Johnson's Vietnam policy drew on the Kennedy legacy for legitimacy. "Is there today," Tom Wicker has asked, "in consequence of the war, any more thoroughly rejected doctrine than this unlimited commitment from Kennedy's Inaugural Address?"

The initial commitment of additional troops to Vietnam came in May 1961 when President Kennedy received an oral report from General Maxwell Taylor on the Bay of Pigs disaster. Robert Kennedy, CIA director Allen Dulles, and Admiral Arleigh Burke had aided in the preparation of the report. The gist of it was that the United States, locked in a "life and death struggle" with the Soviet Union "which we may be losing," must carry any Cold War operation "through to conclusion with the same determination as a military operation." In 1962 Taylor became chairman of the Joint Chiefs of Staff. That January, 2,646 American military personnel were stationed in Vietnam. By October 1963, the total had risen to 16,732. Technological escalation also took place under Kennedy, notably the introduction of artillery and fighter-bomber aircraft.

Once the American presence had been established, however, it was unlikely that its size or character could be limited. When American troops were committed and some were killed, those who advocated escalation employed the irresistible logic that the initial involvement must be redeemed. Kennedy himself may have realized this. He observed that sending troops is a little like taking a drink: the effect wears off, and you have to take another. Each new escalation was carried out with the obsessive certainty that it would ultimately succeed.

Until the missile crisis Kennedy had to direct his abundant energies largely toward foreign policy. But in 1961 Congress did pass several administration measures: a higher minimum wage law; a Housing Act, which granted almost $5 billion for urban-renewal projects; an Area Development Act, which provided funds for retraining in areas of high unemployment; and money for control of water pollution. Although some of his cabinet appointees, such as Stewart L. Udall of the Interior Department, promoted conservation programs, the president did not press Congress for new welfare or social legislation. Udall, after speaking to the president about conservation in the summer of 1961, remarked: "He's imprisoned by Berlin." In 1962 and 1963, few administration bills passed Congress. The president lacked the time or patience necessary to work on details of legislation. When Secretary of Health, Education, and Welfare Anthony Celebrezze tried to engage him in discussion about proposed laws, the president cut him off, saying, "You were the mayor of a large city. You know how to handle these problems. Now handle them."

On the major social issue of the era, that of civil rights, Kennedy brought to the presidency a record of compromise and expediency. He had seemed scarcely aware of the civil rights movement that had crystallized after the Supreme Court school desegregation decision of 1954. In his presidential campaign he sought support from the most truculent segregationist governors. In January 1960 he omitted civil rights from a list of the "real issues of 1960." Along with Richard Nixon, he made promises during the campaign, but he translated few of them into concrete proposals after he took office. His telephone message of sympathy to Mrs. Martin Luther King, Jr., while her husband sat in an Atlanta jail was a symbolic gesture of great political value, but there is no evidence to indicate that it was anything more.

Genuinely fearful of losing support for other programs, Kennedy sent no new civil rights legislation to Congress in 1961 and 1962. During the campaign, he had castigated President Dwight D. Eisenhower for tolerating segregation in federally financed housing, but it took him two years to make good on his promise to eliminate it with "a stroke of the presidential pen." (He received thousands of pens through the mail.) Even then he acted deviously, burying the order among more dramatic acts so that the presidential deed earned him little credit or blame. He did appoint Vice President Johnson to head a new Committee on Equal Employment Opportunity, and that blunt southerner, whose manner and politics were so unappealing to the liberal taste, used his powers of persuasion with some success to insure that blacks would be employed under all types of federal contracts. In addresses at Gettysburg and Detroit in 1963 Johnson spoke sincerely and strongly for full civil rights. Kennedy also appointed a prominent black, Robert C. Weaver, as federal housing administrator. Yet the president generally followed the Eisenhower pattern and seemed not to realize the explosive potential of the race situation. Had he sensed it, he might not have appointed his brother attorney general, for that office would have much white resentment directed at it. It was Robert Kennedy, in fact, who accomplished what little the government did for blacks before 1963. He tried to enforce the weak laws of the 1950's, especially those requiring the desegregation of transportation facilities, although in 1962, the Federal Aviation Agency awarded a $2 million grant for the building of an airport in Jackson, Mississippi, with segregated restaurants and restrooms. Robert Kennedy sped voter registration of southern blacks. The freedom rides of 1961, designed to desegrate bus-station waiting rooms, led the attorney general, who had tried to discourage the project, to send federal marshals into Alabama to protect the riders. His efforts were largely canceled out when his brother appointed several outspoken segregationists to lifetime positions on southern district courts.

The civil rights movement proceeded without John Kennedy, although it eventually forced him to act. Coverage by the media sustained the sense that a new age was coming. Television in particular dramatically transmitted the new tactics of confrontation and the concomitant threat of violence from the racist opposition, and the posing of simple moral demands. The momentum begun in 1961 with the freedom rides continued in the fall of 1962 with James Meredith's attempted enrollment at the University of Mississippi. Federal troops came to the university to enroll Meredith, while the president went on television and radio to appeal for obedience to the law. In the spring of 1963, Vivian Malone and James Hood entered the University of Alabama under the protection of federal soldiers. The most incendiary situation, however, developed in Birmingham, Alabama, that May. The only strategy that could work for the oppressed blacks in that city was the forcing of massive arrests. The scenes and events that transpired placed an overwhelming demand on the national conscience: police dogs, electric cattle prods, fire hoses, rioting, and a church bombing that left four black children dead. Kennedy, foreseeing the "fires of frustration and discord . . . burning in every city, North and South," responded. By now, he, a majority of Congress, the churches, and much of the nation had finally awakened. The president requested a partial ban on discrimination in public places, asked Congress to give the Justice Department the power to sue for school desegregation, and urged broader authority to withhold funds from federally assisted programs in which discrimination occurred. Congressional civil rights leaders pushed Kennedy further, persuading him to give the attorney general power to intervene in all civil rights cases. But Kennedy told a press conference that tax reform was more important than the civil rights bill. A stronger economy, he believed, would help blacks more than anything else. But before his death later that fall, he secured an agreement from congressional leaders that would probably have led to the passage of a civil rights act in 1964.

Martin Luther King, Jr., complained in June 1963 that while Kennedy had perhaps done "a little more" for blacks than Eisenhower, "the plight of the vast majority of Negroes remains the same." King was the hero of the movement. When 250,000 people marched on Washington the next August to be counted for the proposed legislation, King addressed them:

I have a dream that one day on the red hills of Georgia the sons of former slaves and the sons of former slaveholders will be able to sit down together at the table of brotherhood. I have a dream that one day even the state of Mississippi, a desert state sweltering with the heat of injustice and oppression, will be transformed into an oasis of freedom and justice. . . . I have a dream that one day the state of Alabama . . . will be transformed into a situation where little black boys and black girls will be able to join hands with little white boys and white girls and walk together as sisters and brothers.

Yet despite Kennedy's failure to share King's vision, the president's assassination that November resulted in an outpouring of grief in black communities. Efforts to pass legislation gained strength by their being construed as a memorial to Kennedy; Congress easily approved his rights bill in 1964, and others followed in 1965 and 1966.

If the origins of the missile crisis had been Soviet rather than American, Kennedy had nonetheless given it the direction it took; and his television appearance, although the character of the event virtually dictated it, represented his active, decisive engagement. With regard to the civil rights movement, however, the president did scarcely anything that could convincingly be called an initiative. Yet we must include the movement, and indeed give it central placement, within that public collective experience that is associated with Kennedy's presidency. He deserves some credit for this. In 1957 President Eisenhower, in electing to use the Arkansas National Guard and federal troops to enforce integration in the Little Rock school system against the governor's orders, had made a choice far less predictable than we might today think it. Eisenhower had established that, in such cases, a customary American bias in favor of states' rights would not prevent the employment of federal military power against state authority. However late in coming, Kennedy's decision to give governmental countenance to the civil rights movement was comparably innovative, for the tactics of mass demonstrations, religious witness, and civil disobedience directed against institutions that embodied deep, traditional, and popular prejudices were not the kinds of conduct that administrations could ordinarily be expected to deal with on friendly terms. In publicly allying the government with the movement, Kennedy gave the cause a look of inevitability, of being in the main flow of American life. The more general feelings of energy, electricity, and challenge that attended the Kennedy presidency may have made a further, intangible contribution to the struggle for civil rights. The movement itself, of course, was responsible for a good portion of that feeling, and the presidency may have been more its beneficiary than its agent. But this is to say that the relationship of Kennedy to the Kennedy era is elusive.

The early nonviolent civil rights movement died with Kennedy or soon afterward. It had been a fragile coalition. Dependent on keeping the race issue confined to the South, and on receiving the support of poor blacks unable to profit immediately from the achievement of its goals, the movement broke apart during the time of demonstrations in the North, ghetto riots, and growing black nationalism.

In the 1960 campaign Kennedy had charged the Eisenhower administration with failing to maintain as high a national growth rate as that of Western Europe or the Soviet Union. Once in office, however, he began by acting cautiously.

To cure the recession that Nixon later claimed had cost him the presidency, Kennedy relied on piecemeal measures, including the raising of social security payments and the minimum wage—measures akin to those Eisenhower had employed. An increase in military spending, too, helped alleviate unemployment. The new president faced problems that discouraged more forthright fiscal or monetary tactics, notably an adverse balance of payments. Until the third quarter of 1962 his prudent policies held the cost of living steady without causing either much inflation or substantial new unemployment.

A severe drop in the stock market began in May 1962. It threatened the country's somewhat shaky prosperity and persuaded Kennedy to embark upon a more venturesome policy. The patient counsel of Walter Heller, his chief economic adviser, had convinced Treasury Secretary Douglas Dillon, a Republican, of the need for more federal action. For the first time during relatively prosperous times, an administration proposed a budget deficit through tax reduction, an action that was much more acceptable to business than new spending. The Senate concurred in a reversal of its earlier views. Senator Paul Douglas, asking in 1958 for a $6 billion tax cut, had been rebuffed by a vote of 65 to 23. Yet in February 1964, 77 senators favored a tax cut of over $10 billion— and at a time when the economy merely lagged. The economy responded; the tax cuts helped spur a $30 billion yearly increase in stable dollars in the gross national product, and unemployment declined sharply.

Businesses profited enormously from the expansive economy. Kennedy in 1962 signed tax credits and a generous depreciation allowance for business, and in 1963 reduced corporate income taxes by 20 percent. These were gifts of unprecedented generosity. The Trade Expansion Act of 1962 won some economic concessions from the European Common Market through a mutual reduction of tariffs. But business never trusted Kennedy, and in April of that year he had so severe a clash with the steel industry that in the minds of many representatives of business, his name would join in opprobrium that of Franklin Roosevelt.

Late in the afternoon of April 10, 1962, Roger Blough, chairman of the board of United States Steel, appeared at the White House for an appointment with the president. He told Kennedy that even as they spoke press releases were announcing a rise in the price of steel. The president was furious. On the understanding that prices would remain steady, Secretary of Labor Arthur Goldberg had persuaded the unions to settle for a modest wage hike. Kennedy privately quoted his father's denunciation of businessmen as "sons of bitches" and launched an unprecedented government attack on the industry. The Defense Department threatened to shift steel contracts to the small companies that had not yet raised prices; the Justice Department and the Federal Trade Commission warned of antitrust action and the passage of new antitrust laws; the Treasury Department hinted at a tax investigation. Kennedy himself spoke on television: "In this serious hour in our nation's history, when we are confronted with grave crises in Berlin and Southeast Asia, . . . the American public will find it hard, as I do, to accept a situation in which a tiny handful of steel executives whose pursuit of private power and profit exceeds their sense of public responsibility can show such utter contempt of the interests of 185 million Americans." Big steel, following the lead of some smaller companies, grudgingly rescinded the increase.

Belatedly successful in managing the economy, Kennedy late in 1963 was giving genuine promise of responding more to domestic needs. Then, on November 22, he went to Dallas. The city has a Texas way of attaining its objects: its football stadium and its ultra-modern airport are expressions of its will to make for itself, quickly and on a grand scale, the kind of civic life it wanted. The confident American energies that the Kennedy administration wished to marshal and represent were a good deal like that, although the Kennedy rhetoric emphasized the intractable difficulties of the world toward which those energies were to be directed, and the tempering and restraint that must qualify their character. The speech that the president had planned to deliver in Dallas celebrated American military might, but also argued for care in its employment. If delivered, Kennedy's address to Dallas would have provided a minor but telling incident in the Kennedy presidency, a confrontation between two views, only marginally different, of the nature and possibilities of American technological power.

The assassination gave final form to the public that John F. Kennedy's administration had molded. There were the televised funeral procession down Pennsylvania Avenue, the grave at Arlington, the remembrance of a promising presidency that had ended with the dignity of a state funeral. There has also been the continuing public obsession with the idea that the murder must have been the work of a conspiracy, perhaps a plot involving the CIA, or the Mafia, or unknown individuals. The Warren Commission Report on the assassination, which declared that only a single gunman had been involved, was itself so incomplete as to play to the mind that looks for conspiracies. Lee Harvey Oswald, in fact, fits a chilling model of assassins: victims of disrupted childhoods, loners lacking in remorse or any clear idea of what they have done, confused followers of large causes that can give some order and certainty to the world that has provided so little order for their own lives. Oswald had built himself a secret world of schemes. According to a schoolmate, he "seemed to be a boy that was looking for something to belong to, but I don't think anybody was looking for him to belong to them." Conspiracy theories deny the uncertainty and chanciness within life that Oswald had experienced so much of and felt himself compelled to overcome. His upbringing had been disordered and had lacked a spine of principles and projects. His Marxist politics, from which the assassination probably sprang, was probably an attempt to discover order behind an existence that must have seemed maliciously purposeless. The flesh and blood Oswald takes the mystery, and the grandiose conspiracy, out of the story. He fired on Kennedy, we may suppose, to take revenge on an uncaring world. Still, questions about the assassination persist, and in their own way they reflect and help to sustain the memory of the young president.

How did Kennedy and liberalism come into their alliance? It is a reasonable assumption that Kennedy by his later days had developed some genuine convictions that made him and the liberals acceptable to each other: he was, after all, a northeastern, urban Democrat. But it is more revealing of the character of liberalism and of Kennedy to point to matters of circumstance and mental tone that brought them into partnership. Liberals in 1960 desired a more active national enterprise than the Republicans had been providing, and Kennedy's vigorous person promised that. The sheer feeling of activity that his presidency generated was tonic to his liberal supporters. And whatever it was in Kennedy that relished motion and drama, or responded intellectually to the complexities of political and diplomatic strategy, could fix on liberal objectives and on working toward the sort of world in which liberals wanted to live. He could conduct a foreign policy that put a variety of resources into play and anticipated shifts in objectives within the communist nations and a domestic policy that was at least open to most constructive plans for change. The distinctive service of the Kennedy presidency to American liberalism was not to devise a collection of ideas or programs, but rather to create a conjunction of liberalism, government, and some of the most progressive impulses of the time.

The John F. Kennedy Inaugural Address

John F. Kennedy set proud goals for his administration in 1961, promising that "a new generation of Americans" would march forth to do battle with "the common enemies of man: tyranny, poverty, disease and war itself." But the Kennedy administration was to be a brief one —two years and ten months from the "trumpet summons" of the inauguration to the muffled drums and caissons marching slowly up Pennsylvania Avenue in November 1963. This foreshortened story of beginnings and promises, then, is a hard one to interpret. Were the hopes real? Was the vitality an illusion? Was there substance behind the glittering style? Was the New Frontier a beckoning horizon or an armed border, a fresh direction or only a new rhetoric? The answers remain "blowing in the wind"—a phrase directly from the Kennedy era.

Kennedy's inaugural address set the tone for his administration as few such addresses have ever done. The elevation, the magnetic tone of dedication and of hope comes across in the way of words chiseled in granite. Thousands, perhaps millions, of Americans have read these words on Kennedy's tombstone in Arlington National Cemetery. Yet a close reading of this famous speech reveals subtle counterthemes that suggest possible answers to the questions that were subsequently raised after John F. Kennedy's death: about his place in American history, his administration's continuity, or discontinuity, with his predecessors' policies, and the substance lodged beneath the glittering language. Ask yourself what the various publics listening to this speech would have understood by it. What would a civil rights worker have derived from it? A conservative congressman? A Pentagon policy planner? The Soviet foreign ministry? John F. Kennedy was never easy to evaluate, and his untimely death left a legacy of controversy and unanswered questions surrounding him that history may never resolve.

We observe today not a victory of party but a celebration of freedom—symbolizing an end as well as a beginning—signifying renewal as well as change. For I have sworn before you and Almighty God the same solemn oath our forebears prescribed nearly a century and three quarters ago.

The world is very different now. For man holds in his mortal hands the power to abolish all forms of human poverty and all forms of human life. And yet the same revolutionary beliefs for which our forebears fought are still at issue around the globe—the belief that the rights of man come not from the generosity of the state but from the hand of God.

We dare not forget today that we are the heirs of that first revolution. Let the word go forth from this time and place, to friend and foe alike, that the torch has been passed to a new generation of Americans—born in this century, tempered by war, disciplined by a hard and bitter peace,

183

proud of our ancient heritage—and unwilling to witness or permit the slow undoing of those human rights to which this nation has always been committed, and to which we are committed today at home and around the world.

Let every nation know, whether it wishes us well or ill, that we shall pay any price, bear any burden, meet any hardship, support any friend, oppose any foe to assure the survival and the success of liberty.

This much we pledge—and more.

To those old allies whose cultural and spiritual origins we share, we pledge the loyalty of faithful friends. United, there is little we cannot do in a host of cooperative ventures. Divided, there is little we can do—for we dare not meet a powerful challenge at odds and split asunder.

To those new states whom we welcome to the ranks of the free, we pledge our word that one form of colonial control shall not have passed away merely to be replaced by a far more iron tyranny. We shall not always expect to find them supporting our view. But we shall always hope to find them strongly supporting their own freedom—and to remember that, in the past, those who foolishly sought power by riding the back of the tiger ended up inside.

To those peoples in the huts and villages of half the globe struggling to break the bonds of mass misery, we pledge our best efforts to help them help themselves, for whatever period is required—not because the communists may be doing it, not because we seek their votes, but because it is right. If a free society cannot help the many who are poor, it cannot save the few who are rich.

To our sister republics south of our border, we offer a special pledge —to convert our good words into good deeds—in a new alliance for progress—to assist free men and free governments in casting off the chains of poverty. But this peaceful revolution of hope cannot become the prey of hostile powers. Let all our neighbors know that we shall join with them to oppose aggression or subversion anywhere in the Americas. And let every other power know that this Hemisphere intends to remain the master of its own house.

To that world assembly of sovereign states, the United Nations, our last best hope in an age where the instruments of war have far outpaced the instruments of peace, we renew our pledge of support—to prevent it from becoming merely a forum for invective—to strengthen its shield of the new and the weak—and to enlarge the area in which its writ may run.

Finally, to those nations who would make themselves our adversary, we offer not a pledge but a request: that both sides begin anew the quest for peace, before the dark powers of destruction unleashed by science engulf all humanity in planned or accidental self-destruction.

We dare not tempt them with weakness. For only when our arms are sufficient beyond doubt can we be certain beyond doubt that they will never be employed.

But neither can two great and powerful groups of nations take comfort from our present course—both sides overburdened by the cost of modern weapons, both rightly alarmed by the steady spread of the deadly atom, yet both racing to alter that uncertain balance of terror that stays the hand of mankind's final war.

So let us begin anew—remembering on both sides that civility is not a sign of weakness, and sincerity is always subject to proof. Let us never negotiate out of fear. But let us never fear to negotiate.

Let both sides explore what problems unite us instead of belaboring those problems which divide us.

Let both sides, for the first time, formulate serious and precise proposals for the inspection and control of arms—and bring the absolute power to destroy other nations under the absolute control of all nations.

Let both sides seek to invoke the wonders of science instead of its terrors. Together let us explore the stars, conquer the deserts, eradicate disease, tap the ocean depths and encourage the arts and commerce.

Let both sides unite to heed in all corners of the earth the command of Isaiah—to "undo the heavy burdens . . . [and] let the oppressed go free."

And if a beach-head of cooperation may push back the jungle of suspicion, let both sides join in creating a new endeavor, not a new balance of power, but a new world of law, where the strong are just and the weak secure and the peace preserved.

All this will not be finished in the first one hundred days. Nor will it be finished in the first one thousand days, nor in the life of this Administration, nor even perhaps in our lifetime on this planet. But let us begin.

In your hands, my fellow citizens, more than mine, will rest the final success or failure of our course. Since this country was founded, each generation of Americans has been summoned to give testimony to its national loyalty. The graves of young Americans who answered the call to service surround the globe.

Now the trumpet summons us again—not as a call to bear arms, though arms we need—not as a call to battle, though embattled we are —but a call to bear the burden of a long twilight struggle, year in and year out, "rejoicing in hope, patient in tribulation"—a struggle against the common enemies of man: tyranny, poverty, disease and war itself.

Can we forge against these enemies a grand global alliance, North and South, East and West, that can assure a more fruitful life for all mankind? Will you join in that historic effort?

In the long history of the world, only a few generations have been granted the role of defending freedom in its hour of maximum danger. I do not shrink from this responsibility—I welcome it. I do not believe that any of us would exchange places with any other people or any other generation. The energy, the faith, the devotion which we bring to this endeavor will light our country and all who serve it—and the glow from that fire can truly light the world.

And so, my fellow Americans: ask not what your country can do for you—ask what you can do for your country.

My fellow citizens of the world: ask not what America will do for you, but what together we can do for the freedom of man.

Finally, whether you are citizens of America or citizens of the world, ask of us here the same high standards of strength and sacrifice which we ask of you. With a good conscience our only sure reward, with history the final judge of our deeds, let us go forth to lead the land we love, asking His blessing and His help, but knowing that here on earth God's work must truly be our own.

The Port Huron Statement

STUDENTS FOR A DEMOCRATIC SOCIETY

The radical tradition in America is a series of episodes, not a continuous story. Where conservatives and liberals never cease reaching back for real or imaginary forbears, radicals have generally insisted on forgetting the history of radicalism as the first act in any new beginning. In the early 1960's, when the Students for a Democratic Society spread from campus to campus, drawing together activists in the civil rights and peace movements, the group received compliments for precisely this tendency to forget the radical past. It was "pragmatic," "non-ideological," and "non-programmatic." The movement worried little about its intellectual underpinnings; its main concern was action. The Port Huron Statement, drawn up at the first SDS convention in 1962, achieved wide circulation on the campuses as an "agenda for a generation."

The document, written principally by Tom Hayden, is impressive in surprising ways. Its tentative assertions, social science language, and generally nationalistic and cooperative stance contrast sharply with the image of campus militancy of the later 1960's. In its quiet way, however, it states the main themes of the youth political movement: rejection of bureaucracy, anti-communism, alienation, and the lack of community. It is clearly the beginning of a quest, not a set of final answers. Where that quest led was one of the fascinating subjects of the decade. It raises the inevitable question—to what extent did the young radicals relive the experience of earlier radicals because they began by rejecting its lessons?

INTRODUCTION: AGENDA FOR A GENERATION

We are people of this generation, bred in at least modest comfort, housed now in universities, looking uncomfortably to the world we inherit.

When we were kids the United States was the wealthiest and strongest country in the world; the only one with the atom bomb, the least scarred by modern war, an initiator of the United Nations that we thought would distribute Western influence throughout the world. Freedom and equality for each individual, government of, by, and for the people—these American values we found good, principles by which we could live as men. Many of us began maturing in complacency.

As we grew, however, our comfort was penetrated by events too troubling to dismiss. First, the permeating and victimizing fact of human degradation, symbolized by the Southern struggle against racial bigotry, compelled most of us from silence to activism. Second, the enclosing fact of the Cold War, symbolized by the presence of the Bomb, brought awareness that we ourselves, and our friends, and millions of abstract "others" we knew more directly because of our common peril, might die at any time. We might deliberately ignore, or avoid, or fail to feel all other human problems, but not these two, for these were too immediate and crushing in their impact, too challenging in the demand that we as individuals take the responsibility for encounter and resolution.

While these and other problems either directly oppressed us or rankled our consciences and became our own subjective concerns, we began to see complicated and disturbing paradoxes in our surrounding America. The declaration "all men are created equal . . ." rang hollow before the facts of Negro life in the South and the big cities of the North. The proclaimed peaceful intentions of the United States contradicted its economic and military investments in the Cold War status quo.

We witnessed, and continue to witness, other paradoxes. With nuclear energy whole cities can easily be powered, yet the dominant nation-states seem more likely to unleash destruction greater than that incurred in all wars of human history. Although our own technology is destroying old and creating new forms of social organization, men still tolerate meaningless work and idleness. While two-thirds of mankind suffers undernourishment, our own upper classes revel amidst superfluous abundance. Although world population is expected to double in forty years, the nations still tolerate anarchy as a major principle of international conduct and uncontrolled exploitation governs the sapping of the earth's physical resources. Although mankind desperately needs revolutionary leadership, America rests in national stalemate, its goals ambiguous and tradition-bound instead of informed and clear, its democratic system apathetic and manipulated rather than "of, by, and for the people."

Not only did tarnish appear on our image of American virtue, not only did disillusion occur when the hypocrisy of American ideals was discovered, but we began to sense that what we had originally seen as the American Golden Age was actually the decline of an era. The worldwide outbreak of revolution against colonialism and imperialism, the entrenchment of totalitarian states, the menace of war, overpopulation, international disorder, supertechnology—these trends were testing the tenacity of our own commitment to democracy and freedom and our abilities to visualize their application to a world in upheaval.

Our work is guided by the sense that we may be the last generation in the experiment with living. But we are a minority—the vast majority of our people regard the temporary equilibriums of our society and world as eternally-functional parts. In this is perhaps the outstanding paradox: we ourselves are imbued with urgency, yet the message of our society is that there is no viable alternative to the present. Beneath the reassuring tones of the politicians, beneath the common opinion that America will "muddle through," beneath the stagnation of those who have closed their minds to the future, is the pervading feeling that there simply are no alternatives, that our times have witnessed the exhaustion not only of Utopias, but of any new departures as well.

Feeling the press of complexity upon the emptiness of life, people are fearful of the thought that at any moment things might be thrust out of control. They fear change itself, since change might smash whatever invisible framework seems to hold back chaos for them now. For most Americans, all crusades are suspect, threatening. The fact that each individual sees apathy in his fellows perpetuates the common reluctance to organize for change. The dominant institutions are complex enough to blunt the minds of their potential critics, and entrenched enough to swiftly dissipate or entirely repel the energies of protest and reform, thus limiting human expectancies. Then, too, we are a materially improved society, and by our own improvements we seem to have weakened the case for further change.

Some would have us believe that Americans feel contentment amidst prosperity—but might it not be better be called a glaze above deeply-felt anxieties about their role in the new world? And if these anxieties produce a developed indifference to human affairs, do they not as well produce a yearning to believe there *is* an alternative to the present, that something *can* be done to change circumstances in the school, the workplaces, the bureaucracies, the government? It is to this latter yearning, at once the spark and engine of change, that we direct our present appeal. The search for truly democratic alternatives to the present, and a commitment to social experimentation with them, is a worthy and fulfilling human enterprise, one which moves us and, we hope, others today. On such a basis do we offer this document of our convictions and analysis: as an effort in understanding and changing the conditions of humanity in the late twentieth century, an effort rooted in the ancient, still unfulfilled conception of man attaining determining influence over his circumstances of life. . . .

THE STUDENTS

In the last few years, thousands of American students demonstrated that they at least felt the urgency of the times. They moved actively and directly against racial injustices, the threat of war, violations of individual rights of conscience and, less frequently, against economic manipulation. They suceeded in restoring a small measure of controversy to the campuses after the stillness of the McCarthy period. They succeeded, too, in gaining some concessions from the people and institutions they opposed, especially in the fight against racial bigotry.

The significance of these scattered movements lies not in their success or failure in gaining objectives—at least not yet. Nor does the significance lie in the intellectual "competence" or "maturity" of the students involved—as some pedantic elders allege. The significance is in the fact the students are breaking the crust of apathy and overcoming the inner alienation that remain the defining characteristics of American college life.

If student movements for change are still rareties on the campus scene, what is commonplace there? The real campus, the familiar campus, is a place of private people, engaged in their notorious "inner emigration." It is a place of commitment to business-as-usual, getting ahead, playing it cool. It is a place of mass affirmation of the Twist, but mass reluctance toward the controversial public stance. Rules are accepted as "inevitable," bureaucracy as "just circumstances," irrelevance as "scholarship," selflessness as "martyrdom," politics as "just another way to make people, and an unprofitable one, too."

Almost no students value activity as citizens. Passive in public, they are hardly more idealistic in arranging their private lives: Gallup concludes they will settle for "low success, and won't risk high failure." There is not much willingness to take risks (not even in business), no settling of dangerous goals, no real conception of personal identity except one manufactured in the image of others, no real urge for personal fulfillment except to be almost as successful as the very successful people. Attention is being paid to social status (the quality of shirt collars, meeting people, getting wives or husbands, making solid contacts for later on); much, too, is paid to academic status (grades, honors, the med school rat race). But neglected generally is real intellectual status, the personal cultivation of the mind.

"Students don't even give a damn about the apathy," one has said. Apathy toward apathy begets a privately-constructed universe, a place of systematic study schedules, two nights each week for beer, a girl or two, and early marriage; a framework infused with personality, warmth, and under control, no matter how unsatisfying otherwise.

Under these conditions university life loses all relevance to some. Four hundred thousand of our classmates leave college every year.

But apathy is not simply an attitude; it is a product of social institutions, and of the structure and organization of higher education itself. The extracurricular life is ordered according to *in loco parentis* theory, which ratifies the Administration as the moral guardian of the young.

The accompanying "let's pretend" theory of student extracurricular affairs validates student government as a training center for those who want to spend their lives in political pretense, and discourages initiative from the more articulate, honest, and sensitive students. The bounds and style of controversy are delimited before controversy begins. The university "prepares" the student for "citizenship" through perpetual rehearsals and, usually, through emasculation of what creative spirit there is in the individual.

The academic life contains reinforcing counterparts to the way in which extracurricular life is organized. The academic world is founded on a teacher-student relation analogous to the parent-child relation which characterizes *in loco parentis*. Further, academia includes a radical separation of the student from the material of study. That which is studied, the social reality, is "objectified" to sterility, dividing the student from life—just as he is restrained in active involvement by the deans controlling student government. The specialization of function and knowledge, admittedly necessary to our complex technological and social structure, has produced an exaggerated compartmentalization of study and understanding. This has contributed to an overly parochial view, by faculty, of the role of its research and scholarship, to a discontinuous and truncated understanding, by students, of the surrounding social order; and to a loss of personal attachment, by nearly all, to the worth of study as a humanistic enterprise.

There is, finally, the cumbersome academic bureaucracy extending throughout the academic as well as the extracurricular structures, contributing to the sense of outer complexity and inner powerlessness that transforms the honest searching of many students to a ratification of convention and, worse, to a numbness to present and future catastrophes. The size and financing systems of the university enhance the permanent trusteeship of the administrative bureaucracy, their power leading to a shift within the university toward the value standards of business and the administrative mentality. Huge foundations and other private financial interests shape the under-financed colleges and universities, not only making them more commercial, but less disposed to diagnose society critically, less open to dissent. Many social and physical scientists, neglecting the liberating heritage of higher learning, develop "human relations" or "morale-producing" techniques for the corporate economy, while others exercise their intellectual skills to accelerate the arms race.

Tragically, the university could serve as a significant source of social criticism and an initiator of new modes and molders of attitudes. But the actual intellectual effect of the college experience is hardly distinguishable from that of any other communications channel—say, a television set—passing on the stock truths of the day. Students leave college somewhat more "tolerant" than when they arrived, but basically unchallenged in their values and political orientations. With administrators ordering the institution, and faculty the curriculum, the student learns by his isolation to accept elite rule within the university, which prepares him to accept later forms of minority control. The real function of the educational system—as opposed to its more rhetorical function of "searching for truth"—is to impart the key information and styles that will help the student get by, modestly but comfortably, in the big society beyond.

THE SOCIETY BEYOND

Look beyond the campus, to America itself. That student life is more intellectual, and perhaps more comfortable, does not obscure the fact that the fundamental qualities of life on the campus reflect the habits of society at large. The fraternity president is seen at the junior manager levels; the sorority queen has gone to Grosse Pointe; the serious poet burns for a place, any place, to work; the once-serious and never-serious poets work at the advertising agencies. The desperation of people threatened by forces about which they know little and of which they can say less; the cheerful emptiness of people "giving up" all hope of changing things; the faceless ones polled by Gallup who listed "international affairs" fourteenth on their list of "problems" but who also expected thermonuclear war in the next few years; in these and other forms, Americans are in withdrawal from public life, from any collective effort at directing their own affairs.

Some regard these national doldrums as a sign of healthy approval of the established order—but is it approval by consent or manipulated acquiescence? Others declare that the people are withdrawn because compelling issues are fast disappearing—perhaps there are fewer bread-lines in America, but is Jim Crow gone, is there enough work and work more fulfilling, is world war a diminishing threat, and what of the revolutionary new peoples? Still others think the national quietude is a necessary consequence of the need for elites to resolve complex and specialized problems of modern industrial society—but, then, why should *business* elites help decide foreign policy, and who controls the elites anyway, and are they solving mankind's problems? Others, finally, shrug knowingly and announce that full democracy never worked anywhere in the past—but why lump qualitatively different civilizations together, and how can a social order work well if its best thinkers are skeptics, and is man really doomed forever to the domination of today?

There are no convincing apologies for the contemporary malaise. While the world tumbles toward final war, while men in other nations are trying desperately to alter events, while the very future qua future is uncertain—America is without community, impulse, without the in-ner momentum necessary for an age when societies cannot successfully perpetuate themselves by their military weapons, when democracy must be viable because of the quality of life, not its quantity of rockets.

The apathy here is, first *subjective*—the felt powerlessness of ordi-nary people, the resignation before the enormity of events. But subjec-tive apathy is encouraged by the *objective* American situation—the actual structural separation of people from power, from relevant knowledge, from pinnacles of decision-making. Just as the university influences the student way of life, so do major social institutions create the circum-stances in which the isolated citizen will try hopelessly to understand his world and himself.

The very isolation of the individual—from power and community and ability to aspire—means the rise of a democracy without publics. With the great mass of people structurally remote and psychologically hesitant with respect to democratic institutions, those institutions them-selves attenuate and become, in the fashion of the vicious circle, pro-gressively less accessible to those few who aspire to serious participation in social affairs. The vital democratic connection between community and leadership, between the mass and the several elites, has been so wrenched and perverted that disastrous policies go unchallenged time and again.

POLITICS WITHOUT PUBLICS

The American political system is not the democratic model of which its glorifiers speak. In actuality it frustrates democracy by con-fusing the individual citizen, paralyzing policy discussion, and consoli-dating the irresponsible power of military and business interests.

A crucial feature of the political apparatus in America is that greater differences are harbored within each major party than the differences existing between them. Instead of two parties presenting distinctive and significant differences of approach, what dominates the system is a natural interlocking of Democrats from Southern states with the more conservative elements of the Republican party. This arrangement of forces is blessed by the seniority system of Congress which guarantees congressional committee domination by conservatives—ten of 17 committees in the Senate and 13 of 21 in the House of Representatives are chaired currently by Dixiecrats.

The party overlap, however, is not the only structural antagonist of democracy in politics. First, the localized nature of the party system does not encourage discussion of national and international issues: thus problems are not raised by and for people, and political representatives usually are unfettered from any responsibilities to the general public except those regarding parochial matters. Second, whole constituencies are divested of the full political power they might have: many Negroes in the South are prevented from voting, migrant workers are disenfranchised by various residence requirements, some urban and suburban dwellers are victimized by gerrymandering, and poor people are too often without the power to obtain political representation. Third, the focus of political attention is significantly distorted by the enormous lobby force, composed predominantly of business interests, spending hundreds of millions each year in an attempt to conform facts about productivity, agriculture, defense, and social services, to the wants of private economic groupings.

What emerges from the party contradiction and insulation of privately-held power is the organized political stalemate: calcification dominates flexibility as the principle of parliamentary organization, frustration is the expectancy of legislators intending liberal reform, and Congress becomes less and less central to national decision-making especially in the area of foreign policy. In this context, confusion and blurring is built into the formulation of issues, long-range priorities are not discussed in the rational manner needed for policy-making, the politics of personality and "image" become a more important mechanism than the construction of issues in a way that affords each voter a challenging and real option. The American voter is buffeted from all directions by pseudo-problems, by the structurally-initiated sense that nothing political is subject to human mastery. Worried by his mundane problems which never get solved, but constrained by the common belief that politics is an agonizingly slow accommodation of views, he quits all pretense of bothering.

A most alarming fact is that few, if any, politicians are calling for changes in these conditions. Only a handful even are calling on the President to "live up to" platform pledges; no one is demanding structural changes, such as the shuttling of Southern Democrats out of the Democratic Party. Rather than protesting the state of politics, most politicians are reinforcing and aggravating that state. While in practice they rig public opinion to suit their own interests, in word and ritual they enshrine "the sovereign public" and call for more and more letters. Their speeches and campaign actions are banal, based on a degrading conception of what people want to hear. They respond not to dialogue, but to pressure: and knowing this, the ordinary citizen sees even greater inclination to shun the political sphere. The politician is usually a trumpeter to "citizenship" and "service to the nation," but since he is unwilling to seriously rearrange power relationships, his trumpetings only increase apathy by creating no outlets. Much of the time the call to "service" is justified not in idealistic terms, but in the crasser terms of "defending the free world from communism"—thus making future idealistic impulses harder to justify in anything but Cold War terms.

In such a setting of status quo politics, where most if not all government activity is rationalized in Cold War anti-communist terms, it is somewhat natural that discontented, super-patriotic groups would emerge through political channels and explain their ultra-conservatism as the best means of Victory over Communism. They have become a politically influential force within the Republican Party, at a national level through Senator Goldwater, and at a local level through their important social and economic roles. Their political views are defined generally as the opposite of the supposed views of communists: complete individual freedom in the economic sphere, non-participation by the government in the machinery of production. But actually "anti-communism" becomes an umbrella by which to protest liberalism, internationalism, welfareism, the active civil rights and labor movements. It is to the disgrace of the United States that such a movement should become a prominent kind of public participation in the modern world—but, ironically, it is somewhat to the interests of the United States that such a movement should be a public constituency pointed toward realignment of the political parties, demanding a conservative Republican Party in the South and an exclusion of the "leftist" elements of the national GOP.

THE ECONOMY

American capitalism today advertises itself as the Welfare State. Many of us comfortably expect pensions, medical care, unemployment compensation, and other social services in our lifetimes. Even with one-fourth of our productive capacity unused, the majority of Americans are living in relative comfort—although their nagging incentive to "keep up" makes them continually dissatisfied with their possessions. In many places, unrestrained bosses, uncontrolled machines, and sweatshop conditions have been reformed or abolished and suffering tremendously relieved. But in spite of the benign yet obscuring effects of the New Deal reforms and the reassuring phrases of government economists and politicians, the paradoxes and myths of the economy are sufficient to irritate our complacency and reveal to us some essential causes of the American malaise.

We live amidst a national celebration of economic prosperity while poverty and deprivation remain an unbreakable way of life for millions in the "affluent society," including many of our own generation. We hear glib references to the "welfare state," "free enterprise," and "shareholder's democracy" while military defense is the main item of "public" spending and obvious oligopoly and other forms of minority rule defy real individual initiative or popular control. Work, too, is often unfulfilling and victimizing, accepted as a channel to status or plenty, if not a way to pay the bills, rarely as a means of understanding and controlling self and events. In work and leisure the individual is regulated as part of the system, a consuming unit, bombarded by hard-sell, soft-sell, lies and semi-true appeals to his basest drives. He is always told that he is a "free" man because of "free enterprise." . . .

THE MILITARY-INDUSTRIAL COMPLEX

The most spectacular and important creation of the authoritarian and oligopolistic structure of economic decision-making in America is the institution called "the military-industrial complex" by former President Eisenhower—the powerful congruence of interest and structure among military and business elites which affects so much of our development and destiny. Not only is ours the first generation to live with the possibility of world-wide cataclysm—it is the first to experience the actual social preparation for cataclysm, the general militarization of American society. In 1948 Congress established Universal Military Training, the first peacetime conscription. The military became a permanent institution. Four years earlier, General Motors' Charles E. Wilson had heralded the creation of what he called the "permanent war economy," the continuous use of military spending as a solution to economic problems unsolved before the post-war boom, most notably the problem of the seventeen million jobless after eight years of the New Deal. This has left a "hidden crisis" in the allocation of resources by the American economy.

Since our childhood these two trends—the rise of the military and the installation of a defense-based economy—have grown fantastically. The Department of Defense, ironically the world's largest single organization, is worth $160 billion, owns 32 million acres of America and employs half the 7.5 million persons directly dependent on the military for subsistence, has an $11 billion payroll which is larger than the net annual income of all American corporations. Defense spending in the Eisenhower era totaled $350 billions and President Kennedy entered office pledged to go even beyond the present defense allocation of 60 cents from every public dollar spent. Except for a war-induced boom immediately after "our side" bombed Hiroshima, American economic prosperity has coincided with a growing dependence on military outlay—from 1941 to 1959 America's Gross National Product of $5.25 trillion included $700 billion in goods and services purchased for the defense effort, about one-seventh of the accumulated GNP. This pattern has included the steady concentration of military spending among a few corporations. In 1961, 86 percent of Defense Department contracts were awarded without competition. The ordnance industry of 100,000 people is completely engaged in military work; in the aircraft industry, 94 percent of 750,000 workers are linked to the war economy; shipbuilding, radio and communications equipment industries commit 40 percent of their work to defense; iron and steel, petroleum, metal-stamping and machine shop products, motors and generators, tools and hardware, copper, aluminum and machine tools industries all devote at least 10 percent of their work to the same cause.

The intermingling of Big Military and Big Industry is evidenced in the 1,400 former officers working for the 100 corporations who received nearly all the $21 billion spent in procurement by the Defense Department in 1961. The overlap is most poignantly clear in the case of General Dynamics, the company which received the best 1961 contracts, employed the most retired officers (187), and is directed by a former Secretary of the Army. A *Fortune* magazine profile of General Dynamics said: "The unique group of men who run Dynamics are only incidentally in rivalry with other U.S. manufacturers, with many of whom they actually act in concert. Their chief competitor is the USSR. The core of General Dynamics' corporate philosophy is the conviction that national defense is a more or less permanent business." Little has changed since Wilson's proud declaration of the Permanent War Economy back in the 1944 days when the top 200 corporations possessed 80 percent of all active prime war-supply contracts.

MILITARY-INDUSTRIAL POLITICS

The military and its supporting business foundation have found numerous forms of political expression, and we have heard their din endlessly. There has not been a major Congressional split on the issue of continued defense spending spirals in our lifetime. The triangular relations of the business, military, and political arenas cannot be better expressed than in Dixiecrat Carl Vinson's remarks as his House Armed Services Committee reported out a military construction bill of $808 million throughout the 50 states, for 1960-61: "There is something in this bill for everyone," he announced. President Kennedy had earlier acknowledged the valuable anti-recession features of the bill.

Imagine, on the other hand, $808 million suggested as an anti-recession measure, but being poured into programs of social welfare: the impossibility of receiving support for such a measure identifies a crucial feature of defense spending—it is beneficial to private enterprise, while welfare spending is not. Defense spending does not "compete" with the private sector; it contains a natural obsolescence; its "confidential" nature permits easier boondoggling; the tax burdens to which it leads can be shunted from corporation to consumer as a "cost of production." Welfare spending, however, involves the government in competition with private corporations and contractors; it conflicts with immediate interests of private pressure groups; it leads to taxes on business. Think of the opposition of private power companies to current proposals for river and valley development, or the hostility of the real estate lobby to urban renewal; or the attitude of the American Medical

Association to a paltry medical care bill; or of all business lobbyists to foreign aid; these are the pressures leading to the schizophrenic public-military, private-civilian economy of our epoch. The politicians, of course, take the line of least resistance and thickest support: warfare, instead of welfare, is easiest to stand up for: after all, the Free World is at stake (and our constituency's investments, too). . . .

THE STANCE OF LABOR

Amidst all this, what of organized labor, the historic institutional representative of the exploited, the presumed "countervailing power" against the excesses of Big Business? The contemporary social assault on the labor movement is of crisis proportions. To the average American, "big labor" is a growing cancer equal in impact to Big Business—nothing could be more distorted, even granting a sizeable union bureaucracy. But in addition to public exaggerations, the labor crisis can be measured in several ways. First, the high expectations of the newborn AFL-CIO of 30 million members by 1965 are suffering a reverse unimaginable five years ago. The demise of the dream of "organizing the unorganized" is dramatically reflected in the AFL-CIO decision, just two years after its creation, to slash its organizing staff in half. From 15 million members when the AFL and CIO merged, the total has slipped to 13.5 million. During the post-war generation, union membership nationally has increased by four million—but the total number of workers has jumped by 13 million. Today only 40 percent of all non-agricultural workers are protected by any form of organization. Second, organizing conditions are going to worsen. Where labor now is strongest—in industries—automation is leading to an attrition of available work. As the number of jobs dwindles, so does labor's power of bargaining, since management can handle a strike in an automated plant more easily than the older mass-operated ones.

More important, perhaps, the American economy has changed radically in the last decade, as suddenly the number of workers producing goods became fewer than the number in "nonproductive" areas—government, trade, finance, services, utilities, transportation. Since World War II "white collar" and "service" jobs have grown twice as fast as have "blue collar" production jobs. Labor has almost no organization in the expanding occupational areas of the new economy, but almost all of its entrenched strength in contracting areas. As big government hires more, as business seeks more office workers and skilled technicians, and as growing commercial America demands new hotels, service stations and the like, the conditions will become graver still. Further, there is continuing hostility to labor by the Southern states and their industrial interests—meaning "runaway" plants, cheap labor threatening the organized trade union movement, and opposition from Dixiecrats to favorable labor legislation in Congress. Finally, there is indication that Big Business, for the sake of public relations if nothing more, has acknowledged labor's "right" to exist, but has deliberately tried to contain labor at its present strength, preventing strong unions from helping weaker ones or from spreading to unorganized sectors of the economy. Business is aided in its efforts by proliferation of "right-to-work" laws at state levels (especially in areas where labor is without organizing strength to begin with), and anti-labor legislation in Congress.

In the midst of these besetting crises, labor itself faces its own problems of vision and program. Historically, there can be no doubt as to its worth in American politics—what progress there has been in meeting human needs in this century rests greatly with the labor movement. And to a considerable extent the social democracy for which labor has fought externally is reflected in its own essentially democratic character: representing millions of people, not millions of dollars; demanding their welfare, not eternal profit.

Today labor remains the most liberal "mainstream" institution— but often its liberalism represents vestigial commitments, self-interestedness, unradicalism. In some measure labor has succumbed to institutionalization, its social idealism waning under the tendencies of bureaucracy, materialism, business ethics. The successes of the last generation perhaps have braked, rather than accelerated labor's zeal for change. Even the House of Labor has bay windows: not only is this true of the labor elites, but as well of some of the rank-and-file. Many of the latter are indifferent unionists, uninterested in meetings, alienated from the complexities of the labor-management negotiating apparatus, lulled to comfort by the accessibility of luxury and the opportunity of long-term contracts. "Union democracy" is not simply inhibited by labor-leader elitism, but by the related problem of rank-and-file apathy to the tradition of unionism. The crisis of labor is reflected in the co-existence within the unions of militant Negro discontents and discriminatory locals, sweeping critics of the obscuring "public interest" marginal tinkering of government and willing handmaidens of conservative political leadership, austere sacrificers and business-like operators, visionaries and anachronisms—tensions between extremes that keep alive the possibilities for a more militant unionism. Too there are seeds of rebirth in the "organizational crisis" itself: the technologically unemployed, the unorganized white collar men and women, the migrants and farm workers, the unprotected Negroes, the poor, all of whom are isolated now from the power structure of the economy, but who are the potential base for a broader and more forceful unionism.

HORIZON

In summary: a more reformed, more human capitalism, functioning at three-fourths capacity while one-third of America and two-thirds of the world goes needy, domination of politics and the economy by fantastically rich elites, accommodation and limited effectiveness by the labor movement, hard-core poverty and unemployment, automation confirming the dark ascension of machine over man instead of shared abundance, technological change being introduced into the economy by the criteria of profitability—this has been our inheritance. However inadequate, it has instilled quiescence in liberal hearts—partly reflecting the extent to which misery has been overcome, but also the eclipse of social ideals. Though many of us are "affluent," poverty, waste, elitism, manipulation are too manifest to go unnoticed, too clearly unnecessary to go accepted. To change the Cold War status quo and other social evils, concern with the challenges to the American economic machine must expand. Now, as a truly better social state becomes visible, a new poverty impends: a poverty of vision, and a poverty of political action to make that vision reality. Without new vision, the failure to achieve our potentialities will spell the inability of our society to endure in a world of obvious, crying needs and rapid change. . . .

TOWARDS AMERICAN DEMOCRACY

Every effort to end the Cold War and expand the process of world industrialization is an effort hostile to people and institutions whose interests lie in perpetuation of the East-West military threat and the postponement of change in the "have not" nations of the world. Every such effort, too, is bound to establish greater democracy in America. The major goals of a domestic effort would be:

1 *America must abolish its political party stalemate.*

Two genuine parties, centered around issues and essential values, demanding allegiance to party principles shall supplant the current system of organized stalemate which is seriously inadequate to a world in flux. . . . What is desirable is sufficient party disagreement to dramatize major issues, yet sufficient party overlap to guarantee stable transitions from administration to administration.

Every time the President criticizes a recalcitrant Congress, we must ask that he no longer tolerate the Southern conservatives in the Democratic Party. Every time a liberal representative complains that "we can't expect everything at once" we must ask if we received much of anything from Congress in the last generation. Every time he refers to "circumstances beyond control" we must ask why he fraternizes with racist scoundrels. Every time he speaks of the "unpleasantness of personal and party fighting" we should insist that pleasantry with Dixiecrats is inexcusable when the dark peoples of the world call for American support.

2 *Mechanisms of voluntary association must be created through which political information can be imparted and political participation encouraged.*

Political parties, even if realigned, would not provide adequate outlets for popular involvement. Institutions should be created that engage people with issues and express political preference, not as now with huge business lobbies which exercise undemocratic *power* but which carry political *influence* (appropriate to private, rather than public, groupings) in national decision-making enterprise. Private in nature, these should be organized around single issues (medical care, transportation systems reform, etc.), concrete interest (labor and minority group organizations); multiple issues or general issues. These do not exist in America in quantity today. If they did exist, they would be a significant politicizing and educative force bringing people into touch with public life and affording them means of expression and action. Today, giant lobby representatives of business interests are dominant, but not educative. The Federal government itself should counter the latter forces whose intent is often public deceit for private gain, by subsidizing the preparation and decentralized distribution of objective materials on all public issues facing government.

3 Institutions and practices which stifle dissent should be abolished, and the promotion of peaceful dissent should be actively promoted.

The First Amendment freedoms of speech, assembly, thought, religion and press should be seen as guarantees, not threats, to national security. While society has the right to prevent active subversion of its laws and institutions, it has the duty as well to promote open discussion of all issues—otherwise it will be in fact promoting real subversion as the only means of implementing ideas. To eliminate the fears and apathy from national life it is necessary that the institutions bred by fear and apathy be rooted out: the House Un-American Activities Committee, the Senate Internal Security Committee, the loyalty oaths on Federal loans, the Attorney General's list of subversive organizations, the Smith and McCarran Acts. The process of eliminating the blighting institutions is the process of restoring democratic participation. Their existence is a sign of the decomposition and atrophy of participation.

4 Corporations must be made publicly responsible.

It is not possible to believe that true democracy can exist where a minority utterly controls enormous wealth and power. The influence of corporate elites on foreign policy is neither reliable nor democratic; a way must be found to subordinate private American foreign investment to a democratically-constructed foreign policy. . . .

Labor and government as presently constituted are not sufficient to "regulate" corporations. A new re-ordering, a new calling of responsibility is necessary: more than changing "work rules" we must consider changes in the rules of society by challenging the unchallenged politics of American corporations. Before the government can really begin to control business in a "public interest," the public must gain more substantial control of government: this demands a movement for political as well as economic realignments. We are aware that simple government "regulation," if achieved, would be inadequate without increased worker participation in management decision-making, strengthened and independent regulatory power, balances of partial and/or complete public ownership, various means of humanizing the conditions and types of work itself, sweeping welfare programs and regional *public* development authorities. These are examples of measures to re-balance the economy toward public—and individual—control.

5 *The allocation of resources must be based on social needs. A truly "public sector" must be established, and its nature debated and planned.*

At present the majority of America's "public sector," the largest part of our public spending, is for the military. When great social needs are so pressing, our concept of "government spending" is wrapped up in the "permanent war economy." . . .

The main *private* forces of economic expansion cannot guarantee a steady rate of growth, nor acceptable recovery from recession—especially in a demilitarizing world. Government participation will inevitably expand enormously, because the stable growth of the economy demands increasing "public" investments yearly. Our present outpour of more than $500 billion might double in a generation, irreversibly involving government solutions. And in future recessions, the compensatory fiscal action by the government will be the only means of avoiding the twin disasters of greater unemployment and a slackening rate of growth. Furthermore, a close relationship with the European Common Market will involve competition with numerous planned economies and may aggravate American unemployment unless the economy here is expanding swiftly enough to create new jobs.

All these tendencies suggest that not only solutions to our present social needs but our future expansion rests upon our willingness to enlarge the "public sector" greatly. Unless we choose war as an economic solvent, future public spending will be of non-military nature— a major intervention into civilian production by the government. . . .

6 *America should concentrate on its genuine social priorities: abolish squalor, terminate neglect, and establish an environment for people to live in with dignity and creativeness.*

A. A program against *poverty* must be just as sweeping as the nature of poverty itself. It must not be just palliative, but directed to the abolition of the structural circumstances of poverty. At a bare minimum it should include a *housing* act far larger than the one supported by the Kennedy Administration, but one that is geared more to low- and middle-income needs than to the windfall aspirations of small and large private entrepreneurs, one that is more sympathetic to the quality of communal life than to the efficiency of city-split highways. Second, *medical care* must become recognized as a lifetime human right just as vital as food, shelter and clothing—the Federal government should guarantee health insurance as a basic social service turning medical treatment into a social habit, not just an occasion of crisis, fighting sickness among the aged, not just by making medical care financially feasible but by reducing sickness among children and younger people. Third, existing institutions should be expanded so the Welfare State cares for *everyone's* welfare according to need. *Social Security* payments should be extended to everyone and should be proportionately greater for the poorest. A *minimum wage* of at least $1.50 should be extended to all workers (including the 16 million currently not covered at all). Programs for equal *educational opportunity* are as important a part of the battle against poverty.

B. A full-scale public initiative for civil rights should be undertaken despite the clamor among conservatives (and liberals) about gradualism, property rights, and law and order. The executive and legislative branches of the Federal government should work by enforcement *and* enactment against any form of exploitation of minority groups. No Federal cooperation with racism is tolerable—from financing of schools, to the development of Federally-supported industry, to the social gatherings of the President. Laws hastening school desegregation, voting rights, and economic protection for Negroes are needed right now. The moral force of the Executive Office should be exerted against the Dixiecrats specifically, and the national complacency about the race question generally. Especially in the North, where one-half of the country's Negro people now live, civil rights is not a problem to be solved in isolation from other problems. The fight against poverty, against slums, against the stalemated Congress, against McCarthyism, are all fights against the discrimination that is nearly endemic to all areas of American life.

C. The promise and problems of long-range *Federal economic development* should be studied more constructively. It is an embarrassing paradox that the Tennessee Valley Authority is a wonder to most foreign visitors but a "radical" and barely influential project to most Americans. The Kennedy decision to permit private facilities to transmit power from the $1 billion Colorado River Storage Project is a disastrous one, interposing privately-owned transmitters between publicly-owned generators and their publicly (and cooperatively) owned distributors. The contrary trend, to public ownership of power, should be generated in an experimental way.

The Area Redevelopment Act of 1961 is a first step in recognizing the underdeveloped areas of the United States. It is only a drop in the bucket financially and is not keyed to public planning and public works on a broad scale. It consists only of a few loan programs to lure industries and some grants to improve public facilities to lure these industries. The current public works bill in Congress is needed—and a more sweeping, higher-priced program of regional development with a proliferation of "TVAs" in such areas as the Appalachian region are needed desperately. However, it has been rejected already by Mississippi because the improvement it bodes for the unskilled Negro worker. This program should be enlarged, given teeth, and pursued rigorously by Federal authorities.

D. We must meet the growing complex of "city" problems; over 90 percent of Americans will live in urban areas within two decades. Juvenile delinquency, untended mental illness, crime increase, slums, urban tenantry and non-rent controlled housing, the isolation of the individual in the city—all are problems of the city and are major symptoms of the present system of economic priorities and lack of public planning. Private property control (the real estate lobby and a few selfish landowners and businesses) is as devastating in the cities as corporations are on the national level. But there is no comprehensive way to deal with these problems now amidst competing units of government, dwindling tax resources, suburban escapism (saprophitic to the sick central cities), high infrastructure costs and no one to pay them.

The only solutions are national and regional. "Federalism" has thus far failed here because states are rural-dominated; the Federal government has had to operate by bootlegging and trickle-down measures dominated by private interests, with their appendages through annexation or federation. A new external challenge is needed, not just a Department of Urban Affairs but a thorough national *program* to help the cities. The *model* city must be projected—more community decision-making and participation, true integration of classes, races, vocations—provision for beauty, access to nature and the benefits of the central city as well, privacy without privatism, decentralized "units" spread horizontally with central, regional democratic control—provision for the basic facility-needs, for everyone, with units of planned *regions* and thus public, democratic control over the growth of the civic community and the allocation of resources.

E. *Mental health institutions* are in dire need; there were fewer mental hospital beds in relation to the numbers of mentally-ill in 1959 than there were in 1948. Public hospitals, too, are seriously wanting; existing structures alone need an estimated $1 billion for rehabilitation. Tremendous staff and faculty needs exist as well, and there are not enough medical students enrolled today to meet the anticipated needs of the future.

F. Our *prisons* are too often the enforcers of misery. They must be either re-oriented to rehabilitative work through public supervision or be abolished for their dehumanizing social effects. Funds are needed, too, to make possible a decent prison environment.

G. *Education* is too vital a public problem to be completely entrusted to the province of the various states and local units. In fact, there is no good reason why America should not progress now toward internationalizing rather than localizing, its education system—children and young adults studying everywhere in the world, through a United Nations program, would go far to create mutual understanding. In the meantime, the need for teachers and classrooms in America is fantastic. This is an area where "minimal" requirements should hardly be considered as a goal—there always are improvements to be made in the education system, e.g., smaller classes and many more teachers for them, programs to subsidize the education for the poor but bright, etc.

H. America should eliminate *agricultural policies* based on scarcity and pent-up surplus. In America and foreign countries there exist tremendous needs for more food and balanced diets. The Federal government should finance small farmers' cooperatives, strengthen programs of rural electrification, and expand policies for the distribution of agricultural surpluses throughout the world (by Food-for-Peace and related

UN programming). Marginal farmers must be helped to either become productive enough to survive "industrialized agriculture" or given help in making the transition out of agriculture—the current Rural Area Development program must be better coordinated with a massive national "area redevelopment" program.

I. *Science* should be employed to constructively transform the conditions of life throughout the United States and the world. Yet at the present time the Department of Health, Education, and Welfare and the National Science Foundation together spend only $300 million annually for scientific purposes in contrast to the $6 billion spent by the Defense Department and the Atomic Energy Commission. One-half of all research and development in America is directly devoted to military purposes. Two imbalances must be corrected—that of military over nonmilitary investigation, and that of biological-natural-physical science over the sciences of human behavior. Our political system must then include planning for the human use of science: by anticipating the political consequences of scientific innovation, by directing the discovery and exploration of space, by adapting science to improved production of food, to international communications systems, to technical problems of disarmament, and so on. For the newly-developing nations, American science should focus on the study of cheap sources of power, housing and building materials, mass educational techniques, etc. Further, science and scholarship should be seen less as an apparatus of conflicting power blocs, but as a bridge toward supra-national community: the International Geophysical Year is a model for continuous further cooperation between the science communities of all nations.

The Greensboro Sit-Ins

WILLIAM CHAFE

*On February 1, 1960, four black students from North Carolina Agri-
cultural and Technical College walked into a Woolworth's in downtown
Greensboro, North Carolina, purchased a few small items, and then
sat at the lunch counter to seek equal service with white patrons. Their
action sparked the student phase of the "civil rights revolution." Within
days, the sit-in movement had spread to fifty-four cities in nine states.
Two months after the first sit-ins, the Student Non-Violent Coordinating
Committee (SNCC) was formed in Raleigh, North Carolina. Within a
year, more than one hundred cities had engaged in at least some desegregation of public facilities in response to student-led demonstrations.
The memorable era of controversy had begun.*

*In light of subsequent events, it is not surprising that many
people view the Greensboro sit-ins as marking an abrupt turn in the
history of race relations. News accounts at the time emphasized the
immediate events that had spurred the students to action—a recently
viewed television documentary on Gandhi, for example, or an experience
with bus terminal segregation—rather than recognizing long-term causes.
Indeed, some have interpreted sit-ins almost as a miraculously new movement, a transcendence of the earlier behavior of the national black
community.*

*The motivation was simple to understand. The sit-ins ennobled
the ordinary: the right to a Coke and a hamburger at a lunch counter,
or a room in a motel, or a book at a public library. All blacks could
identify with that. The results of the sit-ins were clear-cut: the customer
or patron is either served or not. Victory was instantaneous when it
came and required no elaborate rite of concession by the white community: someone simply put the food on the counter. And the process
could be made general. The demonstrator did not need to know anything about Greensboro, North Carolina, or any place else: the tactic
was as good in one city as in another.*

*The approach was dramatic. Yet Greensboro sit-ins can be under-
stood only as part of an ongoing process of race relations and struggle
within a community. This article examines the conditions out of which
the sit-ins grew and demonstrates that the black quest for equality has
been a continuous process, marked by shifts in direction, each generation transmitting strength and support to its children. The four young
men at Greensboro—and all their imitators—stood on the shoulders of
anonymous men and women throughout black history.*

To a passing observer in the late 1940s, Greensboro might have appeared
either as a striking example of "the new South," ready to set aside old
patterns of racial oppression, or as a smoother version of the traditional

South, disguising its racism with a "progressive" image. Most whites preferred the first interpretation, pointing to the city's cosmopolitan air, the presence of three colleges and two universities, and Greensboro's history of good race relations, which included the election of a Jew as president of the Chamber of Commerce and then mayor of the city. Most blacks, on the other hand, leaned toward the second interpretation. Although the black community in Greensboro had historically ranked ahead of other areas in the state in education, median income and occupation level, one black leader spoke of Greensboro as a "nice-nasty town"; and Nell Coley, a veteran black schoolteacher, commented that "there has been a kind of liberal strand running through the air . . . but make no mistake about it, Greensboro is not all that liberal."

In fact, there was evidence to support both points of view. Some white liberals and black educators had been involved in interracial activities throughout the '40s. The Guilford County Interracial Commission, a private citizens' group, quietly lobbied local merchants to remove Jim Crow signs from the water fountains in downtown stores. United Church Women, an interdenominational group, held interracial social activities and discussion groups, as did a few faculty members of the local colleges. The YWCA integrated its board of directors during the late '40s, and in the early '50s hired a black secretary-receptionist. Perhaps most supportive of the "liberal" Greensboro image was the election in 1951 of Dr. William Hampton—a Negro—to the City Council by one of the largest majorities given any candidate.

On the other hand, a layer of paternalism and resistance to change could be detected in many of these activities. Rev. Edward Edmonds, who came to Greensboro in the 1950s, noted that although a Human Relations Council existed, the "only place it could meet was the YWCA." Furthermore, as soon as the YWCA integrated its board and began to hold interracial luncheons, many of its most prominent members resigned. The hiring of a black secretary proved especially controversial. The director of the United Fund alerted the "Y" leadership that it was alienating people and endangering contributions. Within a few months, the secretary had been hired away at double the salary by the president of predominately black A&T College. When one white liberal benefactor wished to donate a swimming pool to the black YMCA, he attempted to set as a condition that the black YWCA join the "YM" so that there would be only one pool for all blacks, thereby avoiding the prospect of black girls swimming at the downtown "white" YWCA. It seemed that interracial activity was sanctioned only when it involved whites going into the black community, or when it did not visibly offend the traditional racial etiquette of the South.

In this context, the Supreme Court's 1954 *Brown vs. the Board of Education* decision provided a crucial test for the leadership of white Greensboro. The same night the decision was handed down, a group of Greensboro leaders met at the home of school board chairman D. Edward Hudgins to discuss their course of action. The next night, Hudgins brought with him to the regular school board meeting a resolution committing Greensboro to a policy of implementing the Court's edict as the law of the land. The ruling, Hudgins said, was "one of the most momentous events" in the history of education, and he urged his colleagues not to "fight or attempt to circumvent it." School Superintendent Benjamin Smith, a devoutly religious man respected by many black leaders for his support of steps toward racial equality, sounded the same theme: "It is unthinkable that we will try to abrogate the laws of the United States of America, and it is also unthinkable that the public schools should be abolished." Dr. David Jones, the only black member of the school board, supported the responses of Hudgins and Smith. "Isn't there a possibility," he asked, "that we of Greensboro may furnish leadership in the way we approach this problem? Not only to the community, but to the state and to the South?" After a brief debate, the board voted 6-0, with one abstention, to endorse Hudgins' resolution.

The morning newspaper applauded the decision, and within a few days the Greensboro Jaycees and the Ministerial Fellowship added their endorsements. But the hope of Dr. Jones and other blacks that Greensboro would quickly integrate its schools soon gave way before the reality of inaction and resistance. Most of the powerful white churches in the community failed to follow through on the endorsement by the Ministerial Fellowship. More importantly, the leaders of the largest corporations refused to support desegregation actively. Spencer Love, head of Burlington Industries (the state's largest employer, headquartered in Greensboro), decided it was not appropriate for him to become involved in the issue. Other businessmen quickly followed his lead.

A few days after the Hudgins resolution passed, the newspaper provided a harbinger of subsequent policy in an editorial entitled "Time for the Golden Mean." "During 50 years," the Greensboro *Daily News* argued, "the Negro race has moved rapidly to its rightful place in the mainstream of the nation, but these extremists on both sides—the Talmadges and the NAACP—should remember the moderate views held by most Southerners. They cannot be pushed too fast." The question was, what did it mean to be moderate? Governor Luther Hodges gave his answer in the summer of 1955 when he urged North Carolinians to pursue a "moderate" policy of voluntary segregation.

Black Greensboro, meanwhile, pursued its own agenda. There had long been a strong tradition of educational and economic self-improvement within the black community. Nearly three thousand blacks in 1960 had some college education—almost twice as many as in Durham, a comparable city. Many blacks were property owners, taxpayers and registered voters. Furthermore, through such institutions as the YMCA, the Greensboro Men's Club, and various church groups, black citizens had organized for their own protection and advancement.

Nevertheless, there were two different styles of activism in black Greensboro. One directly challenged the oppressiveness of white power, while the other sought to work within the white power structure for black advancement. Randolph Blackwell embodied the first style. Born in Greensboro during the 1920s, he grew up in a family which instilled values of independence and pride. Although Blackwell's parents were not well-off, they would not permit him to hold any jobs that might place him in a position subservient to whites, such as delivery boy or newspaper carrier. Blackwell's father was a railroad worker who was devoted to the teachings of the black nationalist leader Marcus Garvey, and Blackwell recalls attending meetings in Greensboro where as many as 50 followers of Garvey would be present. While Blackwell was still a boy, his father took him to Atlanta to visit the prison where Garvey was held, and to see a black insurance company with all black workers. In high school, he was inspired by two teachers at Dudley High who were active members of the NAACP; and in 1943, after hearing an address by Ella Baker, a field secretary for the NAACP, he helped to start a Youth Chapter in Greensboro. Five years later, as a student at A&T, Blackwell ran for the state assembly on a platform that challenged the entire white power structure. He also organized a voter registration campaign and worked to expose and defeat black politicians who were hired by whites to influence black votes. Eventually, in the 1960s, Blackwell became an important leader in the Southern Christian Leadership Conference.

The second style of leadership was typified by Dr. F. D. Bluford, president of A&T College. Since A&T's existence depended upon white legislative support, Bluford repeatedly found himself accommodating white expectations; he discouraged protest on the campus and performed those public acts of subservience to white leaders necessary to improve A&T's funding. Faculty members quickly got the message that, as one put it, "you could make it here if you didn't go too fast," or protest too much. Participation in the NAACP was discouraged and any form of overt resistance was forbidden. As a price for his accommodation, Bluford was denounced as "the last of the handkerchief heads," and the president's house was referred to by students as "Uncle Tom's Cabin."

In specific situations, the two kinds of leadership occasionally worked together in unpredictable ways, as a private conversation between Blackwell and Bluford illustrates. During his 1948 campaign for the state legislature, Blackwell was lambasting local textile magnates and posting campaign literature around the A&T campus. He knew his actions embarrassed the administration, and he expected reprisals. One day, while Blackwell was talking with some students, Bluford walked by and said, "Blackwell, I'd like to see you in my office." "Here it comes," thought Blackwell. "Now I've had it." Instead, when he arrived at Bluford's office, the president told him that he was free to use one of the college auditoriums if he wished. But he must never ask for permission, because if Bluford were called on the carpet, he needed to be able to say that he had not sanctioned Blackwell's actions. Blackwell concluded that despite Bluford's dissembling before the white community, he was a man with "a sense of dignity . . . a man [who, though] thoroughly discredited and constantly abused . . . also had some of the same yearnings as those of us that were out there raising hell."

The conflict between the two styles of leadership continued into the 1950s with first one, then the other dominating. Some black principals refused to allow teachers in black schools to solicit for NAACP memberships, and many members insisted on paying their dues privately and in cash rather than risking economic reprisal by having their names publicly associated with the NAACP. Nevertheless, other leaders kept the spirit of public protest visible. When Hobart Jarrett arrived in 1949 to teach at Bennett College, a black women's college in Greensboro, he found a newly formed organization, the Greensboro Citizens Association, combating politicians who sold black votes and working for candidates whose programs benefited the black community. The GCA lobbied effectively for paved streets, better lighting and improved sewage, and quickly became identified with Dr. William Hampton's campaign for the city council. Jarrett was also instrumental in a voter registration drive conducted by Bennett College students and faculty. "Greensboro black people saw something they had never seen in their lives," he recalled. "Long lines at the Community Center [of] people waiting in line to get registered." Hampton's election in 1951, together with the appointment of Dr. David Jones to the school board in 1952, suggested that the political self-assertion of the black community was beginning to make a mark.

Throughout the 1950s, the protest movement resisted white attempts to uphold the "old order" and demanded desegregation in schools and public facilities. The *Brown* decision had not caused the protest, recalled Vance Chavis, a teacher and politician, but it helped spur "people to come out and express how they felt more . . . a lot of black people sometimes have a way of answering you the way they thought you wanted to hear." Now, it became more likely that blacks would answer the way they actually felt.

The most dramatic example of overt protest came on the A&T campus itself. North Carolina Governor Luther Hodges had been invited to attend the Founder's Day Ceremony in the fall of 1955. The invitation was extended before Hodges' voluntary segregation speech in August of that year, and before his appeal to the all-black North Carolina Teachers' Association to endorse separate schools—an appeal which they unanimously rejected. Although Bluford had warned students they would lose their jobs if they misbehaved, campus observers knew that if Hodges insulted the audience, he would receive an appropriate response. Arriving 15 minutes after the ceremonies had begun, Hodges in effect gave two speeches. In the first he praised the founders of A&T and scrupulously referred to blacks as "Negroes." Then, he launched an attack on the NAACP, specifically criticizing "some of your unwise leaders." In the process, he began to use the word "Nigra." Almost instantly, the students started to scrape their feet on the floor and cough.

The next day, newspapers throughout the state reported that black students at A&T had humiliated and embarrassed their governor. But the black newspaper, *The Carolina Times*, called the protest "a product of three-quarters of a century of flagrant disrespect for the humanity of the Negro . . . another link in a chain of events showing obvious and outspoken Negro dissatisfaction with an unwise and inept public servant." Two days after the Hodges incident, Dr. Bluford went to the hospital. Within a month, he was dead.

The demonstrations at A&T set the tone for the increasing assertiveness of black protest during the middle and late '50s. A group of black professionals went to the local public golf course in 1955 demanding the right to play. The city had rented the course for a nominal sum to a "private" concession. As the blacks arrived, the golf pro cursed, and asked why they were there. "For a cause—the cause of democracy," they answered. That night, the black protesters were arrested. Eventually, the federal courts ruled that all citizens had a right to play on the course. But then the clubhouse burned down mysteriously and the city ordered the golf course closed. Two years later, another group of blacks demanded that the Lindley Park swimming pool be opened to blacks and whites alike. Again, they were turned down, but this time the city avoided a court contest by immediately closing down the pool and selling it, as well as the black public pool, to private buyers.

The greatest upsurge of activism, however, occurred with regard to the public schools. "One of the things that the NAACP recognized very early," Rev. Edward Edmonds, a protest leader, later recalled, "was that one of the ways to move black folk is to move them about their children. You can't be conditioned for years to achieve, to become somebody, and then have your kids denied. School was a very sensitive thing . . . a pressure point . . . so we had all kinds of support from people willing to go down and confront the school board." Beginning in December, 1955, the parent-teacher associations of two black high schools, Dudley and Lincoln, sent frequent delegations to the monthly school board meeting to demand better facilities for black schools. In the 18 months between October, 1956, and April, 1958, representatives of black organizations appeared at all but two meetings to protest and lobby for their children's education.

Black parents were especially persistent in their demands for a new gymnasium at Dudley High School. With skill and shrewdness, the Dudley delegation demanded that either a new gymnasium be started immediately or that the white high school be opened for black basketball games. The board stalled, but eventually said that the building schedule could not be altered and that the white gym was being used on every occasion that Dudley had a basketball game planned. Not to be outwitted, the Dudley PTA offered to rearrange the schedule to play on the nights when the gym was free. With no other way out, the school board instructed the superintendent to make the Senior High available on nights when it was not in use. Shortly after the Dudley team played its first game at the white school, the board of education shifted its building schedule and constructed a new Dudley gymnasium. As the NAACP leader Rev. Edmonds recalled, "The minute you use their facilities, they find the money."

The persistent campaign of black parents and the NAACP strikingly demonstrated the increased assertiveness of blacks. They would not permit the school board to deny their children a better life. Despite the apparent contradictions between demands for a new black facility and desegregation, these two prongs of the NAACP attack were complementary, reinforcing each other in the quest for a better education for black children. Furthermore, each bespoke a growing commitment to open protest in the black community.

Meanwhile, a number of black parents applied to have their children reassigned to previously all-white schools. Although many whites claimed that these applications came from outside agitators and elite educators, the parents actually reflected a broad cross section of black Greensboro, including a black milkman, a printer, an express handler, a barber, a maid, a student at A&T, a minister and a worker in the stockroom of a local mail-order house. All were willing to undergo social ostracism and economic intimidation in order to seek a better life for their children.

It would be a mistake, of course, to over-emphasize activism and under-emphasize the continued intimidation of protesters. When Rev. Edmonds left Bennett College in 1959, many blacks believed it was at least in part because he was "too far ahead of his time" and had stirred up too much trouble as the head of the NAACP, thereby invoking the hostility of powerful whites and their black allies. Though the tension between assertiveness and caution remained unresolved, there could be little question that by the end of the 1950s black leadership as a whole was moving decisively toward overt challenge to white power.

The white community, meanwhile, remained largely indifferent to black demands, and in particular, failed to implement desegregation quickly. Events soon proved that the near unanimity of the school board's vote for compliance obscured significant differences over what the Hudgins resolution meant. Although board chairman Ed Hudgins had drafted the compliance resolution, he believed that desegregation would be "traumatic for the average white southerner," and did not contemplate any immediate action toward desegregation. John Foster, school board chairman from 1955 to 1958, viewed the board's action as "more or less an easing of conscience." Thus, the primary purpose of the school board action was to neutralize the issue and prevent the kind of disruption that might hurt the city's image. As had been true so often in the past, the promise of change obscured an agenda for continued control.

The dominant view of the school board grew out of a profound misreading of black community sentiments. Foster was convinced that "the average Negro does not want desegregation"—a judgment he based on personal contact with the maid in his home, the man who drove his truck, and the janitor in his place of business. Although he acknowledged that a new assertiveness had "crept" into the manner of blacks who visited school board meetings, he viewed such delegations as atypical. The NAACP, Foster believed, was like a labor union that claimed to have a lot of support but whose members "never paid any dues."

Significantly, the white members of the school board sought corroboration for their point of view from their black colleagues who, given the power relationships surrounding the racial contacts in the South, could only achieve positions of eminence by seeming to accept prevailing white assumptions. Thus, while the black community perceived Dr. William Hampton, who replaced David Jones as the only black school board member, and Dr. J. A. Tarpley, the supervisor of black schools, as strong supporters of racial equality, many white board members saw them as allies working for the common goal of maintaining order and controlling the situation. White leaders praised Hampton as a "level-minded" realist who could be depended upon to help chart a "moderate" course between extremes. Foster noted that when a black activist became particularly "obnoxious," Dr. Hampton could be counted upon to "handle him well." White leaders relied on both men to "look after" the black community; indeed, their presence gave the school board an excuse to discount the more militant assertions of other black activists, since, after all, Hampton and Tarpley "represented" the black community. Both men, of course, were playing other roles than that of accommodationists, and frequently stood up in support of black delegations to the school board. Nevertheless, white officials focused selectively on those cues which conformed to their own preconceptions and needs.

On the state level, meanwhile, Luther Hodges had quickly assumed an antiblack and pro-segregationist position. In the summer of 1955, months before the 1956 gubernatorial election, he charged that the NAACP was trying to destroy the "good race relations" in North Carolina. Although his own advisors assessed public sentiment as apathetic and even tinged with a feeling of inevitability about integration, Hodges warned of a crisis unless the state acted to forestall integrationists.

The state legislature implemented Hodges' retreat from compliance in 1956 when, at a special session, it passed the Pearsall Plan, a series of constitutional amendments that provided "safety valves" against integration. The plan permitted local school districts to close schools if desegregation took place, and granted tuition aid for white students in those districts to attend private schools. Advocates of the plan cleverly ruled out other options and controlled the debate over ratification by the manner in which they defined the issues. The Pearsall Committee claimed that the voters had only two choices: they could either save the public schools by voting yes, or risk losing the schools by voting no.

In this manner, the Pearsall Committee defined the political spectrum by portraying the Pearsall Plan as a middle path between the extremes of the violence of die-hard white racists, and the demands of black integrationists. Through such public opinion manipulation, the committee equated the NAACP with the KKK. The Charlotte *Observer* called the Pearsall Plan a blend of "conscience and common sense . . . an effort to preserve the public schools and at the same time North Carolina's identity with constitutional government." In the words of the Shelby *Star*, the Plan would "maintain separate school systems," but with a "tone of moderation." Although many Greensboro white liberals would later blame Hodges and the Pearsall Plan for preventing a racial breakthrough in their own school system, white executives and politicians had, by their silence, recognized the right of the governor to speak for them. Of the local school hierarchy, only Superintendent of Schools Benjamin Smith opposed the Pearsall Plan. In Greensboro, as in the state-at-large, white leaders simply were not ready to deal with blacks who demanded their rights. As the Pearsall Committee staff wrote on one occasion about a court hearing, "We were shocked at the . . . rudeness and complete self-confidence of the Negro attorneys." The juxtaposition of words did not seem a coincidence.

It is impossible to overestimate the disastrous impact of the plan. It postponed meaningful desegregation in North Carolina for more than a decade—far longer than in some states where "massive resistance" was practiced. It placed the entire burden for seeking justice on the shoulders of the victim, without aid from the state or the law. Above all, it gave the moral sanction of the state to a policy of circumventing significant movement toward racial equality.

The Pearsall Plan provided the context for token desegregation of Greensboro schools in the late summer of 1957. School board members understood that they would have to desegregate, but could proceed slowly, in a manner designed to limit the number of blacks and reduce the possibility of white dissension. Black applicants for transfer to white schools had to fill out complicated forms and have them notarized, while white parents could secure automatic reassignment for their children if they objected to desegregated schools. Most black requests for transfer were denied, notwithstanding the cogent reasons offered in the applications. At the same time, board chairman John Foster arranged with Winston-Salem and Charlotte to announce heir desegregation plans on the same night as Greensboro. If we act separately, he told them, "the segregationists get three shots at us. If we act together, they get one. . . ." One month after the school board meeting, six black students entered previously all-white schools, one in the senior high school, the others together in Gillespie Elementary School.

From a national point of view, Greensboro's action seemed a "progressive" breakthrough. *Newsweek* called the city a symbol of the "new south, astir with new liberalism." A group of Princeton sociologists heaped praise on the city's leadership, predicting that "desegregation will not only surely triumph but will do so quickly." But from the perspective of Greensboro's blacks, such phrases described a city on another planet. By 1957 the hopes raised by the board's 1954 resolution had evaporated. The black community perceived the 1957 desegregation plan as carrying out the spirit of the Pearsall Plan—a spirit they identified as unmistakably racist. "The white power structure was trying to appease," a black activist recalled. "They wanted a token thing . . . so that they could call Greensboro the gateway city, an all-American city—and they got it."

The black perception was accurate. A leader of the Pearsall Committee had written that one of his worst nightmares was being in a federal court trying to defend the school board "when a showing is made that nowhere in all the state . . . had a single Negro been admitted to any of the more than 2,000 schools attended by white students." In this context, the Greensboro decision to desegregate on a token basis constituted an integral part of an effort to protect the state by salvaging the Pearsall Plan. John Foster recalled how angry and frustrated he became when segregationists from eastern counties attacked him for his liberalism. "I tried to tell them," he said, "that dammit, we were holding a big umbrella over them. We're protecting them really, because we are at least getting into a position where the state of North Carolina can't be forced into integrating."

The history of the next three years only confirmed the growing anger of blacks at white duplicity. Black students and parents were frequently victims of harassment and reprisal. Josephine Boyd, the first black girl to attend all-white Senior High School, experienced repeated insults and intimidation. Her dress was splattered with eggs, a boy spit on her sweater, and her mother's car was pelted with rocks. Often, she felt like leaving the situation entirely, and only the support of family, two or three student friends and some teachers sustained her.

The school board's approach to desegregation was perhaps best revealed in 1959 when the parents of four black students sought to restrain the city and state from operating segregated schools through a lawsuit demanding that their children be admitted to the all-white Caldwell High School. Thurgood Marshall, and later Jack Greenberg of the NAACP Legal Defense Fund, argued the case in court. In an effort to forestall what the school attorney called one of the most important suits in North Carolina history, the board merged the all-black Pearson school with Caldwell. Four months later, the board transferred every white student out of Caldwell and redrew the district lines so that Caldwell became an all-black school with an all-black faculty. In the meantime, the board successfully argued in court that the legal action on behalf of the four black students had become moot since the students were now in the school they had applied to. The episode highlighted the gap between promise and performance. As one black minister declared, "these folks were primarily interested in evading, and they weren't even embarrassed."

Not surprisingly, as the decade drew to a close, blacks intensified their protest activities. NAACP membership on a local level rose from 12,000 in 1958 to 23,000 in 1960. When Martin Luther King, Jr., came to Greensboro in 1958, the audience filled not only the chapel at Bennett College, but a number of auditoriums on the campus into which King's address was piped by loudspeaker. Most Greensboro blacks had reached their own conclusion on the sincerity of the white leadership structure in promoting desegregation, seeming to agree with the assessment of a Little Rock school official, writing to an associate in North Carolina: "You North Carolinians have devised one of the cleverest techniques of perpetuating segregation that we have seen."

It was against this background that the student sit-ins of 1960 began. Three of the original four sit-in demonstrators spent their adolescent years in Greensboro attending Dudley High School. There, they encountered teachers who instilled in them a sense of pride and dignity—teachers like Nell Coley, mentioned over and over again by black activists as a model of strength. By her actions, as well as her words, Coley inspired the young to realize their potential. "I had to tell kids that you must not accept," she said. "I don't care if they do push and shove you, you must not accept that. . . . You are who you are." Through the literature she assigned and the discussions she conducted, Coley drove home the message that nothing was beyond the reach of her students if they would only dare boldly. The same message came from Ezell Blair, Sr., a shop teacher and NAACP activist who was the father of one of the sit-in demonstrators, and from Rev. Otis Hairston, who led the NAACP membership drive in 1959 and who was minister to two of the students.

Three of the four initial demonstrators also participated in a revitalized NAACP youth group headed by Rev. Edward Edmonds. Edmonds had been involved in the original March On Washington Movement in 1941 and had helped found the Southern Christian Leadership Conference. Each week from 1956 on, the Youth Chapter met at St. James Presbyterian Church or one of the black colleges in Greensboro to discuss local politics and the freedom struggle. Ezell Blair, Jr., later the spokesman for the sit-in movement, recalled that the Montgomery Bus Boycott provided a focus for many of the NAACP Youth Group's discussions. "It was like a catalyst—it started things rolling." When Martin Luther King, Jr., came to Greensboro in 1958, his presence particularly affected the young. King's sermon was "so strong," Blair recalled, "I could feel my heart palpitating. It brought tears to my eyes."

By the fall of 1959, the three Greensboro natives were freshmen at A&T where they were joined by Joseph McNeill from Wilmington, North Carolina. The students read an anthology with selections from W. E. B. DuBois, Ralph Bunche, and Toussaint L'Ouverture among others. The course work led to numerous late night discussions about blacks in America. In that same fall and winter, the group began a series of conversations with Ralph Johns, a white clothing store owner who had long supported the NAACP and been committed to the idea of some form of demonstrations against segregated public facilities. And one of the students worked in the library with Eula Hudgins, an A&T graduate who in 1948 had participated in freedom rides to test the desegregation of the interstate bus system.

The resolve to act crystallized in late January. In December, McNeill had returned from a trip to New York, angered because he could not get food service at the Greensboro Trailways Bus Terminal. The late night discussions took on a new focus, and on Sunday, January 31, Ezell Blair, Jr., came home and asked his parents if they would be embarrassed if he got in trouble. "Why?" his parents wondered. "Because," he said, "tomorrow we're going to do something that will shake up this town." The next day the four friends—nervous, fearful, but determined—took their historic journey to Woolworth's.

Almost immediately, the students knew they were not alone in their struggle. On the following day, 23 men and four women students sat in at Woolworth's. Wednesday, students occupied 63 out of 66 seats at the lunch counter. By Thursday, three women from the white Woman's College had joined the sit-in. Nearly 300 students participated in the protest on Friday; this time Ku Klux Klan members disrupted the protest with violence. Finally, on Saturday, hundreds of students, including the A&T football team, descended on the downtown area to continue the protest and resist white intimidation. When the A&T student body held a mass meeting on Saturday night to vote on a proposal for a two-week moratorium on the sit-ins, more than 1,600 students participated.

The demonstrations shocked the white community into action—six years after the *Brown* decision. Concerned about the city's image and its continued ability to attract industry, Greensboro's white leadership sought to quell the disruptions and to pressure Woolworth's to change its policy. As in 1954, some turned to Spencer Love, the leading industrialist, for aid. This time, Love responded positively, giving support to the efforts of his close associate, Edward R. Zane, to find a solution. Armed with Love's economic clout as well as his own moral conviction about racial injustice, Zane entered the situation by the end of the first week of demonstrations and established a close relationship with the students. Despite significant local resistance and Governor Hodges' desire to arrest the demonstrators, Zane pushed through a proposal to create a Human Relations Advisory Committee, headed by himself. The students postponed further demonstrations while the Committee sought a negotiated solution. Although the Committee failed initially, a black economic boycott of Woolworth's and further picketing in April and May created pressure that resulted in the desegregation of Greensboro's lunch counters in early summer.

The impact on the black community, however, was perhaps even more significant. The local NAACP endorsed the sit-ins on the second day, and other activists quickly provided similar support. In addition, groups and individuals who previously had adopted accommodationist positions now refused to use their influence to restrain the demonstrators. Despite strong pressure from Governor Hodges, the administrators of A&T basically supported the demonstrators. Under pressure from below, ministers who previously had been conservative now permitted mass meetings in their sanctuaries. Summarizing the impact of the demonstrations, a librarian at A&T commented: "It shook the people up in both ways. Some were happy about it, some were scared to death." But the demonstrations had raised the consciousness of the second group and showed them they no longer had to accept injustice. "They learned something from those four fellows, that if you want something done you've got to go out and fight for it." City leaders had expected adult blacks to put a brake on the students. Instead, the adult community reinforced the student efforts and joined them in pushing for a satisfactory settlement. When the owner of Meyer's, a prestigious local department store, tried to desegregate only his lunch counter and not the Garden Room, where middle-class women lunched, black middle-class customers turned in their charge cards and conducted their own economic boycott until the Garden Room was also desegregated.

Support from the black adult community was perhaps best exemplified by Dr. Willa Player, president of Bennett College. Always a strong woman, she was described by one of her faculty members as "an administrator with a capital A; she went according to the rules, and regulations were carried out to perfection." Some whites saw Player as a potential ally in their efforts to control the protest movement. Shortly after the sit-ins began, Spencer Love wrote her "about certain disturbances with which I am sure you're familiar." Assuring her that he, together with all broad-minded people, wanted to keep "our part of the south on top of the heap as becoming more and more enlightened and progressive," Love offered his own view of the situation. "To people who are younger, progress may seem slow," he wrote, "but as long as it is there, and as long as it is sure, it seems to me best to be patient and not to try to rush the clock too much." Though not an open request for restraint, the letter's message seemed clear. So too was Player's polite response to a subsequent letter from Love. "We hope that you will have time to express in a letter to Mr. Zane and to Mayor Roach," she wrote, "your desire to see us work together in our community for provision of services for all citizens alike." Throughout 1960, as well as later, Player offered complete support to her students. In addition, she was the first black adult to turn in her charge card when Meyer's Department Store refused to desegregate its dining room. As one observer commented, "something happened to Willa Player when the students took the lead and went out . . . she became real impatient. She may have been impatient in her own right all along; it may simply have been that front she was putting up. But then she no longer put up that front."

Although an examination of the Greensboro sit-ins is instructive from many perspectives, a few themes stand out. First, and perhaps most important, the demonstrations continued a long tradition of protest within black Greensboro. To Nell Coley, the sit-ins did not seem unusual because, she said, "we had been teaching those kids things all along." Indeed, a significant number of blacks in Greensboro had always engaged in overt protest, whether in the Garvey movement or the NAACP or the Greensboro Citizens Association. In the 1950s and later, such protest became more pronounced, taking the form of the black PTA's visits to the school board, the revitalization of the NAACP, the challenge to segregated public facilities, and the resurgence of an NAACP youth group. In this context, the sit-in demonstrations were an extension of, rather than a departure from, traditional patterns of black activism in Greensboro.

The second theme involves the forms of social control practiced by the white power structure. The style championed by white leadership was that of "moderation." By proceeding gradually, and with civility on issues of race, white leaders believed that they could both preserve the progressive image of their city and meet the demands for some change from local blacks and from the Supreme Court. The style of moderation, however, served primarily as a guise for inaction. As the sociologist Thomas Pettigrew observed in 1961, "good race relations, for the moderate, refer to the relaxed relations of paternalism when the white man's superior status went unquestioned."

A central ingredient of the "moderate" style was the form of communication which existed between whites and blacks. Whites listened to those blacks who conformed in manner and approach to white expectation and denounced as "unrepresentative" and "extremists" those who failed to so conform. The result was an inescapable trap for men like William Hampton. Forced to cooperate with white officialdom if he were to have any voice at all, Hampton found his cooperation taken as a sign that blacks were satisfied, while his support of protest was discounted as a sop to black militants. Within such a contorted framework, whites dismissed as atypical those delegates from the NAACP and black PTAs who appeared before them in the '50s; the style of moderation thus entailed a ritual of distortion in which honest expression of opinion was subverted. In the end, blacks could get their real message across only by going outside the existing process of communication.

In this sense, the sit-ins contributed a fundamentally new form of expressing protest. The very fact of sitting-in circumvented those forms of fraudulent communication through which whites had historically controlled black self-assertion. A new language was being devised, one which communicated a different message than had been heard before. In a most dramatic way, the sit-ins embodied the dissatisfaction and anger of the black community at white indifference and injustice. From a black point of view, the message was the same as it had been all along, but now it was expressed in a manner that whites could no longer dismiss or ignore. From a white point of view, the message also appeared different because, for the first time, it had to be heard.

The integral relationship between style and content was perhaps best illustrated in the response of Governor Hodges and some local white leaders to black self-assertion. What disturbed the Governor and his aides most was the "intemperate" behavior of blacks seeking social change, their "rudeness . . . and self-confidence." The style of the demonstrators was offensive precisely to the extent that it conveyed a message of discontent which could not possibly be mistaken for acquiescence. The underlying issue was strikingly revealed in a Greensboro *Daily News* editorial on the death of Dr. William Hampton, one week after the sit-ins began. The editorial eulogized Hampton for never engaging in public argument and for never forcing an issue when people disagreed with him. Hampton, it said, was a model for everyone to follow.

Ultimately, then, the sit-ins were both a consequence and cause of black activism. Consistent with the tradition of protest, the sit-ins reinforced and extended that tradition to the entire community, at the same time changing the form through which old as well as young would express their demands for dignity and equality. The sit-ins did not bring victory to the black community. But they provided a new vehicle for carrying on the struggle. Despite the desegregation of lunch counters, white Greensboro did not easily give up its "cherished traditions." In the battle between "civil rights and civilities," as the Greensboro *Daily News* called it, most whites came down solidly on the side of "civilities," preferring the style of moderation, "unimpeded by the threat of force or the worry of economic reprisal." It would be necessary again and again for black students and adults to take to the streets during the 1960s in order to drive their message home. The Greensboro sit-ins of 1960 were not a radical departure from the black past of protest, but they did provide a transition to a new language of self-expression which broke through white patterns of self-deception and control. Thereafter, the forms of communication between white and black would never be the same.

On Revolution

MALCOLM X

*Malcolm X emerged as one of the first to attack the civil rights move-
ment from the left. As a member of the Black Muslims (Nation of
Islam), a black nationalist group, Malcolm X rejected the Christian
millennialism of Martin Luther King, Jr., the belief in nonviolence,
and the notion that whites could be converted to racial integration.
This speech delivered in November 1963, three months after King's "I
Have a Dream" speech, strikes the themes that dominated black power
movements in the ensuing years: solidarity with African nationalism,
emphasis on revolution with the attendant threat of violence, and insistence on black separatism rather than integration with whites.*

*During the years after Malcolm X left the Muslims, he moderated
some of his rhetoric. But overall he remains important as one of the
first major black voices in the 1960's to speak from the city streets rather
than from the rural southern base that King represented. Of course, the
principal successes in the drive against segregation and discrimination
did come in the South; the issues Malcolm X raised—what future lies
beyond civil rights for black Americans—remain to be resolved.*

. . .

Of all our studies, history is best qualified to reward our research.
And when you see that you've got problems, all you have to do is
examine the historic method used all over the world by others who have
problems similar to yours. Once you see how they got theirs straight,
then you know how you can get yours straight. There's been a revolution, a black revolution, going on in Africa. In Kenya, the Mau Mau
were revolutionary; they were the ones who brought the word "Uhuru"
to the fore. The Mau Mau, they were revolutionary, they believed in
scorched earth, they knocked everything aside that got in their way, and
their revolution also was based on land, a desire for land. In Algeria,
the northern part of Africa, a revolution took place. The Algerians were
revolutionists, they wanted land. France offered to let them be integrated into France. They told France, to hell with France, they wanted
some land, not some France. And they engaged in a bloody battle.

So I cite these various revolutions, brothers and sisters, to show you
that you don't have a peaceful revolution. You don't have a turn-the-
other-cheek revolution. There's no such thing as a nonviolent revolution. The only kind of revolution that is nonviolent is the Negro
revolution. The only revolution in which the goal is loving your enemy
is the Negro revolution. It's the only revolution in which the goal is
a desegregated lunch counter, a desegregated theater, a desegregated
park, and a desegregated public toilet; you can sit down next to white
folks—on the toilet. That's no revolution. Revolution is based on land.

Land is the basis for all independence. Land is the basis for freedom, justice, and equality.

The white man knows what a revolution is. He knows that the black revolution is world-wide in scope and in nature. The black revolution is sweeping Asia, is sweeping Africa, is rearing its head in Latin America. The Cuban Revolution—that's a revolution. They overturned the system. Revolution is in Asia, revolution is in Africa, and the white man is screaming because he sees revolution in Latin America. How do you think he'll react to you when you learn what a real revolution is? You don't know what a revolution is. If you did, you wouldn't use that word.

Revolution is bloody, revolution is hostile, revolution knows no compromise, revolution overturns and destroys everything that gets in its way. And you, sitting around here like a knot on the wall, saying, "I'm going to love these folks no matter how much they hate me." No, you need a revolution. Whoever heard of a revolution where they lock arms . . . singing "We Shall Overcome?" You don't do that in a revolution. You don't do any singing, you're too busy swinging. It's based on land. A revolutionary wants land so he can set up his own nation, an independent nation. These Negroes aren't asking for any nation— they're trying to crawl back on the plantation.

When you want a nation, that's called nationalism. When the white man became involved in a revolution in this country against England, what was it for? He wanted this land so he could set up another white nation. That's white nationalism. The American Revolution was white nationalism. The French Revolution was white nationalism. The Russian Revolution too—yes, it was—white nationalism. You don't think so? Why do you think Khrushchev and Mao can't get their heads together? White nationalism. All the revolutions that are going on in Asia and Africa today are based on what?—black nationalism. A revolutionary is a black nationalist. He wants a nation. . . . If you're afraid of black nationalism, you're afraid of revolution. And if you love revolution, you love black nationalism.

To understand this, you have to go back to what the young brother here referred to as the house Negro and the field Negro back during slavery. There were two kinds of slaves, the house Negro and the field Negro. The house Negroes—they lived in the house with the master, they dressed pretty good, they ate good because they ate his food—what he left. They lived in the attic or the basement, but still they lived near the master; and they loved the master more than the master loved himself. They would give their life to save the master's house—quicker than the master would. If the master said, "We got a good house here," the house Negro would say, "Yeah, we got a good house here." Whenever the master said "we," he said "we." That's how you tell a house Negro.

If the master's house caught on fire, the house Negro would fight harder to put the blaze out than the master would. If the master got sick, the house Negro would say "What's the matter, boss, we sick?" We sick! He identified himself with his master, more than his master identified with himself. And if you came to the house Negro and said, "Let's run away, let's escape, let's separate," the house Negro would look at you and say, "Man, you crazy. What you mean, separate? Where is there a better house than this? Where can I wear better clothes than this? Where can I eat better food than this?" That was that house Negro. In those days he was called a "house nigger." And that's what we call them today, because we've still got some house niggers running around here.

This modern house Negro loves his master. He wants to live near him. He'll pay three times as much as the house is worth just to live near his master, and then brag about "I'm the only Negro out here." "I'm the only one on my job." "I'm the only one in this school." You're nothing but a house Negro. And if someone comes to you right now and says, "Let's separate," you say the same thing that the house Negro said on the plantation. "What you mean, separate? From America, this good white man? Where you going to get a better job than you get here?" I mean, this is what you say. "I ain't left nothing in Africa," that's what you say. Why, you left your mind in Africa.

On that same plantation, there was the field Negro. The field Negroes—those were the masses. There were always more Negroes in the field than there were Negroes in the house. The Negro in the field caught hell. He ate leftovers. In the house they ate high on the hog. The Negro in the field didn't get anything but what was left of the insides of the hog. They call it "chitt'lings" nowadays. In those days they called them what they were—guts. That's what you were—gut-eaters. And some of you are still gut-eaters.

The field Negro was beaten from morning to night; he lived in a shack, in a hut; he wore old, castoff clothes. He hated his master. I say he hated his master. He was intelligent. That house Negro loved his master, but that field Negro—remember, they were in the majority, and they hated the master. When the house caught on fire, he didn't try to put it out; that field Negro prayed for a wind, for a breeze. When the master got sick, the field Negro prayed that he'd die. If someone came to the field Negro and said, "Let's separate, let's run," he didn't say "Where we going?" He'd say, "Any place is better than here." You've got field Negroes in America today. I'm a field Negro. The masses are the field Negroes. When they see this man's house on fire, you don't hear the little Negroes talking about *"our* government is in trouble." They say, *"The* government is in trouble." Imagine a Negro: *"Our* government!" I even heard one say *"our* astronauts." They won't even let him near the plant—and *"our* astronauts!" *"Our* Navy"—that's a Negro that is out of his mind, a Negro that is out of his mind.

Just as the slavemaster of that day used Tom, the house Negro, to keep the field Negroes in check, the same old slavemaster today has Negroes who are nothing but modern Uncle Toms, twentieth-century Uncle Toms, to keep you and me in check, to keep us under control, keep us passive and peaceful and nonviolent. That's Tom making you nonviolent. It's like when you go to the dentist, and the man's going to take your tooth. You're going to fight him when he starts pulling.

So he squirts some stuff in your jaw called novocaine, to make you think they're not going to do anything to you. So you sit there and because you've got all of that novocaine in your jaw, you suffer—peacefully. Blood running all down your jaw, and you don't know what's happening. Because someone has taught you to suffer—peacefully.

The white man does the same thing to you in the street, when he wants to put knots on your head and take advantage of you and not have to be afraid of your fighting back. To keep you from fighting back, he gets these old religious Uncle Toms to teach you and me, just like novocaine, to suffer peacefully. Don't stop suffering—just suffer peacefully. As Rev. Cleage pointed out, they say you should let your blood flow in the streets. This is a shame. You know he's a Christian preacher. If it's a shame to him, you know what it is to me.

There is nothing in our book, the Koran, that teaches us to suffer peacefully. Our religion teaches us to be intelligent. Be peaceful, be courteous, obey the law, respect everyone; but if someone puts his hand on you, send him to the cemetery. That's a good religion. In fact, that's that old-time religion. That's the one that Ma and Pa used to talk about: an eye for an eye, and a tooth for a tooth, and a head for a head, and a life for a life. That's a good religion. And nobody resents that kind of religion being taught but a wolf, who intends to make you his meal.

This is the way it is with the white man in America. He's a wolf—and you're sheep. Any time a shepherd, a pastor, teaches you and me not to run from the white man and, at the same time, teaches us not to fight the white man, he's a traitor to you and me. Don't lay down a life all by itself. No, preserve your life, it's the best thing you've got. And if you've got to give it up, let it be even-steven.

. . .

The Great Society

LYNDON B. JOHNSON

Lyndon Johnson announced his Great Society program in a speech delivered at the University of Michigan in 1964. This, in effect, was his "I Have a Dream" speech, and Johnson was indeed a man of large dreams and grandiose vision. He promised to tackle the full range of social problems that American society faced in the mid-1960's: racial injustice, poverty, a decaying environment, as well as the need to improve the quality of life by applying American economic advances in the twentieth century to the resolution of these problems.

In this speech Johnson spoke of leading the nation's intelligentsia toward formulation of social polices to solve the problems he identified. This dream was the source of the Great Society legislation of the mid- and late 1960's. The implementation of this far-reaching social program became sadly tangled with the parallel pursuit of elusive victory in the Vietnam War. The outcome of these noble dreams has had a mixed reception. To some extent, a fair assessment of Johnson's programs is still premature. The Great Society was clearly a major effort in the history of American reform. Much of our opinion of the reform tradition in American politics will be colored by the eventual assessment that American historians reach of the programs that Lyndon Johnson created in a few frenetic years.

I have come today from the turmoil of your capital to the tranquility of your campus to speak about the future of your country.

The purpose of protecting the life of our nation and preserving the liberty of our citizens is to pursue the happiness of our people. Our success in that pursuit is the test of our success as a nation.

For a century we labored to settle and to subdue a continent. For half a century we called upon unbounded invention and untiring industry to create an order of plenty for all of our people.

The challenge of the next half century is whether we have the wisdom to use that wealth to enrich and elevate our national life, and to advance the quality of our American civilization.

Your imagination, your initiative, and your indignation will determine whether we build a society where progress is the servant of our needs, or a society where old values and new visions are buried under unbridled growth. For in your time we have the opportunity to move

Speech at Ann Arbor, Mich., May 22, 1964. *Public Papers of the Presidents of the United States: Lyndon B. Johnson,* Government Printing Office (Washington, D.C., 1965), I (1963-1964), 704-707.

not only toward the rich society and the powerful society, but upward to the Great Society.

The Great Society rests on abundance and liberty for all. It demands an end to poverty and racial injustice, to which we are totally committed in our time. But that is just the beginning.

The Great Society is a place where every child can find knowledge to enrich his mind and to enlarge his talents. It is a place where leisure is a welcome chance to build and reflect, not a feared cause of boredom and restlessness. It is a place where the city of man serves not only the needs of the body and the demands of commerce but the desire for beauty and the hunger for community.

It is a place where man can renew contact with nature. It is a place which honors creation for its own sake and for what it adds to the understanding of the race. It is a place where men are more concerned with the quality of their goals than the quantity of their goods.

But most of all, the Great Society is not a safe harbor, a resting place, a final objective, a finished work. It is a challenge constantly renewed, beckoning us toward a destiny where the meaning of our lives matches the marvelous products of our labor.

So I want to talk to you today about three places where we begin to build the Great Society—in our cities, in our countryside, and in our classrooms.

Many of you will live to see the day perhaps fifty years from now, when there will be 400 million Americans—four-fifths of them in urban areas. In the remainder of this century urban population will double, city land will double, and we will have to build homes, highways, and facilities equal to all those built since this country was first settled. So in the next forty years we must rebuild the entire urban United States.

Aristotle said: "Men come together in cities in order to live, but they remain together in order to live the good life." It is harder and harder to live the good life in American cities today.

The catalogue of ills is long: there is the decay of the centers and the despoiling of the suburbs. There is not enough housing for our people or transportation for our traffic. Open land is vanishing and old landmarks are violated.

Worst of all expansion is eroding the precious and time-honored values of community with neighbors and communion with nature. The loss of these values breeds loneliness and boredom and indifference.

Our society will never be great until our cities are great. Today the frontier of imagination and innovation is inside those cities and not beyond their borders. . . .

A second place where we begin to build the Great Society is in our countryside. We have always prided ourselves on being not only America the strong and America the free, but America the beautiful. Today that beauty is in danger. The water we drink, the food we eat, the very air that we breathe, are threatened with pollution. Our parks are overcrowded, our seashores overburdened. Green fields and dense forests are disappearing.

A few years ago we were greatly concerned about the "Ugly American." Today we must act to prevent an ugly America.

For once the battle is lost, once our natural splendor is destroyed, it can never be recaptured. And once man can no longer walk with beauty or wonder at nature his spirit will wither and his sustenance be wasted.

A third place to build the Great Society is in the classrooms of America. There your children's lives will be shaped. Our society will not be great until every young mind is set free to scan the farthest reaches of thought and imagination. We are still far from that goal. . . .

Each year more than 100,000 high school graduates, with proved ability, do not enter college because they cannot afford it. And if we cannot educate today's youth, what will we do in 1970 when elementary school enrollment will be 5 million greater than 1960? And high school enrollment will rise by 5 million. College enrollment will increase by more than 3 million.

In many places, classrooms are overcrowded and curricula are outdated. Most of our qualified teachers are underpaid, and many of our paid teachers are unqualified. So we must give every child a place to sit and a teacher to learn from. Poverty must not be a bar to learning, and learning must offer an escape from poverty.

But more classrooms and more teachers are not enough. We must seek an educational system which grows in excellence as it grows in size. This means better training for our teachers. It means preparing youth to enjoy their hours of leisure as well as their hours of labor. It means exploring new techniques of teaching, to find new ways to stimulate the love of learning and the capacity for creation.

These are three of the central issues of the Great Society. While our government has many programs directed at those issues, I do not pretend that we have the full answer to those problems. . . .

But I do promise this: We are going to assemble the best thought and the broadest knowledge from all over the world to find those answers for America. I intend to establish working groups to prepare a series of White House conferences and meetings—on the cities, on natural beauty, on the quality of education, and on other emerging challenges. And from these meetings and from this inspiration and from these studies we will begin to set our course toward the Great Society.

The solution to these problems does not rest on a massive program in Washington, nor can it rely solely on the strained resources of local authority. They require us to create new concepts of cooperation, a creative federalism, between the national capital and the leaders of local communities.

Within your lifetime powerful forces, already loosed, will take us toward a way of life beyond the realm of our experience, almost beyond the bounds of our imagination.

For better or for worse, your generation has been appointed by history to deal with those problems and to lead America toward a new age. You have the chance never before afforded to any people in any age. You can help build a society where the demands of morality, and the needs of the spirit, can be realized in the life of the nation.

So, will you join in the battle to give every citizen the full equality which God enjoins and the law requires, whatever his belief, or race, or the color of his skin?

Will you join in the battle to give every citizen an escape from the crushing weight of poverty?

Will you join in the battle to make it possible for all nations to live in enduring peace—as neighbors and not as mortal enemies?

Will you join in the battle to build the Great Society, to prove that our material progress is only the foundation on which we will build a richer life of mind and spirit?

There are those timid souls who say this battle cannot be won; that we are condemned to a soulless wealth. I do not agree. We have the power to shape the civilization that we want. But we need your will, your labor, your hearts, if we are to build that kind of society.

Those who came to this land sought to build more than just a new country. They sought a new world. So I have come here today to your campus to say that you can make their vision our reality. So let us from this moment begin our work so that in the future men will look back and say: It was then, after a long and weary way, that man turned the exploits of his genius to the full enrichment of his life.

The Welfare Explosion

FRANCES FOX PIVEN and RICHARD A. CLOWARD

*One view of the growth of social welfare programs is that of a pro-
gressive liberalization as "rugged individualism" has given way to "wel-
farism." More and more forms of social welfare—relief for the poor,
old age and unemployment insurance, free medical services for the
aged and the indigent—have become increasingly available in an industrial economy that could afford such benefits and had less use for the
labor of old people, mothers and children, and unskilled workers. According to this view, the growth of the welfare roles in the 1960's—
as well as the rising opposition to this development in the 1970's—is
easy to understand as liberal thrust and conservative reaction, Democratic initiative and Republican consolidation, Johnson's New Society
versus Nixon's New American (Counter) Revolution.*

*Frances Fox Piven and Richard A. Cloward contest this consensus
notion of welfare history. They argue that the timing of growth in welfare rolls does not support such a view. They point out how welfare roles
"exploded" in the mid-1960's as well as in other eras extending back
at least to Elizabethan England. In effect, Piven and Cloward argue,
the welfare system responds to political, rather than to social or economic, stimuli; it feeds on fear, not on generosity. Thus when social
fears diminish, so does the number of welfare "cases."*

*The authors raise important questions about the so-called Moyni-
han thesis that attributes a large part of the welfare rise of the 1960's
to the presumed disintegration of the black family under the impact
of migration from country to city. Yet the reader must consider whether
social welfare benefits can be separated from the other developments
in social legislation that seem to show a more steady progress throughout the twentieth century. These include unemployment insurance;
federal Social Security; disability and workmen's compensation systems; and growth of social services, clinics, and government-financed
medicine. Is the function of social welfare programs markedly different
from that of these other social services? Or do these services show some
of the same flaws as the relief-giving system? The welfare issue remains
a subject of live controversy that has taken an increasingly bitter tone
during the 1970's.*

During the 1950's the welfare rolls rose by only 110,000 families or
17 per cent. But from December 1960 to February 1969, some 800,000
families were added to the rolls, an increase of 107 per cent in just
eight years and two months. In the course of the 1960's, then, the
nation experienced a "welfare explosion"; for all practical purposes,
traditional restrictions collapsed and the relief money poured out. As
costs rose, the relief system once again became a major public issue, a

source of political controversy and conflict, and thus an object of proposals for "reorganization" and "reform." The remainder of this essay will deal with the economic and political sources of this relief explosion.

SOME DIMENSIONS OF THE WELFARE RISE

The relief rise was pervasive: even the rural counties of the South showed an increase of 34 per cent (see Table 1). However (and this is important), the rises in some places were much greater than in others. By region, the rolls almost tripled in the Northeast and in the West, while the rolls rose by 78 per cent in the North-Central area and by 54 per cent in the South as a whole.

TABLE I

AFDC Caseload Increase By Area

	% Change 1950–1960	% Change 1960–1969	% of 1960–1969 Change Occurring After 1964
National Total	17%	107%	71%
Regions			
Northeast	26	180	69
North Central	27	78	59
West	38	161	72
South	0	54	86
Deep South	7	57	98
Other South	−3	52	81
121 Major Urban Counties	35	165	71
5 Most Populous	26	217	75
116 Remaining	41	135	68
78 Northern	41	175	70
43 Southern	13	121	80
All Less Urban Rural Counties	6	60	71
Northern	17	87	62
Southern	−3	34	93

Among urban counties, the steepest increase (217 per cent) occurred in the 5 most populous ones—New York, Philadelphia, Cook County (Chicago), Wayne County (Detroit), and Los Angeles. A smaller upsurge took place in the 116 remaining urban centers (135 per cent). The rise was larger in Northern urban centers (175 per cent) than in Southern ones (121 per cent).

The nation's rural counties—many of which, especially in the South, experienced considerable outmigration of their poor—nevertheless had a rise of 60 per cent. The Northern rural rolls almost doubled (87 per cent), and Southern rolls moved up more modestly (34 per cent).

Another way to describe these increases is to ask: How many of the 800,000 additional families on the rolls in February 1969 were located in one region or another, in urban areas or in rural ones? Table 2 [not shown] shows that many families in all parts of the country got on the rolls, although there were great variations by region. The Northeast and West accounted for most of the national increase (39 per cent and 26 per cent respectively). Seventeen per cent of the increase occurred in the North Central region. Finally, the South contributed 18 per cent to the national increase; this fact deserves special note, for the Southern rolls had not changed at all during the 1950's. It also deserves note because the welfare explosion is popularly believed to be a wholly Northern phenomenon.

Urban areas as a whole accounted for the overwhelming share of the national AFDC increases (70 per cent), but it was the "big five" urban centers that experienced the most dramatic rise. During the 1950's, these countries accounted for only 23 per cent of the national increase, while the remaining 116 urban counties accounted for two and a half times as much (57 per cent). In the 1960's, however, the "big five" counties contributed as much to the national increase as all the remaining urban counties in the nation combined (34 and 36 per cent, respectively).

Finally, rural counties contributed 30 per cent to the increase, although the contribution by Northern rural counties (22 per cent) was much greater than by Southern ones (9 per cent). (Still, it is worth remembering that the Southern rural rolls had fallen during the 1950's.)

We come now to the most striking feature of the welfare rise. To speak only of its magnitude and where it took place is to overlook an extraordinary fact: *that the rolls went up all at once*—by 31 per cent in the first four years of the decade, but by 58 per cent in the next four years. Stated another way, fully 71 per cent of the huge welfare increase during the 1960's took place in the four years *after* 1964 (Table 1). It was truly an explosion.

Among the regions, all but the North Central area experienced at least two thirds of their increases after 1964. Indeed, 86 per cent of the total Southern increase and an astonishing 98 per cent of the Deep South increase occurred after 1964!

Urban and rural areas show the same pattern (with the exception of Northern rural counties, where only 62 per cent of the increase took place after 1964). The rural South had an especially abrupt increase— 93 per cent of the rise occurred after 1964. Any explanation of the welfare rise in the 1960's must account for this extraordinary precipitousness.

In summary, the welfare explosion occurred in all regions, and in both urban and rural counties. But the explosion was far greater in urban areas; and among those urban areas it was a handful of the most populous Northern cities that showed the largest rises. Finally, most of the increase occurred all at once, in just a brief period after 1964.

SOME EXPLANATIONS OF THE WELFARE RISE

Of the explanations that have been advanced to account for the welfare explosion, three deserve mention here. One points to continued migration of the black poor from the South. Another attributes the increase to rising formal benefit levels. And the third fixes responsibility on the presumed deterioration of "the Negro family."

We believe that these explanations share a common defect that makes them at best incomplete. All are based on the extremely doubtful premise that *the relief rolls automatically grow when the pool of people eligible for relief grows.* Each of these explanations does, to be sure, point to a factor that increased the pool: the more poor people who migrate from Southern states with restrictive welfare systems to Northern states with more liberal ones, the larger the pool; the higher the formal benefit levels, the larger the pool of eligible families; and the more families without male heads, the larger the pool. But relief-giving does not increase simply because economic deprivation spreads; nor did it increase for this reason in the 1960's. The families who got on the rolls after 1964 were, on the whole, just as much in need of aid before 1964. A pool of eligible people had always been there; and although it grew for the reasons given above, it had also been growing for some time.

If these theories were valid, welfare increases should have occurred where the pool of eligible people was growing. In principle, for example, poor black families in Southern states with low payment levels and severe eligibility restrictions improved their chances of obtaining relief if they migrated to Northern states with higher formal benefit levels and fewer restrictions; some families may even have migrated for that reason. But the principle hardly worked out in practice during the 1950's. Indeed, the number of black families moving northward in the 1950's was greater than in the 1960's, yet the Northern regional increases were from three to seven times larger in the 1960's (Table 1). In the Northeast, for example, the rolls rose by 26 per cent in the 1950's, but by 180 per cent in the 1960's. New York and Los Angeles experienced great in-migration during the 1950's, not only by Southern blacks but by Spanish-speaking families as well; nevertheless, the rolls in these counties went up by only 16 and 14 per cent, respectively.

During the 1960's, however, *the rolls in both counties quadrupled* (300 per cent and 293 per cent respectively), despite the fact that in-migration by blacks had slackened.

Not all of the Southern black poor were dislodged from agriculture in recent decades went North; many migrated to Southern cities. Although such migration might thus account for the decline in Southern rural rolls in the 1950's, it surely would lead us to expect an increase of more than 13 per cent in the Southern cities. The situation in the 1960's is even more puzzling: the rolls in the Southern cities jumped by 121 per cent, and that could be said to be a delayed response to in-migration; but such a speculation is made dubious by the fact that the Southern rural rolls also jumped, and this despite continued out-migration.

The upgrading of benefit levels obviously expands the pool of people who are eligible for assistance. However, even the most cursory examination of the relationship between this factor and changes in the welfare rolls reveals the inadequacy of this explanation. In the 1950's, the national average level of payment per recipient rose almost by half, thus greatly enlarging the pool; but in fact the rolls rose a mere 17 per cent. In the South, furthermore, average payments went up by half but the rolls remained absolutely unchanged. During the 1960's, these patterns were reversed: a national increase of only one-third in average payment was accompanied by more than a doubling of the rolls. In short, neither decade provides evidence to support the rising-payment-level thesis.

The record of individual states also casts serious doubt on this explanation. Between 1960 and early 1969, California increased its average monthly payment per recipient from $43 to $48—a change of 11 per cent. During the same period, California's rolls increased by 219 per cent. In Georgia, the average payment rose by 4 per cent, and the rolls rose 138 per cent. North Carolina raised its average payment by 45 per cent, yet the rolls went up only 4 per cent.

Nor does the evidence from many individual cities bear out the thesis. The quadrupling of New York City's rolls could be explained by a series of substantial payment-level changes enacted by the state beginning in 1960; however, the rolls in Los Angeles also quadrupled although there was no significant upgrading of payment levels in California during the same period.

Before we examine the adequacy of the family-deterioration thesis, it might be well to say a bit more about the thesis itself. This view of the welfare rise was put forward by Daniel P. Moynihan in a much-publicized report on "The Negro Family." Having noted that the number of individuals on the AFDC rolls trebled between 1940 and 1963, and that a disproportionate share of the increase was attributable to black families, he asserted that "the steady expansion of . . . [the AFDC] program, as of public assistance programs in general, can be taken as a measure of the steady disintegration of the Negro family structure over the past generation in the United States."

We find this explanation of the relief rise inadequate, but not because we dismiss the evidence showing that the black family has been weakened by uprooting, urban resettlement, and chronically high rates of urban unemployment. These forces have taken their toll, as they did of other dislocated groups in earlier periods of our history. (Indeed, we will return to the evidence on the erosion of the black family, . . . for we believe it does help to explain the welfare rise, albeit very circuitously. From our perspective, the weakening of the family signified a weakening of social control, especially over the young, and it was the young who were the most prominent in the disorders of the 1960's. Disorder, in turn, was a critical force in producing more liberal relief practices, or so we shall argue.) But Moynihan leaps to the conclusion that AFDC rolls rose simply because the changing structure of the black family increased the pool of families *presumably eligible* for relief; the rolls rose, in other words, as an automatic result of a growing pool of eligibles. But that conclusion does not accord with the facts.

Until 1948, blacks did not appear on the AFDC rolls in significant proportions. Whatever their family structure, they were severely discriminated against prior to that time, especially in the South. Two changes then combined to increase their proportion on the rolls in the years immediately after 1948, neither of which had anything to do with family structure. One was pressure by the federal government on Southern states to relax discriminatory practices, a circumstance that produced a sharp increase in the number of blacks who received aid in the South, especially between 1948 and 1952. . . . The second factor was the steady migration of blacks to more liberal Northern cities, where they were less likely to be disqualified for assistance. These factors (or any other factors, for that matter) did not appreciably increase the *magnitude* of the national AFDC rolls between 1948 and 1960, a remarkable phenomenon on which we have already commented; however, they did significantly alter their *composition,* for the proportion of blacks increased from 31 to 40 per cent.

However worrisome the gradual AFDC rise in the 1950's, the rapid rise beginning in 1960 was a special source of alarm to Moynihan, for he thought he detected in this trend the basis for concluding that the black family had become so disorganized that "the present tangle of pathology is capable of perpetuating itself without assistance from the white world." To arrive at this conclusion, Moynihan compared the trends in black male unemployment rates with trends in the total number of AFDC cases opened. From 1953 to 1958, he shows, the black male unemployment rate rose and the total number of new AFDC cases also rose, as if caused by the rising trend in unemployment. After 1958, the unemployment level slowly moved downward, but the total number of new AFDC cases inexplicably continued to climb. It was this failure of the relief rolls to decline in response to ostensibly improved economic conditions in the late 1950's and early 1960's that led Moynihan to say that the pathology of the black family had become so serious that it "may indeed have begun to feed on itself."

The obvious question to which this conclusion leads is whether the absolute increase in female-headed families was as large as the absolute rise in AFDC cases. In a detailed examination of this question, Lurie found that even if all of the new female-headed families in the period between 1959 and 1966 had received AFDC assistance, only about 10 per cent of the AFDC increase would have been accounted for: "It is clear, then, that the rise in the number of families receiving AFDC cannot be explained by the rise in the number of poor families headed by females."

Furthermore, how is one to reconcile recent AFDC increases in the rural South with an "urbanization leads to family deterioration" thesis? Even the urban data yield little support. The nation's 121 urban counties accounted for most of the recent increase, and at first glance this fact might seem to support the explanation, except that a major shift occurred among the urban communities that contributed to the welfare rise in the 1950's, as contrasted with the 1960's. In the 1950's, as we noted earlier, the "big five" counties accounted for only 23 per cent of the national increase; in the 1960's, however, they represented 34 per cent, or as much as the remaining 116 urban counties combined. A family-deterioration argument would have to explain why, during the 1950's, families were more likely to deteriorate in cities of less than one million persons, whereas in the 1960's the vulnerable families had shifted to cities of over one million persons. What such an explanation would be is not readily apparent.

Finally, and of great importance, none of these explanations, including the family-breakdown thesis, helps to account for the striking fact that 71 per cent of the welfare rise in the 1960's took place after 1964. The extraordinary precipitousness of the Southern rise is clearly incompatible with all three of these theories, for the Southern rolls rose by just half, but virtually all of that increase (86 per cent) took place after 1964.

And so the puzzle remains, for if neither the rate of migration nor formal benefit levels skyrocketed after 1964, the rolls clearly did, and if family life among blacks did not suddenly collapse in those few years, many of the restrictive practices of the relief system clearly did. What must be explained, in short, is not why the pool of eligible families grew, although the existence of a pool of unemployed poor is one precondition for a welfare explosion; what must be explained is why so many of the families in that pool were finally able to get on the rolls.

. . .

The contemporary relief explosion was a response to the civil disorder by rapid economic change—in this case, the modernization of Southern agriculture. The impact of modernization on blacks was much greater than on whites: it was they who were the chief victims of the convulsion in Southern agriculture, and it was they who were more likely to encounter barriers to employment once relocated in the cities, a combination of circumstances which led to a substantial weakening of social controls and widespread outbreaks of disorder. For if un-employment and forced migration altered the geography of black pov-erty, it also created a measure of black power. In the 1960's, the grow-ing mass of black poor in the cities emerged as a political force for the first time, both in the voting booths and in the streets. And the relief system was, we believe, one of the main local institutions to respond to that force, even though the reaction was greatly delayed.

The relationship between increasing black power and the expand-ing welfare rolls is not altogether obvious. Great masses of poor blacks did not rise up in anger against a welfare system that denied them sustenance (although some did). Nor did the increased flow of public aid result from demands made by black political leaders; quite to the contrary, the expanding welfare rolls have often been as much a source of dismay to black elites as to white elites. Finally, there is a puzzling absence of liberalizing legislation. Legislative enactments in the years between 1960 and 1969 were intended not to put more families on the rolls, but to get them off via rehabilitation services (the passage of AFDC-UP is an exception). Indeed, the puzzle deepens because some legislative enactments—particularly the congressional amendments of 1967—actually made the relief system more restrictive. Still, the rolls more than doubled. The policies of the welfare rise, in short, are any-thing but self-evident.

In our previous analysis of why relief restrictions collapsed in the Great Depression, we found that the critical factor was the growing volatility of those dislodged from the occupational order. Mass un-employment alone did not lead to the expansion of relief arrangements —not, that is, until unemployment had generated so much unrest as to threaten political stability. In other words, economic convulsions which also produce mass turbulence—whether riots in the streets or upheavals in electoral alignments—are likely to lead to the temporary liberaliza-tion of relief provisions.

Although unemployment during the Great Depression rapidly pro-duced a political crisis and impelled the expansion of public aid, two decades passed before the unemployment resulting from moderniza-tion and migration after World War II produced mass disorder, and so the relief rolls did not rise appreciably until after 1964. Agricultural modernization and migration to the cities brought blacks within the sphere of electoral politics, to be sure, but larger voting numbers alone did not produce concessions. It was not until this mass of unintegrated people finally became turbulent that both local government and the federal government began to register and react to their presence.

The welfare explosion occurred during several years of the greatest domestic disorder since the 1930's—perhaps the greatest in our history. It was concurrent with the turmoil produced by the civil rights struggle, with widespread and destructive rioting in the cities, and with the for-mation of a militant grass-roots movement of the poor dedicated to the combatting welfare restrictions. Not least, the welfare rise was also con-current with the enactment of a series of ghetto-placating federal pro-grams (such as the antipoverty program) which, among other things, hired thousands of poor people, social workers, and lawyers who, it subsequently turned out, greatly stimulated people to apply for relief and helped them to obtain it. And the welfare explosion, although an urban phenomenon generally, was greatest in just that handful of large metropolitan counties where the political turmoil of the middle and late 1960's was the most acute.

In other words, we shall argue that the expansion of the welfare rolls was a political response to political disorder. If many of the welfare restrictions were not legislated out of existence in the 1960's, *their implementation in many localities (especially in the cities) almost completely broke down*. And that was very much a matter of politics. Moreover, it was a matter of black politics, or so we shall argue . . .

PART FOUR

The 1970's and Beyond

The 1970's did not begin with the sharp assertiveness of the previous decade, when John F. Kennedy announced in his inaugural the coming into power of "a new generation." Rather, the nation was ruled by a man long familiar to the electorate—the man who "got" Alger Hiss in the 1940's, who had given his "Checkers" speech two decades before. The war in Vietnam, already the longest in the history of the United States, dragged on. Gone were the young leaders who gave the early 1960's its special flavor; and the even younger radicals who had colored the rest of the decade grew older and shed their flamboyance. As Eisenhower had done in the 1950's, Nixon could settle a war he had not made, thereby easing world tension generally and in the process calming a nation too long distracted by political agitation.

Yet the history of the 1950's and 1960's was not repeated. The

Vietnam War stretched into Nixon's second administration. The young people's demonstrations ceased, with several of the young shot to death on college campuses. Instead of an expected tranquillity following the resolution of the war came the resignation of a president in the aftermath of the Watergate scandals, and this created a new period of political excitement. Revelations of sinister doings by hitherto respected institutions—the Oval Office, the CIA, the FBI, and the Justice Department of the United States—came as a shock to the public.

Even before the war in Vietnam ended, the economy sagged just short of depression, buffeted by major shifts in world economic relations. People who had once worried about—or boasted of—the overweening power of the United States in the world economy now fretted over the irresponsibility of multinational corporations. Earlier concern for developing the poorer nations turned to fears of economic blackmail by the oil-producing nations. And the threat of ecological disasters, technological time bombs planted in our chemical dumps and nuclear plants and even in our streams and lakes and the very ocean itself, haunted the American dream.

Midway through the decade came the country's 1976 bicentennial celebration. Its unexpected symbol—the event that captured the nation's imagination most fully—was a parade of "tall ships," reminders of an American economic excellence of more than a century before, the swift and beautiful clipper ships of the 1850's that had so rapidly become obsolete. Most of the tall ships sailing up New York harbor were foreign, just as most American goods shipped by sea went on ships of foreign registry. The nautical parade was at once a suitable celebration both of our old independence and our new interdependence—an indication of the mood of quiet realism that marked the era.

The new Democratic administration led by Jimmy Carter appeared just right to lead the nation into a post-Watergate era. Carter was a Southerner, a nuclear engineer, a successful businessman, an outsider to the Washington establishment, a born-again Christian and at the same time a sophisticated politician. He combined themes from the perennial New Deal sensibility with an innate conservatism that seemed to reflect the mood of the seventies. But the promise was never fulfilled. Foreign dilemmas, domestic economic problems, and the failure of efforts to confront the major issue of energy policy doomed the Carter administration. In 1980 the American people overwhelmingly elected Ronald Reagan, who seemed to resemble the Carter of 1976: a conservative political outsider who harkened back to old virtues and old hopes. Ralph Waldo Emerson had long ago spoken of the opposition of the "party of hope" and the "party of memory," but by 1980 hopes and memories had intertwined in a way that the American political system could not disentangle. No one can say whether the election of Ronald Reagan was a last hurrah for a vanishing America or a new beginning, whether the election of 1980 was the formation of a new ruling coalition or just another turn of the wheel in which every presidential election for the past quarter-century has differed markedly from the one four years before.

Report from Vietnam

MICHAEL HERR

The United States war in Vietnam, as Jean-Paul Sartre described it in his remarkable essay "On Genocide," was a "war of example." It was primarily an assertion of American willingness to resist "wars of national liberation" sponsored by major communist powers. Sartre pointed out that such a war could have no specific outcome. The limitlessness of the goal of demonstrating the great price a country would have to pay if it pursued a war of national liberation made genocide a part of strategy. The United States would bomb the smaller nation "back to the Stone Age," "defoliate" its forests and farmlands, "zippo" its villages, "pattern bomb" its towns and countrysides. With mindless destruction raised to a strategic objective, a certain type of rogue warrior would be the only possible hero; the rest were "grunts" mired in the slaughter, having to kill, hoping to survive, breathing in and breathing out, as Michael Herr says, but doomed to live with a horror of purposelessness that they could never share with the everyday world to which they prayed to return. This was not the John Wayne kind of war the generation after World War II grew up with, where purpose and heroism weighed in against the horrors. This was the world of Apocalypse Now, *of an anger without focus that is the only legacy of Vietnam.*

Michael Herr's book Dispatches *has been widely acclaimed as the most successful depiction of the American war in Vietnam. It was a media war: reporters at least represented a bit of the gratuitous heroism, the choosing to live dangerously that we Americans have been pleased to identify with war since the days of Richard Harding Davis and Ernest Hemingway. It was a battle of technology against the silent black-pajama-clad Viet Cong. (And of the modern globalism of the United States set so incongruously against obscurely understood struggles that drifted back through three thousand years of history and may continue for three thousand more.) It was also a defense of Saigon, where, for a scant century or so, the West had comfortably exploited the East. Michael Herr's stacatto prose captures the images the war holds at a point in our experience when its larger meanings for the United States remain still beyond the grasp of our imaginations, which are still glutted by the years of televised horrors witnessed in our living rooms.*

I THE REPORTER

Going out at night the medics gave you pills, Dexedrine breath like dead snakes kept too long in a jar. I never saw the need for them myself, a little contact or anything that even sounded like contact would give me more speed than I could bear. Whenever I heard something outside of our clenched little circle I'd practically flip, hoping to God that I wasn't the only one who'd noticed it. A couple of rounds fired off in the dark a kilometer away and the Elephant would be there kneeling on my chest, sending me down into my boots for a breath. Once I thought I saw a light moving in the jungle and I caught myself just under a whisper saying, "I'm not ready for this, I'm not ready for this." That's when I decided to drop it and do something else with my nights. And I wasn't going out like the night ambushers did, or the Lurps, long-range recon patrollers who did it night after night for weeks and months, creeping up on VC base camps or around moving columns of North Vietnamese. I was living too close to my bones as it was, all I had to do was accept it. Anyway, I'd save the pills for later, for Saigon and the awful depressions I always had there.

I knew one 4th Division Lurp who took his pills by the fistful, downs from the left pocket of his tiger suit and ups from the right, one to cut the trail for him and the other to send him down it. He told me that they cooled things out just right for him, that he could see that old jungle at night like he was looking at it through a starlight scope. "They sure give you the range," he said.

This was his third tour. In 1965 he'd been the only survivor in a platoon of the Cav wiped out going into the Ia Drang Valley. In '66 he'd come back with the Special Forces and one morning after an ambush he'd hidden under the bodies of his team while the VC walked all around them with knives, making sure. They stripped the bodies of their gear, the berets too, and finally went away, laughing. After that, there was nothing left for him in the war except the Lurps.

"I just can't hack it back in the World," he said. He told me that after he'd come back home the last time he would sit in his room all day, and sometimes he'd stick a hunting rifle out the window, leading people and cars as they passed his house until the only feeling he was aware of was all up in the tip of that one finger. "It used to put my folks real uptight," he said. But he put people uptight here too, even here.

"No man, I'm sorry, he's just too crazy for me," one of the men in his team said. "All's you got to do is look in his eyes, that's the whole fucking story right there."

"Yeah, but you better do it quick," someone else said. "I mean, you don't want to let him catch you at it."

But he always seemed to be watching for it, I think he slept with his eyes open, and I was afraid of him anyway. All I ever managed was one quick look in, and that was like looking at the floor of an ocean. He wore a gold earring and a headband torn from a piece of camouflage parachute material, and since nobody was about to tell him to get his hair cut it fell below his shoulders, covering a thick purple scar. Even at division he never went anywhere without at least a .45 and a knife, and he thought I was a freak because I wouldn't carry a weapon.

"Didn't you ever meet a reporter before?" I asked him.

"Tits on a bull," he said. "Nothing personal."

But what a story he told me, as one-pointed and resonant as any war story I ever heard, it took me a year to understand it:

"Patrol went up the mountain. One man came back. He died before he could tell us what happened."

I waited for the rest, but it seemed not to be that kind of story; when I asked him what had happened he just looked like he felt sorry for me, fucked if he'd waste time telling stories to anyone dumb as I was.

His face was all painted up for night walking now like a bad hallucination, not like the painted faces I'd seen in San Francisco only a few weeks before, the other extreme of the same theater. In the coming hours he'd stand as faceless and quiet in the jungle as a fallen tree, and God help his opposite numbers unless they had at least half a squad along, he was a good killer, one of our best. The rest of his team were gathered outside the tent, set a little apart from the other division units, with its own Lurp-designated latrine and its own exclusive freeze-dry rations, three-star war food, the same chop they sold at Abercrombie & Fitch. The regular division troops would almost shy off the path when they passed the area on their way to and from the mess tent. No matter how toughened up they became in the war, they still looked innocent compared to the Lurps. When the team had grouped they walked in a file down the hill to the lz across the strip to the perimeter and into the treeline.

I never spoke to him again, but I saw him. When they came back in the next morning he had a prisoner with him, blindfolded and with his elbows bound sharply behind him. The Lurp area would definitely be off limits during the interrogation, and anyway, I was already down at the strip waiting for a helicopter to come and take me out of there. . . .

II AIRMOBILITY

In the months after I got back the hundreds of helicopters I'd flown in began to draw together until they'd formed a collective meta-chopper, and in my mind it was the sexiest thing going; saver-destroyer, provider-waster, right hand—left hand, nimble, fluent, canny and human; hot steel, grease, jungle-saturated canvas webbing, sweat cooling and warming up again, cassette rock and roll in one ear and door-gun fire in the other, fuel, heat, vitality and death, death itself, hardly an intruder. Men on the crews would say that once you'd carried a dead person he would always be there, riding with you. Like all combat people they were incredibly superstitious and invariably self-dramatic, but it was (I knew) unbearably true that close exposure to the dead sensitized you to the force of their presence and made for long reverberations; long. Some people were so delicate that one look was enough to wipe them away, but even bone-dumb grunts seemed to feel that something weird and extra was happening to them.

Helicopters and people jumping out of helicopters, people so in love they'd run to get on even when there wasn't any pressure. Choppers rising straight out of small cleared jungle spaces, wobbling down onto city rooftops, cartons of rations and ammunition thrown off, dead and wounded loaded on. Sometimes they were so plentiful and loose that you could touch down at five or six places in a day, look around, hear the talk, catch the next one out. There were installations as big as cities with 30,000 citizens, once we dropped in to feed supply to one man. God knows what kind of Lord Jim phoenix numbers he was doing in there, all he said to me was, "You didn't see a thing, right Chief? You weren't even here." There were posh fat air-conditioned camps like comfortable middle-class scenes with the violence tacit, "far away"; camps named for commanders' wives, LZ Thelma, LZ Betty Lou; number-named hilltops in trouble where I didn't want to stay; trail, paddy, swamp, deep hairy bush, scrub, swale, village, even city, where the ground couldn't drink up what the action spilled, it made you careful where you walked.

Sometimes the chopper you were riding in would top a hill and all the ground in front of you as far as the next hill would be charred and pitted and still smoking, and something between your chest and your stomach would turn over. Frail gray smoke where they'd burned off the rice fields around a free-strike zone, brilliant white smoke from phosphorus ("Willy Peter/Make you a buh liever"), deep black smoke from 'palm, they said that if you stood at the base of a column of napalm smoke it would suck the air right out of your lungs. Once we fanned over a little ville that had just been airstruck and the words of a song by Wingy Manone that I'd heard when I was a few years old snapped into my head, "Stop the War, These Cats Is Killing Them-selves." Then we dropped, hovered, settled down into purple lz smoke, dozens of children broke from their hootches to run in toward the focus of our landing, the pilot laughing and saying, "Vietnam, man. Bomb 'em and feed 'em, bomb 'em and feed 'em."

Flying over jungle was almost pure pleasure, doing it on foot was nearly all pain. I never belonged in there. Maybe it really was what its people had always called it, Beyond; at the very least it was serious, I gave up things to it I probably never got back. ("Aw, jungle's okay. If you know her you can live in her real good, if you don't she'll take you down in an hour. Under.") Once in some thick jungle corner with some grunts standing around, a correspondent said, "Gee, you must really see some beautiful sunsets in here," and they almost pissed themselves laughing. But you could fly up and into hot tropic sunsets that would change the way you thought about light forever. You could also fly out of places that were so grim they turned to black and white in your head five minutes after you'd gone.

That could be the coldest one in the world, standing at the edge of a clearing watching the chopper you'd just come in on taking off again, leaving you there to think about what it was going to be for you now: if this was a bad place, the wrong place, maybe even the last place, and whether you'd made a terrible mistake this time.

There was a camp at Soc Trang where a man at the lz said, "If you come looking for a story this is your lucky day, we got Condition Red here," and before the sound of the chopper had faded out, I knew I had it too. . . .

Airmobility, dig it, you weren't going anywhere. It made you feel safe, it made you feel Omni, but it was only a stunt, technology. Mobility was just mobility, it saved lives or took them all the time (saved mine I don't know how many times, maybe dozens, maybe none), what you really needed was a flexibility far greater than anything the technology could provide, some generous, spontaneous gift for accepting surprises, and I didn't have it. I got to hate surprises, control freak at the crossroads, if you were one of those people who always thought they had to know what was coming next, the war could cream you. It was the same with your ongoing attempts at getting used to the jungle or the blow-you-out climate or the saturating strangeness of the place which didn't lessen with exposure so often as it fattened and darkened in accumulating alienation. It was great if you could adapt, you had to try, but it wasn't the same as making a discipline, going into your own reserves and developing a real war metabolism, slow yourself down when your heart tried to punch its way through your chest, get swift when everything went to stop and all you could feel of your whole life was the entropy whipping through it. Unlovable terms.

The ground was always in play, always being swept. Under the ground was his, above it was ours. We had the air, we could get up in it but not disappear in *to* it, we could run but we couldn't hide, and he could do each so well that sometimes it looked like he was doing them both at once, while our finder just went limp. All the same, one place or another it was always going on, rock around the clock, we had the days and he had the nights. You could be in the most protected space in Vietnam and still know that your safety was provisional, that early death, blindness, loss of legs, arms or balls, major and lasting disfigurement— the whole rotten deal—could come in on the freakyfluky as easily as in the so-called expected ways, you heard so many of those stories it was a wonder anyone was left alive to die in firefights and mortar-rocket attacks. After a few weeks, when the nickel had jarred loose and dropped and I saw that everyone around me was carrying a gun, I also saw that any one of them could go off at any time, putting you where it wouldn't matter whether it had been an accident or not. The roads were mined, the trails booby-trapped, satchel charges and grenades blew up jeeps and movie theaters, the VC got work inside all the camps as shoeshine boys and laundresses and honey-dippers, they'd starch your fatigues and burn your shit and then go home and mortar your area. Saigon and Cholon and Danang held such hostile vibes that you felt you were being dry-sniped every time someone looked at you, and choppers fell out of the sky like fat poisoned birds a hundred times a day. After a while I couldn't get on one without thinking that I must be out of my fucking mind. . . .

"Boy, you sure get offered some shitty choices," a Marine once said to me, and I couldn't help but feel that what he really meant was that you didn't get offered any at all. Specifically, he was just talking about a couple of C-ration cans, "dinner," but considering his young life you couldn't blame him for thinking that if he knew one thing for sure, it was that there was no one anywhere who cared less about what *he* wanted. There wasn't anybody he wanted to thank for his food, but he was grateful that he was still alive to eat it, that the mother-fucker hadn't scarfed him up first. He hadn't been anything but tired and scared for six months and he'd lost a lot, mostly people, and seen far too much, but he was breathing in and breathing out, some kind of choice all by itself.

He had one of those faces, I saw that face at least a thousand times at a hundred bases and camps, all the youth sucked out of the eyes, the color drawn from the skin, cold white lips, you knew he wouldn't wait for any of it to come back. Life had made him old, he'd live it out old. All those faces, sometimes it was like looking into faces at a rock concert, locked in, the event had them; or like students who were very heavily advanced, serious beyond what you'd call their years if you didn't know for yourself what the minutes and hours of those years were made up of. Not just like all the ones you saw who looked like they couldn't drag their asses through another day of it. (How do you feel when a nineteen-year-old kid tells you from the bottom of his heart that he's gotten too old for this kind of shit?) Not like the faces of the dead or wounded either, they could look more released than over-taken. These were the faces of boys whose whole lives seemed to have backed up on them, they'd be a few feet away but they'd be looking back at you over a distance you knew you'd never really cross. We'd talk, sometimes fly together, guys going out on R&R, guys escorting bodies, guys who'd flipped over into extremes of peace or violence. Once I flew with a kid who was going home, he looked back down once at the ground where he'd spent the year and spilled his whole load of tears. Sometimes you even flew with the dead.

Once I jumped on a chopper that was full of them. The kid in the op shack had said that there would be a body on board, but he'd been given some wrong information. "How bad do you want to get to Danang?" he'd asked me, and I'd said, "Bad."

When I saw what was happening I didn't want to get on, but they'd made a divert and a special landing for me, I had to go with the chopper I'd drawn, I was afraid of looking squeamish. (I remember, too, thinking that a chopper full of dead men was far less likely to get shot down than one full of living.) They weren't even in bags. They'd been on a truck near one of the firebases in the DMZ that was firing support for Khe Sanh, and the truck had hit a Command-detonated mine, then they'd been rocketed. The Marines were always running out of things, even food, ammo and medicine, it wasn't so strange that they'd run out of bags too. The men had been wrapped around in ponchos, some of them carelessly fastened with plastic straps, and loaded on board. There was a small space cleared for me between one of them and the door gunner, who looked pale and so tremendously furious that I thought he was angry with me and I couldn't look at him for a while. When we went up the wind blew through the ship and made the ponchos shake and tremble until the one next to me blew back in a fast brutal flap, uncovering the face. They hadn't even closed his eyes for him.

The gunner started hollering as loud as he could, "Fix it! Fix it!," maybe he thought the eyes were looking at him, but there wasn't anything I could do. My hand went there a couple of times and I couldn't, and then I did. I pulled the poncho tight, lifted his head carefully and tucked the poncho under it, and then I couldn't believe that I'd done it. All during the ride the gunner kept trying to smile, and when we landed at Dong Ha he thanked me and ran off to get a detail. The pilots jumped down and walked away without looking back once, like they'd never seen that chopper before in their lives. . . .

III   SAIGON

In Saigon I always went to sleep stoned so I almost always lost my dreams, probably just as well, sock in deep and dim under that information and get whatever rest you could, wake up tapped of all images but the ones remembered from the day or the week before, with only the taste of a bad dream in your mouth like you'd been chewing on a roll of dirty old pennies in your sleep. I'd watched grunts asleep putting out the REM's like a firefight in the dark, I'm sure it was the same with me. They'd say (I'd ask) that they didn't remember their dreams either when they were in the zone, but on R&R or in the hospital their dreaming would be constant, open, violent and clear, like a man in the Pleiku hospital on the night I was there. It was three in the morning, scary and upsetting like hearing a language for the first time and somehow understanding every word, the voice loud and small at the same time, insistent, calling, "*Who? Who?* Who's in the next room?" There was a single shaded light over the desk at the end of the ward where I sat with the orderly. I could only see the first few beds, it felt like there were a thousand of them running out into the darkness, but actually there were only twenty in each row. After the man had repeated it a few times there was a change like the break in a fever, he sounded like a pleading little boy. I could see cigarettes being lighted at the far end of the ward, mumbles and groans, wounded men returning to consciousness, pain, but the man who'd been dreaming slept through it. . . . As for my own dreams, the ones I lost there would make it through later, I should have known, some things will just naturally follow until they take. The night would come when they'd be vivid and unremitting, that night the beginning of a long string, I'd remember then and wake up half believing that I'd never really been in any of those places.

Saigon *cafarde*, a bitch, nothing for it but some smoke and a little lie-down, waking in the late afternoon on damp pillows, feeling the emptiness of the bed behind you as you walked to the windows looking down at Tu Do. Or just lying there tracking the rotations of the ceiling fan, reaching for the fat roach that sat on my Zippo in a yellow disk of grass tar. There were mornings when I'd do it before my feet even hit the floor. Dear Mom, stoned again.

In the Highlands, where the Montagnards would trade you a pound of legendary grass for a carton of Salems, I got stoned with some infantry from the 4th. One of them had worked for months on his pipe, beautifully carved and painted with flowers and peace symbols. There was a reedy little man in the circle who grinned all the time but hardly spoke. He pulled a thick plastic bag out of his pack and handed it over to me. It was full of what looked like large pieces of dried fruit. I was stoned and hungry, I almost put my hand in there, but it had a bad weight to it. The other men were giving each other looks, some amused, some embarrassed and even angry. Someone had told me once, there were a lot more ears than heads in Vietnam; just information. When I handed it back he was still grinning, but he looked sadder than a monkey.

In Saigon and Danang we'd get stoned together and keep the common pool stocked and tended. It was bottomless and alive with Lurps, seals, recondos, Green-Beret bushmasters, redundant mutilators, heavy rapers, eye-shooters, widow-makers, nametakers, classic essential American types; point men, *isolatos* and outriders like they were programmed in their genes to do it, the first taste made them crazy for it, just like they knew it would. You thought you were separate and protected, you could travel the war for a hundred years, a swim in that pool could still be worth a piece of your balance.

We'd all heard about the man in the Highlands who was "building his own gook," parts were the least of his troubles. In Chu Lai some Marines pointed a man out to me and swore to God they'd seen him bayonet a wounded NVA and then lick the bayonet clean. There was a famous story, some reporters asked a door gunner, "How can you shoot women and children?" and he'd answered, "It's easy, you just don't lead 'em so much." Well, they said you needed a sense of humor, there you go, even the VC had one. Once after an ambush that killed a lot of Americans, they covered the field with copies of a photograph that showed one more young, dead American, with the punch line mimeographed on the back, "Your X-rays have just come back from the lab and we think we know what your problem is."

Beautiful for once and only once, just past dawn flying toward the center of the city in a Loach, view from a bubble floating at 800 feet. In that space, at that hour, you could see what people had seen forty years before, Paris of the East, Pearl of the Orient, long open avenues lined and bowered over by trees running into spacious parks, precisioned scale, all under the soft shell from a million breakfast fires, camphor smoke rising and diffusing, covering Saigon and the shining veins of the river with a warmth like the return of better times. Just a projection, that was the thing about choppers, you had to come down sometimes, down to the moment, the street, if you found a pearl down there you got to keep it.

By 7:30 it was beyond berserk with bikes, the air was like L.A. on short plumbing, the subtle city war inside the war had renewed itself for another day, relatively light on actual violence but intense with bad feeling: despair, impacted rage, impotent gnawing resentment; thousands of Vietnamese in the service of a pyramid that wouldn't stand for five years, plugging the feed tube into their own hearts, grasping and gorging; young Americans in from the boonies on TDY, charged with hatred and grounded in fear of the Vietnamese; thousands of Americans sitting in their offices crying in bored chorus, "You can't get these people to do a fucking thing, you can't get these people to do a fucking thing." And all the others, theirs and ours, who just didn't want to play, it sickened them. That December the GVN Department of Labor had announced that the refugee problem had been solved, that "all refugees [had] been assimilated into the economy," but mostly they seemed to have assimilated themselves into the city's roughest corners, alleyways, mud slides, under parked cars. Cardboard boxes that had carried air-conditioners and refrigerators housed up to ten children, most Americans and plenty of Vietnamese would cross the street to avoid trash heaps that fed whole families. And this was still months before Tet, "refugees up the gazops," a flood. I'd heard that the GVN Department of Labor had nine American advisors for every Vietnamese.

In Broddards and La Pagode and the pizzeria around the corner, the Cowboys and Vietnamese "students" would hang out all day, screaming obscure arguments at each other, cadging off Americans, stealing tips from the tables, reading Pléiade editions of Proust, Malraux, Camus. One of them talked to me a few times but we couldn't really communicate, all I understood was his obsessive comparison between Rome and Washington, and that he seemed to believe that Poe had been a French writer. In the late afternoon the Cowboys would leave the cafés and milk bars and ride down hard on Lam Son Square to pick the Allies. They could snap a Rolex off your wrist like a hawk hitting a field mouse; wallets, pens, cameras, eyeglasses, anything; if the war had gone on any longer they'd have found a way to whip the boots off your feet. They'd hardly leave their saddles and they never looked back. There was a soldier down from the 1st Division who was taking snapshots of his friends with some bar girls in front of the Vietnamese National Assembly. He'd gotten his shot focused and centered but before he pushed the button his camera was a block away, leaving him in the bike's backwash with a fresh pink welt on his throat where the cord had been torn and helpless amazement on his face, "Well I'll be dipped in shit!"; as a little boy raced across the square, zipped a piece of cardboard up the soldier's shirtfront and took off around the corner with his Paper Mate. The White Mice stood around giggling, but there were a lot of us watching from the Continental terrace, a kind of gasp went up from the tables, and later when he came up for a beer he said, "I'm goin' back to the war, man, this fucking Saigon is too much for me." There was a large group of civilian engineers there, the same men you'd see in the restaurants throwing food at each other, and one of them, a fat old boy, said, "You ever catch one of them li'l nigs just pinch 'em. Pinch 'em hard. Boy, they hate that."

Five to seven were bleary low hours in Saigon, the city's energy ebbing at dusk, until it got dark and movement was replaced with apprehension. Saigon at night was still Vietnam at night, night was the war's truest medium, night was when it got really interesting in the villages, the TV crews couldn't film at night, the Phoenix was a night bird, it flew in and out of Saigon all the time.

Maybe you had to be pathological to find glamour in Saigon, maybe you just had to settle for very little, but Saigon had it for me, and danger activated it. The days of big, persistent terror in Saigon were over, but everyone felt that they could come back again any time, heavy like 1963–5, when they hit the old Brinks BOQ on Christmas Eve, when they blew up the My Canh floating restaurant, waited for it to be rebuilt and moved to another spot on the river, and then blew it up again, when they bombed the first U.S. embassy and changed the war forever from the intimate inside out. There were four known VC sapper battalions in the Saigon-Cholon area, dread sappers, guerrilla superstars, they didn't even have to do anything to put the fear out. Empty ambulances sat parked at all hours in front of the new embassy. Guards ran mirrors and "devices" under all vehicles entering all installations, BOQ's were fronted with sandbags, checkpoints and wire, high-gauge grilles filled our windows, but they still got through once in a while, random terror but real, even the supposedly terror-free safe spots worked out between the Corsican mob and the VC offered plenty of anxiety. Saigon just before Tet; guess, guess again.

Those nights there was a serious tiger lady going around on a Honda shooting American officers on the street with a .45. I think she'd killed over a dozen in three months; the Saigon papers described her as "beautiful," but I don't know how anybody knew that. The commander of one of the Saigon MP battalions said he thought it was a man dressed in an *ao dai* because a .45 was "an awful lot of gun for a itty bitty Vietnamese woman."

Saigon, the center, where every action in the bushes hundreds of miles away fed back into town on a karmic wire strung so tight that if you touched it in the early morning it would sing all day and all night. Nothing so horrible ever happened upcountry that it was beyond language fix and press relations, a squeeze fit into the computers would make the heaviest numbers jump up and dance. You'd either meet an optimism that no violence could unconvince or a cynicism that would eat itself empty every day and then turn, hungry and malignant, on whatever it could for a bite, friendly or hostile, it didn't matter. Those men called dead Vietnamese "believers," a lost American platoon was "a black eye," they talked as though killing a man was nothing more than depriving him of his vigor.

It seemed the least of the war's contradictions that to lose your worst sense of American shame you had to leave the Dial Soapers in Saigon and a hundred headquarters who spoke goodworks and killed nobody themselves, and go out to the grungy men in the jungle who

Ronald Reagan— Where Will He Lead Us, This Embodiment of Our Everyday Existence

GARRY WILLS

Some observers have taken Ronald Reagan's defeat of President Jimmy Carter in the 1980 presidential election, along with the defeat that year of a number of prominent liberal senators, to be indicative of a turn toward conservatism in American politics. But it is uncertain exactly what the election represented and what it can lead to. Although Reagan is known for his commitment to a conservative philosophy and his campaign drew enthusiastic support of conservatives, he worked hard to assure voters that he would not dismantle the federal institutions of social welfare. During the campaign months commentators were convinced that it was the frustrating state of the economy that was uppermost in the minds of the voters; there was little evidence that the electorate was greatly interested in the ideological conservatism. So long as a Reagan administration follows the economic prescriptions of conservatism, moreover, it will be prevented from taking the kinds of action that respond to the greatest needs of the unhappiest citizens; and that will give it, fairly or unfairly, the appearance of inactivity or of accommodation to the wishes of the most prosperous or most selfishly contented segments of the population. Liberals, meanwhile, with their greater confidence in the efficacy of federal intervention will be able to provide a wide range of alternatives to inaction. Perhaps the overriding question—as the liberal moderate might phrase it—is simply whether the conservatives who wield at least some power in every branch of government will concentrate on invigorating the economic system for the benefit of all Americans, as they have promised to do, or will simply try to build into a weakening economy an institutionalized selfishness benefiting established interests.

Garry Wills, in the brief piece that follows, attempts to define President Reagan's appeal and compare it with that of his predecessors Kennedy, Nixon, and Carter.

SOME IMP OF HISTORY
SEEMS TO BE URGING REAGAN ON

He is the serene beneficiary of turmoil, the amateur foil of professionals, the sane relayer of craziness. There is no way to have at him. His very flaws promote him, and weakness prevails. He wins campaigns by being

349

a noncandidate. His lapses rivet his followers closer to him. There is deep magic here.

But he is *old?* Sure; and that reassures. He is walking evidence that the past perdures—it is out there, ambulatory, defying time. Philip Crane's 1980 campaign was supposed to establish that Reagan's unsound mind could exist in a sound body: as Reagan decomposed along the way, there would still be a handsome head swiveling on a mobile body, saying the same decrepit things. How was Crane to know that a modest decomposition was part of the charm? Time softens Reagan, taking sharp edges off. The older he gets, the better he looks, enacting the truth that old values are still viable. Creaky, perhaps, in this joint or that; rambling, not marching. But even the ramble soothes, where marching would disquiet.

So rivals find that age is Reagan's tease, the booby trap he sets for them. Attack his age, and you seem ungallant, the kind of person who would suggest that Mae West's yips of sexual ecstasy have been feigned for the last half-century or so. Who wants to believe *that,* true or not?

Wild inaccuracy is another of the pitfalls he seems to be digging for himself—as he watches others fall into them. But why should his friends care about a fact here, a fact there, when he so obviously does not? Facts come and go; statistics are symbols or persuaders, when they are not lies; reality adjusts to belief, not vice versa. There is a sophisticated calculus to Reagan's naïveté.

Not that he sees all the understructure of his own appeal, girder by girder. That would not fit the very genius of his appeal. He floats above the quibbling because it never touches his self-esteem. He does not, like most politicians, have to defend his arguments. It is his *attitude* that is right, and arguments cannot reach that. His right-wing attitude was unruffled even when he enacted rather left-wing laws in California (such as a permissive abortion program). He rather attended his own administration than became its creature or creator.

Like most politicians, he lacks pride. But, unlike them, he also lacks the vanity that makes a claim, at least, to discursive consistency on issues. He looks unchallengeable, even in error, because he feels secure. He shrugs off attacks as so clearly benighted they scarcely deserve attention, and certainly not anger. He brings to the Right the thing it always needed most—relaxation. Consider how rare has been sheer friendliness on the right wing of our political spectrum. Robert Taft was loved only by a hard effort of those conservatives who threw their hearts into the arctic blast of his number-citing rectitude. Reagan has a shrugging semirectitude that will not stand on ceremony or split hairs: he tugs hearts out before they can be thrown.

Richard Nixon, unlovable himself, was warmly supported for the enemies he made. A hired gun, his very nastiness could be put to an exterminator's use. But Reagan is a *good* guy willing to take on the baddies; and after the shoot-out, he will not rifle the till, like Nixon; he will not save the town only as a way of lining his own pocket.

Reagan's deepest appeal is to those who cheered George Wallace on but who felt a bit shabby and soiled after he worked them over, massaged their hate glands, made them queasy with acrid emotions sweated out of them. Reagan croons, in love accents, his permission to indulge a functional hatred of poor people and blacks. Nothing personal about it. It is really an act of patriotism not to let the hardworking middle class be dragged down to *their* level. Imagine what a godsend this is for right-wingers with some small claim left them to fastidiousness. Poor William Buckley had to fashion a nine-foot pole for dealing with all those Spiro Agnew types a gentleman should not touch with a ten-foot pole. But Ronnie he can walk right up to and hug. Even the caricaturists have a hard time putting Joe McCarthy's scowl or Agnew's dopey viciousness on Reagan's face.

But Reagan would not be important if he just made the right wing giddy with relief at finding a nontawdry spokesman for its tainted views. Reagan has stronger historical tides running in his favor, tides that affect our whole society and not just the right wing. He is the legitimate-looking heir to our government's illegitimacy. Reagan has some of the show biz glitter that right-wingers hated when they misleadingly called it "charisma" in John Kennedy's time. But Kennedy was not charismatic in any but the *Photoplay* sense. Reagan is the man who combines a superficial glamour with real charismatic function.

Max Weber popularized the concept of charismatic leadership, which he contrasted with rational and traditional authority. Tradition gives a sacredness to office, and reason gives a utilitarian vindication to law. It is only when these comparatively stable and everyday channels of authority break down that an entirely personal and arbitrary authority is needed. This can happen when a new society is coming into being, without prior tradition or magic to rely on; Weber thought, here, of the founders of great religious orders whose private vision fired disciples —Saints Benedict and Francis, Dominic and Ignatius. The charismatic leader occurs, as well, in revolutions, when old patterns of authority are called abruptly into question, or utterly effaced, to give birth to a new nation. George Washington is the exemplar, or Mao Tse-tung.

But we have been witnessing for some time a crisis that Weber did not expressly treat in his discussion of charisma—the gradual inanition of institutions, the evanescence of authority, without conscious revolution or new vision. We see a paradoxical new process at work—the undermining of traditional authority by people who think of themselves as conservatives, as guardians of tradition. The enemies of government, of "the establishment," have exactly Reagan's sense of an ideal (unformulated) tradition at war with the actual traditions of our government.

John Kennedy was not a charismatic leader in Weber's sense. Quite the opposite. He relied on all the institutions of authority—Ivy League ties, press camaraderie, bureaucratic myths of efficiency. He loved the symbols of office and thought of the White House as his palace. Robert McNamara was in attendance to explicate rational authority, and Arthur Schlesinger Jr. to weave the rites of tradition stretching from Jackson through Roosevelt. The style was not arbitrary, nor the vision private.

In the common misuse of the term, Nixon lacked charisma. But his was a counterinsurgency presidency, a one-man rule, charismatic in that sense. He occupied the White House as an outpost in enemy territory. He created his secret army of thugs and gumshoes because he did not trust his own official underlings: the bureaucracy, the CIA, the FBI. The hired gun was there to do a job just because the sheriff's star had lost its luster. But, of course, his very presence further tarnished the authority he wielded. It was something alien, to be turned on itself. Nixon brought himself down as part of the larger demolition job he was engaged in. His principal regret was that he did not have time to level more institutions. He thought of his task as breaking the grip of the bureaucracy; but he could do that only by undermining government itself.

Jimmy Carter consciously offered himself as a restorer of decency to scenes still reeking with scandal. But he felt he could do this only by stressing his own qualities as separate from those of his office. His personal concern was the issue. We were to think more of President *Carter* than of *President* Carter. That is why official ceremony was played down. He was just a lone man strolling into town with his wardrobe bag over his shoulder. He would never lie to us, he promised, playing that claim off against implicit recognition that our officialdom lies, and that he could never be part of that officialdom.

This attempt to *re*legitimate office in terms of one's own personal qualities simply *de*legitimates. The office is more suspect, in the long run, if it is redeemed only by men who keep their distance from it. That is the deep and disturbing point of cocktail chatter about Carter's "war on Washington."

NIXON'S AND CARTER'S FAILINGS HAVE BEEN BLESSINGS IN DISGUISE

The office of the President has not been totally discredited because the opponent-holders of that office have had a negative appeal, one that could not entirely supplant the utilitarian authority of law (which did in Nixon) or the sacredness of office (which continues to elude Carter). Nixon was hedged in by his own suspicions, which turned even his private army, as well as his public entourage, against him. Carter is limited by the sectional appeal that made him important to the Democratic party, resolving the anomaly of our postwar politics—the fact that Democrats could outregister Republicans two to one or more, yet have not won the presidency without the South. The very thing that gives Carter his marginal purchase on the South—his loyalty to a clutch of Dogpatchers like Bert Lance and Hamilton Jordan—weakens his links to the everyday experience of Americans less regionally marked.

Reagan, by contrast, has *been* our everyday experience through years of popcorn matinees, through decades of relaxed success as a campaigner. He is by now our neighbor as the orator, the hometown boy as a success. Not only the baseball player and soldier and football hero he actually played on the screen, he has become the inheritor of roles played by his coevals—Jimmy Stewart as Mr. Smith, Gary Cooper as Mr. Deeds, even Judy Holliday as Billie Dawn. He is the innocent as celebrity, and the celebrity as the real authority behind all screens and shams of officialdom. He is the first serious *counter*authority with an *air* of authority; the charismatic leader without a vision, just a role. He is the perfect denier, the double negative that comes out, somehow, as a positive. The disinherited air of his predecessors made us let them into the American psyche through some trapdoor (like Joe McCarthy and Nixon) or side entrance (like Agnew and Carter). But Reagan strides confidently in through the front door.

That, of course, is the scary thing about Reagan: that he does not scare us. He so obviously means well that it is gauche (like mentioning his age) to notice that he means nothing; that he has no alternative vision; that his war on authority is neither radically *founding* (like Ignatius Loyola's) nor revolutionary (like George Washington's). He represents that stage of our government's inanition of authority where it is no longer a wild claim, but mild dogma, to say that the rule of tradition and reason has ended in Washington—that everything depends, now, on one man's personal qualities, on charisma. Facts and evidence are not important in the time of a private vision publicly yearned for. In that situation, to claim authority is to profess illegitimacy, to be one of "them," of "the gummint" that must be got off "our" backs.

· This process—ridding American backs of encumbrance—is entirely negative in logic; but Reagan's approach is not obviously denigrative. He does not mean the meanness of his views. He does not scowl racism at us, like Wallace, nor leer hatred of Ivy League types, like McCarthy or Nixon. He does an actor's walk-through of those men's lines without losing his unruffled air of meaning well—just as he walked through the animosities of both sides in the Hollywood Red-hunt days, coming out an ambiguous half-hero (or at least nonvillain) to all sides. He uses ideology without being trapped inside it. The very thing that frees him of authority keeps him clear of what others take so seriously. If the authority of facts and argument matters so little, how should ideology itself confine its wielder? With Reagan, we get Vietnam defended without Goldwater's bluster, blacks put in their place without Bull Connor's dogs, patriotism defended without Lyndon Johnson's oleaginous defensiveness. Reagan is so patently unmalicious as he speaks for war and divisiveness that he may, indeed, kill us with kindness. He is the wholesome hometown sort who can drop the bomb without a second thought, your basic American Harry Truman.

In a world being emptied of authority, Reagan has some of authority's characteristics. Continuity, for instance. His age does not bother people; rather, it suggests a rootedness in essentially deracinated views. He is unmenacing because he is always around, so much a part of us (and how could *we* be menacing?). He is both Henry Aldrich and Grandpa Walton, our remembered and our present selves, our fantasy of afternoons with popcorn and the "real" world of TV politics. Where so little is stable, the emptiness at the center looks eternal. Reagan is the calm eye of history's hurricane; and we hope, by moving with it, never to slip toward the edges and to chaos. But we will.

Suggested Further Readings

I. 1945 TO 1952

An important revisionist work critical of administration Cold War policy is Gabriel and Joyce Kolko, *The Limits of Power* (New York: Harper & Row, 1972). A more moderate, yet still revisionist, account is Walter La Feber, *America, Russia, and the Cold War, 1945–1966*, rev. ed. (New York: Wiley, 1972). Dean Acheson offers his defense in *Present at the Creation* (New York: Norton, 1969). Alonzo Hamby has written the now standard book on the Truman administration: *Beyond the New Deal* (New York: Columbia University Press, 1973). See also the more critical anthology edited by Barton J. Bernstein and Allen J. Matusow, *The Truman Administration: A Documentary History* (New York: Harper & Row, 1966), as well as Bernstein's *Toward a New Past* (New York: Random House, 1967), and *Politics and Policies of the Truman Administration* (Chicago: Quadrangle, 1970).

II. 1953 TO 1959

The best book on Dwight Eisenhower is Herbert S. Parmet, *Eisenhower and the American Crusades* (New York: Macmillan, 1972). See also Emmet John Hughes, *The Ordeal of Power* (New York: Atheneum, 1963), and Arthur Larson, *Eisenhower: The President Nobody Knew* (New York: Scribner's, 1968). The standard work on Joseph McCarthy is Michael Paul Rogin, *The Intellectuals and McCarthy* (Cambridge, Mass.: Harvard University Press, 1967); still interesting is William F. Buckley, Jr., and L. Brent Bozell's defense, *McCarthy and His Enemies* (Chicago: Henry Regnery, 1954). Some outstanding works of social criticism are David Riesman et al., *The Lonely Crowd* (New Haven: Yale University Press, 1950); Daniel Bell, *The End of Ideology*, rev. ed. (New York: Free Press, 1965); C. Wright Mills, *The Power Elite* (New York: Oxford University Press, 1956); John Kenneth Galbraith, *American Capitalism* (Boston: Houghton Mifflin, 1956).

III. THE 1960's

A Thousand Days by Arthur Schlesinger, Jr. (Boston: Houghton Mifflin, 1965) is still the best book on the Kennedy administration, and Herbert Parmet's *Jack: The Struggles of John F. Kennedy* (New York: Dial, 1980) is the standard biography. Most recent books have been critical, even hypercritical, of Kennedy. See, for example, Henry Fairlie, *The Kennedy Promise* (Garden City, N.Y.: Doubleday, 1973); Louise Fitzsimons, *The Kennedy Doctrine* (New York: Random House, 1972); and Nancy Gager Clinch, *The Kennedy Neurosis* (New York: Grosset and Dunlap, 1973). A book both critical of and sympathetic to President Johnson is *Lyndon Johnson and the American Dream* by Doris Kearns (New York: Harper & Row, 1976). A good book on Martin Luther King, Jr., is John A. Williams, *The King God Didn't Save* (New York: Coward-

McCann, 1970); a statement by a more radical figure is Eldridge Cleaver, *Soul on Ice* (New York: McGraw-Hill, 1967). A good historical account of the Vietnam War is Frances Fitzgerald, *Fire in the Lake* (Boston: Little, Brown, 1972). A good account of the election of 1968—and of the events of that startling year itself—is Lewis Chester et al., *An American Melodrama* (New York: Viking, 1969).

IV. THE 1970's AND BEYOND

The best book on Richard Nixon is the revised *Nixon Agonistes* by Garry Wills (Boston: Houghton Mifflin, 1979). On the economy see Robert Lekachman, *Inflation: The Permanent Problem of Boom and Bust* (New York: Vintage, 1973). On Watergate there are Jonathan Schell, *The Time of Illusion* (New York: Alfred A. Knopf, 1975); John Dean, *Blind Ambition* (New York: Simon & Schuster, 1976); Philip B. Kurland, *Watergate and the Constitution* (Chicago: University of Chicago: University of Chicago Press, 1978); and John A. Labovitz, *Presidential Impeachment* (New Haven: Yale University Press, 1977). On Kissinger there is Roger Morris's Uncertain Greatness: *Henry Kissinger and American Foreign Policy* (New York: Harper & Row, 1977). Betty Glad has written Jimmy Carter: *From Plains to the White House* (New York: Norton, 1980). There is as yet no good study of Reagan. On politics generally, see Kirkpatrick Sale, *Power Shirt: The Rise of the Southern Rim and Its Challenge to the Eastern Establishment* (New York: Random House, 1975); and Sidney Verba, *Political Participation in America* (Ann Arbor, Mich.: Inter-University Consortium for Political Research, 1975). On society, there is Robert Heilbroner's *An Inquiry into the Human Prospect* (New York: Norton, 1980).

talked bloody murder and killed people all the time. It was true that the grunts stripped belts and packs and weapons from their enemies; Saigon wasn't a flat market, these goods filtered down and in with the other spoils: Rolexes, cameras, snakeskin shoes from Taiwan, air-brush portraits of nude Vietnamese women with breasts like varnished beach balls, huge wooden carvings that they set on their desks to give you the finger when you walked into their offices. In Saigon it never mattered what they told you, even less when they actually seemed to believe it. Maps, charts, figures, projections, fly fantasies, names of places, of operations, of commanders, of weapons; memories, guesses, second guesses, experiences (new, old, real, imagined, stolen); histories, attitudes—you could let it go, let it all go. If you wanted some war news in Saigon you had to hear it in stories brought from the field by friends, see it in the lost watchful eyes of the Saigonese, or do it like Trashman, reading the cracks in the sidewalk.

Sitting in Saigon was like sitting inside the folded petals of a poisonous flower, the poison history, fucked in its root no matter how far back you wanted to run your trace. Saigon was the only place left with a continuity that someone as far outside as I was could recognize. Hue and Danang were like remote closed societies, mute and intractable. Villages, even large ones, were fragile, a village could disappear in an afternoon, and the countryside was either blasted over cold and dead or already back in Charles' hands. Saigon remained, the repository and the arena, it breathed history, expelled it like toxin, Shit Piss and Corruption. Paved swamp, hot mushy winds that never cleaned anything away, heavy thermal seal over diesel fuel, mildew, garbage, excrement, atmosphere. A five-block walk in that could take it out of you, you'd get back to the hotel with your head feeling like one of those chocolate apples, tap it sharply in the right spot and it falls apart in sections. Saigon, November 1967: "The animals are sick with love." Not much chance anymore for history to go on unselfconsciously.

You'd stand nailed there in your tracks sometimes, no bearings and none in sight, thinking, *Where the fuck am I?*, fallen into some unnatural East-West interface, a California corridor cut and bought and burned deep into Asia, and once we'd done it we couldn't remember what for. It was axiomatic that it was about ideological space, we were there to bring them the choice, bringing it to them like Sherman bringing the Jubilee through Georgia, clean through it, wall to wall with pacified indigenous and scorched earth. (In the Vietnamese sawmills they had to change the blades every five minutes, some of our lumber had gotten into some of theirs.)

There was such a dense concentration of American energy there, American and essentially adolescent, if that energy could have been channeled into anything more than noise, waste and pain it would have lighted up Indochina for a thousand years. . . .

The Multinational Corporations

RICHARD J. BARNET and RONALD E. MULLER

*The interrelationship between foreign policy and economic develop-
ment is one of the classic themes of twentieth-century historical
thought. A whole school of historians has argued that the search for
markets has dominated American foreign policy, producing periodic
wars and creating the sources for repressive government at home. Students of this struggle for world markets have recently introduced a new
perspective in which international corporations—not national policies—
are the main movers and shakers of the earth. According to Barnet our
conception of foreign relations as transactions and conflicts among
nation states has become outmoded, as global corporations with trans-
national interests have seemingly achieved independence of individual
national bases and gained the ability to manipulate governments and
whole societies for their own narrow ends.*

*Some implications of this new perspective are clear. Economic de-
velopment, according to this model, is unlikely to be a straight-line
advance dividing the world into "developed" and "underdeveloped"
(Third World) countries. Rather, economic development is more likely
to take place in a setting of constant fluctuation as multinational corporations find new pools of cheap labor to form "export platforms,"
to be abandoned as prices and wages begin to rise. Other issues are less
clear-cut. To what extent do these corporations really conflict with
national governments? What means do national governments possess to
manipulate the corporate structures in the interests of maintaining social stability? What counterthrusts are available to multinational corporations? Is this a passing stage of industrialization, the product of
uneven economic development among countries? Or is it a new "stage"
of world capitalism? What (as Marxists would ask) are its "contradictions?" The understanding of these new institutions, whether an evo-
lutionary stage or simply an aberration of international political
economy, is a major item for study on the agenda of the social sciences in this generation.*

The men who run the global corporations are the first in history
with the organization, technology, money, and ideology to make a
credible try at managing the world as an integrated unit. The global
visionary of earlier days was either a self-deceiver or a mystic. When
Alexander the Great wept by the riverbank because there were no more
worlds to conquer, his distress rested on nothing more substantial than
the ignorance of his mapmaker. As the boundaries of the known world
expanded, a succession of kings, generals, and assorted strong men tried

to establish empires of ever more colossal scale, but none succeeded in making a lasting public reality out of private fantasies. The Napoleonic system, Hitler's Thousand Year Reich, the British Empire, and the Pax Americana left their traces, but none managed to create anything approaching a global organization for administering the planet that could last even a generation. The world, it seems, cannot be run by military occupation, though the dream persists.

The managers of the world's corporate giants proclaim their faith that where conquest has failed, business can succeed. "In the forties Wendell Willkie spoke about 'One World,'" says IBM's Jacques G. Maisonrouge. "In the seventies we are inexorably pushed toward it." Aurelio Peccei, a director of Fiat and organizer of the Club of Rome, states flatly that the global corporation "is the most powerful agent for the internationalization of human society." "Working through great corporations that straddle the earth," says George Ball, former Under Secretary of State and chairman of Lehman Brothers International, "men are able for the first time to utilize world resources with an efficiency dictated by the objective logic of profit." The global corporation is ushering in a genuine world economy, or what business consultant Peter Drucker calls a "global shopping center," and it is accomplishing this, according to Jacques Maisonrouge, "simply by doing its 'thing,' by doing what came naturally in the pursuit of its legitimate business objectives."

The global corporation is the first institution in human history dedicated to centralized planning on a world scale. Because its primary purpose is to organize and to integrate economic activity around the world in such a way as to maximize global profit, the global corporation is an organic structure in which each part is expected to serve the whole. Thus in the end it measures its successes and its failures not by the balance sheet of an individual subsidiary, or the suitability of particular products, or its social impact in a particular country, but by the growth in global profits and global market shares. Its fundamental assumption is that the growth of the whole enhances the welfare of all the parts. Its fundamental claim is efficiency.

Under the threat of intercontinental rocketry and the global ecological crisis that hangs over all air-breathing creatures, the logic of global planning has become irresistible. Our generation, the first to discover that the resources of the planet may not last forever, has a particular reverence for efficiency. The global corporations, as Maisonrouge puts it, make possible the "use of world resources with a maximum of efficiency and a minimum of waste . . . on a global scale." Rising out of the post-World War II technological explosion which has transformed man's view of time, space, and scale, global corporations are making a bid for political acceptance beyond anything ever before accorded a business organization. The first enterpreneurial class with the practical potential to operate a planetary enterprise now aspires to become global managers.

"For business purposes," says the president of the IBM World Trade Corporation, "the boundaries that separate one nation from another are no more real than the equator. They are merely convenient demarcations of ethnic, linguistic, and cultural entities. They do not define business requirements or consumer trends. Once management understands and accepts this world economy, its view of the market-place—and its planning—necessarily expand. The world outside the home country is no longer viewed as series of disconnected customers and prospects for its products, but as an extension of a single market."

The rise of the planetary enterprise is producing an organizational revolution as profound in its implications for modern man as the Industrial Revolution and the rise of the nation-state itself. The growth rate of global corporations in recent years is so spectacular that it is now easy to assemble an array of dazzling statistics. If we compare the annual sales of corporations with the gross national product of countries for 1973, we discover that GM is bigger than Switzerland, Pakistan, and South Africa; that Royal Dutch Shell is bigger than Iran, Venezuela, and Turkey; and that Goodyear Tire is bigger than Saudi Arabia. The average growth rate of the most successful global corporations is two to three times that of most advanced industrial countries, including the United States. It is estimated that global corporations already have more than $200 billion in physical assets under their control. But size is only one component of power. In international affairs Mao's dictum that political power grows out of the barrel of a gun shocks no one. To those who question their power, corporate statesmen like to point out that, like the Pope, they have no divisions at their command. The sources of their extraordinary power are to be found elsewhere—the power to transform the world political economy and in so doing transform the historic role of the nation-state. This power comes not from the barrel of a gun but from control of the means of creating wealth on a worldwide scale. In the process of developing a new world, the managers of firms like GM, IBM, Pepsico, GE, Pfizer, Shell, Volkswagen, Exxon, and a few hundred others are making daily business decisions which have more impact than those of most sovereign governments on where people live; what work, if any, they will do; what they will eat, drink, and wear; what sorts of knowledge schools and universities will encourage; and what kind of society their children will inherit.

Indeed, the most revolutionary aspect of the planetary enterprise is not its size but its worldview. The managers of the global corporations are seeking to put into practice a theory of human organization that will profoundly alter the nation-state system around which society has been organized for over 400 years. What they are demanding in essence is the right to transcend the nation-state, and in the process, to transform it. "I have long dreamed of buying an island owned by no nation," says Carl A. Gerstacker, chairman of the Dow Chemical Company, "and of establishing the World Headquarters of the Dow company on the truly neutral ground of such an island, beholden to no nation or society. If we were located on such truly neutral ground we could then really operate in the United States as U.S. citizens, in Japan as Japanese citizens and in Brazil as Brazilians rather than being governed in prime by the laws of the United States. . . . We could even pay any natives handsomely to move elsewhere."

A company spokesman for a principal competitor of Dow, Union Carbide, agrees: "It is not proper for an international corporation to put the welfare of any country in which it does business above that of any other." As Charles P. Kindleberger, one of the leading U.S. authorities on international economics, puts it, "The international corporation has no country to which it owes more loyalty than any other, nor any country where it feels completely at home." The global interests of the world company are, as the British financial writer and Member of Parliament Christopher Tugendhat has pointed out, separate and distinct from the interests of every government, including its own government of origin. Although, in terms of management and ownership, all global corporations are either American, British, Dutch, German, French, Swiss, Italian, Canadian, Swedish, or Japanese (most, of course, are American), in outlook and loyalty they are becoming companies without a country.

It is not hard to understand, however, why American corporate giants, even those whose presidents must still make do with an office in a Park Avenue skyscraper instead of a Pacific island, feel that they have outgrown the American Dream. The top 298 U.S.-based global corporations studied by the Department of Commerce earn 40 percent of their entire net profits outside the United States. A 1972 study by Business International Corporation, a service organization for global corporations, shows that 122 of the top U.S.-based multinational corporations had a higher rate of profits from abroad than from domestic operations. In the office-equipment field, for example, the overseas profit for 1971 was 25.6 percent, compared with domestic profits of 9.2 percent. The average reported profit of the pharmaceutical industry from foreign operations was 22.4 percent as against 15.5 percent from operations in the United States. The food industry reported profits from overseas of 16.7 percent as compared with U.S. profits of 11.5 percent. (Extraordinarily high profit on relatively low overseas investment is not uncommon. In 1972, for example, United Brands reported a 72.1 percent return on net assets, Parker Pen 51.2 percent, Exxon 52.5 percent.) By 1973, America's seven largest banks were obtaining 40 percent of their total profits from abroad, up from 23 percent in 1971.

Department of Commerce surveys show that dependence of the leading U.S.-based corporations on foreign profits has been growing at an accelerating rate since 1964. In the last ten years it has been substantially easier to make profits abroad than in the U.S. economy. The result has been that U.S. corporations have been shifting more and more of their total assets abroad: about one-third of the total assets of the chemical industry, about 40 percent of the total assets of the consumer-goods industry, about 75 percent of those of the electrical industry, about one-third of the assets of the pharmaceutical industry are now located outside the United States. Of the more than $100 billion invested worldwide by the U.S. petroleum industry, roughly half is to be found beyond American shores. Over 30 percent of U.S. imports and exports are bought and sold by 187 U.S.-based multinational corporations through their foreign subsidiaries. It is estimated by the British financial analyst Hugh Stephenson that by the mid-1970's, 90 percent of overseas sales of U.S.-based corporations "will be manufactured abroad by American-owned and controlled subsidiaries." "Investment abroad is investment in America" is the new slogan of the global corporations.

The popular term for the planetary enterprise is "multinational corporation." It suggests a degree of internationalization of management, to say nothing of stock ownership, which is not accurate. A study of the 1,851 top managers of the leading U.S. companies with large overseas payrolls and foreign sales conducted a few years ago by Kenneth Simmonds reveals that only 1.6 percent of these high-level executives were non-Americans. It is well known that non-Americans hold no more than insignificant amounts of the stock of these enterprises.

More important, the term is inadequate because it fails to capture that aspect of the contemporary world business which is most revolutionary. Businessmen have been venturing abroad a long time—at least since the Phoenicians started selling glass to their Mediterranean neighbors. Some of the great trading companies like the sixteenth-century British Company of Merchants Adventurers antedated the modern nation-state. Each of the great nineteenth-century empires—the British, the French, the Dutch, and even the Danish—served as a protector for private trading organizations which roamed the earth looking for the markets and raw-material sources on which the unprecedented comforts of the Victorian Age depended. Nor could it be said that doing business abroad is a new departure for Americans. At the turn of the century, American firms, such as the Singer Sewing Machine Company, were already playing such an important role in the British economy that the book *The American Invaders* was assured an apoplectic reception in the city when a London publisher brought it out in 1902. Ford has had an assembly plant in Europe since 1911, and the great oil companies have been operating on a near-global scale since the early days of the century.

What makes the global corporation unique is that unlike corporations of even a few years ago, it no longer views overseas factories and markets as adjuncts to its home operations. Instead, as Maisonrouge puts it, the global corporation views the world as "one economic unit." Basic to this view, he points out, "is a need to plan, organize, and manage on a global scale." It is this holistic vision of the earth, in comparison with which "internationalism" seems parochial indeed, that sets the men who have designed the planetary corporation apart from the generations of traders and international entrepreneurs who preceded them.

. . .

The managers of the global corporations keep telling one another that there can be no integrated world economy without radical transformations in the "obsolete" nation-state; but however progressive a notion this may be, those who depend on the old-fashioned structures for their careers, livelihood, or inspiration are not easily convinced. The executives who run the global corporations have persuaded themselves that they are far ahead of politicians in global planning because political managers are prisoners of geography. As much as the mayor of Minneapolis or Milan or São Paulo may aspire to a planetary vision, his career depends upon what happens within his territorial domain. Rulers of nations exhibit a similar parochialism for the same reasons. They are jealous of their sovereign prerogatives and do not wish to share, much less abdicate, decision-making power over what happens within their territory.

The new globalists are well aware of the problem. "Corporations that buy, sell, and produce abroad," says George Ball, "do have the power to affect the lives of people and nations in a manner that necessarily challenges the prerogatives and responsibilities of political authority. How can a national government make an economic plan with any confidence if a board of directors meeting 5,000 miles away can by altering its pattern of purchasing and production affect in a major way the country's economic life?" But the World Manager's answer to the charge of being a political usurper is not to deny the extraordinary power he seeks to exercise in human affairs but to rationalize it.

David Rockefeller has called for a "crusade for understanding" to explain why global corporations should have freer rein to move goods, capital, and technology around the world without the interference of nation-states; but such a crusade calls for the public relations campaign of the century. Perhaps the logic of One World has never been so apparent to so many, yet the twentieth century is above all the age of nationalism. There has been no idea in history for which greater numbers of human beings have died, and most of the corpses have been added to the heap in this century. The continuing struggle for national identity is the unifying political theme of our time. The imperial architects of Germany, Italy, and Japan; the guerrilla leaders of liberation movements, Tito, Ho, Castro; and those who are still fighting to free Africa from colonial rule have all been sustained by the power of nationalism. "The nation-state will not wither away," the chairman of Unilever, one of the earliest and largest world corporations, predicts. A "positive role" will have to be found for it.

.   .   .

The World Managers, sensitive to such criticism as UAW President Leonard Woodcock's charge that the companies don't care that they are causing unemployment in the United States, like to minimize their interest in coolie labor. (Woodcock is fond of quoting Thomas Jefferson's observation about merchants without a country: "The mere spot they stand on does not constitute so strong an attachment as that from which they draw their gain.") Their sudden interest in Taiwan, global managers argue, has nothing to do with either their treasure or their heart being there. They want merely to be better able to make use of supply markets. It is not usually considered good taste to talk about 14-cents-an-hour help, but occasionally an entrepreneur breaks loose from the public relations department and gives an honest answer. "In South Korea, Taiwan, and Indonesia," says Henry Ford II, "we see promising markets and we see an attractive supply of cheap labor." William Sheskey told the House Ways and Means Committee how he purchased a modern U.S. shoe factory, shut it down, and shipped the lasts, dies, patterns, management, and much of the leather to Europe:

I am making the same shoes under the same brand name, selling them to the same customers with the same management, with the same equipment, for one reason. The labor where I am now making the shoes is 50 cents an hour as compared to the $3 I was paying. Here is a perfect example of where I took everything American except the labor and that is exactly why I bought it.

Relocating production in Mexico, Taiwan, Brazil, or the Philippines is an even more irresistible way to cut costs. In the office-macinery field, a company must pay its U.S. workers about ten times what it pays its Taiwanese and Korean workers and about six times what it pays its Mexican workers. In the last few years more than 50,000 jobs have been created along the Mexican border, and exports from the area back to the United States have climbed from $7 million in 1966 to $350 million in 1972. During the latter year, imports from Taiwan to the U.S. market amounted to $1.3 billion. No amount of statistical magic can obscure the commonsense conclusion that servicing the U.S. market from Taiwanese and Mexican factories rather than U.S. factories deprives American workers in the affected industries of their jobs.

However, the continuing exodus to the export platforms of the underdeveloped world is creating problems for the American labor movement in addition to structural unemployment. Corporate organization on a global scale is a highly effective weapon for undercutting the power of organized labor everywhere. Capital, technology, and marketplace ideology, the bases of corporate power, are mobile; workers, by and large, are not. The ability of corporations to open and close plants rapidly and to shift their investment from one country to another erodes the basis of organized labor's bargaining leverage, the strike. While it may be true to argue, as IBM's Arthur Watson does, that when a plant is closed in the United States and opened in Korea "we have not lost jobs; one can trade jobs internationally," the trading process does not benefit the worker who has lost his job and cannot afford to sit home until the uncertain day when his town feels the beneficial effects of industrial expansion overseas. Even when World Managers defend their labor policies, they unwittingly attest to their great bargaining edge over organized labor.

The power of corporations to neutralize the strike weapon is not merely theoretical. It is used. Perhaps the most celebrated example is the strike at Ford's British operation in 1970. After a summit conference with the Prime Minister, Henry Ford II delivered a stiff note to the British people. "We have got hundreds of millions of pounds invested in Great Britain and we can't recommend any new capital investment in a country constantly dogged with labor problems. There is nothing wrong with Ford of Britain but with the country." Shortly thereafter he shifted back to Ohio a proposed £30-million operation for building Pinto engines. The following year he pointedly announced that Ford's major new plant would be put in Spain, a country that offered "social peace."

Management finds that its power to close an entire operation in a community and to transfer everything but the workers out of the country produces a marvelously obliging labor force. The threat, real or imagined, of retaliatory plant closings has caused unions in both Europe and the United States to moderate their demands and in a number of cases to give "no-strike" pledges. There have been enough cases in which global corporations have used their superior mobility to defeat unions to make the threat credible. Dunlop Pirelli, to give one example, closed its Milan-area plant and moved it across the Swiss border, where it proceeded to rehire Italian workers as low-wage migrant labor. (The savings in pensions and accumulated seniority rights accomplished by this thrifty maneuver were, one would hope, passed on to the purchasers of rubber tires around the world, but there is no evidence of this.)

There are also less drastic alternatives available to management which further weaken labor's bargaining power. One is the layoff. A Burroughs subsidiary making computers in France suddenly laid off one-third of its workers on orders from its headquarters in New York. (The case is a good illustration of how the interests of subsidiaries are subordinated to the corporation's global strategy, for the plant in question was operating at near capacity and was making good profits. Evidently some company consideration having nothing to do with the French operation itself dictated the layoff.) Neither the French Government nor the outraged local manager could do a thing about it. A global corporation can also protect itself from a strike by establishing what is called "multiple sourcing"—i.e., different plants in different countries producing the same component. It is a strategy by which the corporation can make itself independent of the labor force in any one plant. Chrysler, British Leyland, Goodyear, Michelin, and Volkswagen are among the many firms which use this technique for managing their labor problems. When Ford in Britain was faced with a strike at the plant that was its sole supplier for a crucial component, the company reclaimed the die used in the manufacture from the struck plant and had it flown within five days to a German plant. As *The Times* observed in 1970, "In some cases Ford has beaten strikes by 'pulling' tools and dies in time to start alternative production before employees in the original firm have stopped work." Unions are attempting to organize a campaign to counteract plant juggling as a strike-breaking strategy and are beginning to achieve some successes.

The confrontation of capital and labor, a battle scarcely more than 100 years old, has now moved to the global stage. Because it is easier to write a check than to move a worker and his family, the owners and managers of capital, as we have seen, enjoy certain advantages over labor. Paul Ramadier's studies confirm that strikes in global companies are on the average of shorter duration than strikes in domestic firms in Europe. He attributes this fact to the superior bargaining power of the global companies. (IBM's Jacques Maisonrouge, on the other hand, prefers to explain the fact that his French workers stayed at their jobs during the massive strikes of 1968 as evidence of their international outlook.)

A number of lesser advantages also inure to the global corporation because of its very structure. Because lines of authority are kept deliberately murky in many global enterprises, the local union does not know with whom it should deal. Many union leaders in Europe complain of "buck-passing" in negotiations. They are unable to get a decision out of the local manager and are never sure what issues he has the authority to settle. Labor unions up to this point lack anything comparable to the sophisticated communications system of the corporations. Thus they have difficulty finding out what the corporation may have paid in other countries or whether there are precedents for the concessions they are demanding. Corporations surmount differences in language, customs, and outlook by spending money for translators, language schools, and cram courses on local culture which unions do not have. The airborne executive corps can develop a properly statesmanlike international consciousness as its members dart in and out of the capitals of the world, but for the union organizer in Liège or Milan, without anything equivalent to the global intelligence system of the corporation, the mysteries of the outside world continue to loom large. These mysteries represent a management asset.

The most crucial mysteries concern the company's books. The complexity of intracorporate balance sheets, further obfuscated by the miracles of modern accounting, makes it exceedingly difficult for unions to find out how much money the employer is making or, indeed, if he is really losing money, as he frequently claims. Transfer pricing and other mysterious intracorporate transactions, hidden behind the veil of consolidated balance sheets, are formidable obstacles for union negotiators trying to get an accurate picture of what the local subsidiary of the global company can and should be paying in wages. (Of course, companies seek to maximize or minimize income depending upon whether they are talking to shareholders, tax collectors, or workers. In ITT's frenetic growth campaign, the company bookkeeper has on occasion employed rather unusual accounting methods to demonstrate "record earnings." In 1968, ITT's consolidated balance sheet showed $56 million in "miscellaneous and nonoperating income," of which, a diligent analyst discovered, $11 million was attributable to its having sold off properties and investments in Europe.)

A global company often bargains with several unions representing different parts of its conglomerate empire. Because of the way unions are typically organized, what impact they have is limited to that phase of the global operation in which the labor dispute is taking place. They have little leverage to affect other aspects of the global operation, although, as we shall see, they are trying to develop that leverage. Most unions are nationalistic and cannot afford to risk jobs to support workers in other countries.

Moreover, unions lack a tightly organized structure for dealing with the global corporate hierarchy. Thus they not only are at a disadvantage because they know less about the company than the company knows about them but also lack the common purpose that unites the worldwide operation of a global corporation—i.e., global profit maximization. In Europe the ideological splits of the Cold War that divided Communist and non-Communist unions still persist, though they are growing weaker. Moreover, there are sharp differences between "pragmatic" labor leaders looking for a bigger paycheck and more job security and "ideological" union functionaries who, in Charles Levinson's words, want not merely a bigger piece of the pie but a voice in baking it. In general, European unions are more radical than U.S. unions in demands for a share in management decisions about the workplace, but they are are less well organized and, with few exceptions, appear to have even less comprehension of the nature of the challenge which the global corporation poses to workers. Moreover, legislation hampers organizing efforts in many parts of the world. Like the United States, both Germany and Holland have laws against sympathy strikes and secondary boycotts. Countries such as Greece, Ireland, Singapore, Malaysia, and Indonesia advertise their repressive labor legislation.

Nonetheless, the exploitation of wage differentials in different parts of the world by the global corporations is causing unions to dust off the classic phrase "international worker solidarity" and to try to make it relevant to "bread and butter" bargaining. But even as U.S. union leaders begin to realize that the army, 34,000 strong, of 30-cents-an-hour child laborers in Hong Kong is not only a sin to be deplored at the annual convention but a real and growing economic threat to American workers, they are confused about what to demand. Should the wages in Hong Kong and Detroit be the same? Not even powerful unions in Europe are making demands for parity with U.S. workers. Despite the logic in paying the same wage for the same work for the same company irrespective of race, creed, color, or national origin, the practical union organizer is reluctant to ask for it. Given the risk that the company may decide to pull out altogether, he is happy if he can get a few more francs or marks a day. The only case of an American union's successfully negotiating international wage parity is the United Auto Workers contract covering Canadian automobile workers. But this was a special case because of a long history of governmental and union efforts to harmonize labor policy. International solidarity has yet to extend to Brazil or Singapore, where, of course, there are no local unions. However, the boldness with which such governments are competing with one another in offering their docile labor force to global corporations is posing a challenge to the American union movement which it knows it can no longer ignore.

. . .

The global corporation is the most powerful human organization yet devised for colonizing the future. By scanning the entire planet for opportunities, by shifting its resources from industry to industry and country to country, and by keeping its overriding goal simple—world-wide profit maximization—it has become an institution of unique power. The World Managers are the first to have developed a plausible model of the future that is global. They exploit the advantages of mobility while workers and governments are still tied to particular territories. For this reason, the corporate visionaries are far ahead of the rest of the world in making claims on the future. In making business decisions today they are creating a politics for the next generation.

We have shown that because of their size, mobility, and strategy, the global corporations are constantly accelerating their control over the world productive system and are helping to bring about a profound change in the way wealth is produced, distributed, and defended. There are a number of elements in this extraordinary transformation, but the global corporation is the most dynamic agent of change in a new stage in world capitalism.

In assessing the role the global corporation is playing and ought to play in this sweeping process, the issue is not whether the World Managers wish the global corporation to be a force for peace, stability, and development, but whether it can be. We would put the question this way: Given its drive to maximize world profits, the pressures of global oligopolistic competition, and its enormous bargaining power, can the global corporation modify its behavior in ways that will significantly aid the bottom 60 percent of the world's population—in the rich nations as well as in the poor?

. . .

There has never been a time since the Great Depression when there has been more economic uncertainty around the world. But the corporate prospect of a world without borders offers something more distressing than uncertainty. It is a vision without ultimate hope for a majority of mankind. Our criterion for determining whether a social force is progressive is whether it is likely to benefit the bottom 60 percent of the population. Present and projected strategies of global corporations offer little hope for the problems of mass starvation, mass unemployment, and gross inequality. Indeed, the global corporation aggravates all these problems, because the social system it is helping to create violates three fundamental human needs: social balance, ecological balance, and psychological balance. These imbalances have always been present in our modern social system; concentration of economic power, antisocial uses of that power, and alienation have been tendencies of advanced capitalism. But the process of globalization, interacting with and reinforcing the process of accelerating concentration, has brought us to a new stage.

The role of the global corporation in aggravating social imbalance is perhaps the most obvious. As owner, producer, and distributor of an ever greater share of the world's goods, the global corporation is an instrument for accelerating concentration of wealth. As a global distributor, it diverts resources from where they are most needed (poor countries and poor regions of rich countries) to where they are least needed (rich countries and rich regions).

Driven by the ideology of infinite growth, a religion rooted in the existential terrors of oligopolistic competition, global corporations act as if they must grow or die, and in the process they have made thrift into a liability and waste into a virtue. The rapid growth of the global corporate economy requires ever-increasing consumption of energy. The corporate vision depends upon converting ever-greater portions of the earth into throwaway societies: ever-greater quantities of unusable waste produced with each ton of increasingly scarce mineral resources; ever-greater consumption of nondisposable and nonreturnable packaging; ever-greater consumption of energy to produce a unit of energy; and ever more heat in our water and our air—in short, ever more ecological imbalance.

The processes that lead to psychological imbalance are more difficult to analyze than the processes of social or ecological imbalance. But the World Managers have based their strategy on the principles of global mobility, division of labor, and hierarchical organization—all of which may be efficient, in the short run, for producing profits but not for satisfying human beings. The very size of the global corporation invites hierarchy. The search for economic efficiency appears to require ever more division of labor and to challenge traditional loyalties to family, town, and nation. Another name for mobility is rootlessness. There is nothing to suggest that loyalty to a global balance sheet is more satisfying for an individual than loyalty to a piece of earth, and there is a good deal of evidence that being a "footloose" and airborne executive is not the best way to achieve psychological health—for either the managers themselves or their families. By marketing the myth that the pleasures of consumption can be the basis of community, the global corporation helps to destroy the possibilities of real community—the reaching out of one human being to another. The decline of political community and the rise of consuming communities are related. Each TV viewer sits in front of his own box isolated from his neighbor but symbolically related through simultaneous programmed activity and shared fantasy. How much the pervasive sense of meaninglessness in modern life can be attributed to the organizational strategies and values of the huge corporation we are only beginning to understand, but for the longer run the psychological crises associated with the emerging socioeconomic system are potentially the most serious of all, for they undermine the spirit needed to reform that system.

If we are right that the strategies of growth of the global corporation are incompatible with social, ecological, and psychological balance, why will such growth be permitted to continue? Is the earth—or indeed, the corporation itself—so lacking in self-correcting mechanisms that we are doomed to be diverted with upbeat balance sheets while we and our descendants wait for the air to give out? Stephen Hymer argues that high noon for the global corporation has already come and gone. The highly centralized hierarchical model of organization is simply too much at odds with the aspirations of too many of the 4 billion inhabitants of the planet for greater control over their own lives and greater political participation. (There is instability in every major hierarchical organization, including the Catholic Church, universities, the American and German armed forces, and authoritarian states like the Soviet Union.) Why should the global corporation be successful in establishing its political legitimacy to gather more and more public decisions into private hands at a time of worldwide political awakening?

Public anticorporate criticism is growing. Monkey-wrench politics also threatens the symmetry of the corporate global model (oil boycotts, kidnapping, extortion, bomb threats, trucker stall-ins). The worldwide resource scarcity jeopardizes global planning, which was based on the assumption that transportation costs could be kept low and that ships, trucks, and planes would always be available. Winging components and managers around the world to take advantage of differentials in labor costs, tax rates, and tariffs may no longer be the key to higher profits. If the Global Factory, with its worldwide division of labor, no longer represents the ultimate in economic efficiency, much of the rationale for the global corporation is gone. Is it possible that resource limitations are forcing an alternative model of a world economy in which *decentralization* is the hallmark? Perhaps the wave of the future is not the "Cosmocorp" but the backyard steel factory?

Whether global corporations will continue to increase their power will depend upon how successfully they can adapt to rapid change. They are more adaptable than government, because their goals are simpler, their bureaucracies are often more authoritarian, their planning cycle is shorter, and fewer conflicting interests need be heard. The dependence of advanced capitalist societies on privately controlled sources of power for maintaining employment, transferring money, and distributing technology and services is so great that government as a practical matter can no longer control them. The very advantages the global corporation enjoys over government—principally mobility and control of information—are creating a structural lag. Government is operating under a set of economic assumptions and legal theories which treat the corporation as if it were a private and national institution when it is in fact a social institution of global dimension. While the structural lag makes it possible for the corporation to accumulate more and more power, this lag renders increasingly ineffective the traditional tools of government for trying to achieve social stability. Thus in its continual quest for its own stability the global corporation is helping to create instability for society as a whole. As social, ecological, and psychological imbalances become more pronounced, the temptation increases to maintain the appearance of stability with repressive measures. For example, the gospel of growth requires a tolerant attitude toward inflation, but the management of inflation demands tough governmental controls. "There is little doubt," says Storey-Boekh Associates, bank-credit analysts not given to bleeding-heart rhetoric or to casual predictions of fascism, "that we could correct a lot of problems with a large dose of authoritarianism, at least for a while, but the chances of operating a successful inflationary economy like Brazil within the confines of democracy are just about nil."

The prospect, then, is not the death of the nation-state in a world without borders, but the transformation of the nation-state. The increasing impotence of the nation-state to solve its domestic affairs with traditional economic policies will probably drive it to seek survival by more direct and more violent means. The breakdown in the consensus among the industrialized nations on the international ground rules governing economic activity and the growing struggle over scarce resources signal a return to protectionism and economic nationalism. As oligopolistic competition among U.S., Japanese, and European firms intensifies, they will increasingly call upon their governments to back their efforts. The fading of the Cold War is making modern replays of World War I-type geopolitics more plausible. Despite their laudable vision of world peace through world trade, global corporations are more likely to act as instruments of competitive economic and geopolitical rivalry. In sum, if global corporations do not undergo profound changes in their goals and strategies, or are not effectively controlled, they will continue to act as disturbers of the peace on a global scale.

Women's Liberation

SARA EVANS

"Out of our arguments with others, we make rhetoric; out of our arguments with ourselves, we make poetry," wrote the great Irish poet William Butler Yeats. But the political movements of recent years have changed the relationship between the private sphere and public issues. "There is no private domain of a person's life," writes women's movement activist Charlotte Bunch, "that is not political and there is no political issue that is not ultimately personal." The women's movement of the late 1960's and 1970's exhibited complex shifts from private feeling to the assertion of public rights to a deeper exploration of the personal meaning of the new stance that some women assumed.

At first it seemed a conventional movement not unlike that of the civil rights activists of the 1960's. The movement got its first burst of energy from official sources: the President's Commission on the Status of Women, which John F. Kennedy named in 1961, and Title VII of the Civil Rights Act of 1964, which a hostile southern senator had added as an amendment in hopes of sinking the bill. The movement's early activities incorporated the traditional demands of political, public, and economic rights—more and better jobs, political office, equal pay, the Equal Rights Amendment.

The so-called "bra-burning" at the 1968 Miss America pageant announced that women, like blacks before them, had moved to cultural issues that made more personal statements. Consciousness-raising emerged as a technique for relating political changes to changes in women's personalities and self-images. A longer term revolution in values and sensibilities had emerged that would parallel and perhaps outlive the specific political issues on which the movement had initially arisen. Where once there had been the "New Woman," then the "Suffragist," then the "Flapper," then the "Career Woman," now there was a new sisterhood that did not try to isolate a particular track for some women to take, but was rather a movement to redefine the meaning of being a woman. The revolutionary potential of the movement that Sara Evans stresses eventually became clear to all observers, particularly to its opponents.

I

In the mid-1950s Betty Friedan wrote and edited articles entitled "Millionaire's Wife," "I Was Afraid to Have a Baby," and "Two Are an Island" for *Cosmopolitan*, *McCall's*, and *Mademoiselle*. Robin Morgan was a child-actress playing Dagmar on the popular TV series, "I Remember Mama." Thousands of other future feminists lived in middle-class homes, growing up to be bright, popular, and good. Everything appeared to promise them a future of happy domesticity. Who would have guessed that within a decade they would rise up to challenge that promise, to name it fraud, and to demand fundamental changes in American society under the banner of women's liberation? Feminism had been dead for over thirty years. Even the word had become faintly embarrassing. Feminists were seen as unfulfilled, neurotic, grasping women.

When *Life* magazine produced a special issue on women in December 1956, Mrs. Peter Marshall charged in her introduction that "many of woman's current troubles began with the period of her preoccupation with her 'rights.'" She advised women to turn instead to the most satisfying and "completely fulfilling" moments of their lives: the first formal dance, the first embrace, the first baby. In the same issue Cornelia Otis Skinner denounced the "shrill ridiculous war over the dead issue of feminism." "Ladies," she appealed, "we have won our case, but for heaven's sake let's stop trying to prove it over and over again."

The odor of embarrassment surrounding women's changing roles lingered as a reminder of the acrid attack that had been launched more than a decade before when Philip Wylie had blamed "Mom" for all the evils of American society. Modern industrialization, the critics argued, had undermined the basic functions of the traditional home. Such changes induced severe neurosis in women, they said. According to Wylie, it transformed them into narcissistic "Moms" who devoured their sons and husbands, robbing them of independence and ego strength. Freudians like Marynia Farnham and Ferdinand Lundberg pointed to another "pathological" response in modern women: feminism. They recommended massive use of psychotherapy, government propaganda and awards for good motherhood, cash payments to mothers, and the restoration of such traditional home tasks as cooking, preserving, and decorating. Only through a return to the traditional home, "a social extension of the mother's womb," could "women's inner balance" be reclaimed and the level of hostility in the world reduced.

By the mid-fifties such worries seemed a bit misplaced. Women were marrying younger, having three and four children, and apparently loving it. The vast majority of American women identified themselves as housewives whether they worked outside the home or not. Although growing numbers of them attended college, educators assured the public that they were simply preparing to be better mothers and wives, nothing more. If pickling and preserving had become the province of automated canneries, the work of the suburban housewife expanded in other ways. *Life* described a "typical" housewife under the banner: "Busy Wife's Achievements: Marjorie Sutton is Home Manager, Mother, Hostess, and Useful Civic Worker." No longer a household drudge, Marjorie the housewife had become a glamorized "superwoman" whose husband made $25,000 a year. Married at sixteen, she managed her household with the help of a full-time maid, worked with the Campfire Girls, the PTA, did charity fund raising, and sang in the choir. She cooked, sewed clothes for her four children, entertained 1,500 guests a year, and exercised on a trampoline "to keep her size 12 figure."

While alternative images of womanhood never disappeared alto-gether, for most people they scarcely existed. The mass media pro-claimed the triumph of domesticity. Women's magazines displayed "feminine" fashions with cinched waists, billowing petticoats, and accented bustlines. The movie industry promoted blond, buxom, sexy-but-innocent stars like Marilyn Monroe and Jayne Mansfield. Advertisers peddled a host of new appliances and household products to improve the housewife's ability to serve her family with cleaner, whiter clothes, odor-free kitchens, and "Poppin' Fresh" breads. The family as firmament of a stable social order received a stream of paeans from noted figures who encouraged women to center their energies in the home. Adlai Stevenson, liberal hero and two-time Democratic Party nominee for president, exhorted Smith College graduates in 1955 to remember that marriage and motherhood gave them a unique political duty. A woman could "inspire in her home a vision of the meaning of life and freedom . . . help her husband find values that will give purpose to his specialized daily chores . . . [and] teach her children the uniqueness of each individual human being." Studies indicated that most young women intended to do just that.

How, then, shall we explain the fact that by the early 1960s Betty Friedan had issued her famous denunciation of the "feminine mys-tique"—her term for the identification of womanhood with the roles of wife and mother? Or that Robin Morgan would grow up to organize a demonstration against Miss America in 1968 and use her powerful skills as writer and poet to proclaim herself a radical lesbian feminist in the early 1970s? Or that newspapers would be filled with news of a revival of feminism while feminist organizations and projects sprouted in every city in the country? The feminist resurgence in the 1960s and the 1970s makes sense only when one looks deeper under the surface of the apparent placidity of the 1950s, for there lay a dramatically changed reality for women, one that the old ideologies about women's place could not explain. The "feminine mystique" in operation offered a modernized version of the Victorian notion of women's sphere sharply separated from the public (male) realms of paid work, politics, and "historic" action. As an ideology it shaped women's and men's percep-tions of reality, but its life was limited at the outset.

This undercurrent of change provoked Wylie's rage and Farnham and Lundberg's assault. And it prompted Adlai Stevenson to preface his remarks about the political power of homemakers with an ac-knowledgment that many women in that role "feel frustrated and far apart from the great issues and stirring debate for which their educa-tion has given them understanding and relish. Once they wrote poetry. Now it's the laundry list." The reassertion of domesticity and its ap-parent hegemony in the 1950s constituted an attempt to ignore and contain the altered conditions of the twentieth century that had begun to culminate in new life patterns for women. But women's lives could no longer be encompassed by the older definitions of a "woman's place."

Within the home women with more and more education found that they had less and less to do. Despite the baby boom, their families were smaller than their grandmothers' had been. Technology abbreviated the physical labor of housework while consumer items complicated and, in effect, expanded it again. Laundry could be done by an automatic machine, but it required the appropriate detergents, bleaches, and rinses to meet changing standards of cleanliness. Children spent their days in school and afternoons at the playground, but a model mother had to be constantly available, both physically—to drive car pools, lead Scout troops, entertain bored children—and emotionally to avoid inflicting irreparable psychic damage. The suburban supermom, as illustrated by Marjorie Sutton, fulfilled a complex round of community activities and enhanced her husband's career opportunities with her well-kept home and lavish entertaining. Other women attempting a similar burden with less money and no full-time maid felt anxious, guilty, and inadequate. For all their busyness, little of what they did felt like work. Women's function in the home had shifted from producing food and clothing for family use to maintaining the family as an emotional community, making sure that everyone was healthy and above all happy. Led to fantasize that marriage would provide them with total emotional and intellectual fulfillment, more and more women experienced acute disappointment and then guilt when it fell below the mark. In particular, educated suburban housewives, the women who attempted to live out the mystique in its fullest form, found that their goal had become a trap.

Large numbers of them now attended college, where they performed to intellectual standards that made no allowances for sex. Although educators defensively proclaimed that they were educating women to be better wives and mothers, they nonetheless offered women essentially the same training as that which prepared men for future careers in professions and business. Thus women entered marriage with heightened expectations of companionship and fulfillment and with a growing knowledge of their own diverse capabilities. Yet they arrived to find that suburbia had become a female ghetto. Their husbands worked miles away; parents and relatives lived in other cities. The social isolation of modern housewives and the automation of housework, combined with a rising awareness of what they were missing "out there," produced, inevitably, a high degree of loneliness and boredom. Life seemed to be passing them by: shopping trips became forays into the outside world, and husbands, who had less and less time to spend with their families, were now their major link to the public realm.

Even more important than these changes in the home was the fact that many housewives were also leaving home for up to eight hours a day to shoulder additional jobs as secretaries, social workers, teachers, sales clerks, stewardesses, and waitresses. These were not the dreaded "career women." They had jobs, not professions. But the fact that most of them were older, married women shattered the notion that work outside the home was a male preserve, to be shared only with young, single women filling in a gap between childhood and marriage. Furthermore, they were not all victims of grinding poverty. Throughout the fifties women from middle-income families entered the labor force faster than any other group in the population.

If Harvard seniors in 1955 were concerned to limit the boundaries of their future wives' aspirations, then they had reason to worry. "She can be independent on little things, but the big decisions will have to go my way," said one. "The marriage must be the most important thing that ever happened to her." Another would permit his wife to work until she had children, after which she must stay home. A third wanted an "Ivy League type," who "will also be centered in the home, a housewife." Writers like Ashley Montagu bemoaned women's failure to understand that homemaking was the world's most important occupation and exhorted them to look to the model of European women, who focused their lives on the happiness of their husbands and children. Such women, he noted wistfully, "seem to behave as if they love their husbands." The fear of female competition with men had become a thread running through contemporary fiction, while the funny pages featured strong-minded Blondies married to foolish, ineffectual Dagwoods. . . .

The election of John Fitzgerald Kennedy in 1960 marked a shift in the public mood. Change became a positive rather than a negative value. Together with the southern civil rights movement, programs like the Peace Corps and VISTA sparked a resurgence of idealism and active involvement in social change. The child-mother no longer fit the times. She was too static, too passive, maybe even too safe. A rising number of voices in the late 1950s urged the abandonment of outmoded myths, though usually with a qualifying clause about the importance of mothers to very young children and the primacy of the family. Many social scientists moved from using "role conflict" as an argument for women to refuse outside work, to a more realistic appraisal of the problems of the "working wife," who could not and would not evade such conflicts by returning to the home. Thus such observers had finally achieved the level of adjustment to changing reality accomplished already by millions of American families. Jobs for women were becoming legitimate as extensions of the housewife role.

With the growing public acceptance of women's work outside the home, the mass media suddenly discovered the "trapped housewife." Betty Friedan pointed out that in 1960 the housewife's predicament was examined in *The New York Times, Newsweek, Good Housekeeping, Redbook, Time, Harper's Bazaar*, and on CBS Television. *Newsweek* entitled a Special Science Report and cover story: "Young Wives with Brains: Babies, Yet—But What Else?" The editors reported that the American middle-class woman "is dissatisfied with a lot that women of other lands can only dream of. Her discontent is deep, pervasive, and impervious to the superficial remedies which are offered at every hand." Both seriously and superficially, most articles in the issue treated women's problems of boredom, restlessness, isolation, over-education, and low esteem.

Educators also responded to the changing mood. Beginning in about 1960, a series of educational experiments and innovations appeared to meet the newly recognized malaise of the middle-class housewife. The "continuing education movement" focused on shaping the educational system to meet the demands of women's "dual role." Educational and career interruptions due to marriage and children were presumed inevitable. The problem, therefore, was to allow middle-class educated women to reenter the work force either full or part time without being forced into low-skilled, low-paid work.

Even the federal government began to treat women's roles as a public issue and to explore public policy alternatives to meet changing conditions. On December 14, 1961, President Kennedy established the President's Commission on the Status of Women, chaired by Eleanor Roosevelt. The purpose, in fact, may have been to quell a growing pressure for an Equal Rights Amendment, but unwittingly the government organized its own opposition. The existence of the commission and in subsequent years of state commissions on the status of women provided a rallying point for professional women. Such commissions constituted a tacit admission that there was indeed a "problem" regarding women's position in American society, that the democratic vision of equal opportunity had somehow left them out. Furthermore, they furnished a platform from which inequities could be publicized and the need for women's rights put forth. The President's Commission's report, entitled *American Women* and published in 1963, was moderate in tone. Yet despite obeisance to the primacy of women's roles within the family, it catalogued in great detail the inequities in the lives of women, the discrimination women faced in employment, and the need for proper child-care centers.

The importance of the report and the commission itself lay less in the specific changes they generated directly than in the renewed interest in "women's place in society" which they reflected. The following year women's rights advocates gained a crucial legal victory in the passage of Title VII of the Civil Rights Act, which prohibited discrimination by private employers, employment agencies, and unions on the basis of sex as well as race, color, religion, and national origin. Though introduced by a southern senator in a facetious gesture of hostility to the entire act, Title VII provided women with a legal tool with which to combat pervasive discrimination in hiring and promotion in all aspects of the economy.

The renewed discussion and activism took place primarily among professional women, who did not see themselves as housewives. Precisely because these professional women thought their work important and because they resented being patronized as if they had fled housework to get a little excitement, they felt even more acutely the discrimination leveled against them. Having openly admitted a certain level of drive and ambition, they were far more likely to experience discriminatory hiring, training, promotion, and pay rates as unfair. Other women could justify their unwillingness to fight against such barriers by saying, "I wouldn't be here if I didn't have to be," or "I'm only doing this for my family, not for myself." But for professional women, long-term careers were involved. Discrimination could close off opportunities they had invested years of training and hard work to attain. And it could deny them the positive reinforcement of respect from their colleagues. Since they took their work seriously, they were more vulnerable to the contempt that underlies patronage.

In general such women embraced the American ideology of equal opportunity, believing in advancement according to individual merit and achievement. Between 1940 and 1960, while the numbers of professional women declined relative to men, they also grew in absolute numbers by 41 percent. With more and more women in professional jobs, there were more examples to prove that women could excel at any occupation they chose. The individual professional woman was not a fluke or a freak of nature. On the other hand, there were also multiplying examples of blatant discrimination as their salaries and promotions increasingly lagged behind those of men with the same training and experience.

The new public attention to women's roles finally generated an overtly feminist position in 1963 in Betty Friedan's book, *The Feminine Mystique.* In a brilliant polemic she declared that housework was intrinsically boring, that the home had become a "comfortable concentration camp" which infantilized women. She took dead aim at the educational establishment, Freudians, women's magazines, and mass advertising, which she believed had combined to limit women's horizons and to force them back into the home. More academic but equally critical reassessments of women's traditional roles soon followed.

By the mid-sixties these angry professional women were developing an oppositional ideology and a strong network within governmental commissions on the status of women. As participants and consultants, they articulated the discrepancy between the ideals of equal opportunity and the actual treatment of women by employers. They mobilized to press for the passage of Title VII and then for its enforcement. A growing circle of women, including Friedan, Rep. Martha Griffiths, and the lawyers Mary Eastwood and Pauli Murray, urged the creation of an action group to pressure a government that continued to issue provocative reports but showed little sign of taking effective action. When, at a national conference of state commissions on the status of women in 1965, activists were informed that they could pass no resolutions and take no action in their capacity as state commissioners, a group broke away to resolve to found the National Organization for Women (NOW). These women had become convinced that, for real change to occur, a new civil rights group must be formed that could pressure the government to enact and enforce laws against sexual discrimination. Thus NOW became the "women's rights" branch of a renewed feminism.

In general, the professional women who created NOW accepted the division between the public and private spheres and chose to seek equality primarily in the public realm. Betty Friedan's devastating critique of housewifery ended up with a prescription that women, like men, should be allowed to participate in both realms. In effect she urged women to do it all—to be superwomen—by assuming the dual roles of housewife and professional. She made no serious assault on the division of labor within the home. For Friedan it was easier to imagine a professional woman hiring a "professional housewife" to take her place in the home than to challenge the whole range of sex roles or the division of social life into home and work, private and public, female and male domains.

In contrast, however, the oppression of most American women centered on their primary definition of themselves as "housewife," whether they worked solely inside the home or also outside it. Although they could vote, go to college, run for office, and enter most professions, women's primary role identification created serious obstacles both internally and in the outside world. Within themselves, women were never sure that they could be womanly when not serving and nurturing. And such doubts were reinforced by a long series of experiences: the advice and urging of high school and college counselors; discrimination on the job; pressure from family and friends; a lack of social services such as child care; and social expectations on the job that continually forced women back into traditional roles. Somehow women in every position from secretary to executive all too often ended up making the coffee.

At the same time that women acknowledged the social judgment that their work counted for very little—by accepting lower pay and poor jobs outside the home, or describing themselves as "just a housewife"—they also felt uncomfortable in any role other than that of the housewife. To admit discontent was to face a psychic void. The choices were there in a formal sense, but the price they exacted was a doubled workload and loss of both self-approval and public approval. Thus, though the *Newsweek* article on "Young Women with Brains" generated a storm of response from women, many who responded in writing denied the existence of a problem altogether. Others advised volunteer work and hobbies to fill the time, or else criticized women for their unhappiness. Only a few women echoed the article and discussed their distress.

If women found housewifery unfulfilling, they also on some level believed it was their own fault, thus turning their guilt and anger back in upon themselves. In a culture that offered no support for serious alternatives, women clung to the older definitions. If such roles did not reflect changing options or their real desires, at least they were familiar.

The tenacity of traditional roles and their internalization by most women meant that any successful revolt that drew on women's discontent would finally neither accept a traditional view of "female nature" as particularly suited to home and motherhood nor restrict itself simply to a critique of inequities in the public realm. For this reason, the emergence of the National Organization for Women did not provoke a massive grass-roots feminist movement. As a civil rights lobbying group, it could and did raise the public policy issues of discrimination in education, employment, and media in accordance with its stated purpose:

... to take action to bring women into full participation in the mainstream of American society *now*, exercising all the privileges and responsibilities thereof in truly equal partnership with men.

But while the professional women in NOW's constituency militantly demanded equality in the public realm, they were not prepared to question the mainstream itself, nor to carry their critique into the operation of sex roles in every aspect of life.

Yet the initiation of a mass movement required that the problem be addressed at its core. The pressures on most women were building up not on the level of public discrimination but at the juncture of public and private, of job and home, where older structures and identities no longer sufficed but could not simply be discarded either. The growing emotional strains of providing nurture for others with nowhere to escape to oneself, of rising expectations and low self-esteem, of public activity and an increasingly private, even submerged, identity required a radical—in the literal sense—response. A new movement would have to transform the privacy and subjectivity of personal life itself into a political issue.

Once such issues were raised by the radical young feminists in the late sixties, the challenge to traditional roles penetrated the mainstream of American society within a few years. Outrageous assaults on such cultural icons as Miss America, motherhood, and marriage caught the attention of the mass media. Americans were both shocked and intrigued by the sudden questioning of fundamental assumptions. As ever-widening circles of women joined in the process, a range of institutions—from corporations to families—began to experience angry insurgency from within. The *Ladies' Home Journal*, its offices seized by female journalists, agreed to print in August 1970 a special section written and produced by feminists; soon afterwards, women at *Newsweek* and *Time* staged their own rebellions. No institution, it seemed, was sacred or safe. Nuns organized within the Catholic Church; female seminary students began to agitate for full equality within Protestant churches. In 1975 they wracked the Episcopal Church with controversy, when eleven women defiantly joined in an unauthorized ordination service. And in the privacy of thousands of bedrooms and kitchens across the country, revolutions over housework, child care, family decisionmaking, and sexuality raged on or reached quiet resolution.

The young are prominent in most revolutions. In this case in particular it seemed logical and necessary that the initiative should come from young women who did not have marriages and financial security to risk or years invested in traditional roles to justify. Within the context of cultural unrest and the attack on tradition made by women like Friedan, the catalyst for a profounder criticism and a mass mobilization of American women proved to be the young female participants in the social movements of the 1960s. These daughters of the middle class had received mixed, paradoxical messages about what it meant to grow up to be women in America. On the one hand, the cultural ideal—held up by media, parents, and school—informed them that their only true happiness lay in the twin roles of wife and mother. At the same time they could observe the reality that housewifery was distinctly unsatisfactory for millions of suburban women and that despite the best efforts of *Ladies' Home Journal*, most American women could expect to work outside the home a substantial part of their lives. Furthermore, having grown up in an era that commoditized sexual titillation while it reasserted repressive norms, they found themselves living on the ambiguous frontiers of sexual freedom and self-control opened up by the birth control pill. Such contradictions left young, educated women in the 1960s dry tinder for the spark of revolt.

The stage was set. Yet the need remains to unravel the mystery of how a few young women stepped outside the assumptions on which they had been raised to articulate a radical critique of women's position in American society. For them, a particular set of experiences in the southern civil rights movement and parts of the student new left catalyzed a new feminist consciousness. There they found the inner strength and self-respect to explore the meaning of equality and an ideology that beckoned them to do so. There they also met the same contradictory treatment most American women experienced, and it spun them out of those movements into one of their own.

II

By the late 1960s it was dramatically apparent that most American women's lives bore no relation to the happy housewife image of the 1950s. And like the proverbial child who pointed out that the emperor had no clothes, it was America's youth who first heralded the discrepancy between myth and reality. Young women from the new left had torn away with intrepid zeal and directness the shrouds of ambiguity and mystification surrounding women's roles. Kathie Sarachild compared their new examination of personal experience with the seventeenth-century struggle against the scholastics and dogmatists who clung to ancient texts on anatomy despite the very different facts revealed by dissection: "So they'd deny what they saw in front of their eyes, because Galen didn't say it was there." Thus the women's liberation movement was initiated by women in the civil rights movement and the new left who dared to test the old assumptions and myths about female nature against their own experience and discovered that something was drastically wrong. And they dared because within these movements they had learned to respect themselves and to know their own strength. They could do so because the new left provided an egalitarian ideology, which stressed the personal nature of political action, the importance of community and cooperation, and the necessity to struggle for freedom for the oppressed. They had to dare because within the same movement that gave them so much they were simultaneously thrust into subservient roles—as secretary, sex object, housekeeper, "dumb chick."

The feminine mystique of the 1950s had blinded American women to the realities of their experience. It had depicted happiness where there was frustration. It projected the idea of pleasant housework where that often meant the additional burden of another full-time job. The mystique drew on centuries of tradition and specifically on the separation between the home and work spheres in the modern economy. Yet industrial capitalism, which once had pushed women to the periphery of the paid economy and remodeled the family into a private enclave, now drew women back into the labor force. While the expansion of government and the service sector of the economy pulled women into jobs outside the home, such workers still found themselves performing subservient tasks. And they received in the public sphere, as they had in the private, a low evaluation of their work and worth—this time expressed in the form of low pay and job discrimination. As the public and private spheres interpenetrated, the inherited roles proved less and less adequate as sources of identity and self-esteem. Traditional definitions could not encompass, explain, or help women to cope with the new realities of their lives. Thus, only a movement that simultaneously challenged their roles in both the home and the outside workplace could have tapped the pain and anger of most women and moved them to action.

The new feminist movement made its explosive debut in the Miss America demonstration of August 1968. With a sharp eye for flamboyant guerrilla theater, young women crowned a live sheep to symbolize the beauty pageant's objectification of female bodies, and filled a "freedom trashcan" with objects of female torture—girdles, bras, curlers, issues of *Ladies' Home Journal.* Peggy Dobbins, dressed as a stockbroker, auctioned off an effigy of Miss America: "Gentlemen, I offer you the 1969 model. She's better every year. She walks. She talks. She smiles on cue. *And* she does housework." Even though the coverage of such events was likely to be derogatory—in reports of the Miss America demonstration the media coined the term "bra-burner"—the dramatic rise in media coverage in 1969 and 1970 provoked a massive influx of new members into all branches of the feminist movement.

The experiences of the first few women's liberation groups were repeated hundreds of times over. Young women's instinctive sharing of their personal experiences soon became a political instrument called "consciousness-raising." The models for consciousness-raising ranged from the earliest SNCC meetings, to SDS's "Guatemala Guerrilla" organizing approach, to the practice of "speaking bitterness" in the Chinese resolution. It evolved into a kind of phenomenological approach to women's liberation. Kathie Sarachild advocated that women should junk all the old theories and start from scratch, relying on their own experience: "In our groups, let's share our feelings and pool them. Let's let ourselves go and see where our feelings lead us. Our feelings will lead us to ideas and then to actions." Thus consciousness-raising became both a method for developing theory and a strategy for building up the new movement.

Consciousness-raising exemplified both the frontal assault on sex roles and the personalized approach to politics that soon became hallmarks of the proliferating new feminist groups. The radical democracy of the new left carried over into an unequivocal assertion of sexual equality and an impatience with any belief that women should be treated or expected to act differently from men. The notion that women were different but equal, argued by biological determinists, sounded to the new movement like the "separate but equal" rhetoric of southern segregationists. And their demands led beyond equal *rights*, in formal terms, to a demand for equality of power. Thus they inspired a thorough critique of personal life and of the subtleties of an oppression that was at once internal and external.

The focus on the personal experience of oppression, moreover, led to the creation of small groups within which women could share with mutual trust the intimate details of their lives. Formed almost instinctively at first as radical women gathered in each others' living rooms to discuss their needs, these small groups quickly became the primary structure of the women's revolt. They provided a place, a "free space," in which women could examine the nature of their own oppression and share the growing knowledge that they were not alone. The qualities of intimacy, support, and virtual structurelessness made the small group a brilliant tool for spreading the movement. Anyone could form a group anywhere: an SDS women's caucus, a secretarial pool, a friendship circle, a college dorm, a coffee klatsch.

Each small group—and soon there were thousands—created a widening impact among the families, friends, and co-workers of its members. Soon the radical ideas and cooperative forms of the women's movement were reshaping the more conservative, tightly structured "women's rights" branch of the movement. Within a few years NOW had strengthened its positions on issues like abortion and lesbianism and had considerably changed its style. In several cities NOW became the chief instigator of new consciousness-raising groups. Individual leaders responded as well, for the new movement awakened them to the broader aspects of their feminism. For instance, theologian Mary Daly advocated "women's rights" in the Church when she wrote *The Church and the Second Sex* in 1968. Several years later she had become a leading exponent of a feminist theology that challenged patriarchal images of God.

As feminist ideas and rebellions spread into mainstream institutions—business offices, churches, and the mass media—the advertising and publishing industries, quick to perceive a shift in public mood, tried to make the best of it. By the mid-seventies advertisers had added new appeals to their repertory; in addition to the old standbys about women as sex objects and the glories of housework, they sought to capitalize upon the frustrations of the housewife who feels harried and unappreciated ("You deserve a break today") and even upon the anxieties of the husband who must prepare dinner when his wife is late from work. A spate of books and novels after 1969 by and about women signaled the publishing industry's assessment of the importance of women's liberation. Textbooks were revised to eliminate blatant sexual and racial stereotypes. New words appeared in print: "Ms.," "chairperson," "congressperson." Editors thought twice about using some of the old ones, like "mankind." Liberation, it seemed, was becoming big business.

The combined impact of women's liberation and the women's rights branches of the new feminism rocked institutions of higher education. Women in the New University Conference, a new left group, joined with a large constituency of professional women, many already active in NOW, to form women's caucuses within academic professions. Normally staid professional meetings began to ring with acrimony as women cried "foul" about hiring, admissions, and promotion practices. Then exercising the intellectual tools of their disciplines on the substance of the disciplines themselves, they criticized the male biases involved in the treatment of women and sex roles. Thus armed with new questions and mutually supportive organizations, women generated an outpouring of scholarly studies on the sociology of family and sex roles, female psychology, women's history, and literature by and about women. Women's studies programs encouraged interdisciplinary cross-fertilization and provided points of intersection with the women's movement itself.

The dramatic growth of feminism—a term that itself signaled the blurring lines between women's liberation and women's rights—affected political institutions as well. The women's rights movement had first coalesced around support for the Equal Rights Amendment and Title VII of the Civil Rights Act. Younger radical women pushed hardest for the issues that they felt struck closer to women's fundamental oppression—abortion and child care. As imaginative public presentations, mass demonstrations, and widespread publicity reinforced their lobbying, liberal politicians leaped on the bandwagon and for a moment all the bulwarks seemed to be crumbling. In 1972, after more than fifty years of sporadic debate, Congress passed the Equal Rights Amendment and sent it to the states for ratification. The EEOC and HEW stopped treating discrimination against women as a joke. The Supreme Court ruled that abortion in the first three months of pregnancy was a medical problem to be settled privately between patient and doctor. A bill for massive federal funding of child care found heretofore unheard of support in Congress. For a time it seemed that the power of an aroused, united mass movement of women was irresistible.

Within a few years the women's liberation movement had spread through many layers of American society. Where the public ideology of groups like NOW had originally focused on legal inequities and formal rights, the newer revolt made a critique of family and personal life the very cornerstone of its existence. Without such a critique there would likely have been a strong feminist lobby, for the severe pressures on professional women ensured that they would participate in the reform impetus of the sixties. But there would have been no mass insurgency. For most American women only a movement that addressed the oppression at the core of their identity could have generated the massive response that in fact occurred. Women from the new left had been able to penetrate to the essence of their roles because of their specific experiences in the 1960s, which facilitated the emergence of an insurgent group consciousness. . . .

Women from the new left explained the sources of their new awareness by pointing to the discrepancy between the movement's egalitarian ideology and the oppression they continued to experience within it. What they failed to perceive, however, was the fact that the new left did more than simply perpetuate the oppression of women. Even more importantly, it created new arenas—social space—within which women could develop a new sense of self-worth and independence; it provided new role models in the courage and capability of southern black women and female community leaders; and having heightened women's self-respect, it also allowed them to claim the movement's ideology for themselves. The point at which they did so came when the movement that had opened for them a new sense of their own potential simultaneously thrust them into menial domestic roles. Feminism was born in that contradiction—the threatened loss of new possibility.

Moreover, as conditions within the new left permitted young women to reexamine and reinterpret their own experiences, their situation also proved parallel to that of millions of American women far beyond the enclaves of the left. Indeed, it represented in microcosm the dilemma of most American women, trapped in an obsolete domestic role while new realities generated an unarticulated sense of greater potential. Although women's liberation was shocking and alienating to many, especially as seen through the magnifying lens of a hostile media, the reactions to the outcry on behalf of women's equality indicated that feminism had tapped a vein of enormous frustration and anger. The Harris Survey found in 1971 that 62 percent of American women believed that women had to "speak up" in order to accomplish anything, although most of them disapproved the tactics of picketing and protest and did not support "efforts to strengthen and change women's status in society." Nearly five years later, after the intervening upsurge of activism, 65 percent endorsed such efforts. Previously, ambivalence and fear of change had made women even less likely than men to advocate greater sexual equality. But by 1975 a new sense of rights and possibilities had led women to assert their belief in equal rights and opportunities for females in greater numbers and with greater intensity than men. Similarly, on specific issues such as abortion, child care, and the Equal Rights Amendment, opinion polls recorded a steady shift in public opinion toward the endorsement of feminist programs. By the bicentennial year, 1976, the *Reader's Digest* conceded: "Women's Liberation has changed the lives of many Americans and the way they look at family, job and sexual equality." Nearly a decade after the women's movement began, the confused response of most American women would be: "I'm not a women's libber, but . . . I believe women ought to be equal."

Within the context of such massive shifts of opinion, as millions of women readjusted their view of themselves and of the world, many thousands also moved to activism and into the burgeoning women's liberation movement. But success was not without its problems: neither the leaders nor the organizational structures could maintain a unified movement. And at the same time that the issue of sexual equality had become a subject of dinner conversation in households across the nation, the new revolt suffered from internal weaknesses inherited from the new left.

Radical women had used their organizing skills to set up literally thousands of small groups within which hundreds of thousands of women transformed their perceptions of personal inadequacy into a political analysis of women's oppression. They created dozens of journals and newspapers through which they could share and develop these new ideas and actions. The dynamic excitement of such groups sprang in part from their infusion with the anarchist democracy and spirit of radical egalitarianism characteristic of the early new left. Yet the anti-leadership consensus proved inadequate as a basis for organization. A preoccuption with internal process—the effort to live out the revolutionary values of egalitarianism and cooperation within the movement itself—took precedence over program or effectiveness. As a result, women's groups tended to oscillate between total formlessness at one extreme or a kind of collective authoritarianism on the other. To avoid hierarchies, some groups invented systems of lots for selecting who would be on committees or write or type a press release, even who would speak in meetings. A former member of the Feminists in New York City described how "they made the lot system into a religion, lotting each other to death. The principle of equality was distorted into an anti-individualist mania." Keen insights into the way in which women had been repressed by hierarchical structures thus developed into moral imperatives that were out of touch with the necessary tension between means and ends. Women who developed an ability for public leadership within the insurgency received harsh criticism for being "stars." On the one hand, if they shared the movement's anti-authoritarianism, they quickly withdrew, stung by the criticism. Naomi Weisstein, for instance, felt that the women's movement had given her a voice and then taken it away again; as a result, the women's revolt wasted the very talents it needed most. And on the other hand, women who refused to withdraw from public view operated as spokeswomen for women's liberation when in fact there was no structural means of holding them responsible for what they said and did. Thus, Roxanne Dunbar, brilliant, charismatic, and authoritarian, traveled the country representing only a small group of followers, but to the media she became an important symbol of the new feminism.

The lack of structure and of responsible leadership led, inevitably, to a loss of internal coherence as the women's liberation movement expanded. This fragmentation was intensified by the obstacles and defeats that the women's movement encountered, analogous to those of the civil rights movement and the anti-war protest. New left women, emerging from a movement high on visions of immediate revolution, failed to perceive initially that the profound changes they desired would arouse intense opposition and that the process of change itself would of necessity be long and laborious. As a result, they often deprecated their achievements and failed to claim the concrete victories that were won.

In the beginning, radical women believed that if they pointed out the inequities in women's position, at the very least their comrades on the left would understand. And with a united, egalitarian movement, they would quickly be able to revolutionize society. They rapidly met the full force of social tradition on the one hand, however, and the realities of the left culture on the other. After a child-care bill had sailed through Congress, Richard Nixon explained his ringing veto by saying that the family must be protected and women should stay at home with their children. And on the left, while a few men responded openly and honestly, others paid guilty lip service and many were obscenely hostile. "Take her off the stage and fuck her," shouted members of the audience as Marilyn Salzman Webb spoke to an anti-war rally in January 1969. Thus, young women in their small groups found themselves floundering in a morass of left-wing hostility and establishment derision. As both left and right labeled them "man-haters" when they demanded equality, they became acutely sensitized to the way in which it seemed that the whole culture was biased against women. One new recruit described her change in consciousness: "I couldn't walk down the street, read advertisements, watch TV, without being incensed . . . at the way women are treated." Robin Morgan's anger grew in the year that she edited *Sisterhood Is Powerful*, an anger that came "from deep down and way back, something like a five-thousand-year buried anger." She continued, "It makes you very sensitive—raw, even, this consciousness."

The rage, the sensitivity, and the overwhelming, omnipresent nature of "the enemy" drove parts of the women's movement into ideological rigidities, and the movement splintered as it grew. Who could say what was *the* central issue: equal pay? abortion? the nuclear family? lesbianism? welfare policies? capitalism? Groups formed around particular issues, constituencies, and political styles, many sure that they had found the key to women's liberation. After 1970, women's liberation groups in all parts of the country suffered painful splits variously defined as politico/feminist, gay/straight, anti-imperialist/radical feminist.

Yet while some became disillusioned at the fragmentation, the movement continued to spread. Certain more radical branches mellowed and grew critical of their own purism. They recognized that consciousness-raising, as an essentially intellectual mode of radicalization, could not address the daily needs for health care, child care, equal pay, and decent housing of minority and working-class women. At the same time former conservatives were radicalized. The National Organization for Women gradually assumed primary responsibility for creating new consciousness-raising groups and absorbed much of the new left heritage with its slogan: "Out of the mainstream—and into the revolution." But no single organization was able to capture the energy and enthusiasm aroused by the women's revolt and convert it into a sustained power base from which women could demand political and social change.

The difficulties of achieving change grew further as the spread of feminist ideas provoked opposition. Predictably, the traditionalists organized a reaction to turn back the Equal Rights Amendment, proscribe abortion, punish homosexuality, and in general return women to a subservient domesticity. But for all their vehemence and occasional victories, their arguments drew on visions of a mythic past in which women and men knew their places and the patriarchal family served as the stable foundation of a static social order. Although there was reaction, there could be no return.

Watergate

JONATHAN SCHELL

The Watergate crisis with its bizarre, abrupt rhythm of mysterious events following one upon another, each out of beat with the one before—trivial burglaries, odd dealings with reclusive billionaires, Saturday night massacres during which no blood was shed, statements that the President of the United States is not a "crook," unseemly hassles with reporters, the impeachment and resignation of a president—was perhaps the greatest piece of political theatrics in American history. The story dominated not just the news but the national imagination for many months. Since its dramatic conclusion, theories about its meaning, even about its cause, flourish like weeds in a horticulturist's nightmare. Impeachment is such a drastic measure that a president must experience almost every kind of failure to fall under its threat. He must find his political support hopelessly collapsed, his morality highly suspect, his associates seriously tainted, his policies in disarray. But even then he must be unlucky as well. It is almost impossible for a president to be forced to resign. But this happened to Richard M. Nixon.

Jonathan Schell offers one of the more persuasive and even-tempered views of the spectacle. Schell emphasizes the problems of conducting foreign policy in secret as well as Nixon's personality as contributing influences leading to the Watergate scandals. Other writers, however, have with equal plausibility emphasized entirely other explanations. The journalists J. Anthony Lucas and Norman Mailer have viewed Nixon's involvements with the eccentric billionaire Howard Hughes as a key element in the coverup. Other arguments emphasize different issues: new Nixon men undermining old party arrangements, new Texas and California money threatening the East. In many ways, we must understand the whole history of the Cold War, the intelligence apparatus it spawned, and the domestic political and economic arrangements that it influenced before a full assessment of this catastrophe will become apparent.

In mid-1972, as President Nixon returned to the United States from his trip to Russia—where he had signed the first Soviet-American agreements on the limitation of nuclear arms—and as his reëlection campaign got under way, the systemic crisis that had been threatening the survival of Constitutional government in the United States ever since he took office was deepening. The crisis had apparently had its beginnings in the war in Vietnam. Certainly the lines connecting the crisis to the war were numerous and direct. The war had been the principal issue in the struggle between the President and his political opposition—a struggle that had provoked what he called the Presidential Offensive, which was aimed at destroying independent centers of authority in the

281

nation. In more specific ways, too, the evolution of the Administration's usurpations of authority had been bound up with the war. Almost as soon as the President took office, he had ordered a secret bombing campaign against Cambodia (theretofore neutral). When details of the campaign leaked out, he had placed warrantless wiretaps on the phones of newsmen and White House aides. And when J. Edgar Hoover, the Director of the Federal Bureau of Investigation, seemed to be on the verge of getting hold of summaries of those tapped conversations, the President, in his efforts to prevent this, had entered into a venomous hidden struggle with the Director, and the Nixon White House had tried to damage the Director's reputation in the press. In another incident growing out of the war, the White House had hired undercover operatives to "nail" Daniel Ellsberg (as their employers expressed it) after Ellsberg gave the Pentagon Papers to the press; and then some of these operatives had been transferred to the Committee for the Re-Election of the President, where they went on to plan and execute criminal acts against the Democrats.

The evolution of the warrantless-wiretap incident and of the Pentagon Papers incident illustrated one of the ways in which the crisis of the Constitutional system was deepening. Large quantities of secret information were building up in the White House, first in connection with the war policy and then in connection with the President's plans to insure his reëlection. Every day, as the White House operatives went on committing their crimes, the reservoir of secrets grew. And the very presence of so many secrets compelled still more improper maneuverings, and thus the creation of still more secrets, for to prevent any hint of all that information from reaching the public was an arduous business. There had to be ever-spreading programs of surveillance and incrasing efforts to control government agencies. Only agencies that unquestioningly obeyed White House orders could be relied upon to protect the White House secrets, and since in normal times it was the specific obligation of some of the agencies to uncover wrongdoing, wherever it might occur, and bring the wrongdoers to justice, some agencies had to be disabled completely. In effect, investigative agencies such as the F.B.I. and the Central Intelligence Agency had to be enlisted in the obstruction of justice.

At some point back at the beginning of the Vietnam war, long before Richard Nixon became President, American history had split into two streams. One flowed aboveground, the other underground. At first, the underground stream was only a trickle of events. But during the nineteen-sixties—the period mainly described in the Pentagon Papers—the trickle grew to a torrent, and a significant part of the record of foreign affairs disappeared from public view. In the Nixon years, the torrent flowing underground began to include events in the domestic sphere, and soon a large part of the domestic record, too, had plunged out of sight. By 1972, an elaborate preëlection strategy—the Administration strategy of dividing the Democrats—was unfolding in deep secrecy. And this strategy of dividing the Democrats governed not only a program of secret sabotage and espionage but the formation of

Administration policy on the most important issues facing the nation. Indeed, hidden strategies for consolidating Presidential authority had been governing expanding areas of Administration policy since 1969, when it first occurred to the President to frame policy not to solve what one aide called "real problems" but to satisfy the needs of public relations. As more and more events occurred out of sight, the aboveground, public record of the period became impoverished and misleading. It became a carefully smoothed surface beneath which many of the most significant events of the period were being concealed. In fact, the split between the Administration's real actions and policies was largely responsible for the new form of government that had arisen in the Nixon White House—a form in which images consistently took precedence over substance, and affairs of state were ruled by what the occupants of the White House called scenarios. The methods of secrecy and the techniques of public relations were necessary to one another, for the people, lacking access to the truth, had to be told something, and it was the public-relations experts who decided what that something would be.

When the President made his trip to Russia, some students of government who had been worried about the crisis of the American Constitutional system allowed themselves to hope that the relaxation of tensions in the international sphere would spread to the domestic sphere. Since the tensions at home had grown out of events in the international sphere in the first place, it seemed reasonable to assume that an improvement in the mood abroad would give some relief in the United States, too. These hopes were soon disappointed. In fact, the President's drive to expand his authority at home was accelerated; although the nation didn't know it, this was the period in which White House operatives advanced from crimes whose purpose was the discovery of national-security leaks to crimes against the domestic political opposition. The Presidential Offensive had not been called off; it had merely been routed underground. The President spoke incessantly of peace, and had arranged for his public-relations men to portray him as a man of peace, but there was to be no peace—not in Indo-China, and not with a constantly growing list of people he saw as his domestic "enemies." Détente, far from relaxing tensions at home, was seen in the White House as one more justification for its campaign to crush the opposition and seize absolute power.

On Sunday, June 18, 1972, readers of the front page of the *Times* learned, among other things, that heavy American air strikes were continuing over North Vietnam, that the chairman of President Nixon's Council of Economic Advisers, Herbert Stein, had attacked the economic proposals of Senator George McGovern, who in less than a month was to become the Presidential nominee of the Democratic Party, and that the musical "Fiddler on the Roof" had just had its three-thousand-two-hundred-and-twenty-fifth performance on Broadway. Readers of page 30 learned, in a story not listed in the "News Summary and Index," that five men had been arrested in the headquarters of the Democratic National Committee, in the Watergate office building, with burglary tools, cameras, and equipment for electronic surveillance in their possession. In rooms that the men had rented, under aliases, in the adjacent Watergate Hotel, thirty-two hundred-dollar bills were found, along with a notebook containing the notation "E. Hunt" (for E. Howard Hunt, as it turned out) and, next to that, the notation "W. H." (for the White House). The men were members of the Gemstone team, a White House undercover group, which had been attempting to install bugging devices in the telephones of Democrats.

Most of the high command of the Nixon Administration and the Nixon reëlection committee were out of town when the arrests were made. The President and his chief of staff, H. R. Halderman, were on the President's estate in Key Biscayne, Florida. The President's counsel, John Dean, was in Manila, giving a lecture on drug abuse. John Mitchell, the former Attorney General, who was then director of the Comimttee for the Re-Election of the President, and Jeb Magruder, a former White House aide, who had become the committee's assistant director, were in California. In the hours and days immediately following the arrests, there was a flurry of activity at the headquarters of the committee, in a Washington office building; in California; and at the White House. Magruder called his assistant in Washington and had him remove certain papers—what later came to be publicly known as Gemstone materials—from his files. Gordon Liddy, by then the chief counsel of the Finance Committee to Re-Elect the President, went into the headquarters himself, removed from his files other materials having to do with the break-in, including other hundred-dollar bills, and shredded them. At the White House, Gordon Strachan, an aide to Haldeman, shredded a number of papers having to do with the setting up of the reëlection committee's undercover operation, of which the break-in at the headquarters of the Democratic National Committee was an important part. Liddy, having destroyed all the evidence in his possession, offered up another piece of potential evidence for destruction: himself. He informed Dean that if the White House wished to have him assassinated he would stand at a given street corner at an appointed time to make things easy. E. Howard Hunt went to his office in the Executive Office Building, took from a safe ten thousand dollars in cash he had there for emergencies, and used it to hire an attorney for the burglars. In the days following, Hunt's name was expunged from the White House telephone directory. On orders from John Ehrlichman, the President's chief domestic-affairs adviser, his safe was opened and his papers were removed. At one point, Dean—also said to have been acting under instructions from Ehrlichman—gave an order for Hunt to leave the country, but then the order was rescinded. Hunt's payment to an attorney for the burglars was the first of many. The President's personal attorney, Herbert Kalmbach, was instructed by Dean and, later, by Ehrlichman, Haldeman, and Mitchell to keep on making payments, and he, in turn, delegated the task to Anthony Ulasewicz, a retired New York City policeman who had been hired to conduct covert political investigations for the White House. Theirs was a hastily improvised operation. Kalmbach and Ulasewicz spoke to each other from phone booths. (Phone booths apparently had a strong attraction for Ulasewicz. He attached a change-maker to his belt to be sure to have enough coins for his calls, and he chose to make several of his "drops" of the payoff money in them.) He and Kalmbach used aliases and code language in their conversations. Kalmbach became Mr. Novak and Ulasewicz became Mr. Rivers—names that seem to have been chosen for no specific reason. Hunt, who had some forty mystery stories published, was referred to as "the writer," and Haldeman, who wore a crewcut, as "the brush." The payoff money became "the laundry," because when Ulasewicz arrived at Kalmbach's hotel room to pick up the first installment he put it in a laundry bag. The burglars were "the players," and the payoff scheme was "the script." Apparently, the reason the White House conspirators spoke to one another from phone booths was that they thought the Democrats might be wiretapping them, just as they had wiretapped the Democrats. In late June, the President himself said to Haldeman, of the Democrats, "When they start bugging us, which they have, our little boys will not know how to handle it. I hope they will, though." Considerations like these led Kalmbach, Ulasewicz, and others working for the White House to spend many unnecessary hours in phone booths that summer.

All these actions were of the sort that any powerful group of conspirators might take upon the arrest of some of their number. Soon, however, the White House was taking actions that were possible only because the conspirator occupied high positions in the government, including the highest position of all—the Presidency. For almost four years, the President had been "reorganizing" the executive branch of the government with a view to getting the Cabinet departments and the agencies under his personal control, and now he undertook to use several of these agencies to cover up crimes committed by his subordinates. In the early stages of the coverup, his efforts were directed toward removing a single evidentiary link: the fact that the Watergate burglars had been paid with funds from his campaign committee. There was a vast amount of other information that needed to be concealed—information concerning not just the Watergate break-in but the whole four-year record of the improper and illegal activities of the White House undercover operators, which stretched from mid-1969, when the warrantless wiretaps were placed, to the months in 1972 when the secret program for dividing the Democrats was being carried out—but if this one fact could somehow be suppressed, then the chain of evidence would be broken, and the rest of it might go undetected. On June 23rd, the President met with Haldeman and ordered him to have the C.I.A. request that the F.B.I. halt its investigation into the origin of the Watergate burglars' funds, on the pretext that C.I.A. secrets might come to light if the investigation went forward The problem, Haldeman told the President, was that "the F.B.I. is not under control, because Gray doesn't exactly know how to control it." Patrick Gray was Acting Director of the F.B.I. "The way to handle this now," he went on, "is for us to have Walters call Pat Gray and just say, 'Stay to hell out of this.' " The reference was to Vernon Walters, Deputy

Director of the C.I.A. A moment later, Haldeman asked the President, concerning the F.B.I., "And you seem to think the thing to do is get them to stop?" "Right, fine," the President answered. But he wanted Haldeman to issue the instructions. "I'm not going to get that involved," he said. About two hours later, Haldeman and Ehrlichman met with C.I.A. Director Richard Helms and Deputy Director Walters, and issued the order.

The maneuver gave the White House only a temporary advantage. Six days later, on June 29th, Gray did cancel interviews with two people who could shed light on the origin of the burglars' funds. (On the twenty-eighth, Ehrlichman and Dean had handed him all the materials taken from Hunt's safe, and Dean had told him that they were never to "see the light of day." Gray had taken them home, and later he burned them.) But soon a small rebellion broke out among officials of the F.B.I. and the C.I.A. Meetings were held, and at one point Gray and Walters told each other they would rather resign than submit to the White House pressure and compromise their agencies. Several weeks after the request was made, the F.B.I. held the interviews after all. The rebellion in the ranks of the federal bureaucracy was not the first to break out against the Nixon White House. As early as 1969, some members of the Justice Department had fought Administration attempts to thwart the civil-rights laws. In 1970, members of the State Department and members of the Office of Education, in the Department of Health, Education, and Welfare, had protested the invasion of Cambodia. In 1970, too, J. Edgar Hoover had refused to go along with a White House scheme devised by a young lawyer named Tom Huston for illegal intelligence-gathering. The executive bureaucracy was one source of the President's great power, but it was also acting as a check on his power. In some ways, it served this function more effectively than the checks provided by the Constitution, for, unlike the other institutions of government, it at least had some idea of what was going on. But ultimately it was no replacement for the Constitutional checks. A President who hired and fired enough people could in time bring the bureaucracy to heel. And although a Gray, a Walters, or a Helms might offer some resistance to becoming deeply involved in White House crimes, they would do nothing to expose the crimes. Moreover, the bureaucracy had no public voice, and was therefore powerless to sway public opinion. Politicians of all persuasions could—and did— heap abuse on "faceless," "briefcase-toting" bureaucrats and their "red tape," and the bureaucracy had no way to reply to this abuse. It had only its silent rebellions, waged with the passive weapons of obfuscation, concealment, and general foot-dragging. Decisive opposition, if there was to be any, had to come from without.

With respect to the prosecutorial arm of the Justice Department, the White House had aims that were less ambitious than its aims with respect to the F.B.I. and the C.I.A., but it was more successful in achieving them. Here, on the whole, the White House men wished merely to keep abreast of developments in the grand-jury room of the U.S. District Court, where officials of the Committee for the Re-Election of the President were testifying on Watergate, and this they accomplished through the obliging coöperation of Henry Petersen, the chief of the Criminal Division, who reported regularly to John Dean and later to the President himself. Dean subsequently described the coöperation to the President by saying, "Petersen is a soldier. He played —he kept me informed. He told me when we had problems, where we had problems, and the like. Uh, he believes in, in, in you. He believes in this Administration. This Administration had made him." What happened in the grand-jury room was further controlled by the coördinating of perjured testimony from White House aides and men working for the campaign committee. As for the prosecutors, a sort of dim-wittedness—a failure to draw obvious conclusions, a failure to follow up leads, a seeming willingness to construe the Watergate case narrowly—appeared to be enough to keep them from running afoul of the White House.

While all these moves were being made, the public was treated to a steady stream of categorical denials that the White House or the President's campaign committee had had anything to do with the break-in or with efforts to cover up the origins of the crime. The day after the break-in, Mitchell, in California, described James McCord, one of the burlars, as "the proprietor of a private security agency who was employed by our Committee months ago to assist with the installation of our security system." Actually, McCord was the committee's chief of security at the moment when he was arrested. Mitchell added, "We want to emphasize that this man and the other people involved were not operating either in our behalf or with our consent. . . . There is no place in our campaign or in the electoral process for this type of activity, and we will not permit nor condone it." On June 19th, two days after the break-in, Ronald Ziegler, the President's press secretary, contemptuously dismissed press reports of White House involvement. "I'm not going to comment from the White House on a third-rate burglary attempt," he said. On June 20th, when Lawrence O'Brien, the chairman of the Democratic Party, revealed that the Party had brought a one-million-dollar civil-damages suit against the Committee for the Re-Election of the President and the five burglary suspects, charging invasion of privacy and violation of the civil rights of the Democrats, Mitchell stated that the action represented "another example of sheer demagoguery on the part of Mr. O'Brien." Mitchell said, "I reiterate that this committee did not authorize and does not condone the alleged actions of the five men apprehended there."

Among the nation's major newspapers, only one, the Washington Post, consistently gave the Watergate story prominent headlines on the front page. Most papers, when they dealt with the story at all, tended to treat it as something of a joke. All in all, the tone of the coverage was not unlike the coverage of the Clifford Irving affair the previous winter, and the volume of the coverage was, if anything, less. "Caper" was the word that most of the press settled upon to describe the incident. A week after the break-in, for instance, the Times headlined its Watergate story "WATERGATE CAPER." When another week had passed, and Howard Hunt's connection with the break-in had been made known, *Time* stated that the story was "fast stretching into the most provocative caper of 1972, an extraordinary bit of bungling of great potential advantage to the Democrats and damage to the Republicans in this election year." In early August, the *Times* was still running headlines like "THE PLOT THICKENS IN WATERGATE WHODUNIT" over accounts of the repercussions of the burglary. "Above all, the purpose of the break-in seemed obscure," the *Times* said. "But these details are never explained until the last chapter." The President held a news conference six weeks after the break-in, and by then the story was of such small interest to newsmen that not one question was asked concerning it.

Disavowals such as those made by Mitchell and Ziegler carried great weight in the absence of incontrovertible evidence refuting them. The public had grown accustomed to deception and evasion in high places, but not yet to repeated, consistent, barefaced lying at all levels. The very boldness of the lies raised the cost of contradicting them, for to do so would be to call high officials outright liars. Another effective White House technique was to induce semi-informed or wholly uninformed spokesmen to deny charges. One of these spokesmen was Clark MacGregor, a former member of Congress from Minnesota, who became reëlection-campaign director early in July, when John Mitchell resigned, pleading family difficulties. A few weeks later, when Senator McGovern described the break-ins as "the kind of thing you expect under a person like Hitler," MacGregor called McGovern's remark "character assassination." The practice of using as spokesmen officials who were more or less innocent of the facts was one more refinement of the technique of dissociating "what we say" from "what we do." In this manner, honest men could be made to lend the weight of their integrity to untruths. They spoke words without knowing whether the words were true or false. Such spokesmen lent their vocal cords to the campaign but left their brains behind, and confused the public with words spoken by nobody.

On Septembter 15th, the five men who had been caught in the Democratic National Committee headquarters were indicted—together with E. Howard Hunt and G. Gordon Liddy, who were elsewhere in the Watergate complex at the time of the break-in—for the felonies of burglary, conspiracy, and wiretapping. A few days later, the seven defendants pleaded not guilty. As the case stood at that moment, their crimes were officially motiveless. The prosecutors had not been able to suggest who might have asked employees of the Committee for the Re-Election of the President to wiretap the Democratic headquarters, or why a check belonging to that committee should have found its way into the bank account of Bernard Barker. That afternoon, the President met with Haldeman and Dean, and congratulated Dean on his work, "Well," he said, "the whole thing is a can of worms. . . . But the, but the way you, you've handled it, it seems to me, has been very skillful, because you— putting your fingers in the dikes every time that leaks have sprung here and sprung there." Representative Wright Patman, the chairman of the House Banking and Currency Committee, was planning to hold hearings on the Watergate break-in, and the President, Dean, and Haldeman went on to discuss ways of "turning that off," as Dean put it. Dean reported to the two others that he was studying the possibility of blackmailing members of the Patman committee with damaging information about their own campaigns, and then the President suggested that Gerald Ford, the minority leader of the House, would be the man to pressure Patman into dropping the hearings. Ford should be told that "he's got to get at this and screw this thing up while he can," the President said. Two and a half weeks later, a majority of the members of the committee voted to deny Patman the power to subpoena witnesses. But Patman made the gesture of carrying on anyway for a while, and asked questions of an empty chair.

At the end of September—more than a month before the election —the Washington *Post* reported that John Mitchell had had control of a secret fund for spying on the Democrats. Throughout October, denials continued to pour out from the Administration. As before, some were outright lies by men who knew the facts, and others were untruths spoken by men who were simply repeating what they had been told. On October 2nd, Acting Director Gray of the F.B.I. said that it was unreasonable to believe that the President had deceived the nation about Watergate. "Even if some of us [in federal law enforcement agencies] are crooked, there aren't that many that are. I don't believe everyone is a Sir Galahad, but there's not been one single bit of pressure put on me or any of my special agents." In reality, of course, Gray had once considered resigning because the pressure from the White House to help with the coverup had been so intense, and even as he spoke he was keeping the contents of E. Howard Hunt's safe in a drawer of a dresser at his home in Connecticut. Gray went on to say, "It strains the credulity that the President of the United States—if he had a mind to —could have done a con job on the whole American people." Gray added, "He would have to control the United States."

In the months since the election, the issue of Watergate had faded, and the papers had devoted their front pages to other news. Shortly after the trial began, however, the front-page news was that all the defendants but two had pleaded guilty. In the courtroom, Judge John Sirica, who presided, found himself dissatisfied with the questioning of witnesses by the government prosecutors. The prosecutors now had a suggestion as to the burglars' motive. They suggested that it might be blackmail. They did not say of whom or over what. At the trial, the key prosecution witness, the former F.B.I. agent Alfred Baldwin, related that on one occasion he had taken the logs of the Watergate wiretaps to the headquarters of the Committee for the Re-Election of the President. But this suggested nothing to the Justice Department, one of whose spokesmen had maintained when the indictment was handed up in September that there was "no evidence" showing that anyone except the defendants was involved. Sirica demurred. "I want to know where the money comes from," he said to the defendant Bernard Barker.

"There were hundred-dollar bills floating around like coupons." When Barker replied that he had simply received the money in the mail in a blank envelope and had no idea who might have sent it, Sirica commented, "I'm sorry, but I don't believe you." When the defense lawyers protested Sirica's questioning, he said, "I don't think we should sit up here like nincompoops. The function of a trial is to search for the truth."

All the Watergate defendants but one were following the White House scenario to the letter. The exception was James McCord. He was seething with scenarios of his own. He hoped to have the charges against him dismissed, and, besides, he had been angered by what he understood as a suggestion from one of his lawyers that the blame for the Watergate break-in be assigned to the C.I.A., his old outfit, to which he retained an intense loyalty. There was some irony in the fact that McCord's anger had been aroused by an Administration plan to involve the C.I.A. in its crimes. McCord believed that Nixon's removal of C.I.A. director Richard Helms, in December of 1972—at the very time that McCord himself was being urged to lay the blame for Watergate at the door of the C.I.A.—was designed to pave the way for an attempt by the Administration itself to blame the break-in on the agency and for a takeover of the agency by the White House. He had worked for the White House, but he did not see the reorganizational wars from the White House point of view. He saw them from the bureaucrats' point of view; in his opinion, President Nixon was attempting to take over the C.I.A. in a manner reminiscent of attempts by Hitler to take control of German intelligence agencies before the Second World War. The White House, that is, belatedly discovered that it had a disgruntled "holdover" on its hands. And this particular holdover really was prepared to perform sabotage; he was prepared, indeed, to sabotage not just the President's policies but the President himself, and, what was more, he had the means to do it. McCord was putting together a scenario that could destroy the Nixon Administration. In a letter delivered to his White House contact, the undercover operative John Caulfield, McCord pronounced a dread warning: If the White House continued to try to have the C.I.A. take responsibility for the Watergate burglary, "every tree in the forest will fall," and "it will be a scorched desert." Piling on yet another metaphor of catastrophe, he wrote, "Pass the message that if they want it to blow, they are on exactly the right course. I am sorry that you will get hurt in the fallout." McCord was the first person in the Watergate conspiracy to put in writing exactly what the magnitude of the Watergate scandal was. Many observers had been amazed at the extreme hard line that the President had taken since his landslide reëlection—the firings in the bureaucracies, the incomprehensible continuation of the attacks on Senator McGovern, the renewed attacks on the press, the attacks on Congress's power of the purse, the bombing of Hanoi. They could not know that at the exact moment when President Nixon was wreaking devastation on North Vietnam, James McCord was threatening to wreak devastation on him.

On February 7th, the Senate, by a vote of seventy-seven to none, established a Select Committee on Presidential Campaign Activities, to look into abuses in the Presidential campaign of 1972, including the Watergate break-in; and the Democratic leadership appointed Senator Sam Ervin, of North Carolina, the author of the resolution to establish the Select Committee, to be its chairman. Three days later, the Administration secretly convened a Watergate committee of its own, in California—at the La Costa Resort Hotel and Spa, not far from the President's estate in San Clemente, with John Dean, H. R. Haldeman, John Ehrlichman, and Richard Moore, a White House aide, in attendance. The meeting lasted for two days. Its work was to devise ways of hampering, discrediting, and ultimately blocking the Ervin committee's investigation.

The President's drive to take over the federal government was going well. By the end of March those legislators who were worried about the possibility of a collapse of the Constitutional system were in a state of near-hopelessness. It seemed that the President would have his will, and Congress could not stop him; as for the public, it was uninterested in Constitutional matters. Senator Muskie had now joined Senator McGovern in warning against the dangers of "one-man rule," and he said that the Administration's proposal for preventing the release of "classified" information, no matter how arbitrarily the "classified" designation had been applied, could impose "the silence of democracy's graveyard." Senator William Fulbright, of Arkansas, had expressed fear that the United States might "pass on, as most of the world has passed on, to a totalitarian system." In the press, a new feeling seemed to be crystallizing that Congress had had its day as an institution of American life. Commentators of all political persuasions were talking about Congress as though it were moribund. Kevin Phillips, a political writer who had played an important role in formulating "the Southern strategy," and who had once worked in John Mitchell's Justice Department, wrote, in an article in *Newsweek* called "Our Obsolete System," that "Congress's separate power is an obstacle to modern policy-making." He proposed a "fusion of powers" to replace the Constitution's separation of powers. "In sum," he wrote, "we may have reached a point where separation of powers is doing more harm than good by distorting the logical evolution of technology-era government." In *The New Republic,* the columnist TRB, who, like Senator McGovern and Senator Muskie, was worried that "one-man rule" was in prospect, wrote, "President Nixon treats Congress with contempt which, it has to be admitted, is richly deserved. We have a lot of problems—the economy, inflation, the unfinished war, Watergate —but in the long run the biggest problem is whether Congress can be salvaged, because if it can't, our peculiar 18th-century form of government, with separation of powers, can't be salvaged," And he wrote, "A vacuum has to be filled. The authority of Congress has decayed till it is overripe and rotten. Mr. Nixon has merely proclaimed it." At the Justice Department, Donald Santarelli, who was shortly to become head of the Law Enforcement Assistance Administration, told a reporter, "Today, the whole Constitution is up for grabs." These observers took the undeniable fact that the Congress was impotent as a sign that the Congress was obsolete. And the executive branch, having helped reduce the Congress to helplessness, could now point to that helplessness as proof that the Congress was of no value.

The coverup and the takeover had merged into a single project. For four years, the President's anger at his "enemies" had been growing. As his anger had grown, so had that clandestine repressive apparatus in the White House whose purpose was to punish and destroy his enemies. And as this apparatus had grown, so had the need to control the Cabinet departments and the agencies; and the other branches of government, because they might find out about it—until, finally, the coverup had come to exceed in importance every other matter facing the Administration. For almost a year now, the coverup had been the motor of American politics. It had safeguarded the President's reëlection, and it had determined the substance and the mood of the Administration's second term so far. In 1969, when President Nixon launched his Presidential Offensive, he had probably not foreseen that the tools he was developing then would one day serve him in a mortal struggle between his Administration and the other powers of the Republic; but now his assault on the press, the television networks, the Congress, the federal bureaucracy, and the courts had coalesced into a single, coordinated assault on the American Constitutional democracy. Either the Nixon Administration would survive in power and the democracy would die or the Administration would be driven from power and the democracy would have another chance to live. If the newly reëlected President should be able to thwart investigations by the news media, the agencies of federal law enforcement, the courts, and Congress, he would be clear of all accountabiilty, and would be above the law; on the other hand, if the rival institutions of the Republic should succeed in laying bare the crimes of his Administration and in bringing the criminals to justice, the Administration would be destroyed.

In the latter part of March, the pace of events in this area of the coverup quickened. Under the pressure of the pending sentences, two of the conspirators were breaking ranks: James McCord and Howard Hunt. McCord, who had been threatening the White House with exposure since December, now wrote a letter to Judge Sirica telling what he knew of the coverup. Hunt, for his part, was angry because he and the other defendants and their lawyers had not been paid as much money as they wanted in return for their silence. In November, 1972, he called Charles Colson to remind him that the continuation of the coverup was a "two-way street," and shortly after the middle of March he told Paul O'Brien, an attorney for the reëlection committee, that if more funds weren't forthcoming immediately he might reveal some of the "many things" he had done for John Haldeman—an apparent reference to the break-in at the office of Daniel Ellsberg's psychiatrist. Shortly thereafter, O'Brien informed Dean of Hunt's demand. These events on one edge of the coverup had an immediate influence on the chemistry of the whole enterprise. On March 21st, John Dean, convinced now that the coverup could not be maintained, met with the President and told him the story of it as he knew it from beginning to end. The President's response was to recommend that the blackmail money be paid to Hunt. "I think you should handle that one pretty fast," he said. And later he said, "But at the moment don't you agree that you'd better get the Hunt thing? I mean, that's worth it, at the moment." And he said, "That's why, John, for your immediate thing you've got no choice with Hunt but the hundred and twenty or whatever it is. Right?" The President was willing to consider plans for limited disclosure, and the meeting ended with a suggestion from Haldeman, who had joined the two other men: "We've got to figure out where to turn it off at the lowest cost we can, but at whatever cost it takes."

The defection of Hunt and McCord had upset the delicate balance of roles demanded by the coverup. Information that had to be kept secret began to flow in a wide loop through the coverup's various departments. Not only Hunt and McCord but Dean and Magruder began to tell their stories to the prosecutors. The prosecutors, in turn, relayed the information to Attorney General Kleindienst and Assistant Attorney General Petersen, who then relayed it to the President, who then relayed it to Haldeman and Ehrlichman, who in this period were desperately attempting to avoid prosecution, and were therefore eager to know what was happening in the Grand Jury room. Any defections placed the remaining conspirators in an awkward position. In order to get clear of the collapsing coverup, they had to become public inquisitors of their former subordinates and collaborators. Such a transformation, however, was not likely to sit well with the defectors, who were far from eager to shoulder the blame for the crimes of others, and who, furthermore, were in possession of damaging information with which to retaliate.

Notwithstanding these new tensions, the President sought to continue the coverup. In the weeks following his meeting with Dean on March 21st, his consistent strategy was what might be called the hors d'oeuvre strategy. The President described the strategy to Haldeman and Ehrlichman after a conversation with Dean on April 14th by saying, "Give 'em an hors d'oeuvre and maybe they won't come back for the main course." His hope was that by making certain public revelations and by offering a certain number of victims to the prosecutors he could satisfy the public's appetite, so that it would seek no more revelations and no more victims. (This technique, which Ehrlichman, on another occasion, called a "modified limited hang-out," was also what Haldeman had had in mind when he suggested that they should "turn it off at the lowest cost" they could.) Hors d'oeuvres of many kinds came under consideration. Some were in the form of scapegoats to be turned over to the prosecutors, and others were in the form of incomplete or false reports to be issued to the public. By now, the country's appetite for revelations was well developed, and in the White House it was decided that no less a man than Mitchell was needed to satisfy it.

As Ehrlichman explained the new plan to the President, Mitchell would be induced to make a statement saying, "I am both morally and legally responsible."

"How does it redound to our advantage?" the President asked.

"That you have a report from me based on three weeks' work," Ehrlichman replied, "that when you got it, you immediately acted to call Mitchell in as the provable wrongdoer, and you say, 'My God, I've got a report here. And it's clear from this report that you are guilty as hell. Now John . . . go on in there and do what you should.'"

That way, the President could pose as the man who had cracked the conspiracy.

Shortly thereafter, Mitchell was called down to the White House, and Ehrlichman proposed the plan. Mitchell did not care for it. He not only maintained his innocence but suggested that the guilt lay elsewhere; namely, in the White House. Ehrlichman told the President when Mitchell had left that Mitchell had "lobbed, uh, mud balls at the White House at every opportunity." Faced with Mitchell's refusal to play the scapegoat, the President, Haldeman, and Ehrlichman next invited Dean to step into the role. Soon after Ehrlichman's unsatisfactory experience with Mitchell, the President met with Dean and attempted to induce him to sign a letter of resignation because of his implication in the scandal.

The President approached the subject in an offhand manner. "You know, I was thinking we ought to get the odds and ends, uh . . . we talked, and, uh, it was confirmed that—you remember we talked about resignations and so forth," he said.

"Uh huh," Dean replied.

"But I should have in hand something, or otherwise they'll say, 'What the hell did you—after Mr. Dean told you all of this, what did you do?'" the President went on.

Again Dean answered "Uh huh."

The President then related that even Henry Petersen had been concerned about "this situation on Dean," and Dean once more answered with an "uh huh."

"See what I mean?" the President asked the uncommunicative Dean.

"Are we talking Dean, or are we talking Dean, Ehrlichman, and Haldeman?" Dean finally asked.

"Well, I'm talking Dean," the President answered.

But Dean, like Mitchell before him, was talking Ehrlichman and Haldeman, too, and would not resign unless they also resigned. He did not want to be an hors d'oeuvre any more than Mitchell did. And since Dean was in possession of highly detailed information that implicated not only Haldeman and Ehrlichman but the President as well, the President was unable to "bite the Dean bullet," as he put it, until he also was willing to let Haldeman and Ehrlichman go. Their turn came quickly. By now the President was under intense pressure to act soon. If he did not, he could hardly pose as the man who had cracked the case. On April 17th, the day after the unproductive conversation with Dean, the President said to Haldeman and Ehrlichman, "Let me say this. . . . It's a hell of a lot different [from] John Dean. I know that as far as you're concerned, you'll go out and throw yourselves on a damned sword. I'm aware of that. . . . The problem we got here is this. I do not want to be in a position where the damned public clamor makes, as it did with Eisenhower, with Adams, makes it necessary or calls—to have Bob come in one day and say, 'Well, Mr. President, the public—blah, blah, blah—I'm going to leave.' " But Ehrlichman was not willing to throw himself on a sword. The person he was willing to throw on a sword was Dean. "Let me make a suggestion," he responded. It was that the President give Dean a leave of absence and then defer any decision on Ehrlichman and Haldeman until the case had developed further. However, the President pursued the point, seeming at times to favor Haldeman's and Ehrlichman's resignation, and finally Ehrlichman did what McCord, Hunt, Mitchell, and Dean had done before him. He lobbed mud balls at the White House—which in this case meant the President.

If he and Haldeman should resign, Ehrlichman observed, "we are put in a position of defending ourselves." And he went on, "The things that I am going to have to say about Dean are: basically that Dean was the sole proprietor of this project, that he reported to the President, he reported to me only incidentally."

" 'Reported to the President'?" the President inquired.

A moment later, speaking in his own defense, the President said, "You see the problem you've got there is that Dean does have a point there which you've got to realize. He didn't see me when he came out to California. He didn't see me until the day you said, 'I think you ought to talk to John Dean.' "

At this point, Ehrlichman retreated into ambiguity, and said, "But you see I get into a very funny defensive position then vis-à-vis you and vis-à-vis him, and it's very damned awkward. And I haven't thought it clear through. I don't know where we come out."

On April 17th, the President made a short statement saying simply that there had been "major developments in the case concerning which it would be improper to be more specific now." He was unable to offer any diversionary reports or propitiatory victims to deflect the public's wrath at the forthcoming disclosures. He and his aides had talked over countless schemes, but all of them had foundered on the unwillingness of any of the aides to sacrifice themselves for him—or for "the Presidency," as he had asked them to do. The coverup was all one piece, and it cohered in exposure just as it had cohered in concealment.

The President had become adept at recollecting whatever was needed at a particular moment. By April of 1973, he and his aides were spending most of their time making up history out of whole cloth to suit the needs of each moment. Unfortunately for them, the history they were making up was self-serving history, and by April their individual interests had grown apart. Each of them had begun to "recollect" things to his own advantage and to the detriment of the others. As their community of interests dissolved under the pressure of the investigation, each of them was retreating into his own private, self-interested reality. The capacity for deception which had once divided them from the country but united them with one another now divided them from one another as well.

In the White House, the fabric of reality had disintegrated altogether. What had got the President into trouble from the start had been his remarkable capacity for fantasy. He had begun by imagining a host of domestic foes. In retaliating against them, he had broken the law. Then he had compounded his lawbreaking by concealing it. And, finally, in the same way that he had broken the law although breaking it was against his best interests, he was bringing himself to justice even as he thought he was evading justice. For, as though in anticipation of the deterioration of his memory, he had installed another memory in the Oval Office, which was more nearly perfect than his own, or anyone else's merely human equipment: he had installed the taping system. The Watergate coverup had cast him in the double role of conspirator and investigator. Though the conspirator in him worked hard to escape the law, it was the investigator in him that gained the upper hand in the end. While he was attempting to evade the truth, his machines were preserving it forever.

At the moment when the President announced "major developments" in the Watergate case, the national process that was the investigation overwhelmed the national process that was the coverup. The events that followed were all the more astounding to the nation because, at just the moment when the coverup began to explode, the President, in the view of many observers, had been on the point of strangling the "obsolete" Constitutional system and replacing it with a Presidential dictatorship. One moment, he was triumphant and his power was apparently irresistible; the next moment, he was at bay. For in the instant the President made his announcement, the coverup cracked—not just the Watergate coverup but the broader coverup, which concealed the underground history of the last five years—and the nation suffered an inundation of news. The newspaper headlines now came faster and thicker than ever before in American history. The stories ran backward in time, and each day's newspaper told of some event a little further in the past as reporters traced the underground history to the early days of the Administration, and even into the terms of former Administrations. With the history of half a decade pouring out all at once, the papers were stuffed with more news than even the most diligent reader could absorb. Moreover, along with the facts, nonfacts proliferated as the desperate men in the White House put out one false or distorted statement after another, so that each true fragment of the story was all but lost in a maze of deceptions, and each event, true or false, came up dozens of times, in dozens of versions, until the reader's mind was swamped. And, as if what was in the newspapers were not already too much, television soon started up, and, in coverage that was itself a full-time job to watch, presented first the proceedings of the Ervin committee and then the proceedings of the House Judiciary Committee, when it began to weigh the impeachment of the President. And, finally, in a burst of disclosure without anything close to a precedent in history, the tapes were revealed—and not just once but twice. The first set of transcripts was released by the White House and was doctored, and only the second set, which was released by the Judiciary Committee, gave an accurate account of the President's conversations.

As the flood of information flowed into the public realm, overturning the accepted history of recent years, the present scene was also transformed. The Vice-President was swept from office when his bribe-taking became known, but so rapid was the pace of events that his departure was hardly noticed. Each of the institutions of the democracy that had been menaced by the President—and all had been menaced—was galvanized into action in its turn: the press, the television networks, the Senate, the House of Representatives, and, finally, in a dispute over release of the tapes, the Supreme Court. The public, too, was at last awakened, when the President fired the Special Proscutor whom he had appointed to look into the White House crimes. In an outpouring of public sentiment that, like so much else that happened at the time, had no precedent in the nation's history, millions of letters and telegrams poured in to Congress protesting the President's action. The time of letters sent by the President to himself was over, and the time of real letters from real people had come. No one of the democracy's institutions was powerful enough by itself to remove the President; the efforts of all were required—and only when those efforts were combined was he forced from office.

The Environmental Decline

BARRY COMMONER

The 1970's may well become known to historians as the age of environmentalism. Important initiatives in conserving the natural environment date back nearly one hundred years, but mass public awareness of environmental problems and the development of an elaborate legal structure to deal with them have been phenomena of recent times. After a moment in the late 1960's and early 1970's, when everyone was "for" the environment, the issues to which Barry Commoner speaks became major sources of controversy in a society worried as much about economic stagnation as about the quality of the environment.

Commoner, one of the nation's most distinguished environmental scientists (and the Citizens Party presidential candidate in 1980), analyzes the connection between the nature of economic growth and its impact on the environment. He shows that environmental pollution is the result not of economic growth alone, but rather of alterations in the kinds of products the economy produces. The substitution of plastics and aluminum for wood and steel, synthetic fibers for cotton and wool, and fertilizer for the use of additional acreage needlessly consumes resources and degrades the environment. While much political debate pits environmental quality against economic needs, Commoner's analysis points to a convergence between these issues. More dependence on renewable energy, Commoner argues, will both solve the energy problem and improve the environment while maintaining the nation's standard of living. Clearly, the issues he addresses in the selection that follows will be lively concerns during the decades ahead.

We have now arrived at the following position in the search for the causes of the environmental crisis in the United States. We know that *something* went wrong in the country after World War II, for most of our serious pollution problems either began in the postwar years or have greatly worsened since then. While two factors frequently blamed for the environmental crisis, population and affluence, have intensified in that time, these increases are much too small to account for the 200 to 2,000 per cent rise in pollution levels since 1946. The product of these two factors, which represents the total output of goods (total production equals population times production per capita), is also insufficient to account for the intensification of pollution. Total production—as measured by GNP—has increased by 126 per cent since 1944 while most pollution levels have risen by at least several times that rate. Something else besides growth in population and affluence must be deeply involved in the environmental crisis. . . .

The growth of the United States economy is recorded in elaborate detail in a variety of government statistics—huge volumes tabulating the amounts of various goods produced annually; the expenditures involved, the value of the goods sold, and so forth. Although these endless columns of figures are rather intimidating, there are some useful ways to extract meaningful facts from them. In particular, it is helpful to compute the rate of growth of each productive activity, a procedure that nowadays can be accomplished by committing the tables of numbers to an appropriate programmed computer. In order to compare one kind of economic activity with another, it is useful to arrange the computer to yield a figure for the percentage increase, or decrease, in production or consumption.

Not long ago, two of my colleagues and I went through the statistical tables and selected from them the data for several hundred items, which together represent a major and representative part of overall United States agricultural and industrial production. For each item, the average annual percentage change in production or consumption was computed for the years since 1946, or since the earliest date for which the statistics were available. Then we computed the overall change for the entire twenty-five year period—a twenty-five-year growth rate. When this list is rearranged in decreasing order of growth rate, a picture of *how* the United States economy has grown since World War II begins to emerge.

The winner of this economic sweepstakes, with the highest postwar growth rate, is the production of nonreturnable soda bottles, which has increased about 53,000 per cent in that time. The loser, ironically, is the horse; work animal horsepower has declined by 87 per cent of its original postwar value. The runners-up are an interesting but seemingly mixed bag. In second place is production of synthetic fibers, up 5,980 per cent; third is mercury used for chlorine production, up 3,920 per cent; succeeding places are held as follows: mercury used in mildew-resistant paint, up 3,120 per cent; air conditioner compressor units, up 2,850 per cent; plastics, up 1,960 per cent; fertilizer nitrogen, up 1,050 per cent; electric housewares (such as can-openers and corn-poppers), up 1,040 per cent; synthetic organic chemicals, up 950 per cent; aluminum, up 680 per cent; chlorine gas, up 600 per cent; electric power, up 530 per cent; pesticides, up 390 per cent; wood pulp, up 313 per cent; truck freight, up 222 per cent; consumer electronics (TV sets, tape recorders), up 217 per cent; motor fuel consumption, up 190 per cent; cement, up 150 per cent.

Then there is a group of productive activities that, as indicated earlier, have grown at about the pace of the population (i.e., up about 42 per cent): food production and consumption, total production of textiles and clothes, household utilities, and steel, copper, and other basic metals.

Finally there are the losers, which increase more slowly than the population or actually shrink in total production: railroad freight, up 17 per cent; lumber, down 1 per cent; cotton fiber, down 7 per cent; returnable beer bottles, down 36 per cent; wool, down 42 per cent; soap, down 76 per cent; and, at the end of the line, work animal horsepower, down 87 per cent.

What emerges from all these data is striking evidence that while production for most basic needs—food, clothing, housing—has just about kept up with the 40 to 50 per cent or so increase in population (that is, production *per capita* has been essentially constant), the *kinds* of goods produced to meet these needs have changed drastically. New production technologies have displaced old ones. Soap powder has been displaced by synthetic detergents; natural fibers (cotton and wool) have been displaced by synthetic ones; steel and lumber have been displaced by aluminum, plastics, and concrete; railroad freight has been displaced by truck freight; returnable bottles have been displaced by nonreturnable ones. On the road, the low-powered automobile engines of the 1920's and 1930's have been displaced by high-powered ones. On the farm, while per capita production has remained about constant, the amount of harvested acreage has decreased; in effect, fertilizer has displaced land. Older methods of insect control have been displaced by synthetic insecticides, such as DDT, and for controlling weeds the cultivator has been displaced by the herbicide spray. Range-feeding of livestock has been displaced by feedlots.

In each of these cases, what has changed drastically is the technology of production rather than overall output of the economic good. Of course, part of the economic growth in the United States since 1946 has been based on some newly introduced goods: air conditioners, television sets, tape recorders, and snowmobiles, all of which have increased absolutely without displacing an older product.

Distilled in this way, the mass of production statistics begins to form a meaningful pattern. In general, the growth of the United States economy since 1946 has had a surprisingly small effect on the degree to which individual needs for basic economic goods have been met. That statistical fiction, the "average American," now consumes, each year, about as many calories, protein, and other foods (although somewhat less of vitamins); uses about the same amount of clothes and cleaners; occupies about the same amount of newly constructed housing; requires about as much freight; and drinks about the same amount of beer (twenty-six gallons per capita!) as he did in 1946. However, his food is now grown on less land with much more fertilizer and pesticides than before; his clothes are more likely to be made of synthetic fibers than of cotton or wool; he launders with synthetic detergents rather than soap; he lives and works in buildings that depend more heavily on aluminum, concrete, and plastic than on steel and lumber; the goods he uses are increasingly shipped by truck rather than rail; he drinks beer out of nonreturnable bottles or cans rather than out of returnable bottles or at the tavern bar. He is more likely to live and work in air-conditioned surroundings than before. He also drives about twice as far as he did in 1946, in a heavier car, on synthetic rather than natural rubber tires, using more gasoline per miles, containing more tetraethyl lead, fed into an engine of increased horsepower and compression ratio.

These primary changes have led to others. To provide the raw materials needed for the new synthetic fibers, pesticides, detergents, plastics, and rubber, the production of synthetic organic chemicals has also grown very rapidly. The synthesis of organic chemicals uses a good deal of chlorine. Result: chlorine production has increased sharply. To make chlorine, an electric current is passed through a salt solution by way of a mercury electrode. Consequently, mercury consumption for this purpose has increased—by 3,930 per cent in the twenty-five-year postwar period. Chemical products, along with cement for concrete and aluminum (also winners in the growth race), use rather large amounts of electric power. Not surprisingly, then, that item, too, has increased considerably since 1946.

All this reminds us of what we have already been told by advertising—which incidentally has *also* grown; for example, the use of newsprint for advertising has grown faster than its use for news—that we are blessed with an economy based on very modern technologies. What the advertisements do not tell us—as we are urged to buy synthetic shirts and detergents, aluminum furniture, beer in no-return bottles, and Detroit's latest creation—is that *all this "progress" has greatly increased the impact on the environment.*

This pattern of economic growth is the major reason for the environmental crisis. A good deal of the mystery and confusion about the sudden emergence of the environmental crisis can be removed by pinpointing, pollutant by pollutant, how the postwar technological transformation of the United States economy has produced not only the much-heralded 126 per cent rise in GNP, but also, at a rate about ten times faster than the growth of GNP, the rising levels of environmental pollution.

Agriculture is a good place to start. . . . Between 1949 and 1968 total United States agricultural production increased by about 45 per cent. Since the United States population grew by 34 per cent in that time, the overall increase in production was just about enough to keep up with population; crop production *per capita* increased 6 per cent. In that period, the annual use of fertilizer nitrogen increased by 648 per cent, surprisingly larger than the increase in crop production. One reason for this disparity also turns up in the agricultural statistics: between 1949 and 1968 harvested acreage *declined* by 16 per cent. Clearly, more crop was being produced on less land (the yield per acre increased by 77 per cent). Intensive use of fertilizer nitrogen is the most important means of achieving this improvement in yield per acre. Thus, the intensive use of fertilizer nitrogen allowed "agribusiness" to just about meet the population's need for food—and at the same time to reduce the acreage used for that purpose.

These same statistics also explain the resulting water pollution problem. In 1949, an average of about 11,000 tons of fertilizer nitrogen were used *per USDA unit of crop production*, while in 1968 about 57,000 tons of nitrogen were used for the *same* crop yield. This means that the efficiency with which nitrogen contributes to the growth of the crop declined fivefold. Obviously, a good deal of the fertilizer nitrogen did not enter the crop and must have ended up elsewhere in the ecosystem. . . .

What the new fertilizer technology has accomplished for the farmer is clear: more crop can be produced on less acreage than before. Since the cost of fertilizer, relative to the resultant gain in crop sales, is lower than that of any other economic input, and since the Land Bank pays the farmer for acreage not in crops, the new technology pays him well. The cost—in environmental degradation—is borne by his neighbors in town who find their water polluted. The new technology is an economic success—but only because it is an ecological failure. . . .

In marketing terms, detergents are probably one of the most successful of modern technological innovations. In a scant twenty-five years this new invention has captured more than two-thirds of the laundry market from one of man's oldest, best-established, and most useful inventions—soap. This technological displacement is typical of many that have occurred since World War II: the replacement of a natural organic product by an unnatural synthetic one. In each case the new technology has worsened the environmental impact of the economic good.

Soap is produced by reacting a natural product, fat, with alkali. A typical fat used in soap making is palm oil. This is produced by the palm tree, using water and carbon dioxide as raw materials, and sunlight to provide the necessary energy. These are all freely available, renewable resources. No environmental impact results from the synthesis of the palm oil molecule. Of course, with inadequate husbandry a palm plantation can deplete the soil, and when the oil is extracted from the coconut, fuel is used and the resultant burning contributes to air pollution. The manufacture of soap from oil and alkali also consumes fuel and produces wastes.

Once used and sent down the drain, soap is broken down by the bacteria of decay—for the natural fat is readily attacked by the bacterial enzymes. In most places, this bacterial action takes place within the confines of a sewage treatment plant. What is then emitted to surface waters is only carbon dioxide and water, since fat contains only carbon, hydrogen, and oxygen atoms. Hence there is little or no impact on the aquatic ecosystem due to biological oxygen demand (which accompanies bacterial degradation of organic wastes) arising from soap wastes. Nor is the product of soap degradation, carbon dioxide, usually an important ecological intrusion since it is already in plentiful supply from other environmental sources. In its production and use, soap has a relatively light impact on the environment.

In comparison with soap, the production of detergents is likely to exert a more intense environmental impact. Detergents are synthesized from organic raw materials originally present in petroleum along with a number of other substances. To obtain the raw materials, the petroleum is subjected to distillation and other energy-consuming processes—and the burned fuel pollutes the air. Then the purified raw materials are used in a series of chemical reactions, involving chlorine and high temperatures, finally yielding the active cleaning agent. This is then mixed with a variety of additives, designed to soften hard water, bleach stains, "brighten" wash (this additive strongly reflects light and dazzles the eye to achieve a simulated whiteness), and otherwise gladden the heart of the advertising copywriter. Suitably boxed, this is the detergent. The total energy used to produce the active agent alone—and therefore the resultant air pollution—is probably three times that needed to produce oil for soap manufacture. And to produce the needed chlorine, mercury is used—and released to the environment as a pollutant. In substituting man-made chemical processes for natural ones, detergent manufacture inevitably produces a greater environmental stress than does the manufacture of soap. . . .

Another pollution problem arises from the phosphate content of detergents, whether degradable or not, for phosphate can stimulate algal overgrowths, which on their death overburden the aquatic ecosystem with organic matter. Phosphate is added to detergents for two purposes: to combat hard water (because it helps to tie up materials, such as calcium, which cause water hardness) and to help suspend dirt particles so that they can be readily rinsed away. Soap itself accomplishes the second of these functions, but not the first. In hard water, soap is rather ineffective, but can be improved by adding a water-softening agent such as phosphate. Thus, phosphate is needed only to solve the hard-water problem. But where water is hard, it can be treated by a household water-softener, a device which could also be built into washing machines. In other words, successful washing can be accomplished without resorting to phosphate, which when added to detergents, worsens their already serious environmental effects. Thus the actual need to replace soap is slight. As a recent chemical engineering textbook states: "There is absolutely no reason why old-fashioned soap cannot be used for most household and commercial cleaning." . . .

Electric power is one of the fast-growing features of the postwar United States economy. This industry is also the source of major pollution problems: sulfur dioxide, nitrogen oxides, and dust emitted by fossil-fuel burning plants; radioactive emissions and the small but enormously catastrophic potential of an accident from the operation of nuclear power plants; and the emission of waste heat to the air and nearby surface waters by both types of plants. This growth in the use of electric power is, justifiably, associated with the modernity of our economy and—with much less cause—to our supposed "affluence." The statistics appear to be straightforward enough. In the United States, annual power consumption is about 20,540 kilowatt hours per capita (the United States consumes 34 per cent of the world's electric power output), as opposed to about 2,900 kw-h per capita for Chile, 260 kw-h per capita for India, and 230 kw-h per capita for Thailand. However, electric power, unconverted, is not in itself capable of satisfying any known human need, and its contribution to human welfare needs to be measured in terms of the economic goods that power can produce. Here we discover another serious failing—when measured in terms of human welfare—of postwar technology: the new productive technologies are more costly than the technologies they have displaced, in consumption of electric power and other forms of fuel-generated energy *per unit economic good*. For example, aluminum, which has increasingly displaced steel and lumber as a construction material, requires for its production about 15 times more fuel energy than steel and about 150 times more fuel energy than lumber. Even taking into account that less aluminum, by weight, is needed for a given purpose than steel, the power discrepancy remains. For example, the energy required to produce metal for an aluminum beer can is 6.3 times that needed for a steel beer can.

The displacement of natural products by synthetic organic chemicals and of lumber and steel by concrete has a similar effect, for both chemical manufacturing and the production of cement for concrete are intense consumers of electric power. Aluminum and chemical production alone account for about 28 per cent of total industrial use of electric power in the United States. Thus the expansion of power production in the United States is not an accurate measure of increased economic good, being badly inflated by the growing tendency to displace power-thrifty goods with power-consumptive ones. The cost of this inefficiency is heavily borne by the environment.

Another technological displacement is readily visible to the modern householder in the daily acquisition of rubbish, most of it from packaging. It is a useful exercise to examine the statistics relevant to some economic good—beer, let us say—and determine from them the origin of the resultant impact on the environment. We can begin the exercise by recalling that the relevant economic good is chiefly the beer, not the bottle or can in which it is delivered. The relevant pollutant is the non-returnable bottle or can, for these, when "disposed of" in rubbish, cannot be assimilated in any natural ecological cycle. Therefore, they either accumulate or must be reprocessed at some expenditure of energy and cost in power-produced pollutants. The exercise consists in determining the relative effects of the three factors that might lead to an increased output of pollution, in this case, in the period from 1950 to 1967. In that time, the total consumption of nonreturnable beer bottles increased by 595 per cent and the consumption of beer increased by 37 per cent. Since the population increased by 30 per cent, the "affluence" factor, or the amount of beer consumed per capita, remained essentially constant (actually a 5 per cent increase). The remainder of the increased output of pollutant—beer bottles—is due to the technological factor—that is, the number of nonreturnable bottles produced per gallon of beer, which increased by 408 per cent. The relative importance of the three factors is evident.

It will be argued, of course, that the use of a nonreturnable beer bottle is more desirable than a returnable one to the individual beer drinker. After all, some human effort must be expended to return the bottle to the point of purchase. We can modify the earlier evaluation, then, by asserting that for the sake of whatever improvement in well-being is involved in avoiding the effort of returning the bottle, the production of beer in nonreturnable bottles incurs a 408 per cent intensification of environmental impact. No such subtlety is involved in comparing the environmental impacts of two alternative nonreturnable beer containers: steel beer cans and aluminum ones. The energy involved in producing the aluminum can—and therefore the amount of combustion and the resultant output of pollutants—is 6.3 times that required for a steel can.

Similar computations can be made for the added environmental impact incurred when extra layers of packaging are added to foods and other goods or when plastic wrappers (nondegradable) are substituted for degradable cellulosic ones. In general, modern industrial technology has encased economic goods of no significantly increased human value in increasingly larger amounts of environmentally harmful wrappings. Result: the mounting heaps of rubbish that symbolize the advent of the technological age.

It should be recognized that such computations of environmental impact are still in a primitive, only partially developed stage. What is needed, and what—it is to be hoped—will be worked out before long, is an ecological analysis of every major aspect of the production, use, and disposition of goods. What is needed is a kind of "ecological impact inventory" for each productive activity, which will enable us to attach a sort of pollution price tag to each product. We would then know, for example, for each pound of detergent: how much air pollution is generated by the electric power and fuel burned to manufacture its chemical ingredients; how much water pollution is due to the mercury "loss" by the factory in the course of manufacturing the chlorine needed to produce it; the water pollution due to the detergent and phosphate entering sewage systems; the ecological effect of fluoride and arsenic (which may contaminate the phosphate), and of mercury, which might contaminate any alkali used to compound the detergent. Such pollution price tags are needed for all major products if we are to judge their relative *social* value. The foregoing account shows how far we are from this goal, and once again reminds us how blind we are about the environmental effects of modern technology.

Cambodia and Kent State: Two Memoirs

RICHARD NIXON and HENRY KISSINGER

The war question that ripped domestic politics in the Vietnam years was without a successful resolution. Several administrators supported a war effort that piled up bodies of Vietnamese and Americans with what we now know was no chance of military success. Yet the conduct of the communist governments that have since seized Indochina have given little cause for satisfaction at the outcome.

The American and South Vietnamese incursion into Cambodia in 1970 raised anger among various segments of the political opposition— those who opposed the entire American cause and those who believed the invasion would interfere with the achievement of an orderly negotiated peace. In any event, Vietnam was a war beyond solutions.

President Richard Nixon and Secretary of State Henry Kissinger, the individuals most responsible for the invasion, were not simplistic right-wingers who tried to reduce international politics to a confrontation between communism and anticommunism; they had respect for the subtle compositions and shifts of international power. Still, the war and the situation in Cambodia eluded their logic of power and revealed a perhaps questionable morality that each in his way labors to justify.

I RICHARD NIXON

The whole situation over Cambodia and Vietnam was becoming so tense that I felt I had to make a very painful personal decision. Although I knew how much Pat and Julie were counting on it, I canceled our plans to attend David's graduation from Amherst and Julie's graduation from Smith later in the spring. Pat had never known the joy of having a parent attend any of her graduations, and I knew that she had been looking forward to Julie's. Julie was also terribly disappointed. She tried to hold back her tears, and she pointed out that only a few small radical groups were involved, and that everyone she knew—including students who opposed the war and my administration—felt that I should be able to attend the ceremony.

Ted Agnew felt particularly strongly about this. "Don't let them intimidate you, Mr. President," he said, barely restraining his indignation. "You may be President, but you're her father, and a father should be able to attend his daughter's graduation." The Secret Service, however, had received reports of several protest demonstrations that were already being planned against me, and the possibility of an ugly incident that would mar the graduation, not just for us but for all the other students and parents, was too great a risk.

Despite the impasse in the secret talks and the worsening military situation in Cambodia, I decided to go ahead with the troop withdrawal scheduled for April 20 [1970]. I discussed the issue at length with Kissinger, and we agreed that the time had come to drop a bombshell on the gathering spring storm of antiwar protest.

Vietnamization had progressed to the point that, for the first time, we felt we could project our troop withdrawals over the next year. We decided, therefore, that instead of announcing a smaller number over a shorter period, I would announce the withdrawal of 150,000 men over the next year.

The withdrawal figure came as a dramatic surprise when I revealed it in a speech on April 20. The only Communist reaction was an escalation of the fighting.

By the end of April, the Communists had a quarter of Cambodia under control and were closing in on Phnom Penh. It was clear that Lon Nol needed help to survive. If the Communists succeeded in overthrowing him, South Vietnam would be threatened from the west as well as the north. This situation would jeopardize our troop withdrawal program and would also virtually assure a Communist invasion of South Vietnam as soon as the last American had left. . . .

The Communist sanctuaries in Cambodia were in two main areas. The Parrot's Beak is a sliver of land that pushes into South Vietnam and reaches within thirty-three miles of Saigon. A particularly strong ARVN [South Vietnamese Army] force was stationed on the border in this area. Our intelligence reports indicated that the heaviest Communist concentration was in another border area, the Fishhook, a thin, curving piece of Cambodian territory jutting right into the heart of South Vietnam, about fifty miles northwest of Saigon. This was the primary area of operation for what intelligence referred to as COSVN—the Central Office of South Vietnam. COSVN was the Communists' floating command post of military headquarters, supplies, food, and medical facilities. The Fishhook was thus the nerve center of the Communist forces in the sanctuaries, and it would be strongly defended. The initial intelligence estimates projected that the heavy fortifications and the concentration of Communist troops in the area might result in very high casualties in the first week of operation.

I began to consider letting the ARVN go into the Parrot's Beak and sending a mixed force of American and South Vietnamese troops into the Fishhook. Giving the South Vietnamese an operation of their own would be a major boost to their morale as well as provide a practical demonstration of the success of Vietnamization. It would also be a good diversionary cover for the more important and more difficult Fishhook operation.

I never had any illusions about the shattering effect a decision to go into Cambodia would have on public opinion at home. I knew that opinions among my major foreign policy advisers were deeply divided over the issue of widening the war, and I recognized that it could mean personal and political catastrophe for me and my administration.

On Sunday night, April 26, I reached my decision. We would go for broke. The ARVN would go into the Parrot's Beak and a joint ARVN–U.S. force would go into the Fishhook.

On Monday morning I met with Rogers, Laird, and Kissinger. It was a tense meeting, because even though Rogers and Laird had by now given up hope of dissuading me from taking some action in Cambodia, they still thought they could convince me not to involve American troops. Rogers said, "It will cost us great casualties with very little gain. And I just don't believe it will be a crippling blow to the enemy." Laird said, "I'm not really opposed to going after the COSVN, but I'm not happy with the way this is being implemented." He was more upset, it seemed, with an apparent snub of the Pentagon in our decision-making process. He also suggested that General Abrams might not approve of the COSVN operation, but backed away when Kissinger contradicted him. Nevertheless, immediately after our meeting I sent a back-channel cable to Abrams, ordering him to send me the "unvarnished truth" about the way he felt.

A joint response from Abrams and U.S. Ambassador Ellsworth Bunker indicated full support on their part. Speaking specifically of the attack on the Fishhook, they wrote: "We both agree that attack on this area should have maximum unsettling effect on the enemy, who has considered until now his sanctuaries immune to ground attack." Abrams added his personal views in a separate paragraph: "It is my independent view that these attacks into the enemy's sanctuaries in Cambodia are the military move to make at this time in support of our mission in South Vietnam both in terms of security of our own forces and for advancement of the Vietnamization program."

That night I sat alone going over the decision one last time. It was still not too late to call the operation off: the Parrot's Beak action would not begin until the next morning, and the Fishhook not until two days after that. I took a pad and began to make a list of the pluses and minuses of both operations. The risk and danger involved were undeniably great; there was no assurance of success on the battlefield and there was the certainty of an uproar at home. But there was also no question that the continued existence of the Cambodian sanctuaries would threaten the safety of the remaining American troops in South Vietnam and almost guarantee a Communist invasion as soon as we had pulled out.

Early the next morning I showed Kissinger my notes. He blinked his eyes as he took a piece of paper from the folder he was carrying and handed it to me. It was a list almost identical to mine. "I did the same thing, Mr. President," he said, "and it looks like we're both able to make a good case both ways on it."

I said that as far as I was concerned, the simple fact of showing the Communists that we intended to protect ourselves and our allies put all the weight on one side. "Now that we have made the decision there must be no recriminations among us," I said. "Not even if the whole thing goes wrong. In fact, *especially* if the whole thing goes wrong."

South Vietnam's announcement of the Parrot's Beak operation came over the wires on Wednesday, April 29. Within minutes the leading Senate doves were in front of the TV cameras, demanding that I disavow Thieu's offensive and not send any American troops into Cambodia. All during the day I continued to work on the speech I would deliver the next night announcing the operation. I asked Rose to call Julie for me. "I don't want to get her upset, but it's possible that the campuses are really going to blow up after this speech," I said, "so could you just say I asked if she and David could come down from school to be with us."

That night I found it difficult to get to sleep. After tossing fitfully for an hour or so, I got up and sat in the Lincoln Sitting Room until 5:30. At nine o'clock I walked over to my EOB office to go over the first pages of the typed speech. That afternoon I had Haldeman and Kissinger come over so I could read the announcement to them. I asked Kissinger to brief George Meany, because I knew that labor support would be vital. A little later he reported that Meany supported my decision wholeheartedly. Kissinger had less success with his own NSC staff. Three of his top assistants decided to resign in protest over my decision.

Shortly before delivering the speech from the Oval Office, I went to the White House Theatre to brief the bipartisan congressional leadership. I said I understood that many of them would oppose the decision I had made. I knew how they felt about it, and I respected their feelings. "I just want you to know that whether you think it's right or wrong, the reason I have decided to do this is that I have decided it's the best way to end the war and save the lives of our soldiers," I told them.

I looked around the room. The faces were intent and strained. Some of the strongest doves were there: Fulbright, Mansfield, Aiken, Kennedy. The sincerity of my words must have reached them, even though they remained opposed to the decision I had made. As I left the room, everyone stood and applauded.

I began the speech by describing how the Communists had responded to my recently announced troop withdrawal by stepping up their attacks throughout Indochina. "To protect our men who are in Vietnam and to guarantee the continued success of our withdrawal and Vietnamization programs," I said, "I have concluded that the time has come for action."

I used a map to explain the geographic and strategic importance of the Cambodian sanctuaries and to describe the South Vietnamese operation in the Parrot's Beak. Then I announced that a joint U.S.–Vietnamese force would go into the Fishhook.

I stressed that this was not an invasion of Cambodia. The sanctuaries were completely occupied and controlled by North Vietnamese forces. We would withdraw once they had been driven out and once their military supplies were destroyed. The purpose, I said, was not to expand the war into Cambodia, but to end the war in Vietnam by making peace possible.

Setting my decision in its widest context, I continued, "If, when the chips are down, the world's most powerful nation, the United States of America, acts like a pitiful, helpless giant, the forces of totalitarianism and anarchy will threaten free nations and free institutions throughout the world."

For an hour after the speech I sat with my family in the Solarium while they discussed the speech and tried to gauge the reactions to it. Then I went to the Lincoln Sitting Room and began returning calls that had come in after the speech.

Just after 10:30 I was informed that Chief Justice Warren Burger was at the gate with a letter for me. I instructed the Secret Service agent on duty to have him shown up immediately.

"I didn't want to disturb you, Mr. President," Burger said, "but I wanted you to know that I think your speech tonight had a sense of history and destiny about it."

I said that the critics had already begun denouncing the speech and the decision, but he said that he was sure it would be supported by the people. "I think anyone who really listened to what you said will appreciate the guts it took to make the decision," he added. He also pointed out that anyone who thought about it would realize that, as a shrewd politician, I would obviously not do anything that might damage Republican chances in the November elections unless I felt that it was absolutely necessary for national security.

"Speaking in the greatest confidence, Mr. Chief Justice," I said, using his formal title as I always did when addressing him, "I am realist enough to know that if this operation doesn't succeed—or if anything else happens that forces my public support below a point where I feel I can't be re-elected—I would like you to be ready to be in the running for the nomination in 1972." . . .

Despite very little sleep, I was up early on the morning after the speech. I went to the Pentagon for a firsthand briefing on the Cambodian operation from the Joint Chiefs and their top advisers. As I walked through the halls to the briefing room, I was mobbed by people cheering and trying to shake my hand. "God bless you!" "Right on!" "We should have done this years ago!" they shouted.

The atmosphere in the briefing room was generally positive if somewhat more restrained. A huge map of the battle area almost covered one wall. Different colored pins indicated the positions and movements of the various forces. As the briefers described the initial success of the operation, I found myself studying the map more and more intently. I noted that in addition to the Parrot's Beak and the Fishhook, four other areas were marked as occupied by Communist forces.

Suddenly I asked, "Between the ARVN and ourselves, would we be able to mount offensives in all of those other areas? Could we take out *all* the sanctuaries?"

The reply to my question emphasized the very negative reaction any such action would receive in the media and Congress.

"Let me be the judge as far as the political reactions are concerned," I said. "The fact is that we have already taken the political heat for this particular operation. If we can substantially reduce the threat to our forces by wiping out the rest of the sanctuaries, now is the time to do it."

Everyone seemed to be waiting for someone else to speak. Usually I like to mull things over, but I made a very uncharacteristic on-the-spot decision. I said, "I want to take out all of those sanctuaries. Make whatever plans are necessary, and then just do it. Knock them all out so that they can't be used against us again. Ever."

As I left the Pentagon after the briefing, once again employees rushed into the halls. By the time I reached the lobby, I was surrounded by a friendly, cheering crowd. One woman was particularly emotional as she thanked me on behalf of her husband, who was serving in Vietnam. As I thought of these men and women with loved ones fighting in Vietnam, I could not help thinking about those students who took advantage of their draft deferments and their privileged status in our society to bomb campuses, set fires, and tyrannize their institutions.

"I have seen them," I said about our soldiers in Vietnam. "They're the greatest. You see these bums, you know, blowing up the campuses. Listen, the boys that are on the college campuses today are the luckiest people in the world, going to the greatest universities, and here they are burning up the books, storming around about this issue. . . . Then out there, we have kids who are just doing their duty. And I have seen them. They stand tall, and they are proud."

That afternoon, while the tempest of reaction over Cambodia continued to build, I decided to get my family away from the White House for at least a few hours of relaxation after the great tension we had all experienced. It was a warm, clear day, so I suggested that we sail down the Potomac to Mount Vernon on the *Sequoia*.

It is the custom for all naval vessels passing Mount Vernon to honor George Washington, who is buried there. When we neared the spot, I had everyone move onto the deck and face the shore. Pat was next to me, then David, Julie, and Bebe Rebozo. As we passed by the first President's tomb, over the *Sequoia*'s loudspeaker came "The Star-Spangled Banner." We all stood at attention until the last note died away.

By the time the *Sequoia* had returned to Washington, the indignant reaction to my "bums" statement that morning at the Pentagon had almost overwhelmed the response to the Cambodia speech itself.

All through the spring of 1970 the country had faced wave after wave of violent campus unrest. As with the disturbances at the beginning of 1969, the issues were largely campus-oriented, dealing with disciplinary regulations, campus administration, and minority admissions.

What distinguished many of the 1970 campus disturbances from all earlier ones was the increase in bombings and violence connected with them. Radical groups openly encouraged the bombing of institutions of which they disapproved.

In the academic year 1969–70 there were 1,800 demonstrations, 7,500 arrests, 462 injuries—two-thirds of them were to police—and 247 arsons and 8 deaths.

April 1970 had been a particularly violent month. For the second time, a bank near the University of California at Santa Barbara was set on fire. A fire was set at the University of Kansas that destroyed buildings worth $2 million. At Ohio State University protesters demanding the admission of more black students and the abolition of ROTC on campus engaged in a six-hour battle with police. There were 600 arrests and 20 wounded. Governor James Rhodes finally had to call in 1,200 national guardsmen and impose a curfew to quiet the campus.

It was criminal and barbarous to burn banks as a protest against capitalism or to burn ROTC buildings as a protest against militarism. But to me the most shocking incidents were those that I considered to be directed at the very quality of intellectual life that should characterize a university community. In March, an arsonist caused $320,000 damage to the University of California library at Berkeley. At the end of April, as part of a demonstration in support of Black Panthers charged with murder in New Haven, $2,500 worth of books were set on fire in the basement of the Yale Law School.

The most shameful incident occurred at Stanford University. On April 24 an anti-ROTC group set a fire at the university's center for behavioral studies. One of the offices that was completely gutted belonged to a visiting Indian anthropologist, Professor M. N. Srinivas. His personal notes, files, and manuscripts went up in flames.

When Pat Moynihan told me about this tragedy, I wrote to Professor Srinivas:

As did countless other Americans, I responded with disbelief at the news that your study at the Center for Advanced Studies in the Behavioral Sciences had been firebombed, and that much of the work of a lifetime had been destroyed.

It can be small consolation for you to know that the overwhelming proportion of the American people, and of the American academic community, utterly reject the tactics of the person or persons who did this. To say that they are deranged, does not excuse them. To say, what is more probably the case, that they are simply evil, does not make them go away.

I hope that the great insights of social anthropology that you have brought to your studies might serve in this moment to help you understand this tragedy. Please at all events know that you are an honored and welcome guest, whose work is appreciated and valued in this nation as indeed throughout the world.

I do not think that anyone who heard my comments at the Pentagon or who heard the tape recording of it had any doubt that when I talked about "bums" burning up the books and blowing up the campuses, I was referring to the arsonists at Berkeley and Yale and the Stanford firebombers and others like them. The Washington *Post* headline the next morning accurately reflected my meaning: *Nixon Denounces Campus "Bums" Who Burn Books, Set Off Bombs.*

But the front-page headline in the New York *Times* conveyed a slightly different meaning: *Nixon Puts "Bums" Label on Some College Radicals*; and the inside continuation of the story was headlined: *Nixon Denounces "Bums" on Campus.*

Within a few days, it was the widespread impression that I had referred to all student protesters as "bums."

The media coverage and interpretation of the "bums" statement added fuel to the fires of dissent that were already getting out of control on many campuses. The National Student Association called for my impeachment, and editors of eleven Eastern colleges, including most of the Ivy League schools, ran a common editorial in their campus newspapers calling for a nationwide academic strike.

At the University of Maryland, just outside Washington, fifty people were injured when students ransacked the ROTC building and skirmished with police. In Kent, Ohio, a crowd of hundreds of demonstrators watched as two young men threw lighted flares into the Army ROTC building on the campus of Kent State University, and burned it to the ground. Governor Rhodes called in the National Guard. He said that 99 percent of the Kent State students wanted the school to remain open, and that the rest were "worse than the brownshirts."

On Monday, May 4, I asked Haldeman to come to the EOB office to go over trip schedules with me. He looked agitated. "Something just came over the wires about a demonstration at Kent State," he said. "The National Guard opened fire, and some students were shot."

I was stunned. "Are they dead?" I asked.

"I'm afraid so. No one knows why it happened."

It appeared that an uneasy confrontation had begun brewing around noon. Finally, a large crowd of students began throwing rocks and chunks of concrete at the guardsmen, forcing them up a small hill. At the top the soldiers turned, and someone started shooting.

In the newspaper the next day I saw the pictures of the four young people who had been killed. Two had been bystanders; the other two had been protesting a decision they felt was wrong. Now all four were dead, and a call was going out for nationwide demonstrations and student strikes. Would this tragedy become the cause of scores of others? I could not get the photographs out of my mind. I could not help thinking about the families, suddenly receiving the news that their children were dead because they had been shot in a campus demonstration. I wrote personal letters to each of the parents, even though I knew that words could not help.

Those few days after Kent State were among the darkest of my presidency. I felt utterly dejected when I read that the father of one of the dead girls had told a reporter, "My child was not a bum."

Kent State also took a heavy toll on Henry Kissinger's morale.

Members of his staff had resigned because of Cambodia, and former Harvard colleagues whom he had considered among his most loyal friends wrote bitter letters to him demanding that he make his professed moral position credible by resigning.

On a day several of these letters arrived, he came into my office and sat staring disconsolately out the window. Finally he said, "I still think you made the right decision as far as foreign policy considerations were involved. But in view of what has happened I fear I may have failed to advise you adequately of the domestic dangers."

I told him that I had been fully aware of both the military and the political risks. I had made the decision myself, and I assumed full responsibility for it. Finally I said, "Henry, remember Lot's wife. Never turn back. Don't waste time rehashing things we can't do anything about."

I was shocked and disappointed when an apparently intentional leak to the press revealed that Bill Rogers and Mel Laird had been opposed to my Cambodian decision. The operation was still in a critical stage, and I called Rogers and told him that I felt the Cabinet should get behind a decision once it had been made by the President.

Walter Hickel, the Secretary of the Interior, chose a more public way to express his conviction that I should listen to the students and spend more time with the Cabinet. In what he later explained as a mishap, a copy of a letter he had written to me raising these points was already going out over the AP wire before it had been delivered to the White House. Several other Cabinet and administration members also took public positions of less than full support.

In the midst of all the furor, it meant a great deal to me when one of the two living Americans who could really know what I was going through wrote to me.

I received a note from Johnson City: "Dear Mr. President," it read, "I hope you have a chance to read this. My best always. LBJ." Attached to it was a recent column by one of Johnson's former assistants, John P. Roche, entitled "The President Makes the Decisions." It began: "What distinguishes the Republican regime from that of Lyndon Johnson is that Mr. Nixon announced an 'open administration,' with the consequence that everyone above the rank of GS-15 feels free to comment on the wisdom of the President's actions." After noting examples of Cabinet members dissociating themselves from my Cambodian decision, Roche concluded by making the point that "Nixon was elected to make a choice and he made it. One can attack it on the merits if he so chooses, that is, say it was mistaken. Or one can support his actions (as I do). But under the Constitution no one has the right to impeach his decision because he did not consult Senator Fulbright, Secretary Finch, Pat Moynihan or the International Security Affairs section of the Pentagon."

Kent State triggered a nationwide wave of campus protests. The daily news reports conveyed a sense of turmoil bordering on insurrection. Hundreds of college campuses went through a paroxysm of rage, riot, and arson. By the end of the first week after the killings, 450 colleges and universities were closed by student or faculty protest strikes. Before the month was over, the National Guard had been called out twenty-four times at twenty-one campuses in sixteen states.

A national day of protest was hastily called to take place in Washington on Saturday, May 9. I felt that we should do everything possible to make sure that this event was nonviolent and that we did not appear insensitive to it. Ehrlichman urged that we make whatever gestures of communication were possible. Kissinger, however, took a particularly hard line on the demonstrators. He was appalled at the violence they provoked and at the ignorance of the real issues they displayed. He felt strongly that I should not appear more flexible until after the Cambodian operation was successfully completed. As he put it, we had to make it clear that our foreign policy was not made by street protests.

I decided to try to defuse the tension by holding a press conference. The risks were high, and my staff was deeply divided about the wisdom of having one at this time. Most of the reporters and commentators were bound to be bitterly critical, and it was highly possible that an acrimonious session would only make things worse. Nonetheless I decided to go ahead, and the conference was announced for prime time on Friday evening, May 8.

I could feel the emotions seething beneath the hot TV lights as I entered the East Room at ten o'clock Friday night. Almost all the questions were about the Cambodian operation and Kent State.

The first question was whether I had been surprised by the intensity of the protests and whether they would affect my policy in any way. I replied that I had not been surprised by the intensity of the protests. I knew that those who protested did so because they felt that my decision would expand the war, our involvement in it, and our casualties. "I made the decision, however, for the very reasons that they are protesting," I said. "I am concerned because I know how deeply they feel. But I know that what I have done will accomplish the goals that they want. It will shorten this war. It will reduce American casualties. It will allow us to go forward with our withdrawal program. The 150,000 Americans that I announced for withdrawal in the next year will come home on schedule. It will, in my opinion, serve the cause of a just peace in Vietnam."

One reporter asked what I thought the students were trying to say in the demonstration that was about to take place in Washington. I wanted my answer to this question to be compassionate but not weak. I said, "They are trying to say that they want peace. They are trying to say that they want to stop the killing. They are trying to say that they want to end the draft. They are trying to say that we ought to get out of Vietnam. I agree with everything that they are trying to accomplish. I believe, however, that the decisions that I have made, and particularly this last terribly difficult decision of going into the Cambodian sanctuaries which were completely occupied by the enemy—I believe that that decision will serve that purpose, because you can be sure that everything that I stand for is what they want."

Immediately after the press conference I began returning some of the dozens of phone calls that had come in and placing calls to others. I was agitated and uneasy as the events of the last few weeks raced through my mind.

I slept for a few hours and then went to the Lincoln Sitting Room. I put on a record of Rachmaninoff's Second Piano Concerto and sat listening to the music. Manolo heard that I was up and came in to see if I would like some tea or coffee. Looking out the windows I could see small groups of young people beginning to gather on the Ellipse between the White House and the Washington Monument. I mentioned that I considered the Lincoln Memorial at night to be the most beautiful sight in Washington, and Manolo said that he had never seen it. Impulsively I said, "Let's go look at it now."

This event was spontaneous on my part and I purposely did not take any staff members along or alert any reporters to accompany me. Thus it was especially frustrating when the newspapers reported that I had been unable to communicate with the young people I met, and that I had shown my insensitivity to their concerns by talking about inconsequential subjects like sports and surfing. Some of this mistaken impression apparently came from the students themselves. One of them told a reporter, "He wasn't really concerned with why we were here." Another said that I had been tired and dull and rambled aimlessly from subject to subject. . . .

II HENRY KISSINGER

Historians rarely do justice to the psychological stress on a policymaker. What they have available are documents written for a variety of purposes—under contemporary rules of disclosure, increasingly to dress up the record—and not always relevant to the moment of decision. What no document can reveal is the accumulated impact of accident, intangibles, fears, and hesitation.

March and April of 1970 were months of great tension. My talks with Le Duc Tho were maddeningly ambiguous. We faced what looked like a significant offensive in Laos; there was the coup in Cambodia soon to be followed by North Vietnamese attacks all over the country; Soviet combat personnel appeared in Egypt—the first time that the Soviet Union had risked combat outside the satellite orbit. Amid all these events, the President was getting testy. Nixon blamed his frustrations on the bureaucracy's slow and erratic response to his wishes, which he ascribed to the legacy of thirty years of Democratic rule. Haldeman joked that the President was in a "charming mood"; in the course of covering one subject on the telephone Nixon had hung up on him several times.

On April 13, just as Cambodia was approaching the decisive turn, an extraneous event occurred that took a heavy toll of Nixon's nervous energy: the mishap of *Apollo 13*. Soon after its launch on April 11 it became apparent that there was a severe malfunction and that the astronauts might have to circumnagivate the moon in the cramped and fragile vehicle designed for the brief lunar landing. I learned of the accident around 11:00 P.M. I sought to inform the President but ran into one of the mindless edicts by which Haldeman established his authority: The President could not be awakened without his specific authorization. This he refused to give for what he considered a technical problem involving no foreign policy considerations. I warned Haldeman that keeping the President ignorant would be hard to explain; he insisted that public relations was his province. The next morning Ron Ziegler had to go through verbal contortions to imply, without lying outright, that the President had been in command all night. . . .

Revisionist history has painted a picture of a peaceful, neutral Cambodia wantonly assaulted by American forces and plunged into a civil war that could have been avoided but for the American obsession with military solutions. The facts are different. Sihanouk declared war on the new Cambodian government as early as March 20, two days after his overthrow, throwing in his lot with the Communists he had held at bay and locating himself in Peking, then still considered the most revolutionary capital in the world and with which, moreover, we had no means of communication whatever. April saw a wave of Communist attacks to overthrow the existing governmental structure in Cambodia. Le Duc Tho on March 16 had rejected all suggestions of de-escalation of military activities and on April 4 had rejected all suggestions of neutralization. He had asserted that the Cambodian, Laotian, and Vietnamese peoples were one and would fight shoulder to shoulder to win the whole of Indochina. By the second half of April, the North Vietnamese were systematically expanding their sanctuaries and merging them into a "liberated zone." They were surrounding Phnom Penh and cutting it off from all access—using the very tactics that five years later led to its collapse.

If these steps were unopposed, the Communist sanctuaries, hitherto limited to narrow unpopulated areas close to the Vietnamese border, would be organized into a single large base area of a depth and with a logistics system which would enable rapid transfer of units and supplies. We would have preferred the old Sihanouk government, I told a group of Republican Senators on April 21. But Sihanouk's pronouncements left little doubt that this option was no longer open to us. If Lon Nol fell, the Sihanouk who returned would no longer balance contending forces in neutrality but lead a Communist government. His necessities (as well as his outraged vanity) would force him to purge the moderate groups on which his freedom of maneuver between contending factions had previously depended; he would be reduced to a figurehead. Sihanoukville would reopen to Communist supplies. Security throughout the southern half of South Vietnam would deteriorate drastically.

By April 21 the basic issue had been laid bare by Hanoi's aggressiveness; it was whether Vietnamization was to be merely an alibi for an American collapse or a serious strategy designed to achieve an honorable peace. If the former, neither the rate of withdrawal nor events in neighboring countries were important; in fact, anything that hastened the collapse of South Vietnam was a blessing in disguise. Some of the opposition, like Senator George McGovern, took this position. Though I considered it against the national interest, it was rational and honest. My intellectual difficulties arose with those who pretended that there was a middle course of action that would avoid collapse in Vietnam and yet ignore the impending Communist takeover in Cambodia.

There was no serious doubt that Hanoi's unopposed conquest of Cambodia would have been the last straw for South Vietnam. In the midst of a war, its chief ally was withdrawing forces at an accelerating rate and reducing its air support. Saigon was being asked to take the strain at the very moment Hanoi was increasing reinforcements greatly over the level of the preceding year. If Cambodia were to become a single armed camp at this point, catastrophe was inevitable. Saigon needed time to consolidate and improve its forces; the United States had to pose a credible threat for as long as possible; and Hanoi's offensive potential had to be weakened by slowing down its infiltration and destroying its supplies. It was a race between Vietnamization, American withdrawal, and Hanoi's offensives.

Strategically, Cambodia could not be considered a country separate from Vietnam. The indigenous Cambodian Communist forces—the murderous Khmer Rouge—were small in 1970 and entirely dependent on Hanoi for supplies. The forces threatening the South Vietnamese and Americans from Cambodia were *all* North Vietnamese; the base areas were part of the war in Vietnam. North Vietnamese forces that were busy cutting communications had already seized a quarter of the country. The danger of being "bogged down in a new war in Cambodia" was a mirage; the enemy in Cambodia and Vietnam was the same one. Whatever forces we fought in Cambodia we would not have to fight in Vietnam and vice versa. The war by then was a single war, as Le Duc Tho had proclaimed; there was turmoil in Cambodia precisely because Hanoi was determined to use it as a base for its invasion of South Vietnam and to establish its hegemony over Indochina.

By April 21 we had a stark choice. We could permit North Vietnam to overrun the whole of Cambodia so that it was an indisputable part of the battlefield and then attack it by air and sea—even Rogers told me on April 21 that if the Communists took over Cambodia, he believed all bombing restrictions should be ended. Or we could resist Cambodia's absorption, supporting the independence of a government recognized by the United Nations and most other nations, including the Soviet Union.

Momentous decisions are rarely produced by profound discussions. By the time an issue reaches the NSC [National Security Council], it has been analyzed by so many lower-level committees that the Cabinet members perform like actors in a well-rehearsed play; they repeat essentially what their subordinates have already announced in other forums. In the Nixon NSC there was the additional factor that every participant suspected that there was almost certainly more going on than he knew. As usual, there was also an ambivalence between taking positions compatible with their complicated chief's designs and fear of the domestic consequences. There was a sinking feeling about anything that could be presented as escalation in Vietnam. No one around the table questioned the consequences of a Communist takeover of Cambodia. But we all knew that whatever the decision another round of domestic acrimony, protest, and perhaps even violence was probable. If Cambodia collapsed we would be even harder pressed to pull out unilaterally; if we accepted any of the other options we would be charged with "expanding the war." There was no middle ground.

The initial decision to attack the sanctuaries was thus taken at a subdued and rather random NSC meeting. Rogers opposed substantial cross-border operations even by South Vietnamese, but he took it for granted that unrestricted bombing of Cambodia would follow the overthrow of the government in Phnom Penh. Laird had been the strongest advocate of shallow cross-border operations, but he opposed General Abrams's recommendation of destroying the sanctuaries altogether. Helms was in favor of any action to neutralize the sanctuaries. Nixon normally announced his decisions after, not during, an NSC meeting; he would deliberate and then issue instructions in writing or through intermediaries. He did this to emphasize that the NSC was an advisory, not a decision-making, body and to avoid a challenge to his orders. On this occasion Nixon altered his usual procedure. He told his colleagues that he approved attacks on the base areas by South Vietnamese forces with US support. Since the South Vietnamese could handle only one offensive, Wheeler recommended that they go after Parrot's Beak. This led to a debate about American participation; Laird and Rogers sought to confine it to an absolute minimum, opposing even American advisers or tactical air support.

At this point Vice President Spiro Agnew spoke up. He thought the whole debate irrelevant. Either the sanctuaries were a danger or they were not. If it was worth cleaning them out, he did not understand all the pussyfooting about the American role or what we accomplished by attacking only one. Our task was to make Vietnamization succeed. He favored an attack on *both* Fishhook and Parrot's Beak, including American forces. Agnew was right. If Nixon hated anything more than being presented with a plan he had not considered, it was to be shown up in a group as being less tough than his advisers. Though chafing at the bit, he adroitly placed himself between the Vice President and the Cabinet. He authorized American air support for the Parrot's Beak operation but only "on the basis of demonstrated necessity." He avoided committing himself to Fishhook. These decisions were later sent out in writing. After the meeting, Nixon complained bitterly to me that I had not forewarned him of Agnew's views, of which I had in fact been unaware. I have no doubt that Agnew's intervention accelerated Nixon's ultimate decision to order an attack on all the sanctuaries and use American forces. . . .

I was becoming increasingly restless with the decision at the NSC meeting that was in effect my recommendation: to limit the attack on the sanctuaries to South Vietnamese forces. Agnew was right; we should either neutralize all of the sanctuaries or abandon the project. It was hard to imagine how a limited operation into just one sanctuary, in which South Vietnamese forces had at best strictly limited American air support, could make a decisive difference. We were in danger of combining the disadvantages of every course of action. We would be castigated for intervention in Cambodia without accomplishing any strategic purpose.

Before I could present these views to Nixon, there occurred another of those seemingly trivial events that accelerate the process of history. Journalist William Beecher in the *New York Times* reported the contents of a highly classified cable informing our chargé in Phnom Penh that we had decided to provide captured Communist rifles to the Cambodian government. Nixon exploded. Leaks infuriated him in the best of circumstances; this one seemed to him a clear attempt by the bureaucracy to generate Congressional and public pressures against any assistance to Cambodia. To make matters worse, at about the same moment Nixon found out that the signal equipment and CIA representative that he had ordered into Phnom Penh on April 1 and again on April 16 had still not been sent.

He flew into a monumental rage. On the night of April 23 he must have called me at least ten times—three times at the house of Senator Fulbright, where I was meeting informally with members of the Senate Foreign Relations Committee. As was his habit when extremely agitated he would bark an order and immediately hang up the phone. He wanted our chargé, Rives, relieved immediately; he ordered Marshall Green fired; on second thought his deputy Bill Sullivan was to be transferred as well; an Air Force plane with CIA personnel aboard should be dispatched to Phnom Penh immediately; everybody with access to the cable should be given a lie-detector test; a general was to be appointed immediately to take charge of Cambodia.

In these circumstances it was usually prudent not to argue and to wait twenty-four hours to see on which of these orders Nixon would insist after he calmed down. As it turned out, he came back to none of them. (I did get the CIA communications sent into Phnom Penh by military plane.) But his April 23 outburst did finally propel him to accept Agnew's advice: to proceed against Fishhook and Parrot's Beak simultaneously, using American forces against Fishhook. He called a meeting on the morning of April 24 with Admiral Moorer, Acting Chairman of the Joint Chiefs, and Helms and Cushman of the CIA. Nixon wanted to discuss the feasibility of a combined US–South Vietnamese operation against Fishhook, in parallel with the Parrot's Beak operation. It was a reflection of his extreme irritation at bureaucratic foot-dragging that he excluded both Rogers and Laird, on the pretext that he merely wanted a military and intelligence briefing. Helms and Moorer were both strongly in favor of an attack on the Fishhook sanctuary. They felt it would force the North Vietnamese to abandon their effort to encircle and terrorize Phnom Penh. The destruction of supplies would gain valuable time for Vietnamization. But Nixon was not prepared to announce a decision yet. Instead, he helicoptered to Camp David to reflect further and to figure out a way to bring along his Cabinet on a course toward which he was increasingly tending. In the meantime he left me to manage the bureaucracy.

The situation had its bizarre aspects. The departments were still dragging their feet on American air support of a South Vietnamese operation against *one* sanctuary when the President was beginning to lean more and more toward *combined* South Vietnamese–American operations against *all* sanctuaries. I did not think it right to keep the Secretary of Defense ignorant of a meeting between the Acting Chairman of the Joint Chiefs and the President; I therefore called Laird, describing it as a military briefing of options. including an American attack on Fishhook. Laird stressed that it would be highly desirable to avoid authorizing any American operation before Rogers's testimony to the Senate Foreign Relations Committee on April 27; this would enable Rogers to state truthfully that no Americans were involved in Cambodia. Laird reported that even the usually hawkish Armed Services Committees were restive about American involvement in Cambodia. Laird also argued—as he was to do on several occasions over the next few days—that Abrams and Wheeler were really opposed to the Fishhook operation. I checked with Admiral Moorer, who claimed (in a rough translation from his more colorful naval jargon) that his Secretary was under a misapprehension.

Once he was launched on a course, Nixon's determination was equal to his tactical resourcefulness. He decided to adopt Rogers's suggestion of scaring the Congress with the prospect of monumental aid requests from Cambodia but to use it to justify *American* operations in the sanctuaries, which Rogers never intended. . . .

The final decision to proceed was thus not a maniacal eruption of irrationality as the uproar afterward sought to imply. It was taken carefully, with much hesitation, by a man who had to discipline his nerves almost daily to face his associates and to overcome the partially subconscious, partially deliberate procrastination of his executive departments. It was a demonstration of a certain nobility when he assumed full responsibility. The decision was not made behind the backs of his senior advisers, as has been alleged—though later on others were. Nixon overruled his Cabinet members; he did not keep them in the dark. This is the essence of the Presidency, the inescapable loneliness of the office, compounded in Nixon's case by the tendency of his senior Cabinet colleagues to leave him with the burden and to distance themselves publicly from him. His secretive and devious methods of decision-making undoubtedly reinforced their proclivity toward selfwill. But his views were well known; the agencies had had many opportunities to argue their case. The fact remains that on the substance of Cambodia, Nixon was right. And he was President. There is no doubt that the procrastination in carrying out direct Presidential directives, the exegesis of clear Presidential wishes in order to thwart them, helped confirm Nixon's already strong predilection for secretive and isolated decision-making from then on.

A confrontation with people who disagreed with him took a lot out of Nixon. After the meeting in the Oval Office he withdrew to his hide-away in the Executive Office Building, not to emerge until he delivered his speech of April 30 announcing the Cambodian incursion. I spent hours with him every day, bringing him up to date on the planning. Pat Buchanan drafted the basic speech from a rough outline supplied by my staff. But its major thrust was Nixon's. He supplied the rhetoric and the tone; he worked for hours each day on successive drafts. . . .

On the fateful day of April 30 the President delivered his speech at 9:00 P.M., explaining to an anxious public that "the actions of the enemy in the last ten days clearly endanger the lives of Americans who are in Vietnam now and would constitute an unacceptable risk to those who will be there after withdrawal of another 150,000." He opened by explaining, with a map, that the North Vietnamese had begun to threaten Phnom Penh and expand their previously separated base areas into "a vast enemy staging area and a springboard for attacks on South Vietnam along 600 miles of frontier." We had three options: to do nothing; to "provide massive military assistance to Cambodia itself"; to clean out the sanctuaries. The decision he now announced was a combined US–South Vietnamese assault on "the headquarters for the entire Communist military operation in South Vietnam." The action was limited, temporary, not directed against any outside country, indispensable for Vietnamization and for keeping casualties to a minimum.

Adding rhetoric out of proportion to the subject though not to the stresses of the weeks preceding it, the President emphasized that America would not be "humiliated"; we would not succumb to "anarchy"; we would not act like a "pitiful, helpless giant." Nor would he take "the easy political path" of blaming it all on the previous administrations. It was vintage Nixon. He had "rejected all political considerations":

Whether my party gains in November is nothing compared to the lives of 400,000 brave Americans fighting for our country and for the cause of peace and freedom in Vietnam. Whether I may be a one-term President is insignificant compared to whether by our failure to act in this crisis the United States proves itself to be unworthy to lead the forces of freedom in this critical period in world history. I would rather be a one-term President and do what I believe is right than to be a two-term President at the cost of seeing America become a second-rate power and to see this Nation accept the first defeat in its proud 190-year history. . . .

None of these successes had any effect on the eruptions of the spring of 1970, thereby turning the period of the Cambodian incursion into a time of extraordinary stress. I had entered government with the hope that I could help heal the schisms in my adopted country by working to end the war. I sympathized with the anguish of the students eager to live the American dream of a world where ideas prevailed by their purity without the ambiguities of recourse to power. The war in Vietnam was the first conflict shown on television and reported by a largely hostile press. The squalor and suffering and confusion inseparable from any war became part of the living experience of Americans; too many ascribed its agony to the defects of their own leaders.

Repellent as I found the self-righteousness and brutality of some protesters, I had a special feeling for the students. They had been brought up by skeptics, relativists, and psychiatrists; now they were rudderless in a world from which they demanded certainty without sacrifice. My generation had failed them by encouraging self-indulgence and neglecting to provide roots. I spent a disproportionate amount of time in the next months with student groups—ten in May alone. I met with protesters at private homes. I listened, explained, argued. But my sympathy for their anguish could not obscure my obligation to my country as I saw it. They were, in my view, as wrong as they were passionate. Their pressures delayed the end of the war, not accelerated it; their simplifications did not bring closer the peace, of the yearning for which they had no monopoly. Emotion was not a policy. We had to end the war, but in conditions that did not undermine America's power to help build the new international order upon which the future of even the most enraged depended.

Nor is it fair to blame the upheaval primarily on Nixon's inflated rhetoric or even on the events at Kent State. The dialogue in our democracy had broken down previously. The antiwar movement had been dormant since November, awaiting a new opportunity. In mid-April there were protests in some two hundred cities and towns, and the temper was such that the April 28 news of the purely South Vietnamese operation in the Parrot's Beak evoked condemnation as a major escalation of the war. This was two days before the involvement of American soldiers or Nixon's speech. North Vietnamese forces had been romping through Cambodia for well over a month, without a word of criticism of Hanoi. Yet the South Vietnamese response was denounced in the *New York Times* ("a virtual renunciation of the President's promise of disengagement from South East Asia"), the *Wall Street Journal* ("Americans want an acceptable exit from Indochina, not a deeper entrapment") and the *St. Louis Post-Dispatch* ("a shocking escalation"). The South Vietnamese thrust was intended to assist our orderly retreat. But in Congress barriers were being erected almost immediately against helping Cambodia, itself suffering a savage invasion by the same enemies and indeed the identical units that were fighting us in Vietnam. Senator J. William Fulbright, Chairman of the Senate Foreign Relations Committee, told NBC news on April 27 after the briefing that had given Rogers so much anticipatory anguish that the Committee was virtually unanimous in the view that assisting Cambodia in its resistance to North Vietnamese conquest "would be an additional extension of the war."

All the critical themes of the later explosion were present before the President's speech: We were escalating the war. No military action could possibly succeed; hence, claims to the contrary by the government were false. We were alleged to be so little in control of our decisions that the smallest step was seen as leading to an open-ended commitment of hundreds of thousands of American troops. A credibility gap had been created over any effort to achieve an honorable exit from the war. Thus, the press greeted the arguments in Nixon's speech on April 30 with a simple counterassertion: They did not believe him. It was "Military Hallucination—Again" according to the *New York Times:* "Time and bitter experience have exhausted the credulity of the American people and Congress." To the *Washington Post* it was a "self-renewing war" supported by "suspect evidence, specious argument and excessive rhetoric." To the *Miami Herald* "the script in Cambodia shockingly is the same as the story in Vietnam in the days of Kennedy and Johnson. We have heard it all before—endless times." Debate was engulfed in mass passion.

Just as it was burgeoning before April 30, the new increase in tempo had begun with calls for strikes and marches by the student leaders, who had proved their skill in producing confrontation in previous seasons of protest. The President's statements, oscillating between the maudlin and the strident, did not help in a volatile situation where everything was capable of misinterpretation. His May 1 off-the-cuff reference to "bums . . . blowing up campuses," a gibe overheard by reporters during a visit to the Pentagon, was a needless challenge, although it was intended to refer only to a tiny group of students who had firebombed a building and burned the life's research of a Stanford professor. When on May 4, four students at Kent State University were killed by rifle fire from National Guardsmen dispatched by Ohio Governor James Rhodes to keep order during several days of violence, there was a shock wave that brought the nation and its leadership close to psychological exhaustion.

The Administration responded with a statement of extraordinary insensitivity. Ron Ziegler was told to say that the killings "should remind us all once again that when dissent turns to violence it invites tragedy."

The momentum of student strikes and protests accelerated immediately. Campus unrest and violence overtook the Cambodian operation itself as the major issue before the public. Washington took on the character of a besieged city. A pinnacle of mass public protest was reached by May 9 when a crowd estimated at between 75,000 and 100,000 demonstrated on a hot Saturday afternoon on the Ellipse, the park to the south of the White House. Police surrounded the White House; a ring of sixty buses was used to shield the grounds of the President's home.

After May 9 thousands more students, often led by their faculty, descended on the capital to denounce "escalation" and the "folly" of their government. A thousand lawyers lobbied Congress to end the war, followed by thirty-three heads of universities, architects, doctors, health officers, nurses, and one hundred corporate executives from New York. The press fed the mood. Editorials expressed doubts about the claims of success in Cambodia emanating from the Pentagon. Beyond these peaceful demonstrations antiwar students proved adept at imaginative tactics of disruption merging with outright violence. Some two thousand Columbia University students sat down in the road in the rush hour. Fires were set on several college campuses as bonfires for peace. At Syracuse University fire destroyed a new building as twenty-five hundred students demonstrated nearby. Students demonstrated in the financial district of New York City on May 7 and 8. In retaliation, construction workers building the World Trade Center descended on Wall Street and beat the protesters with clubs and other makeshift weapons. The incident shocked some into the realization that a breakdown of civil order could backfire dangerously against the demonstrators. But it did not slow down the pace of protest; it only encouraged Nixon in the belief that the masses of the American public were on his side.

Indeed, the Gallup Poll showed considerable support for the President's action. When people were asked, "Do you think the US should send arms and material to help Cambodia or not?" 48 percent of those questioned responded yes, 35 percent no, 11 percent expressed no opinion, while 6 percent gave a qualified answer. When they were asked, "Do you approve or disapprove of the way President Nixon is handling the Cambodian situation?" 50 percent expressed approval; 35 percent expressed disapproval; 15 percent expressed no opinion. And 53 percent of those questioned expressed approval of the way President Nixon was handling the situation in Vietnam; 37 percent expressed disapproval; 10 percent had no opinion.

The tidal wave of media and student criticism powerfully affected the Congress. From not unreasonable criticism of the President's inadequate consultation it escalated to attempts to legislate a withdrawal from Cambodia and to prohibit the reentry of American troops. On May 13 debate began in the Senate on the Foreign Military Sales Bill, to which Senators Frank Church and John Sherman Cooper proposed an amendment prohibiting the extension of US military aid to, and US military activities in, Cambodia after June 30. On the other hand, an amendment offered by Senator Robert Byrd would have granted the President authority to take whatever action he deemed necessary to protect US troops in South Vietnam. This amendment was narrowly defeated, 52–47, on June 11, in what was seen as a trial heat. Senate debate and parliamentary skirmishing lasted seven weeks, until on June 30 the Senate approved the Cooper-Church amendment in a 58–37 roll-call vote. The Senate had voted to give the Communists a free hand in Cambodia even though in the judgment of the Executive Branch this doomed South Vietnam. The bill then went to a House-Senate Conference. The entire Foreign Military Sales Bill remained in conference for the remainder of 1970, deadlocked over the House's refusal to agree to the Senate-passed amendment. By then the damage was substantially done; in the middle of a blatant North Vietnamese invasion, the enemy was being told by the Senate that Cambodia was on its own.

Whereas the Cooper-Church amendment focused on Cambodia, the McGovern-Hatfield amendment to the Defense Procurement Bill aimed at ending the Indochina war by the simple expedient of cutting off all funds by the end of 1970, later extended to December 31, 1971. The move was finally defeated by the Senate on September 1 by a 55–39 margin. But the pattern was clear. Senate opponents of the war would introduce one amendment after another, forcing the Administration into unending rearguard actions to preserve a minimum of flexibility for negotiations. Hanoi could only be encouraged to stall, waiting to harvest the results of our domestic dissent.

All this accelerated the processes of disenchantment. Conservatives were demoralized by a war that had turned into a retreat and liberals were paralyzed by what they themselves had wrought—for they could not completely repress the knowledge that it was a liberal Administration that had sent half a million Americans to Indochina. They were equally reluctant to face the implications of their past actions or to exert any serious effort to maintain calm. There was a headlong retreat from responsibility. Extraordinarily enough, all groups, dissenters and others, passed the buck to the Presidency. It was a great joke for undergraduates when one senior professor proclaimed "the way to get out of Vietnam is by ship." The practical consequence was that in the absence of any serious alternative the government was left with only its own policy or capitulation.

The Carter Presidency

BETTY GLAD

*In the waning days of Jimmy Carter's administration, a noted columnist
forecast that the soon-to-be ex-President would likely wake in the middle
of the night for the rest of his days wondering what went wrong with
his administration.*

*Since Eisenhower's two terms ended in 1961, the White House has
seen five one-term presidents come and go, although only two of the
five, Ford and Carter, were rejected by the electorate. The credit for
Carter's victory over Ford in 1976 is generally given to Carter's chief
political adviser, Hamilton Jordon, and others in the "Georgia Mafia,"
who skillfully and successfully manipulated the campaign issues. As
President, though, Carter could no longer rail against the system, the
Congress, Washington power brokers, and the Republican record.*

*Analysts generally agree that it was Carter's poor record that led
to his defeat. On the plus side in foreign affairs, however, were his
successes in arranging the Camp David accords and the Salt II agreement, although the Russian invasion of Afghanistan and the Iranian
seizure of the American embassy in Teheran killed the chances for Senate approval of the arms agreement.*

*Carter's successes at home were few and far between. By his last
year in office double-digit inflation and record-high interest rates had
stalled economic growth. The passage of the Alaskan Lands Bill represented a real achievement—but one that appealed to a small constituency. It was Carter's vacillation and failure in the economic sphere
that touched the lives of all Americans. At midterm Carter, frustrated
in his efforts to gain Congress's cooperation, and seeking a means to
jolt the nation to attention, delivered a television address in which he
diagnosed the country as suffering a national "malaise." The result was
less a jolt to the country than a call to political commentators to analyze
Carter's leadership. In the selection that follows, Betty Glad discusses
some of the psychological and political traits that underlay Carter's
performance in office.*

STYLISTIC POPULISM

Carter's populism is unique in American politics. In the 1976 campaign he offered what one observer called an insurgency of the middle.
Or as James W. Caesar noted, Carter managed to "pit virtually the entire
population against no one." Rhetorically, he tapped resentments against
the "big shots," a privileged few whom he portrayed as wheeling and
dealing with each other; yet the specific reforms he backed reflected
mostly the good government values associated with middle-class reform
movements. Public business should be conducted in the open and leaders should be available to the people. Policies should be based on

reason and offices awarded on the basis of excellence, not political contributions. The bureaucracies should be organized in accord with the
businesslike principles of efficiency that govern private enterprise. These
changes would be accomplished simply by selecting an outsider like
himself, a man who was from the people, who could represent them
because he was more in tune with their needs and wishes than those he
would bust. Unlike the populists of the 1890s, he called for no trust
busting, no major policy shifts, no developments of countervailing
political groups to oppose the politically or economically entrenched.

In power, Carter was neither as "populistic" nor as naïve as his
campaign rhetoric suggested. As governor, he had worked comfortably
with big business, and as a presidential candidate in 1976, he had indicated that a similar arrangement would exist during his presidency.
In the governorship and the presidency he would function politically as
an "insider" once he had obtained the office he sought. In his various
"people-to-people" techniques he showed a keen sensitivity to the magnetic pull that association with power has for all kinds of people. And
for all his talk of the merit system in choosing officeholders, in practice
Carter has had the traditional politician's bent for putting his own
people in key governmental positions and channeling discretionary resources at his command to build his own political base.

Given his centrist views and his practical knowledge of how to win
and exercise power, as President, Carter might have turned out to be
an effective consolidator, a middle-of-the-road leader who could restore
faith in government by his manifest personal honesty and make government more efficient through his management skills.

He has his failings, however, even as a mainstream politician. He
lacks, it seems, a well-thought-out conceptual framework to guide his
concrete political choices. He immerses himself in the technical details
of programs that interest him, testing various strategies and rhetorical
appeals. Yet he fails to bring the components together in an integrated
approach that would give him a sense of direction and set up priorities
for his various program.

POWER

At the most basic level, Carter fails to address directly the relevance
of power to the political process. Although his "populism" is based on
the premise that the people should have a larger voice in government,
it projects no clear vision of the institutional mechanisms for guaranteeing wider participation; nor does Carter seem to be aware of the
possibility that even leaders brought into office through popular ac-
claim may misuse their power or use it to reinforce the status quo.

Rather, Carter's whole approach is based on the assumptions that
good will and connection with the people are sufficient guarantees that
political power will be used for the good. A good person need not have
any institutional checks on his behavior. To deal with the misdeeds of
the CIA, Carter promised during the 1976 campaign to tell the people
if the CIA did something wrong and punish those responsible. As Presi-

dent, he told the country the United States could safely develop the neutron bomb because he would never use it for a first strike. The magical quality of this transformation he seeks was portrayed in a commercial used in the 1976 campaign (rather appropriately called "Dreams"). The camera showed vignettes of typically American people and places, then a shot of the presidential greats chiseled in the stone at Mount Rushmore, then a panoramic view of the White House. As the announcer asked if the people have felt shut off from government, the camera panned to a close-up of the White House, which dissolved into a portrait of Jimmy Carter, earlier identified with a collage of faces representing the melting pot of America.

Nor does Carter appear to have a clear view of the historical process by which the people are to assume power. Mainly he seems to embrace the old American notion that progress is inevitable. In his earlier career as a businessman and farmer, and in his reorganization efforts as governor, he had embraced the concept of planning as the primary tool for improvement, a manifestation of an increasing rationality that is central to the historical progress. As governor, he added to that notion: the people are demanding and will inevitably receive a greater voice in their government. In *Why Not the Best?* Carter interprets Tolstoy's *War and Peace* as a populistic saga. Ignoring the table of contents (which lists princes, princesses, counts, and generals as the main characters), he interprets the book, not as being about the Emperor or the Czar, "but mostly about the students, farmers, barbers, housewives, and common soldiers." The purpose of the book is "to show that the course of human events—even the greatest historical events—is determined ultimately not by the leaders, but by the common, ordinary people."

VIRTUE

Carter's political views rest on a simplistic moralism. We should honor the same high moral standards "in our home, our office or our government," he told a group of Southern Baptists in 1974.

In *Why Not the Best?* he made a similar point:

Our personal problems are magnified when we assume different standards of morality and ethics in our own lives as we shift from one responsibility or milieu to another. Should elected officials assume different levels of concern, compassion, or love toward their own family or loved ones? Should a businessman like me have a lower standard of honesty and integrity in dealing with my customers than I assume as a Sunday School teacher or a church deacon? Of course not. But we do.

He advocated purity for all government officials, even for those who must engage in covert operations.

Public officials, the President, the Vice-President, Members of Congress, Attorneys General, federal judges, the head of the CIA, the head of the FBI and otherwise, ought to set a standard that is absolutely exemplary. We ought to be like Caesar's wife. We ought to be free of any criticism or allegation. We ought to be open about mistakes that we make, not try to hide from the public what is done. It's erroneous. In that way, mistakes can be more quickly corrected.

His international human rights campaign is based on a missionary assumption that we must not permit violations of the American Bill of Rights in the world at large and that it is our duty to take the lead.

Private virtues, then, become civic virtues. Self-sacrifice and abnegation, which Carter views as the highest goal for an individual (one should love God and his neighbor before himself), is also a value for the citizen in his relations with the government. He told one group during the 1976 campaign: "If you think I'd be the best President, support me in a sacrificial way." Conversely, placing one's interests first is a vice. Both as governor and President, Carter has inveighed against the "special interests"—i.e., those who put their own goals above the public good. Moreover, intimacy and love—values in small and permanent groups—may connect a political leader to the people. (As Carter told Bill Moyers in 1976, he can relate, on a personal level, to people he meets on the campaign trail.) Helping and caring for others—an important and healing virtue in small hometowns like Plains—can be applied directly to the country's relations with other nations. As governor, Carter had embraced the "people-to-people" exchange as a way of building international good will. As candidate, he argued that such volunteer efforts could have a positive effect on international relations. So, too, frugality and hard work, virtues in managing a household or small business, are virtues in the management of the affairs of larger, more complex political enterprises. Indeed, political leadership should provide the same kind of moral stewardship that is relevant in the church. And virtue and adherence to duty will be rewarded by responsibility: political office is a kind of prize to be awarded to the one who works hardest and is "the best"—even the presidency of the United States.

True, he recognizes that both nations and individuals fall short of the perfectionist standard. Reform—salvation—is apt to flow out of a renewed commitment to the higher standard, and in public life reform will often take the form of wider popular participation in government. This is what he means in his frequent quote from Reinhold Niebuhr, "The sad duty of politics is to establish justice in a sinful world."

But the seamlessness of this morality covers potential conflicts between religious and political values. Carter could not foresee a situation in which he would have to choose between his religion and political necessity. He didn't see any conflict between religion and politics, he told a black audience early in 1976. "The purposes are the same—to establish justice in a sinful world." As President, Carter told the Southern Baptist Brotherhood Commission that he has "never detected nor experienced any conflict between God's will and my political duty. It's obvious that when I violate one, I . . . violate the other."

To the contrary, Carter has suggested that religious faith is the source of political virtue. His own faith allows him to be more serene and confident in facing problems. "I know the reassurance I get from my own religion, and it helps me to take a more objective viewpoint and a calmer approach to crisis. I have a great deal of peace with my-self and with other people because of my religious convictions. I think that sort of personal attitude—environment—within which I live helps me to do a better job in dealing with the transient and quite often controversial decisions that have to be made in political life, or in business life, or in a family life."

Most important, his religion provides moral vision. In his speech before the African Methodist Episcopal conference in Atlanta in 1976, Carter said, "I believe there's an eagerness among our people to search for a higher standard of ethics, morality, excellence, greatness that can be derived from those who have a knowledge of that higher standard. We Christians have that knowledge, we have a perfect example [Jesus] of what a person ought to be. We can't meet that example, measure up to those standards, but we know what it is." Indeed, political leadership is a special form of moral stewardship. In an interview with religious broadcasters Carter said, "I cling to the principles of the Judeo-Christian ethic. Honesty, integrity, compassion, love, hope, charity, humility are integral parts of any person's life, no matter what his position in life may be. But when someone is elected and trusted by others to help determine one's own life quality, it puts an additional responsibility on the pastor or the schoolteacher or someone who has a public life. So, the Christian or the religious commitment is one that's especially use-ful to me."

Beyond this, Carter overlooks the possibility that religion might be diluted by making it so public. In 1976, for example, Carter watchers discussed the following: Did the candidate believe in a literal hell or not? What are his views on the literal interpretation of the Bible? Did he and Rosalyn kneel down to pray when they had conflicts? (She said she first heard about that in the newspapers.) His answers to such ques-tions could lose him votes from fundamentalists if he gave one answer, and from liberals if he gave another.

But by submitting his religious life to such public scrutiny in an election campaign, a candidate subjects it to the same pressures for hedging and bland stances that influence his specifically political com-mitments. Thus, Carter did not say whether he believes in a literal heaven and hell. (Even one former minister did not know Carter's stance on this for sure.) The statement in the *Playboy* interview that he was guilty of lust in his heart was in response to a question about his views about the legal rights of homosexuals, which question he never did answer. When pushed on his notion of women's roles, in view of Bibli-cal accounts of creation, he said that he believed in the literal interpre-tation of Genesis but did not say what he understood that to mean. And after the election, when the Plains Baptist Church split in two and Carter's neighbors and friends had to choose one group or another, Carter backed off again. He avoided Plains on Sundays for a while. (His mother went to a third church in Americus.) When he finally did return to Plains on a Sunday, he compromised by attending the services at both the old and the new church.

These beliefs—that the same values are relevant to private and public life and that moral rejuvenation in one area automatically spills over into the other—are deeply ingrained in the American political tradition. Indeed, the melding of the private and public virtues, of the sacred with the secular, has been the source of what sociologist Robert Bellah has called the American civic religion—a "set of religious beliefs, symbols, and rituals growing out of the historical American experience interpreted in the dimension of transcendence." It assumes that the American people, because of their piety, are special people with a special moral mission.*

This particular "gestalt," however, does not provide a very good map of the political world and it suggests, at its base, a superficial understanding of the human situation. Certainly it is antithetical to the tragic perceptions of the existential theologians Carter has so often quoted. It tends to obscure the fact that different virtues are applicable to different realms. Killing a neighbor is generally forbidden—yet men are expected to kill enemies in times of war. An individual may sacrifice his own virtues for a higher good—but it is not considered legitimate for a statesman to sacrifice the national security for some higher goal. One may depend on individual compassion for the care of the weak and sick in the family, but organized supports (jobs, health insurance, retirement programs) are necessary to give substance to compassion in the public realm.

Aside from obscuring such moral dilemmas, the tendency to equate private and public virtues may also mask aspects of power relationships. As Niebuhr has pointed out, love is not the relevant virtue in the political realm. Indeed, to speak of love at the political level is to mask power relationships central to the political process. Justice, Niebuhr argues, is the relevant virtue for the political order, and justice requires that power be confronted and somehow constrained. Further, in international affairs moral reductionism can provide a rationalization of attempts by one nation to extend its influence abroad in the guise of moral salvation. Indeed, the introduction of religious symbols into the public sector, Niebuhr argues, tends to provide support for power. In giving power a dimension of the sacred, one limits the searching inquiry into what government does. To question may become sacrilegious and unpatriotic.

HUMILITY AND PRIDE

Such a perspective on the world is apt to be accompanied by a sanguine personal philosophy, a tendency to gloss over personal vulnerabilities as well as any ultimate ironies or tragedies.

---

* Carter's recent predecessors in the presidency were in this tradition. Lyndon Johnson, as Doris Kearns pointed out, embraced a faith in the relevance of American values to the world as a whole as he tried to bring war on poverty to Southeast Asia. Richard Nixon, as Reinhold Niebuhr pointed out, used religious services in the White House for his own political power and made claims for American moral leadership in the world based, in part, on our spiritual and technological superiority.

Take, for example, Carter's handling of the problem of Christian humility. Pride had been his chief failing before his born again experiences. But during the 1976 campaign he suggested he had mostly overcome these tendencies. He often said he thought himself no better than others. Like all persons, he is subject to the temptations of the flesh. As President, he vowed, he would do his best to remain humble. Thus, in an interview with religious broadcasters in October, 1976, he said: "I would always remember the admonitions of Christ on humility and absence of pride, a prohibition against judging other people. I would try not to consider myself better than others." In another setting he said: "Christ in many ways admonishes us against self-pride, against the condemnation of others, when we have within ourselves sinfulness as well. This is the kind of attitude that I would try to adopt as President."

Yet, Carter does not admit to many politically relevant failings. His confidence in his capacity to resist the temptations of power is manifest in his *Playboy* interview. His religion and his character, he suggested, would keep him from "lying, cheating and distorting the truth," the way Johnson or Nixon did. Earlier he had assured Bill Moyers that he had no unhealthy power drives, no "unpleasant sense of being driven." And when Moyers asked, "Do you need power?" Carter responded, "Well, I think so," in what may have been a slip of the tongue. Then he went on to say that he had no "all-obsessive hunger" for power, that he only wanted to correct social inequities and protect those who are not strong. At another point in the interview he indicated he would not be too upset should he lose the race. "I don't feel that I've got to win, or that I, you know, that I'll be terribly disappointed if I don't win. I feel a sense of equanimity about it." The presidency, he said, would only give him "a chance to serve."

Not only did Carter gloss over the possibility that, like others, he might be motivated by self-regarding as well as altruistic concerns in the pursuit of position and power, he found it difficult to admit that he had personal failings which could obtrude on his performance in office. His tendency to lash out at his critics, he explained while he was still governor, is simply a legitimate use of his office to defend the programs he considers important. His stubbornness is a political asset, an aid in bargaining and a sign he will be tenacious in pursuit of the good.

Moreover, the failings he admits to stop short of full admissions. In the *Playboy* interview, he agreed that he could have spoken out earlier on the Vietnam war and the issues of racial integration. But there were good reasons for his reticence. He did not deal with the Vietnam issue until March, 1971, because "it was the first time anybody had asked me about it. I was a farmer before then and wasn't asked about the war until I took office as governor of Georgia." (His recollections are wrong, here. See above.) "It is easy to say in hindsight what you would have done if you had had the information you now have." Finally: "If there are issues I'm avoiding because of a lack of courage, either I don't recognize them or I can't make myself recognize them." Even Carter's admission, in the last campaign debate in 1976, that he made a "mistake" by being interviewed by *Playboy* has the appearance of a strategic retreat. He had only been unwise in his choice of a format. About the same time he pointed out to a religious group that in his *Playboy* interview he had been engaged in Christian witnessing.

His admissions, as President, that he lacked some expertise when he first came to Washington can also be viewed as strategic retreats. He clearly had drastic losses in his public and congressional support in his first eighteen months in office. It was clearly more preferable to credit that to inexperience rather than more deeply ingrained faults. One confession of error is particularly puzzling. A few days after the Russian invasion of Afghanistan, Carter told Frank Reynolds on ABC that "the action of the Soviets had made a more dramatic change in my opinion of what the Soviets' ultimate goals are than anything they've done in the previous time that I've been in office." Yet from the earliest draft of his speech announcing his candidacy for the presidency, through campaign commercials in 1976, to his Wake Forest University and Annapolis speeches in 1978, Carter had never talked as if he thought the Soviet Union was a peace-loving, moderate state. Perhaps he was trying to dramatize, in the Reynolds interview, the uniqueness of this particular Soviet challenge and justify an increase in defense spending, contrary to his earlier commitments.

Most of Carter's confessions to faults, then, are to private or minor ones (or hidden virtues) or they are face-saving explanations of why he has been doing poorly. His prevailing motif, as Robert Scheer wrote in *Playboy*, is that he has always been virtuous. "Despite Carter's acts of courage [during the earlier civil rights struggle in the South], he didn't always act courageously. He was caught in a terrible time and he was only human—which means often he didn't do the right thing. *But Jimmy Carter won't admit it!* The real heroes of the era were less than ten miles up the road in either direction from his home all his life, taking the most terrible punishment, and he won't admit that he shunned them like everyone else. Like all of us."

Pride can also be manifested in claims to emotional invulnerability—and Carter has shown these tendencies. During the 1976 campaign he indicated, as we have seen, that he had no social insecurity, no ultimate doubts about God or life or his faith. The idea of being President scared him not at all. Indeed he has never been afraid—not even of death.

This kind of self-assurance, on the face of it, is apt to be based on a repression of complex feelings. It certainly reflects a perspective on life that radically differentiates Carter from the existentialist philosopher, Sören Kierkegaard, whom he often quotes. As Ernest Becker has pointed out, Kierkegaard's most basic insight was that peace can only come once one has confronted the ultimate anxiety. "This is the terror: to have emerged from nothing, to have a name, consciousness of self, deep inner feeling, an excruciating inner yearning for life and self-expression and with all this yet to die." It is only by the confronting of this truth that human beings can find self-transcendence and a deeper contact with reality. That is the ultimate education.

CREATIVITY

A person who lives on the surface of things is not likely to have high creative ability, i.e., "the capacity to find new and unexpected connections . . . to find new relationships in time and space, and thus new meanings." Lawrence Kubie, who has given this definition, notes that creativity flows from the preconscious processes, as evident in free association, and that it is impeded when a person insists on complete rationality and control. As he says:

. . . free associations are the most natural and spontaneously creative process of which the mind is capable. . . . There are individuals for whom the process is impossible, except where they are entirely off guard. . . . These are individuals for whom this mental leap-in-the-dark is so fraught with guilt or terror that they can no more allow their thoughts to roam freely than they could run down a flight of stairs with closed eyes. Such individuals have to stretch out their mental toes to feel carefully for each next step before they can trust themselves to express a next word. Logical and chronological sequences are the hand-rail to which they always cling.

Jimmy Carter seems like a man who insists on such control. According to his sister Ruth, he is "a very logical, methodical, punctual, well-programmed man with a mind like a steel trap. I would not say that he's particularly creative or innovative." There is other evidence that Carter has a mechanical approach to problem solving. He makes lists. On one occasion (the *Playboy* interview) he explained how he had derived his program as governor of Georgia: "I remember keeping a check list and every time I made a promise during the campaign I wrote it down in a notebook. I believe I carried out every promise I made." The same procedure was used during the 1976 presidential campaign. Working with Stu Eizenstat on his issues stances, Carter moved through the alphabet from Abortion to Zero-based budgeting, discussing the issues, not on the basis of their importance, but in their alphabetical order. As President, he had a list of his campaign promises made up to provide guidance to his policymaking team. He uses a similar method for composing speeches. He says: "I list the points that I want to make, just like an engineer. In a non-sequential way. I just turn 30 or 35 different items in my mind and then try to drive them into four or five themes. I go down the list and put A, B, C, D, and E by each one of those 35 or so points. I rearrange those and then write individual paragraphs in the structure." (His Annapolis speech, according to James Fallows, was written this way. Carter just spliced together the often contradictory viewpoints of his advisers Cyrus Vance and Zbigniew Brzezinski.)

To understand poetry he works in a similar fashion. When *New York Times Book Review* writer Harvey Shapiro asked how he came to understand Dylan Thomas's "A Refusal to Mourn the Death, by Fire, of a Child in London," Carter replied, "I didn't understand the poem when I read it, but the last line said, 'After the first death there is no other.' And I thought about it for a while and I went back and read the poem again. I couldn't understand it still, so then I went back up to my little desk in the front [of the warehouse in Plains] and I diagrammed all the sentences and I finally understood what Dylan Thomas was saying." A Carter friend, Anne Robbins of Rockville, Maryland, observes how Carter explained the poem to her: "I kept questioning him about it. So he would recite it again and again."

There are other cues that Carter does not deeply understand many of the philosophers and poets he quotes. When asked about their views, he usually elaborates on certain external facts of their lives or how he came to know their work, but does not engage in reflection on the meaning of what they say. When Norman Mailer offered a passionate soliloquy on Kierkegaard during his interview with Carter in August, 1976, he drew only a smile, and Mailer realized that "Carter was not necessarily one of America's authorities on Kierkegaard. How foolish of Mailer to expect it of him—as if Norman in his turn had never quoted an author he had not lived with thoroughly." When asked in May, 1977, whether the quotations from Niebuhr, Bob Dylan, and Dylan Thomas used as epigraphs in *Why Not the Best?* "describe a mental landscape for you?" Carter responded: "I don't know. I think in some ways you can tell the interrelationship between Dylan Thomas' poems that I cherish and the Reinhold Niebuhr quote." What the connection might be he did not specify, but went on to say that he had always wanted to meet Niebuhr.

But if Carter lacks high creativity, how does one then explain the rhetorical genius of his 1976 presidential campaign? Carter seems to have used a kind of trial-and-error approach—he tested a wide variety of themes, and when they worked, he incorporated them into his repertoire. Richard Reeves, in August, 1979, noted this:

Carter did not know what he was doing and did not understand the emotions he had tapped. He had just taken advantage of the unique opportunity of trying out a presidential campaign on the road. No one covered him in the beginning and he had memorized and tested a script that he had figured out worked with crowds—the words weren't the product of inspiration, but of trial and error. Still, it was a pretty good show and some of us bought it: a government as good and decent . . . I'll never lie . . . cut the bureaucracy . . . put the big shots in jail . . .

These themes were already in the air prior to his election. The love-and-intimacy theme had been tried, tested, and found useful by Joseph Biden in his winning campaign for the Senate from Delaware in 1972. And Biden, who was cochairman of the Carter National Steering Committee in 1974, had discussed the potency of this approach with Carter at the governor's mansion in Georgia. Fletcher Knebel's 1972 novel *Dark Horse* has an interesting parallel to Carter's own campaign. The protagonist of the novel is an unknown New Jersey highway commissioner who nearly wins the presidency with an anti-Washington, anti–big shot campaign in which he promises, "I'll never tell a lie." And Carter's "roots" theme was anticipated by Robert Altman's 1975 film

Nashville. The presidential candidate in that film (Hal Phillip Walker) and his Replacement Party campaigned on the theme "New Roots for America," complete with tributes to the superiority of the people and the value of their common sense over the machinations of the politicians and the lawyers.

Supporting this interpretation is Carter's tendency to go on automatic when using some of his themes. He acted, at times, as if he had a formula, using a theme whether it was suited to a particular situation or not. He took his search for a common ground with audiences sometimes to absurd extremes: While campaigning in Idaho in 1976, he told one audience that he identified with them because the major products of Idaho and Georgia were raised underground—Idaho potatoes and Georgia peanuts. Later he noted that both Oregon and Georgia have important lumber industries. To a West Virginia crowd Carter said: "You have tremendous coal deposits under your surface lands. As you know peanuts grow under the ground also, so I have a lot in common with you there." (Norman Mailer, who was in the audience, thought he was telling a bad joke.) During a visit to the West Coast in August, 1976, Carter observed that even Hollywood reminded him of Plains. When a startled listener asked him "Why?" Carter explained that both towns had trees. And in September at Brooklyn College, Carter found himself "much at home," observing that "both a neighborhood and a small town have their own special character, their own distinctive life. I don't come from Americus, or Vienna, or Cordele. I come from Plains. You come from Flatbush—and not Sunnyside or Bay Ridge or Brooklyn Heights. We feel most at home where our roots run deep."

Similarly, at times Carter took his intimacy theme to points that were potentially embarrassing—for himself or others. As governor, he had addressed a conference of psychiatrists, saying: "There were a few months when I was deathly afraid that I was going to get sick and would have to go out of state or come to one of you for treatment. I was hoping that if I did get sick it would be some emotional problem and not some physical problem, because I doubt that I could have found a doctor in Georgia who would have treated me with love and compassion . . ." Later, writing about his childhood desire to attend Annapolis, Carter confessed his anxieties about a disability called "retention of urine." He wrote: "I was always ashamed to ask whether the last clinging drop would block my entire naval career." (This last admission provided the reporters who were traveling with Carter with much material for in-group jokes.) His response in February, 1979, to some Yankee baiting by President José López Portillo in Mexico—a recollection that he had first taken up running years ago, between Mexico City's Palace of Fine Arts and the Majestic Hotel where he was staying, only to find that he was afflicted with "Montezuma's Revenge"—created a nervous embarrassment in his audience on the spot and won him stories around the world. His offer of sympathy to Baltimore Orioles manager Earl Weaver on the death of Weaver's mother (he spoke of how upset he and his family were about it) was misplaced because

Weaver's mother had not died, Pirates' manager Chuck Tanner was the one who had been bereaved.

Overall, Carter's thought possesses a surface quality, and he lacks both creative ability and a basic philosophy to guide him in his political choices. James Fallows, who has worked with Carter as a speechwriter, has made a detailed analysis of his intellectual characteristics and their ramification for Carter's leadership.

. . . Carter has not given us an *idea* to follow. The central idea of the Carter Administration is Jimmy himself, his own mixture of traits, since the only thing that finally gives coherence to the items of his creed is that he happens to believe them all. . . . I came to think that Carter believes fifty things, but no one thing. He holds explicit, thorough positions on every issue under the sun, but he has no large view of the relations between them, no line indicating which goals (reducing unemployment? human rights?) will take precedence over which (inflation control? a SALT treaty?) when the goals conflict. Spelling out those choices makes the difference between a position and a philosophy, but it is an act foreign to Carter's mind. He is a smart man, but not an intellectual, in the sense of liking the play of ideas, of pushing concepts to their limits to examine their implications. Values that others would find contradictory complement one another in his mind.

In an ordinary leadership position, this deficiency might not be of any particular consequence. As President of the United States, however, coming to the office with the promises he made, these intellectual characteristics were almost bound to create problems for him in setting his political agenda and to make him disappointing to those who expected some special moral and political creativity from him. Moreover, these characteristics cannot be changed by admonitions to do better—which is what Fallows attempts to do in his critique of Carter's approach to problems. They are ordinarily too deeply rooted in the personality structure for that.

The Zero-Sum Society

LESTER C. THUROW

For over half a century since political scientist Arthur F. Bentley began the development of the "interest group theory" of American politics, American social scientists have generally extolled the benefits of American "pluralism." They reasoned that so large and varied a society as that of the United States could only be organized in small groups, each composed of individuals sharing particular interests. With many such groups in the field, each would be under a powerful incentive to come to short-term agreements with others in order to logroll its own interests through. For example, conservationists might vote in favor of social security increases if senior citizens supported the Environmental Protection Agency, or industrialists might agree to increases in the minimum wage if labor supported tariff protection or subsidies for their industries. No one group or set of groups could permanently dominate government, and all citizens were free to form whatever and however many interest groups they wished to meet their changing needs. What could better ensure freedom? What could be more democratic?

In recent decades, however, social scientists such as Grant McConnell, C. Wright Mills, Gabriel Kolko, and economist Lester C. Thurow have begun to analyze the perils of pluralism. Mills and other radical scholars have argued that interest groups on the "noisy middle levels of power" mask the continued dominance of a narrow "power elite." Other critics of pluralism like Thurow have pointed to a different outcome: the fragmentation of government and politics into a set of separate, uncontrolled, and greedy principalities that make planning difficult and prevent leaders on every level from making unpopular decisions. Interest groups are organized only to get benefits from government. Where they dominate, there can never be policies to abolish benefits that help the few and harm the majority. And when systemic decisions must be made to reduce the standard of living of segments of the population as a response to problems—such as that of energy or of national security—that affect the entire society, entrenched pluralism may indeed threaten the nation's future. Perhaps only with the revival of ideological debate on a serious level will the American political system be able to heal itself.

I stood in an amphitheater classroom at Harvard University and asked a group of alumni and their spouses what turned out to be an embarrassing question.

All things being equal, I said, an economy that invests 20 percent of its gross national product in new, productive facilities (Japan, for instance) will dominate an economy that invests only 15 percent (West

Germany)—and both will dominate an economy that invests 10 percent (the United States). From an American point of view, the prescription for a brighter future is very clear: increase the share of G.N.P. invested in new, productive facilities. Given our basically stagnant economy, however, some Americans will have to accept a decrease in their own share of the G.N.P. for several years if more of it is to go where it will do the most good for all in the long run.

I asked the Harvard group this question: "Whose standard of living should be trimmed?" One three-piece-suited alumnus in his 40's suggested the elimination of welfare payments for the poor. I pointed out that welfare—public assistance, food stamps, aid to families with dependent children—represents less than 1 percent of the gross national product. What other groups would they nominate for a loss in income? Not another hand went up.

In the months since then, the nation has been buffeted by inflation and unemployment, and foreign competition has driven some American industries—notably, the auto makers—to the wall. American productivity, the output of goods and services per hour of work, has been falling for an unprecedented 18 months. Congress has entered into its annual budget-making roundelay with no sign of a willingness to take on the "Harvard" question. Recession has arrived, precipitated by dramatic increases in interest rates in March and April; the decline has been long awaited by the Administration as an inflation antidote, but the President apparently has no plans to use this opportunity for a major economic policy overhaul.

If only, the public cries, someone knew what to do. If only the problems weren't so insoluble. But, in fact, there is nothing all that mysterious about America's economic woes. Solutions exist. The essential difficulty with them all, be they "liberal" or "conservative," is this: they require that large numbers of people accept a substantial, short-term reduction in their standards of living. And our political institutions are at such a pass that the Government has been incapable of making that happen.

There are fresh and provocative proposals about how to stem America's economic decline. One of the more interesting, and controversial, for example, would essentially bribe people to accept necessary economic dislocations. Another would have Government encourage the trend toward giant industrial conglomerates to soften the effect of economic change on the work force. What is lacking is the political means to such ends, a Government that can respond to particular interest groups and still function in the interests of the majority.

The economy is a kind of multiheaded, nonstop machine that cranks out goods and services while, at the same time, allocating the incomes of those who will consume them. The G.N.P. represents the total of those goods and services. As long as it is rising, there is no necessity to trim the incomes of any substantial group of citizens. Economic growth means that all segments of the society can fatten up, consuming ever larger slices of an ever larger pie.

Today, lacking that kind of healthy growth, we are faced with some unattractive alternatives. We could, for instance, decide to dispense with economic growth altogether. Or, we could eliminate the economic safety net we have placed under our citizens—the assurance of a stable, dependable income—and leave them to the not-so-tender mercies of an unfettered free-enterprise economy. Or, we could democratically determine whose income will be reduced to get the economy growing again.

The ranks of the no-growth advocates have swelled in recent years as the nation has become concerned about environmental quality and the exhaustion of our natural resources. The theory is that, by freezing the economy in place, the air could be cleansed and the parks saved from exploitation. But small is particularly beautiful for those who have already arrived. As a Colorado cynic put it, a developer is a man who wants to build a mountain cabin this year; a conservationist is a man who built his cabin last year. There are too many Americans who are not satisfied with their current standard of living to make the no-growth alternative viable

Conservatives would have us retreat into a mythical past. The American economy flourished best, they claim, when Government interference was least and the individual citizen had sole responsibility for keeping the wolf from the door. In fact, our per capita G.N.P. growth has been higher since the interference-minded New Deal than it was before, and the record of other nations offers little support for the laissez-faire argument.

Just over 30 percent of our gross national product is absorbed by Government activities ranging from public schools to welfare programs to military bases, but West Germany uses up more than 50 percent of its G.N.P. for similarly "unproductive" purposes and consistently outperforms us as to economic growth. Fifteen other industrial countries collect a larger fraction of their G.N.P. in taxes.

Moreover, many Governments with better economic records are far more intrusive in economic affairs. Some of them actually own or control major firms—West Germany's Volkswagen, for instance. In Japan, the Government is a major allocator of investment funds, and an employee may be laid off only if the company goes bankrupt. In Scandinavia, the Government encourages the cooperative arrangements between management and labor under which management shares its responsibilities and profits with the workers.

Our salvation lies with economic growth, but any realistic path to growth will entail tough decisions for Government leaders and painful economic losses for some Americans. But just how realistic are we?

When President Kennedy sought to put a man on the moon, he had little trouble winning popular and Congressional support. But when Presidents Nixon, Ford and Carter sought to initiate much more important energy projects, they were denied. The moon project could be paid for out of a rapidly growing economic pie, and no American had to lose his job or his home over Project Apollo. We all want to be independent of the Arab sheiks and their oil, but any way we pick to achieve that independence is going to cause some of us to face for a time a lower standard of living. Nations have little trouble uniting on issues like war and space exploration, but domestic issues of income distribution are tough for a democracy. It is not we versus them, but us versus us.

Consider one solution to the energy problem, a large tax on gasoline. Other industrial nations typically levy taxes of a dollar or two a gallon, and we could go them a dollar or two better. Such a move would quickly reduce our demand for imported oil by causing Americans to drive somewhat less. However, since the automobile is basic to the way most of us live, we would end up spending more dollars on gasoline, leaving us less to spend for other goods and services. Thus, our standard of living would fall.

That prospect would be difficult enough for Americans to swallow— witness the defeat in Congress of President Carter's effort to impose a mere 10 cents-a-gallon conservation fee. What might seem even more difficult to swallow: the same large gasoline taxes that would hurt some Americans would inevitably benefit others. Any program financed by the enormous new tax revenues would make some folks happy; the builders of mass transit systems, for example.

Much like that first, small heart attack, the first sign of a nation's economic vulnerability can be disconcerting—a hint that one is mortal. The 1973–74 Arab oil embargo performed that function for the United States. And when the gasoline-line convulsions reappeared last year, it was clearly past time for us to take our economic problems seriously.

By 1978, the United States had slipped to fifth place among the industrialized nations of the world in per capita G.N.P., surpassed by Switzerland, Denmark, West Germany and Sweden, with Japan, the world's fastest economic entry, gaining on the outside rail. We had for years been comforting ourselves with a variety of delusions.

There was, for instance, our disdain for the rich Middle East sheikdoms as their per capita G.N.P. passed us by. These were simple cases of countries inheriting wealth, we said, rather than earning it in the good old American way. What we ignored was that our own global supremacy was, in large measure, based upon a vast inheritance of resources, mineral and climatic. We were not the little poor boy who meritoriously worked his way to the top, but the little rich boy who inherited a vast fortune. Perhaps we had squandered it. Perhaps we could not survive without it.

Another favorite notion was that the rising economies of the world would simply adopt our advanced technology, rather than bother about developing their own, and thus would automatically slow down as they caught up with us. We watched amusedly while Japanese engineers ran through our factories, cameras clicking away, and assured ourselves that their genius was derivative rather than creative. But between 1972 and 1978, while American productivity was rising about 1 percent a year, West Germany's productivity was growing at a 4 percent annual rate, Japan's at a 7 percent rate.

Our competitors had developed their own unique economic institutions and technologies. Once-proud American companies were reduced to marketing new products like video recorders bearing the once-derided label "Made in Japan." Now, clearly, it would be camera-carrying American engineers running through Japanese factories—or so one might have expected. In the event, instead of adopting the new technologies of other nations, or—even better—producing serious new technologies of their own, many of our companies decided to sit tight and get the Government to ease their pains. Instead of junking obsolete open-hearth furnaces, for example, and installing the new equipment pioneered by the Japanese, many steel companies complained that their Japanese counterparts were guilty of unfair pricing practices and prevailed upon Washington to artificially increase the cost of imported Japanese steel. Only within the last year or so have such companies as the United States Steel Corporation started calling in Japanese experts or licensing Japanese technology.

Productivity losses have a major impact upon American pocketbooks. Imagine the economy as a factory with 10 workers engaged in turning out a product much cited by economists—widgets. Assume, for the sake of discussion, that there are no overhead or materiel costs. The goal is to produce 100 widgets a day to be sold for $1 each, the proceeds to be divided among the workers.

During the course of 1979, the American economy suffered a 2 percent decrease in productivity. Using our widget model, the loss in productivity means that we are producing only 98 widgets; to cover our $100 labor costs, we will have to charge $1.02 cents per widget. The dollar buys less than it did before.

The economy was also hit, during 1979, by oil price increases imposed by the Organization of Petroleum Exporting Countries. We had to give OPEC an extra 2 percent of our G.N.P. to get the same amount of oil we had purchased a year earlier. As a result, we essentially lost two widgets' worth of output, which caused about 2 percentage points of inflation.

Thus, between productivity losses and foreign-oil price increases, the economic pie available to be divided among American workers was reduced by 4 percent. The price of each of the remaining 96 widgets had to be pegged at $1.04 in order to maintain $10-a-day wages in the widget factory. Of course, because of inflation, that wage now bought the workers 4 percent fewer goods and services.

There are ways to stop inflation. If the workers in the widget factory were willing to accept a 4 percent cut in their wages, there would be no need to increase widget prices and hence no inflation. On the national level, salaries can be held down by Federal controls or, as should shortly be evident, by a major recession. But the essential point remains: given our stagnant economy, there is no way to stop inflation without cutting someone's income. Once again, it boils down to the Harvard question: someone's income, yes, but whose?

The question takes on a certain urgency when the economy is in disarray, but it is always central to our lives. Economic progress is usually portrayed in terms of bright new products and processes, but every new product replaces an old one and every new process makes someone's skills obsolete. There are always losers as well as winners, and Government is inevitably asked to do something to ease the losers' pain.

The democracies of the Western industrial nations and Japan all have majority and minority parties. Theoretically, the majority party is expected to resolve economic problems, and failure brings its punishment—loss of office. Theoretically, each of the political parties is made up of people who have common solutions to the nation's problems and will apply them if elected.

These theories are put into practice abroad. Last year, for example, the Conservative Party in Britain campaigned for office on a platform of tax cuts for the rich and tax increases for the middle class. It was voted into office and has proceeded to implement that platform. It will almost certainly be voted out of office if the policy fails.

In the United States, in lieu of a two-party system, we have free-lance legislators. A farm-state senator reports to his constituents that he has a solution to their low incomes—an increase in the Federal program to prop up farm prices. Of course, that raises the cost of food, but in such a way that most of the economic losses are borne by residents of other states who have to spend a greater share of their income for food. Naturally, the senators from those states are working to kill the idea, but our farm-state senator has not given up hope. Meanwhile, he has joined with senators from other farm states to kill the proposal by an urban senator to set price controls on food. Having offered proposals that would have helped and having stopped proposals that would have hurt, he can be re-elected by his constituents with the problem still unsolved. (Two years ago, 92 percent of all Congressional incumbents running for re-election won their contests.)

A Presidential candidate cannot pass the buck that way; he has to appeal to all the states. He solves the dilemma by assuring the nation that he will conquer everyone's problems and hurt no one in the process. Elected on that platform, he has no electoral mandate to impose economic losses—and any effort to do so is greeted with rage and fierce political resistance.

There was a time when a President could boost an ailing economy by making a politically weak group absorb such losses. Back in 1967, 30 percent of the elderly in this country were living below the poverty line as compared to 14 percent of the total population. Today, the elderly are an organized and ever-more-powerful interest group, and that income gap has been virtually erased. Their political clout was dramatically illustrated earlier this year. Reports appeared in the press that the Carter Administration was considering a cutback in the cost-of-living adjustments in the Social Security program, and though the idea was never even formally proposed, more than half of Congress signed a statement opposing it.

The growth in the numbers and sophistication of interest groups has contributed to the emasculation of our political system. And now we lack the party responsibility we must have if President and Congress are to make the tough decisions our economic situation in the world demands.

Liberal and conservative Democrats may coexist with mainstream Democrats under the party flag, but they must be held responsible for a Democratic President's policies and voted out of office if the policies fail. Ticket splitting, voting for "the man, not the party," may satisfy one's individual urge to support like-minded politicians, but in the long run it destroys party discipline and party responsibility. And those are the characteristics that enable a democracy to make the tough decisions.

By and large, the American economy machine performs the job of allocating income, but the Federal Government has long played a role in the process. Today, that role is larger than ever.

One major form of Government intervention is a kind of economic safety net, intended to protect individuals exposed to the high-wire act known as the market economy. Welfare payments, food stamps, Social Security, Medicaid and unemployment insurance define a minimum standard of living below which no citizen should fall. The standard is supposed to apply equally to all persons who have suffered economic misfortune, regardless of the cause.

As it turns out, the net is higher for some than for others. Unemployment insurance has to suffice for the checkout clerk when the corner grocer goes bankrupt, but when auto plants or textile mills are threatened, the Government rushes in. These workers keep getting their full salaries. Chrysler, having failed to develop cars that can successfully compete in the marketplace, has been given Federal loan guarantees. An import duty has been added to what would have been cheaper fabric made in India.

The special rescue measures that politically powerful unions and companies have lobbied through Congress are inequitable, given the treatment accorded the checkout clerk and similarly powerless individuals. The measures are costly to the general public, which pays for them in higher prices. And they stand in the way of economic growth.

The manufacture of fabric, for instance, is a labor-intensive operation requiring simple technology, ready-made for a developing nation like India. For a high-wage, high-technology country like the United States, such manufacture is foolhardy. It ties up capital and manpower that should be used more productively.

If society is going to maintain a safety net, it must do the job in a way that does not impede economic progress. The net should be set at a level that Americans are willing to tolerate, and then we should insist that auto workers as well as grocery-store clerks take the consequences of economic misfortune.

The second major area of Government intervention in the distribution of income is the tax system. Its particular role, other than financing essential Government activity, is to take much of the sting out of the workings of the market economy. By definition, then, a tax policy must be clear, consistent and fair. Our tax policy fails that test.

Two basic questions: how are Federal, state and local taxes distributed across different income groups? How are they applied to people with the same income? The progressivity of our taxes, the degree to which we soak the rich, is a social-ethical issue more than an economic one. Self-interest tends to determine a citizen's feelings, and views differ widely. They are more united on the second question. Most Americans believe that people with the same income should be treated equally— but in fact they are not.

We have, instead, an ad hoc tax system that is changed not in reasoned response to economic developments but because of emotional winds and the force of special-interest groups. For example, we all wish we were millionaires and have some covetous thoughts about those who are. However, in our market economy, there is nothing inherently inequitable about the fact that American oilmen will reap fortunes because of an OPEC-oil price increase—as long, that is, as they are subject to a standard, consistent tax system that makes sure they will pay out an appropriate share of their new wealth in taxes.

Because we lack such a system, we are trying to make up for it by imposing a windfall profits tax on the oilmen. Inevitably, such a tax is ad hominem in nature and unfair; none such was levied against owners of silver, for example, when at one point last year the price of that metal had soared by 800 percent. What's more, the oil tax is inefficient; it will take away much of the benefit of allowing domestic oil to rise to world price levels, namely, the incentive the higher price gives oilmen to invest in finding new energy supplies. The lack of a fair tax structure prevents the market economy from solving the kinds of problems it is capable of solving.

As the Carter Administration has made abundantly clear in recent months, recession is one means of dealing with inflation. The public demand for products dips, the number of workers needed to meet that demand goes down and unemployment rises. That leads to a drop in incomes, and as products pile up on shelves, prices begin to halt their upward spiral.

There is a temptation when recession arrives to soften the blow. Unions complain that their members should not have to suffer. Some politicians call for income tax cuts to make more money available to the public and thereby boost consumption. Yet such softening of the effects of unemployment undercuts its effectiveness as an inflation fighter.

The fact is that any tax changes should go in the other direction, toward tax cuts that encourage investment in new factories and productive facilities. Such equipment will enable companies to increase productivity, which in turn will raise the G.N.P. A temporary increase in consumption is a kind of Band-Aid, while new production facilities represent a long-term benefit to the economy. But the odds are strong that, given our current political-economic system, we'll be getting Band-Aids.

Are there techniques by which economic progress can be regained, approaches that allocate losses fairly across the whole society? One such proposition envisions a system of cash compensations.

The Congress has passed a measure whereby the Government will subsidize initial coal gasification plants until the process proves economically viable. Vast quantities of coal will be turned into gas and then into liquid fuel, to power our cars—and trim our oil import bill. Assume that the ideal site for one of the plants, according to expert studies, is Westchester County.

There will be local opposition, of course, to the prospect of air pollution, water shortages (the process uses a lot of it), the rumble of coal trains at all hours of the day and night, the danger of fire, the increase in traffic. That kind of opposition has prevented the construction of scores of nuclear plants and oil refineries in recent years. But some form of compensation could pave the way. Specifically, cash.

Residents within, say, a 10-mile radius of the coal gasification plant would be bribed to endure it. That might mean that some wealthy executives will receive funds, along with residents of more modest means, but once again, that is only inequitable if they are not paying their fair share of the tax burden. The solution, in that case, is to correct the tax system.

The private sector can also be organized to help provide more economic security without getting in the way of economic progress. Conglomerates represent a means to that end.

Over the last two decades, these huge corporate entities, consisting of companies in a wide variety of fields, have multiplied enormously. Given the inevitability of this trend, we would do well to forgo traditional antitrust reservations and take advantage of it, by giving these corporations greater responsibility for the economic security of their work forces rather than placing the entire burden on Government.

In Japan, for example, the Government has deliberately encouraged the organization of conglomerates and expects them to shift their resources, labor as well as capital, in the most efficient and humane manner. Thus, there is a constant flow of money and workers from low-productivity, low-wage parts of the corporation to high-productivity, high-wage segments. Workers and managers do not try to stop economic change, because they know they will benefit by the change; people are retrained for new roles, not dismissed. Such measures can help the United States regain its economic vigor.

Unless that vigor is regained, this country will pay a heavy penalty on the international scene. The Soviet Union has become America's military and political equal in the world by the simple expedient of putting a much larger share of its G.N.P. into military hardware. The

Japanese have been helped in their economic miracle by the fact that they have put virtually none of their G.N.P. into military hardware.

It may be that Americans will gradually refuse to maintain a strategic military capability in order to defend countries richer than we are. Of course, under those circumstances our wealthier allies would gradually take over such burdens, along with the decisive vote in geo-political matters that the United States once exercised.

For the foreseeable future, however, Americans must face up to the unpleasant fact that only by means of a temporary reduction of individual income can we turn our faltering economy around. And if that sacrifice is to have any permanent value, our political system is going to have to undergo some major revisions so that it can respond efficiently and fairly to economic change.